D1602250

The Land Beyond

The Land Beyond

ITALIAN MIGRANTS
IN THE
WESTWARD MOVEMENT

An Anthology of Essays on the
Italian Settlers' Experience
in the American West

Edited by
GLORIA RICCI LOTHROP

Introduction by
ANDREW F. ROLLE

PATRONS OF ITALIAN CULTURE
San Marino, California
2007

ISBN 978-0-9791359-0-3
ISBN 0-9791359-0-7
Library of Congress Control Number: 2007922307

Table of Contents

Illustrations 7

Preface 9

INTRODUCTION: The Immigrant Experience:
Reflections of a Lifetime, *Andrew F. Rolle* . . . 13

PART ONE: THE PIONEERS 21

Francesco Vigo: Italian on the American Frontier, *Eric Pumroy* 27

Count Andreani: A Forgotten Traveler, *G. Hubert Smith* . 43

Giacomo Costantino Beltrami and the Indians of
North America, *Luciano G. Rusich* . . . 51

The Middle West in 1837: Translations from the Notes of
an Italian Count, Francesco Arese, *Lynn M. Case* . . 71

PART TWO: THE MISSIONARIES 93

Eusebio Francisco Kino, From *The Padre On Horseback:
A Sketch of Eusebio Kino, S.J., Apostle to the Pimas,
Herbert Eugene Bolton* 101

Samuel Charles Mazzuchelli: Gifted Pioneer of the Midwest,
Flora Breidenbach 117

The Neapolitan Jesuits on the Colorado Frontier, 1868–1919,
Manuel Espinosa 129

Frances Xavier Cabrini: Foundress of the Queen of Heaven
Institute, *Sister M. Lilliana Owens* . . . 139

Part Three: The Settlers 147
Italian Immigrant Women in the Southwest,
   Phylis C. Martinelli 157
Adjustment and Integration: The Italian Experience
   in Colorado, *Janet E. Worrall* 173
Reno's Little Italy: Italian Entrepreneurship and Culture
   in Northern Nevada, *Albin J. Cofone* . . . 187

Part Four: The Laborers 203
California's Fishermen's Festivals, *Charles Speroni* . . 213
The AFL, the IWW and Bay Area Cannery Workers,
   Elizabeth Reis 233
Go East, Paesani: Early Italian American Major Leaguers
   from the West Coast, *Lawrence Baldassaro* . . 259

Part Five: Italians Who Made a Difference . 273
Arrival in San Francisco: Excursions into the Interior of
   California. *California and the Overland Diaries of Count
   Leonetto Cipriani From 1853 Through 1871, Ernesto Falbo, trans.* 279
Life Sketch of Sister Blandina Segale, 1850–1941. *At the End
   of the Santa Fe Trail, Sr. Theresa Martin, S.C.* . . 291
Close Calls: An Interview with Charles A. Siringo,
   Daring Adventurer in the Old West, *Neil M. Clark* . 299
Creative Responses to the Italian American Experience in
   California: Baldassare Forestiere's "Underground Gardens"
   and Simon Rodia's "Watts Towers," *Kenneth Scambray* . 311

Bibliography 327
Index 329

Illustrations

Map of Indiana Featuring Vincennes on the Wabash River . 28
Sioux Indians Racing at Fort Pierre 57
Sketch of Missionary Eusebio Kino, S. J. . . . 102
Sister Frances Xavier Cabrini, M.S.S.H. . . . 141
Salvatore Fallico Family, Colorado 163
Rietta and Bucola Wedding Party 164
Outing Participants, Rancho Cucamonga, California . 183
Interior of De Mateis Winery 199
Piuma's Italian Pharmacy 202
Fishermen's Fiesta, Monterey Bay, California . . 216
Cannery Strike, Bay Area, California . . . 232
Oakland Oaks Pitcher Ernie Lombardi . . . 261
Ping Bodie and Babe Pinelli 266
Portrait of Count Leonetto Cipriani . . . 280
Sister Blandina Segale, S.C. 291
Cover of *A Texas Cowboy: Fifteen Years on the
    Hurricane Deck of a Spanish Pony* by Charles Siringo . 298
Simon Rodia's Watts Towers 321

Preface

RECENT DECADES HAVE WITNESSED significant revisions in approaches to interpreting Italian migration history. The traditional model began with the assumption that the Italian migrant had been uprooted from pastoral harmony and plunged into the throes of an impersonal industrial revolution that had created an urban abyss from which the newcomers could rarely escape. That commonly accepted stereotype of the dispossessed immigrant tenement dweller has finally been dispelled in *Westward the Migrants*, previously published as *The Immigrant Upraised*, where, as a result of exhaustive research, Professor Andrew Rolle has demonstrated that those Italian migrants daring enough and sufficiently well-equipped to participate in the westward transit of the continent shared in the same opportunity, the consequent optimism, and sense of enterprise which characterized the American pioneer.

At the same time, a major revision has occurred in the field of Western American history, challenging established assumptions and introducing factors heretofore not considered. As a result, the traditional model of a heroic male subduing the land and its inhabitants, using whatever forces necessary to access its wealth and the treasure beneath it, and declaring it all in the name of patriotic conquest, has been all but displaced. The new Western history recognizes that American territorial expansion west of the Mississippi River reaped consequences in terms of spoliation of the land and its resources and the dispossession and displacement of a native people.

No longer is the frontier narrative populated solely by men who were sure of shot and had nerves of steel. More thorough historical research has revealed that those heroic figures were joined by women. Furthermore, the restless migration of pioneer settlers moving expectantly from one economic frontier to another has assumed added variety. There remain fur men, missionaries, and Oregon Trail pioneers, as well as miners, cowmen who began to roam the plains at the end of the Civil War, and finally the farmers of the great American prairies. All these have assumed an inviting variety of names and tongues and cultural pasts. The optimistic enterprise engaged Europeans as well as Americans, along with Chinese and Blacks, often building on a colonial Indo-Hispanic culture.

Such a story would not be complete without the tales of the audacious Italian explorers, visionary missionaries, dream-drawn gold seekers, of Italian cowboys and townsfolk who labored and ran businesses across the American West.

Only after the positive response to the initial volume, *Fulfilling the Promise of California: Essays on the Italian American Experience,* was the broader prospect of the Italian migrant experience in the American West considered. Just as the essays drawn from publications of the California Historical Society compiled in the first volume yielded a nuanced image of the Italian settler in California, so too do these selections from published narratives, biographies, and scholarly journals from Montana to California, from Oregon to Colorado and beyond. The number of historical narratives and the variety of westering Italians presented have been limited only by publication considerations. We are grateful for permission to reproduce them in *The Land Beyond: The Italian Migrant in the Westward Movement.*

This volume focuses not only path makers and land developers, on missionaries and sisters, on miners, fishermen, and cannery workers, but also on lawmen and townsfolk who operated all manner of enterprises. Among them are a number of individuals who heroically transacted their destinies in the sometimes unyielding land west of the one hundredth meridian. Diverse though they were, they were all drawn by the possibilities posed by their pioneer venture, and they were, as well, joined by common roots of history and culture.

I am grateful for the assistance in completing this project provided by The Huntington Library, the California Historical Society, the Archives of the Archdiocese of Los Angeles, and the American Italian

Historical Association. I am especially indebted to Professor Andrew Rolle for his scholarly example and contributions, and for his unfailing support.

Above all, I wish to convey thanks to the Di Lorreto Foundation, the Patrons of Italian Culture, and especially the Barbera Foundation, which has so faithfully reflected Robert Barbera's commitment to conveying the fullness of the Italian migration experience, placing it in the broadest panorama which historical research has revealed. That deeply held commitment has led to the publication of this anthology.

The Immigrant Experience
Reflections of a Lifetime

By *Andrew Rolle*
Huntington Library

IN 1950 I WAS a young American Vice Consul in Genoa, Italy. That very year, Professor Oscar Handlin of Harvard University won the Pulitzer Prize for his book *The Uprooted.* His assumptions were based heavily upon Eastern European peasants who ended up in high-intensity urban settings so untypical of the American West. His approach to American immigration seemed terribly wrongheaded, for I had renewed dozens of U.S. entry visas of immigrants who in no way fitted Handlin's stereotype. Unfortunately, he persuaded an entire generation of scholars to adopt his views about downward mobility.

To counter that pessimistic approach, I began to write articles entitled "Italy in California" and "Success in the Sun: The Italians in California." Next, in a book of wider scope, I offered an alternative view of the immigrant experience,[1] focussing on the immigrant as upraised, not uprooted. My years in Genoa, and growing up among immigrant neighbors out West, led me to believe that its foreigners had experienced a different way of life from those immigrants who remained in America's largest urban centers.

---

[1] This essay is adapted from a keynote address given on November 12, 1999, at the American Italian Historical Association meetings in San Francisco. It was published in 1965 as *The Immigrant Upraised: Italian Adventurers and Colonists in an Expanding America.* Mondadori, a Milano publisher, issued an Italian version of that book, entitled *Gli Emigrati Vittoriosi* (1972) with a preface by Luigi Barzini. That volume was republished in 1999, with a new title and preface, as *Westward the Immigrants.* See also Andrew Rolle, *The Italian Americans: Troubled Roots* (1980, reprinted in 1984), which is psychiatrically based.

One purpose of studying history is to escape from commonly accepted assumptions by carefully examining the past. What happened to those
Italians who moved West was also met by other nationalities. One cannot, indeed, fasten a behavioral grid onto the immigrant experience
across an entire continent. America's geography, society, and culture are
simply too immense to sustain such generalizations.

Nowhere is negative stereotyping about foreigners harder to sustain
than in California. This was a new land for both resident Americans
and immigrants as well. No region of the United States saw so varied a
mingling of people whose story was yearning to be told. The scenery
and mildness of California's seasons proved especially attractive to Italians. Even the rainfall pattern resembled Italy's with the heaviest in the
north. Almost anything grown back home could be raised there. All
were invariably struck by the similarities between California and ancient
Tuscany or Campania. The terraced bluffs around Santa Barbara reminded newcomers of the Riviera's Santa Margherita, San Remo, and Rapal-
lo. Blue skies, olive trees, and craggy cliffs took immigrants back mentally
to Posilippo on the Bay of Naples.

Architecturally too, the Mediterranean influence became apparent in
dozens of California locations. The facade of Stanford University's chapel
is an example of the mosaics that adorn churches like Rome's Saint-
Paul-Outside-the-Walls. The Romanesque red-brick and tile style of
U.C.L.A.'s central quad and of Saint Andrew's Church in Pasadena
resulted from the unique skills of Italian craftsmen. Other artisans were
employed by architects who built the Mediterranean campuses of Scripps
College and Occidental College, as well as the Henry E. Huntington
Library and Art Gallery in San Marino.

In California, such workers seemed to have more in common with
their American neighbors than with villagers left behind in Sicily or
Calabria. Westernized foreigners of all nationalities might even be pictured as a new breed whose ambitions often transcended the *campanilismo* of the past. Also left behind were America's large eastern cities.
Some escaped from cramped iron balconies and cold-water tenement
flats. The stereotype of the pathetic, mustachioed organ-grinding Italian peasant with rings in his ears and a monkey on a leash did not fit
well out West. Tradition-free, it offered the immigrant opportunities
not found in the mills and factories of large eastern cities.

As for discrimination, of course it happened. Some immigrants—east or west—were indeed cut out of the American dream. I have never denied the shamefulness of Colorado's 1914 Ludlow massacre. Professor Paola Sensi-Isolani has examined another unfortunate labor dispute, the 1909 McCloud lumber fracas in California. Life was not always a bucolic garden patch out West. Some workers undeniably encountered anti-immigrant prejudice. In mining and lumber camps the most militant strikers were viewed as disruptive anarchists from abroad.

The record of Italians who deserted New York's Mulberry Street surely deserves at least some of the attention lavished upon Indians, outlaws, and vigilantes. But historians of western America continue to emphasize the sensational, the erratic, and the pathological. As TV writers parade the gun slingers, bartenders, gamblers, English lords, white heroes, and swarthy villains across the stage of western history, too few writers have remembered immigrants on America's frontiers.

Alongside the surface cliches of a dime-novel approach to western history, there also stands the solidifying record of the foreigner. Many writers still take for granted a nineteenth-century West without immigrants. Yet, business records, travel accounts, and newspapers all record a conspicuous cosmopolitan element that shaped the life of many a cattle ranch, mine, logging camp, and railroad across the wide Missouri River.

In California, the Italian contribution has been immense. One thinks of A. P. Giannini's giant Bank of America (originally called the Bank of Italy) as well as of the state's renowned vintner families—among them the Martinis and the Mondavis. The bulk shipments of the Gallos have made them the largest worldwide wholesalers of wine. Much earlier, in 1883, at Cucamonga in Southern California, Secondo Guasti began to transform thousands of acres of arid bushlands into vineyards. Soon he was shipping out 400,000 gallons of wine from what came to be called "the largest vineyard in the world."

Italians were also involved with intensive fruit and vegetable ranches. Giannini began his banking empire by lending funds to immigrant produce growers in the lower Sacramento Valley. With such backing, the Di Giorgio Corporation became one of the largest produce-distributing firms in the world. Joseph Maggio was known as the "carrot king of the United States."

Whether in San Francisco, San Pedro, or Monterey, the sardine fleets were mostly owned by Italians. Indeed, Monterey's Sicilians formed that city's largest ethnic community. By 1935, 90 percent of its 150 fishing boats were owned by them. Fishing, a definite Mediterranean way of life, was successfully replicated in California.

Gastronomy, too, has been heavily influenced by the Italian cuisine in restaurants like the Fior D'Italia and the Blue Fox in San Francisco. In Los Angeles, Bert Rovere's singing waiters accompanied dining at the Paris Inn. Alex Perino later set a higher standard of cooking at his Wilshire Boulevard restaurant. Nearby, in Hollywood, the Musso and Frank Restaurant remains a hangout for film actors, writers, and directors, including the late Frank Capra, a graduate of Caltech.

Whereas Domenico Ghirardelli introduced chocolate delicacies to San Francisco during the 1849 California gold rush, Joe DiMaggio played his first baseball on the city's vacant lots. His family, originally Sicilian fishermen, like the Aliotos, owned a North Beach waterfront restaurant. These and other high achievers possessed the entrepreneurial drive— sometimes even the capital—needed to gain financial and social independence. San Francisco's Sbarboro, Petri, and Rossi families had mostly arrived before 1910. Many of these millionaires came from northern Italy, where education was more available than in its south. In Lombardy, Piedmont, and Tuscany the ability to read and write, even on a simple village level, had become increasingly common. Most "successful" immigrants did not, however, come from upper-class families. Yet they wanted a better life for their children.

Not only in the Napa and Sonoma valleys did they encounter an outdoor rusticity similar to rural Italy. Elsewhere, too, experiencing less acculturative friction, they were quite quickly accepted by their neighbors. In fact, assimilation proceeded so rapidly that the story of western immigrants can be reconstructed only with difficulty. Manuscript letters, journals, and memoirs in private hands have been subjected to house cleaning, even incineration, by subsequent generations who did not know the language of either their parents or grandparents. Much of the foreign-language press in California was wiped out by the attrition of time. Whole runs of newspapers were used to wrap garbage by descendants with virtually no sense of their own history.

Professor Alan Balboni's book *Beyond the Mafia* (1996) shatters persistent stereotypes. He has found that Nevada's Italian immigrants were well-represented not only among musicians and other stage performers, but also as architects, contractors, and real-estate developers. Similarly, Nicholas Ciotola has written about the constructive community role of Italians in Albuquerque, New Mexico. Philip Notarianni tells us that Utah's Italians were not only employed by the Union Pacific and Denver & Rio Grand Western railroads, but also broke out of the laboring class, soon owning saloons, grocery stores, and tailor shops in Salt Lake City.

Charlie Siringo, the son of Italian immigrants, went from cowboy hero in Texas to a role as Pinkerton detective. In Arizona after 1913, Columbus Giragi and his brother Carmel took over the *Tombstone Epitaph*, a proto-typical Anglo newspaper. They were the sons of Sicilians who had come to Arizona in the 1880s to work in its silver mines. The Giragis eventually owned a small string of newspapers.

Professor Liping Zhu of Eastern Washington University has recently challenged the stereotypical image of his fellow Chinese in the American West. In his pathbreaking book, *A Chinaman's Chance: The Chinese on the Rocky Mountain Mining Frontier* (1997), he argues that Asians had as equal access to upward mobility as other western miners. This stands in sharp contrast to the notion that these particular immigrants never had "a Chinaman's chance" to succeed.

Out West, what ultimately proved as important as national origins were such matters as how well one could establish a homesite, break the prairie sod, or clear a field of boulders and tree stumps. Although life also had its grubby side, settlers who stuck to their goals and worked hard were generally rewarded by a better life than they had ever known. Relatively few immigrants were too old or dour to change. Most became anything but refugees or mafiosi, a non-stop imagery perpetuated by an obsessed media. Mafia stereotypes have now become almost comical.

Virtually forgotten is the role of such pioneer priests as Fathers John Nobili and Michael Accolti who, as early as 1850, established the groundwork for today's Santa Clara University in California. These Jesuits were followed by Anthony Maraschi who in 1855 became the founder of Saint Ignatius College, now the University of San Francisco. Piedmontese clerics, they had been sent to the new world by their supervising provincial, located in Turin. Among them was Father Joseph Cataldo, founder of Gonzaga University in the state of Washington. The Jesuit missions of Montana were also begun by foreign-born Jesuits.

Elsewhere, as well, foreigners affected the general culture. San Francisco, for example, has always enjoyed a strong infusion of Italian, as well as French, influence from the days of opera diva Madame Adelina Patti to today's popular cappuccino bars. At Los Angeles, visitors flock to Simon Rodia's Watts Towers, which as early as 1921 he began to construct out of bits of discarded tile and bottles. In the post–World War II period, Leo Politi's colorful sketches have preserved for posterity the demolished Victorian mansions of that city's Bunker Hill district where he once lived.

The children of immigrants also achieved prominence as entertainers, especially in Hollywood. Some became celebrities like Frank Sinatra, Perry Como, or Anne Bancroft. Dean Martin came from a family named Croscetti. Others, including composer Frank Mancini, became shapers of popular culture with such songs as "Moon River" and "The Last Time I Saw Paris." Another song writer, of Calabrian parentage. Harry Warren (whose real name was Salvatore Guaragna), wrote such songs as "Chattanooga Choo Choo," "Don't Give Up the Ship," and "The Atchison, Topeka, and the Santa Fe."

Were there unhappy immigrants—east or west—who regretted coming to America? Of course. The mother of Edward Corsi, United States commissioner of immigration, never adjusted to life here. The mother of Luigi Barzini, journalist and author, also could not wait to return to Italy. However, most western immigrants stayed on as hard-working, middle-class folk. Casting off old-world nostalgias, and prejudices too, these came to embrace the American belief that all persons could be masters of their environment. Omaha, Dallas, and Pasadena were not Palermo, Bari, or Naples. Rigidity and closed privilege were eventually replaced by new opportunities. Whether Germans, Italians, or Frenchmen, they sought that better life they had heard of across the seas. In Nebraska, Texas, or California, most went as far as their talents would take them.

Today, relatively few Americans of European descent are immigrants—a luxury which their forbears did not enjoy. Third-generation defensiveness about family origins has finally begun to subside. Ethnicity is also less full of either prejudice or boasting about a lineage back to Dante or Columbus. Fortunately, a new immigration ethos repeats fewer of the cliches about filiopietism, bigotry, racial melting pots, or endless disillusionment.

We have finally come to acknowledge that when pioneering foreigners encountered discrimination, most sought to wear it down—just as they withstood adversities of climate or dire economic realities. Because these folk became the upraised, not the uprooted, we need to be fair to their achievements and to their memory.

PART ONE

The Pioneers

C OLUMBUS, VESPUCCI, Cabot, and Verrazano, mariners from trading states located on the Italian peninsula, represent the vanguard of European expansion into the Western Hemisphere. In the fifteenth century the first European nation states emerged from the checkerboard of minor principalities that had provided a semblance of stability to Western Europe in the centuries following the decline of the Roman empire.

Only with the rise of commerce stimulated by the urge to acquire exotic foreign luxuries, first discovered through foreign contact, did European travel increase along market routes forged by crusaders. The new commerce was dependent upon political stability and a reliable monetary exchange. Assuring these two conditions required the centralized authority of nation states. Spain was the first to fashion a unified rule under the dyarchy administered by the heads of Aragon and Castille, which concluded seven centuries of conflict with the invading Moslem forces and soon blazed new trails of mercantilist commerce across the Western Hemisphere. Spain quickly became the leading political power in Europe, though soon challenged by Bourbon France and Tudor England, which also emerged as nation states in the same fateful fifteenth century.

Spain's colonization of the New World would involve the services of several notable Italians for whom no nation state was yet established. These included Fray Marco da Nizza, a Franciscan friar who was a subject of the House of Savoy. He inadvertently inspired early sixteenth-century Spanish exploration of the American Southwest by passing on an apocryphal tale gleaned from native travelers describing towering cities of gold. The images, reminiscent of the seven holy cities of Spanish legend, lured Francisco de Coronado's expedition into the heartland of the American Southwest and to the discovery of the plateau dwellings of the Zuñi Indians.

A century later the unexplored territory north of Sonora, Mexico, was to be surveyed by the Jesuit missionary and explorer Father Eusebio Kino, whose cartographic record of Spanish land claims from the Gulf of Mexico to the Colorado River remains a monumental accomplishment.

Less than a century later settlements along the Alta California coast were visited by members of a scientific expedition headed by Captain Alessandro Malaspina, who, sailing under the Spanish flag, had successfully circumnavigated the globe. In May 1791 he sailed his two corvettes north from Acapulco to sixty degrees north latitude in futile pursuit of the fabled Northwest Passage, the elusive Passage to India also known as the Straits of Anian, giving his name to several sites along the way. Sailing southward he made landfall at Monterey, then continued his survey southward to Cabo San Lucas. His detailed account, published in Madrid (1885), describes his twelve-day visit to Alta California during which he surveyed the coast, made astronomical observations, and collected all manner of local flora. Throughout, he speaks feelingly about colonial hospitality and, above all, the climate. A more recent edition has been edited by Andrew David, *et al.* (The Hakluyt Society and the Museó Naval, 2001).

An Italian ship's doctor, Paolo Emilio Botta, who later distinguished himself as an archeologist and naturalist, sailed along the California coast between 1827 and 1828 aboard the French ship *Héros*, as part of a global scientific expedition under Captain Auguste Duhaut-Cilly. Botta's personal observations during one of the most extensive scrutinies of Mexican colonial life in California are appended to the captain's 500-page report. In 1841 Botta's father, historian and poet Carlo Botta, translated his son's three sets of observations into Italian and published the volume in Turin.

Botta's account encouraged migration to America as did earlier descriptions of the New World written by Milanese Girolamo Benzoni (1565), Giovanni Careri's autobiographical narrative of a voyage east across the Pacific aboard a treasure-laden Manila galleon (1719), and the adventurous recollections of Lorenzo Boturini (1746).

Some Italians provided services to French colonial settlements, where pursuit of the lucrative fur trade made them among the first Europeans to penetrate the lands west of the Mississippi River. At the vanguard was Enrico (Henri) Tonti, a wounded veteran who had lost his hand in the Sicilian wars, who with Robert de La Salle explored the Mississippi to its mouth and in 1683 jointly claimed the lands drained by the great river for the king of France. After La Salle's violent death near his new colony on the Texas coast, Tonti administered the vast territory for the French crown for a decade and a half. His countless exploits included the construction of Fort Niagara and building the first ship, *The Griffin*, to sail the Great Lakes. His many achievements, including building a fort on the Arkansas River, once called Tonty's River, led him to be declared the "Father of Arkansas."

New Orleans, at the mouth of the Mississippi, soon became a cosmopolitan center, attracting Italian shipping entrepreneurs as well as professionals and public servants. Among them was Sicilian sea captain Salvatore Pizzati, whose maritime shipping activities extended to Central America. Displaying singular business acumen, Pizzati invested his profits in banks, insurance companies, and a vast plantation, making him one of the wealthiest Italians in the United States. Another Italian settler worthy of historical note was Orazio de Attelis, Marquis de Santangelo, who, fleeing the consequences of his political activism in Tuscany and Naples, finally settled in New Orleans, where he conducted a language school and edited *Il Correo Atlantico*. He was a supporter of Texas independence and a bold critic of President James K. Polk's policy of territorial expansion. In 1848 he decamped for Italy to rejoin the independence efforts.

Francesco Vigo was at the forefront of Italian pioneer explorers in the eighteenth century. His life mirrors the history of the American Midwest. A Piedmontese, he became a fur trader in the Arkansas country, having had earlier experience with fur traders while part of the Spanish army occupying the Louisiana Territory after the Seven Years' War.

In the region of St. Louis, where Spanish mercantilist policy limited all colonial trade exclusively to the mother country, the exchange of

Indian furs with French and English trading partners was strictly pro-
hibited. But the superiority of British goods offered by the Hudson's
Bay Company gave rise to a surreptitious and highly profitable alter-
native economy which advanced the fortunes of young Vigo. As Eric
Pumroy explains in the essay "Francesco Vigo: Italian on the American
Frontier," in due course, he established an extensive trade network with
Americans through Kentucky and Pennsylvania, as well as through the
Great Lakes and, later, the mouth of the Mississippi.

As the battles of the American Revolution extended northwestward
toward the British Fort Detroit, Vigo became a welcome ally of the
American patriot fighter George Rogers Clark. The intelligence that
Vigo transmitted significantly aided the Americans in their successful
claim to the Ohio Valley. The fortunes of war being unpredictable, the
$12,000 in supplies that Vigo provided the American colonial forces was
not entirely reimbursed until the passage of the Act of Compensation
in the 1780s.

Vigo's final days, passed in poverty, were not attributable to the Americans' deferred compensation. He accepted the inevitability of the growing American presence and welcomed and supported the stability that
presence engendered. By 1790 he had been the leading land owner in
Vincennes. In 1792 he owned two-thirds of the land Congress had made
available to French settlers. He soon built the town's most expensive
home where for several months he hosted the future United States president William Henry Harrison. But in 1804 he lost the home as well as
his fortune to lawsuits.

Although ultimately bereft of his fortune, Pumroy reminds the reader that Vigo was an inextricable part of the history of European settlement of the Old Northwest. He had served as a Spanish colonial soldier,
a fur trader, and a supporter of the American Revolution. He was, as
well, a highly successful land speculator and a prominent leader in the
Northwest Territory.

In the essay "Count Paolo Andreani: A Forgotten Traveler," G. Herbert writes of a European scientist visiting the unfamiliar American continent. In 1790 Andreani, a Milanese famed for making one of the earliest
balloon ascensions in Europe, arrived in the United States with several
impressive letters of introduction. During the following year he traveled

extensively, making various astronomical observations and, quite possibly, circumnavigating Lake Superior in a birch canoe. During that trip he made observations to determine whether the earth was a sphere, using geographic measurements deemed accurate by later travelers.

In the course of his travels Andreani wrote an account of the fur trade, which was included in the significant study by Duke de la Rochefoucauld Liancourt, *Travels Through the United States of North America* (1799). Having visited one of the major trading sites shortly after the apex of the trade had attracted up to two thousand trappers to a rendezvous, he was blunt in his description and in his discussion of the competitive rivalries between the traders.

Andreani's scientific credentials were such that in 1791 he was made a member of the American Philosophical Society, meeting with the most learned savants as well as with George Washington and James Madison. His return trip to Europe was marred by illness and pirate attacks. Beyond that, his later fortunes are obscure.

In his essay "Giacomo Costantino Beltrami and the Indians of North America," Luciano Rusich writes of the first Italian to venture as far west as Minnesota and the Dakotas. Beltrami arrived in 1823 in the aftermath of the Napoleonic conflicts. Like other trailblazers he was attracted to the uncharted lands of the Louisiana Territory where he attempted to find the headwaters of the Mississippi River.

Beltrami was outfitted for his adventure by Indian agent Major Lawrence Tagliaferro, who had met him aboard the steamboat *Virginia* bound for Fort St. Anthony. Tagliaferro described the middle-aged Beltrami as tall and having a noble bearing. He added that Beltrami's appearance was commanding, but his manner was short-tempered. Together, the two navigated the Ohio and Mississippi rivers to reach Fort Snelling, where they joined Major Stephen H. Long's historic United States Topological Expedition into the interior.

A native of Bergamo, Beltrami had served as a judge in northern Italy, but in the aftermath of the Napoleanic conflict he sought exile in the American West, where he became absorbed with the study of Native Americans. An intrepid explorer, Beltrami traveled with several Indian tribes and guides until, alienated by his imperious commands, they abandoned him, forcing him to travel alone by canoe, sometimes compelled to tow it by drag rope while waist-deep in water. In the course of his travels Beltrami named what he believed to be the source of the Mississippi, Lake Julia, in honor of the Countess Giulia Medici-Spada.

The document "The Middle West in 1837: Translations from the Notes of an Italian Count, Francesco Arese," edited by Lynn Case, provides the reader with an informal narrative containing impressions of the Ohio and Kentucky fur trade, including its environmental impact upon the territory. There is a memorably moving account of Arese's shipboard life on the Mississippi with its attendant dangers. He drafts brutally frank portraits of his fellow passengers, including a company of actors and provides examples of the impact of the fur-trade economy on the cosmopolitan city of St. Louis. At another point, the young Arese describes newly settled Chicago in 1837 as a mere "44 blocks long by 40 wide." Although no more than five years old, he predicts that the city is "destined to become a great city." Finally, the writer is unsparingly frank in his depiction of the inhuman treatment of Blacks.

This young aristocrat dispatched to America at the behest of Queen Hortense to serve as a companion to her exiled son, Louis Napoleon, arrives at some of the same conclusions that earlier traveler Alexis de Tocqueville imparted in *Democracy in America* (1835). Comparing the U.S. system of government with his own European experiences, Arese discusses the relative advantages of a less democratic government. He also reveals an understanding of such impinging factors as the vast expanse of land available for settlement, the fragility of newly established political institutions, and the effect of the continuing influx of immigrant cultures upon the nation.

Despite his reservations, Arese concedes that in America what Europeans would not dare to dream is accomplished. It is in his estimation "an astonishing, magical and miraculous country where many, many things must be seen before you can begin to believe them."

Francesco Vigo
ITALIAN ON THE
AMERICAN FRONTIER

By Eric Pumroy

T HE STANDARD WAY of looking at the settlement of the American Midwest is through the lives of people from the East, principally of English descent, who moved westward from the Appalachians in the last quarter of the eighteenth century. But there is also another story. Prior to the establishment of American settlements west of the Appalachians, there were already European communities in the West, and a very sophisticated and prosperous commercial network in place based upon the fur trade with the Indians. One of the leading figures in this region was an Italian, Francesco Vigo. Vigo was a successful trader, but more important, during the American Revolution and the early years of the American Republic, he risked his life and his fortune to help the United States win the American Midwest.

Francesco Vigo was born in 1747 in Mondovi, a village in the Piedmont region of northwest Italy. He joined the Spanish army as a young man, and the Spanish sent him to New Orleans in 1769 as part of its force occupying Louisiana, which France had ceded to Spain at the end of the Seven Years' War. New Orleans was the principal Spanish outlet for the fur trade with the Indians up the Mississippi, and there he undoubtedly met a number of men connected with the business. The fur trade obviously appealed to him more than soldiering, for he soon obtained his discharge from the army and embarked upon his new career.

Francesco Vigo, a native of Mondavi, Italy, started trading with English and French colonial settlements in 1772, which placed him in a unique position to assist American independence efforts a few years later. After the Revolution, he traded along the Mississippi to the Great Lakes and became a respected figure in Vincennes, where he was the leading land owner.

He apparently started by trading in the Arkansas country, but by 1772 he had established himself at St Louis, along with his partner, Emilien Yosti, another Italian.[1]

St. Louis was one of a number of French settlements in the Midwest at that time. It had been established as a trading post ten years earlier and its location near the outlets of the Missouri, Ohio, and Illinois rivers helped it to prosper quickly. It gained additional importance as a refuge for French families from the eastern side of the Mississippi after France surrendered the area to the British. When the Spanish took control of Louisiana, they made St. Louis the seat of government for Upper Louisiana, and installed a lieutenant governor and a small number of troops there. In 1780, the town's population was about 900.[2] Near St. Louis, but across the river in British territory, were a number of French settlements which had been established early in the century, principally Kaskaskia and Cahokia on the Mississippi, and Vincennes on the lower Wabash River. In 1787, the total adult male population of these towns was estimated at 1,280, including 328 at Kaskaskia, 239 at Cahokia, and 623, or about half, in Vincennes.[3] Most of the people in these towns made at least a part of their living from the Indian trade, although many were also farmers, or had their lands farmed by their Black slaves.[4]

The entry of the British and Spanish into the middle of the American continent disrupted what had been, under the French, a single trading zone linking all of mid-America from New Orleans to Montreal. The Spanish promptly installed the restrictive trading practices which they used in their other colonies, in an attempt to secure a monopoly on the Indian trade in Louisiana. The flaw in this policy, however, was that Spain could not match the quantity, quality, or price of British manu-

---

[1] Bruno Roselli, *Vigo: A Forgotten Builder of the American Republic.* (Boston: The Stratford Co., 1933), 41–42; Dorothy Riker, "Francis Vigo," *Indiana Magazine of History* 26 (March 1930): 12–13.

[2] Louis Houck, *A History of Missouri* (Chicago: R.R. Donnelley & Co., 1905), 2:6–14; John Francis McDermott, "The Myth of the 'Imbecile Governor': Captain Fernando de Leyba and the Defense of St. Louis in 1780," in *The Spanish in the Mississippi Valley, 1762–1804*, ed. John Francis McDermott (Urbana: University of Illinois Press, 1974), 361–62.

[3] Enumeration of male inhabitants of Vincennes and Illinois by Bartholomei Tardiveau, 1787, Pierre Menard Papers, Illinois State Historical Library, Springfield (microfilm, Indiana State Library).

[4] For a good, brief description of the lives of the French settlers in the late eighteenth century, see John Francis McDermott, "French Settlers and Settlements in the Illinois Country in the Eighteenth Century," in *The French, the Indians, and George Rogers Clark in the Illinois Country* (Indianapolis: Indiana Historical Society, 1974), 3–33.

facturers. Faced with losing their trade to British competitors across the river, the St. Louis traders began a lucrative business smuggling English goods into Louisiana.[5] Vigo was undoubtedly involved in this trade, since by the late 1770s he was already a well-known and respected figure in the Illinois towns across the river which were supposed to be off limits to Spanish traders. He was also extremely successful at the trade, and when the new Spanish lieutenant governor, Don Fernando de Leyba, arrived in St. Louis in 1778, he recruited Vigo to enter into a business partnership with him.

That same year, the American Revolution came to the Illinois Country. In July 1778, George Rogers Clark and a small band of Kentucky militiamen occupied Kaskaskia, Cahokia, and Vincennes, all of which had been virtually abandoned by the British a few years before. Clark's plans were not entirely clear, but he apparently intended to capture these towns as a preliminary step to a move against Detroit. Detroit was the principal British post in the northwest and the center from which Indian raids had been directed against the small American settlements in Kentucky the previous year. By taking the Illinois towns, Clark controlled the river routes to Detroit, gained an opportunity to win the disaffected French to his cause, and came into contact with the Spanish, who had quietly begun aiding the American rebels. The aid from the Spanish and French turned out to be particularly important when, in December, British lieutenant governor Henry Hamilton marched down the Wabash from Detroit with about 500 men, most of them Indians, and recaptured Vincennes. Because of the lateness of the season, he disbanded most of his army and settled in for the rest of the winter at Vincennes, where he laid plans for a major expedition against Clark at Kaskaskia in the spring.[6]

At this point, Vigo played a critical role in saving Clark's mission. Even before the British move against Vincennes, Clark's men were

[5] Kouck, *History of Missouri*, 2:32–33; Paul Chrisler Phillips, *The Fur Trade* (Norman: University of Oklahoma Press, 1961), 2:11.

[6] James A. James, *The Life of George Rogers Clark* (Chicago: The University of Chicago Press, 1928), 109–40. For more recent analyses of Clark's motives, see George C. Chalou, "George Rogers Clark and Indian America, 1777–1780," in *The French, the Indians, and George Rogers Clark*, 34–46; and George M. Waller, "Target Detroit: Overview of the American Revolution West of the Appalachians," in *The French, the Indians and George Rogers Clark*, 47–66.

endangered by a lack of supplies, Clark had no means of securing additional supplies from the East, and his funds to purchase new supplies consisted only of promissory notes which he could issue on the state of Virginia. These were payable at New Orleans by the merchant Oliver Pollock, who served as Virginia's agent. The French traders were reluctant to accept these notes, and the Spanish authorities in St. Louis had no supplies to offer. But the Spanish lieutenant governor did have his partner, Francesco Vigo, to help. Probably at de Leyba's request, Vigo met with the French merchants and urged them to provide Clark with the necessary provisions. Vigo's most persuasive argument may have been his example, for he extended a loan of supplies worth nearly $9,000 in December 1778, and eventually provided more than $12,000 worth of supplies to keep Clark's men in the field. The other traders, with renewed confidence in the value of Clark's notes, supplied the army with provisions valued at approximately $70,000 from late 1778 to early 1780, with Vigo's $12,000 by far the largest single contribution. As it turned out, Vigo's confidence in Pollock and the state of Virginia was not justified. Pollock's funds were quickly exhausted, and Virginia was insolvent for a number of years to come. Vigo eventually sold several of the smaller notes at a fraction of their value, but he continued to hope for repayment of the $9,000.[7]

If Vigo's only service to Clark had been financial assistance, he would have earned a substantial amount of credit for the ultimate success of the expedition. But Vigo did more. On December 24, 1778, one week after the British had retaken Vincennes, a British patrol arrested Vigo and a Canadian trader as they approached the town. Lt. Gov. Hamilton saw no threat in Vigo, but he nonetheless confined him to the town for the following three weeks.[8] Vigo was apparently on a business trip, since he could not have known that the British were in Vincennes prior to his departure from Kaskaskia. Once confined, however, he used his time to

[7] Virginia Creditors to Clark, *George Rogers Clark Papers, 1781–1784*, ed. James A. James, vol. 19 of *Collections of the Illinois State Historical Library* (Springfield, 1926), 274–75; House Committee on Revolutionary Claims, *Colonel Francis Vigo* [To accompany bill H.R, No. 3301], 24th Cong., 1st sess., 1836, H. Rept. 317, 11–12.

[8] Henry Hamilton's Journal, 24 December 1778, January 14, 1779, *Henry Hamilton and George Rogers Clark in the American Revolution, with the Unpublished Journal of Lieut. Gov. Henry Hamilton*, ed. John D. Barnhart (Crawfordsville, Ind.: R.E. Banta, 1951), 155,163.

determine the strength of the British forces, the attitudes of the French
inhabitants, and Hamilton's plans for the spring. When the British commander released him in mid-January, Vigo returned to St. Louis, as he
had promised, but then promptly reported to Clark at Kaskaskia. There
he gave Clark the first definite news the Americans had received on what
had happened at Vincennes, as well as a thorough analysis of the British
situation there. Vigo completed the report by noting that since the British
did not expect that the Americans could act before spring, an immediate attack might have a chance of succeeding, Clark accepted Vigo's
advice, and on February 7, he and fewer than 200 men, nearly half of
them French, set out on a dramatic march across the flooded lowlands
of southern Illinois, forded the swollen Wabash River, and forced the
surrender of Hamilton and his men after a brief skirmish.[9]

There has been considerable dispute over the significance of Clark's
campaign, with some historians maintaining that the capture of Vincennes won the Ohio Valley for the United States, and others contending that this campaign was nothing more than a raid, and had no effect
on the negotiations which ended the war.[10] At the very least, Clark's capture of Hamilton and Vincennes saved his men from almost certain defeat
the following spring, and it also checked the British plan to mount a
major assault upon the American settlements in Kentucky. The British
turned their attention to strengthening the posts at Detroit and Michilimackinac against Clark's expected attack, while the Indians, disheart-
ened by the British failure, largely stopped their raids for a time. The
temporary peace achieved by Clark's victories encouraged a flood of new
settlers to come into Kentucky in the summers of 1779 and 1780. When
the British and Indian attacks resumed in 1780 and 1781, the Kentucky

---

[9] George Rogers Clark to Patrick Henry, February 3, 1779, *George Rogers Clark Papers, 1771–1781*,
  ed. James A. James, vol. 8 of *Collections of the Illinois State Historical Library* (Springfield: Illinois State Historical Library, 1912), 97–100; James, *George Rogers Clark*, 136–38.

[10] Those emphasizing Clark's importance include Reuben Gold Thwaites, "How George Rogers
  Clark Won the Northwest," in *How George Rogers Clark Won the Northwest, and Other Essays in
  Western History* (Chicago: A.C. McClurg & Co., 1903), 3–72; James, *George Rogers Clark*; and
  Waller, "Target Detroit." Historians who have de-emphasized the importance of Clark's suc-
  cess have included Clarence W. Alvord, "Virginia and the West: an Interpretation," *Mississip-
  pi Valley Historical Review* 3 (June 1916); 19–38; Jack Sosin, *The Revolutionary Frontier, 1763–1783*
  (New York: Holt, Rinehart and Winston, 1967); and Dwight L. Smith. "The Old Northwest
  and the Peace Negotiations," in *The French, the Indians, and George Rogers Clark*, 92–105.

settlements were much more securely in place, and better able to withstand the assault. It is a moot point whether the United States would have gained the northwestern country in the treaty negotiations at the end of the revolution if Clark had failed, but Clark's success, which Vigo's help made possible, insured that the peace negotiations were conducted with American settlements firmly in place west of the Appalachians.

Vigo was certainly critical to Clark's success, but we must be careful about accepting the later portrayal of Vigo as a dedicated American patriot. Vigo was a Spanish subject, had served a number of years in the Spanish army, and was a friend and business partner of the Spanish lieutenant governor. The Spanish had been antagonistic toward the British since losing Florida to them in the early 1760s. They had been quietly supporting the Americans since the beginning of the revolution, and finally, in 1779, formally joined the war against England. Considering Vigo's background and the Spanish attitude toward the revolution, it would not be surprising if Vigo considered his actions on behalf of Clark to be those of a Spanish patriot, more than an American one. Lt. Governor de Leyba apparently thought so, for when it became clear that Virginia would not honor its debts to Vigo and the rest of the Illinois merchants, he sent Vigo's $900 note to Spain for repayment. Unfortunately, de Leyba died in the summer of 1780, and Vigo never heard anything further from Spain.[11] This note would in fact remain unpaid until 1876, when the U.S. Congress finally agreed to honor it.

A legend has grown up around Vigo that he sacrificed his fortune for the American cause, and that he lived the rest of his days in poverty because an ungrateful country refused to repay its debts to him. While it is true that Vigo died a poor man, and that he was unable to collect on Clark's notes during his lifetime, it is not true that his loans to Clark were the immediate cause of his later financial problems. In fact, Vigo continued to be one of the leading merchants in the middle west for the next twenty years.

Sometime in the early 1780s, Vigo moved from St. Louis to Vincennes. At least in part this was undoubtedly a business decision. At Vincennes, he was connected with Detroit through the Wabash and Maumee rivers, and he was also much closer to the growing settlements in Kentucky than

---

[11] H. Rept. 317,12.

he would have been at St. Louis. Detroit and Michilimackinac were the principal centers of the fur trade in the Great Lakes area. In spite of the Treaty of Paris, which had called for these posts to be turned over to the United States, the British retained them after the war, in large part because of their enormous commercial value. For nearly twenty years after the revolution, most of the world's supply of furs came from British North America, and half of the monetary value of these furs came from Detroit and Michilimackinac. In the late 1780s, Detroit merchants annually collected furs valued at approximately $200,000. The principal source for these furs was the territory south of the Great Lakes, which meant that the Wabash river towns of Vincennes and Miamis (now Fort Wayne) became important subsidiary posts.[12] As for Kentucky, the population was rapidly growing, from only a few hundred at the beginning of the war, to 30,000 in 1784.[13] Since it was difficult for the Kentucky settlers to obtain supplies from over the mountains in the east, this also became a profitable market for the Illinois traders.

By 1784, Vigo had already established good business relationships with a number of leading Detroit merchants. In that year, for example, he exchanged goods valued at more than four thousand British pounds with John Askin of Detroit, and Askin entrusted him to collect a debt owed by another trader.[14] But even though Detroit was the center of Vigo's business world, it presented some political difficulties for him. When Vigo visited the town in 1784, the British authorities arrested him for his role in Clark's campaign, and he might have had to face charges as a spy had not his business acquaintances come to his aid. One Detroit merchant, Alexander Macomb, posted a $5,000 bond to secure his release, and other merchants apparently prevailed on the authorities to drop the matter. Nothing further ever came of the arrest, and Vigo continued to make business trips to Detroit throughout the 1780s.[15]

---

[12] Phillips, *Fur Trade*, 2:102–4; Gayle Thornbrough, ed., *Outpost on the Wabash, 1787–1791. Letters of Brigadier General Josiah Harmar and Major John Francis Hamtramck and other letters and documents selected from the Harmar Papers in the William L. Clements Library*, Indiana Historical Society Publications, vol. 19 (Indianapolis, 1957), 10–11.

[13] Malcolm J. Rohrbough, *The Trans-Appalachian Frontier: People, Societies, and Institutions* (New York: Oxford University Press, 1978), 25.

[14] Account of Vigo with Askin, September 1784; Askin to unidentified, September 28, 1784, Francis Vigo Papers, Indiana Historical Society Library, Indianapolis.

[15] Vigo to the editor of the *Aurora*, October 18, 1807, Vigo Papers.

In 1786, Vigo's relations with Detroit changed, as Askin and five other leading Detroit merchant houses formed a consortium called the Miami Company, with the purpose of pooling capital for outfitting traders and limiting competition for furs.[16] Vigo worked as an independent agent for the company in Vincennes, outfitting other traders who visited the Indian tribes, and then gathering the furs at the end of the season and sending them to Detroit. Askin regarded Vigo as one of his best men, and recruited and outfitted him in 1786 in the expectation that Vigo would make it possible for the company to dominate the trade through Vincennes.[17] The company was not successful. The fur-trading system depended on an extensive network of credit, stretching from the auction houses in London to the individual traders in the American backwoods. The network functioned well in times of stable or rising prices, but when prices were gradually declining, as they were in the 1780s, the merchants who extended credit could run into trouble.[18]

Vigo's situation provides a good example. In June 1786, Vigo sent nearly one hundred packs of furs to Askin at Detroit. Askin valued the furs at about 2,000 British pounds, but Vigo thought this appraisal too low, and rather than selling them outright to Askin, he sent them on consignment for sale in London. Even though Askin did not purchase the furs, he still credited Vigo's account for their estimated value so that Vigo would have trading goods for the following season while they awaited the outcome of the sale in London. The furs were then sent to the large Montreal firm of Todd, McGill & Company which repacked them and sent them to England, where they finally were sold in June 1787, one year after the initial transaction in Detroit. London prices had declined in the meantime, and instead of selling for more than Askin offered, Vigo's furs fetched 145 pounds less. It was undoubtedly many more months before Askin was informed of the results of the sale and received payment. Since the traders rarely came to Detroit more than once a year, it would be common for transactions such as these to take at least two years to settle. For Vigo and Askin, however, it took much longer, for Askin's accounts seem to have become confused in the demise of the

---

[16] Phillips, *The Fur Trade*, 2:9–10.
[17] Askin to Todd & McGill, June 22, 1786, *The John Askin Papers*, ed. Milo M. Quaife (Detroit: Detroit Historical Commission, 1928), 1:251–55.
[18] Phillips, *Fur Trade*, 2:108.

Miami Company in the late 1780s, and so he did not present Vigo with a full accounting of the situation until 1799.[19]

At the same time as he was connected with John Askin, Vigo was also engaged with the French merchant Bartholomei Tardiveau in trading with the American settlements in Kentucky and Tennessee. Their principal trading expedition was to the new American settlements in the Cumberland River area in 1785, although they also traded in Kentucky that year. Vigo did some trading for furs with the Indians along the Tennessee River as well. Trading with American settlers involved dealing in goods different from the blankets, powder, and knives so common in the Indian trade. These staple articles were sold to the Americans, along with a large supply of corn meal and flour. But Americans were interested in other items as well. Tardiveau's account with Col. John Montgomery of Cumberland, for example, shows sales of handkerchiefs, women's gloves and hats, ribbon, chocolate, a teapot, six large mahogany mirrors, and eighteen mirrors with painted frames. The same year, Vigo sold Tardiveau a table service for twelve, complete with plates, soup bowls, teacups and saucers, coffee cups and saucers, chocolate cups and saucers, a set of six silver knives and forks, assorted serving dishes, and a service of glass oil cruets.[20] Life on the frontier was not without its amenities.

In the mid-1780s, this extensive trading network was endangered by the growing hostility between Indians and whites in the region. The Indians, with good reason, feared that the Americans had designs on their lands. They saw the Kentucky settlements rapidly expanding south of the Ohio, and noted the increasing American claims north of the river. To put a stop to further American encroachments, the northwestern Indian tribes formed a confederation and, late in 1785, began attacking Kentucky settlers. The United States Congress was reluctant to provide defense for the frontier, until after George Rogers Clark provoked an international incident when he arrested three Spanish merchants on a counter-raid to Vincennes in 1786. Concluding that it was dangerous to leave defense in the hands of unruly frontiersmen, Congress finally appropriated funds for troops in the West. In 1787, Gen.

[19] Askin to Johnston, March 20, 1800, *Askin Papers*, 2:281–82; Askin to Vigo, May 6, 1799, Vigo Papers.
[20] Account of Col. John Montgomery, July 1785; Account of Tardiveau with Vigo, 1785, Pierre Menard Papers.

Josiah Harmar was given the western command, and later that year he established a permanent garrison at Vincennes under Maj. John Francis Hamtramck.[21]

It is not clear what Vigo's attitude toward the Americans was prior to the arrival of the troops, although as a businessman he seems to have preserved his neutrality as he traded equally with British, Indians, and Americans. But after 1787, he threw in his lot with the United States. Vigo was among the town leaders who welcomed Hamtramck's troops to Vincennes, and on their first night in town he entertained the officers. Far more important than these social courtesies, however, was Vigo's assistance during the following winter. When the army's contractors failed to deliver the necessary provisions for the Vincennes troops, Vigo kept the soldiers from starving by supplying them from his own store of goods, a considerable act of generosity considering Vigo's still unpaid debts from the Clark expedition.[22]

The arrival of American troops created a problem for the Vincennes merchants, for the Americans threatened to cut their trading connections with the British at Detroit. In the spring of 1788, Hamtramck wrote to Harmar asking for instructions on how to handle this situation. The Vincennes merchants were pressing him for permission to import British goods from Detroit, for they feared they would lose their old Indian customers if they could not acquire new trading goods. Hamtramck thought that the best solution would be for American traders to begin coming west to compete with the British.[23]

Vigo saw another solution. If the American traders would not come west, he would go east. In 1788, he made the first of what would become annual trips to Pittsburg and the east coast. His new route consisted of an initial trip in the spring to L'Anse a la Graisse (later known as New Madrid), near the confluence of the Ohio and the Mississippi rivers in Spanish territory. Here he apparently traded for furs from Indians and other traders. From L'Anse a la Graisse, he travelled up the Ohio, frequently stopping at Kentucky for further trading, and then continued upriver to Pittsburg, and from there to Philadelphia, New York, or Bal-

---

[21] Thombrough, ed., *Outpost on the Wabash*, 9–16.

[22] Hamtramck to Harmar, April 13, 1788, *Outpost on the Wabash*, 70; *Military Journal of Major Ebenezer Denny* (Philadelphia: J.B. Lippincott & Co., 1839), 103.

[23] Hamtramck to Harmar, May 21, 1788, *Outpost on the Wabash*, 77.

timore, where he sold the furs and purchased new trading goods.[24] Either Vigo or one of his agents made the trip nearly every year between 1788 and 1798, so it must have been a profitable route for him, and yet few other merchants followed his lead. The Canadian merchant houses continued to dominate the fur market, and so most traders continued their ties with Detroit, despite some feeble American attempts to stop this trade. Even Vigo continued to trade occasionally through Miami and Detroit.[25]

During the summer of 1788, Indian raids continued into Kentucky, and Indian attacks upon military boats on the Ohio became frequent. Kentucky counterraids also continued, generally against peaceful Indian villages, which served only to provoke further Indian raids. Violence came to Vincennes that summer when Kentucky militiamen under Patrick Brown attacked the Piankeshaw village across the river from the town, in spite of Major Hamtramck's attempts to stop them. Later that year the Piankeshaw removed to the less dangerous Kaskaskia area, but only after retaliating by killing two women and an infant living on Vigo's farm.[26] Despite their attempts at neutrality, the French traders came increasingly under Indian attack. In the spring of 1789, Hamtramck reported the murders of several Frenchmen at Indian hands.[27] In July 1790, several of Vigo's men were killed when a band of Indians fired on his boats on the Ohio River west of Louisville. After escaping this ambush, Vigo fell in with a group of military boats near the mouth of the Wabash. When the two parties began to ascend the river, they came under Indian attack. The soldiers escaped, but the Indians captured Vigo and his men and confiscated their goods. They warned that the traders would be killed if they were ever caught with American soldiers again.[28]

In spite of the danger, Vigo continued to work as a friend of the American government. His trading connections, from the Mississippi

---

[24] Thornbrough, ed., *Outpost on the Wabash*, 89, 177; Carter, ed., *Territorial Papers*, 2:405–6; Duver letter, 1791, Lasselle Collection, Indiana State Library, Indianapolis; Vigo accounts with Ghequiere & Holmes, Baltimore, September 28, 1792, September 10, 1798.

[25] Phillips, *Fur Trade*, 2:12; Christopher Coleman, ed., "Letters from Eighteenth Century Indiana Merchants," *Indiana Magazine of History* 15 (December 1909): 156.

[26] Hamtramck to Harmar, August 31, 1788, November 28, 1788, *Outpost on the Wabash*, 114–15, 139.

[27] Hamtramck to Harmar, May 27, 1789, *Outpost on the Wabash*, 169–70.

[28] Arthur St. Clair to Secretary of War, September 19, 1790, *The Territory Northwest of the River Ohio, 1787–1803*, ed. Clarence E. Carter, vol. 2 of *The Territorial Papers of the United States* (Washington, D.C.: Government Printing Office, 1934), 307.

to the Great Lakes, gave him access to information about Spanish, British, and Indian plans, which he freely shared with American officials. Hamtramck and Harmar relied on his judgement and advice, and each frequently entrusted him to discuss sensitive issues with the other officer rather than commit the matter to writing.[29] Through his connections with Harmar, Vigo secured access to higher American officials in the East. In 1789, he met President Washington in Philadelphia to discuss his outstanding claims from the Clark expedition.[30] In turn, Washington asked Vigo in 1790 to carry to the Chickasaw and Choctaw Indians along the Tennessee River his proclamation assuring American goodwill and willingness to live up to its earlier treaties.[31]

The situation in the West continued to deteriorate in the early 1790s. British support for the Indians became more open, the possibility of conflict with Spain over navigation rights to the Mississippi arose, and to make matters worse, the increasingly powerful confederation of northwestern Indians soundly defeated American armies under Harmar and Gen. Arthur St. Clair. In 1792, President Washington placed Gen. Anthony Wayne in charge of the American army in the West, with orders to break the British and Indian forces in the Ohio country. In preparing for the campaign, which would end in the rout of the Indians at Fallen Timbers, Wayne recruited Vigo as an agent to secure information about Indian, British, and Spanish plans. In May 1794, he wrote Vigo requesting him to recruit spies to visit an enemy encampment on the Great Lakes to determine their strength and the state of their fortifications. He also requested that Vigo find a means of intercepting official Spanish dispatches from New Orleans to Detroit, in order to learn if the Spanish and British were planning combined actions against the Americans. Vigo accepted both commissions, but was unable to accomplish either task before Wayne's victory in August rendered the assignments unnecessary. Vigo did, however, write Wayne a number of letters

---

[29] Hamtramck to Harmar, July 14, 1788, July 29, 1789, August 17, 1789, *Outpost on the Wabash*, 90–91, 178–83, 187.

[30] Pierre Menard to Vigo, August 9, 1834, Vigo Papers.

[31] The President to the Chickasaw Nation, December 30, 1790, *The Territory South of the River Ohio, 1790–1796*, ed. Clarence E. Carter, vol. 4 of *The Territorial Papers of the United States* (Washington, D.C.: U.S. Government Printing Office, 1936), 41–42; Henry Knox to Vigo, December 30, 1790, H. Rept. 317, 20–21.

during the spring and summer of 1794 giving information on Spanish movements, and on the strains developing within the British and Indian alliance.[32] The following year, when Wayne negotiated the Treaty of Greenville, bringing to a close the ten years of Indian wars in the Midwest, Vigo was present as an observer.[33]

Vigo's enthusiasm for the United States was uncommon among the Illinois traders. Most of the French at Vincennes resented the Americans for taking over their town, antagonizing the Indians, and destroying the fur trade. But as a European immigrant rather than a native, Vigo was less distressed at the destruction of the traditional way of life in the West. Having lived under established governments in his earlier years, an experience which most of the French had not had, he seems to have been more appreciative of the advantages that a strong United States presence could bring. The most important advantage was security. Under the chaotic conditions that prevailed in the West in the 1780s and 1790s, trading could be neither a safe nor a profitable occupation. Vigo seems to have recognized that American immigration was unstoppable, and as a consequence, that the United States was the only power capable of imposing order in the area. He continued his business connections with the Spanish, the British, and the Indians after 1787, but from that point he was politically committed to the United States.

By the early 1790s, Vigo also had a substantial financial investment in an American victory, for by that point he was Vincennes's leading landowner. He had begun purchasing land in the Vincennes area by 1784, and he had continued purchasing small quantities of land from the French inhabitants throughout the rest of the decade.[34] In the late 1780s, however, a larger opportunity presented itself. At that time, the French in Illinois were growing concerned over the increasing number of American settlers who were coming to Vincennes and settling on lands that the French considered to be theirs, but to which they had no formal title. To protect their rights, the French commissioned Vigo's old trading partner, Bartholomei Tardiveau, to go to Congress with a petition asking that lands be set aside for them. In 1791, Congress granted tracts of

---

[32] Wayne to Vigo, May 27, 1794, July 5, 1794, September 29, 1794, Vigo to Wayne, June 24, 1794, H. Rept. 317, 21–23.

[33] Treaty of Greenville, August 3, 1795, *Territorial Papers*, 2:533.

[34] Contract between Vigo and Vodry, June 2, 1784; Contract between Vigo and Harpin, April 20, 1787; contract between Vigo and Brouillet, July 28, 1789, Lasselle Collection.

four hundred acres to each of the French families who could prove residence prior to 1783. Most of the French in Vincennes were not actually very interested in these undeveloped tracts, which were too far from town to be of any immediate use. Vigo, however, saw that continued American migration to the West would eventually make the land valuable, and so began buying up the French family claims. By 1792 he had purchased 101 of the 158 tracts donated to Vincennes families, most for only $50. Vigo did not immediately become wealthy as a result of this speculation, for the number of American settlers in the area was still small. Still, the land did promise to be profitable, for in 1796 he sold 12 of the tracts to settlers from Pennsylvania and Virginia for about $1 an acre, an eightfold increase in value in just four years.[35]

By 1800, Vigo had largely abandoned the fur trade, primarily due to poor health. For the better part of four years, beginning in 1798, Vigo was unable to travel because of illness, and indeed for a long time he was confined to his bed and not expected to live.[36] He eventually recovered his health, but by that point he was nearly sixty, and he seems to have decided to retire to Vincennes and live off the proceeds of rents and land sales. He was then by far the largest landowner in Vincennes, owning not only the donation tracts but also numerous lots within the borough of Vincennes. He had a new house built in 1801, a two-story white frame house with parqueted floors. An 1802 tax assessment put its value at $2,500, the most expensive house in town, and many times more valuable than the majority of the houses, which were valued at between $200 and $400. When William Henry Harrison arrived in town in 1801 to assume his duties as governor of the newly formed Indiana Territory, he stayed at Vigo's house for a number of months until he could have his own home built.[37]

Vigo's prosperity was short-lived. In 1804, suit was brought against him in the territorial courts for the repayment of debts contracted with John Askin and the Miami Company nearly twenty years earlier. Vigo

[35] Leonard Lux, *The Vincennes Donation Lands*, Indiana Historical Society Publications, vol. 15 (Indianapolis, 1949), 473–74; Contracts between Vigo and Purcell, and Vigo and Dye, June 20, 1796, Vigo Papers.

[36] Deposition of Francis Vigo, August 1, 1807, Vigo Papers.

[37] Lee Burns, *Early Architects and Builders of Indiana*, Indiana Historical Society Publications, vol. 11 (Indianapolis, 1935), 183; Return of the valuation of each house in town, Harrison Township, Vincennes, June 30, 1802, Knox County Commissioners Records, Lewis Historical Library. Vincennes University.

claimed that he had been misinformed about the nature of some of the debts, and that the company had not properly credited him for deliveries of furs that he believed would have offset the remaining debts. He admitted, though, that his position had been weakened by his inability to read and write, which had caused him to depend upon the good faith of others and on the record-keeping of his assistants.[38] Vigo's arguments failed to convince the courts, however, and in 1806 he lost the case. To pay the judgement against him, he disposed of more than 12,000 acres of land, valued at more than $15,000, including thirty donation tracts and his prized home in Vincennes.[39]

Vigo was not left totally destitute by this settlement. He continued to own a good deal of property in the Vincennes area, part of which he periodically sold to raise money.[40] Unfortunately, his property was not adequate to meet the needs of his uncommonly long life. When he died in 1836, nearly all of his property was gone. Since he had no children, he spent the last years of his life living either with a nephew or with a woman whom he and his wife had raised. At his death, the only thing of value that he still owned was the unpaid claim on the United States for supplies provided to George Rogers Clark sixty years earlier.

Vigo's career paralleled the history of the American Midwest in the late eighteenth and early nineteenth centuries. He was a fur trader when the area was largely a wilderness; he became a land speculator when American farmers began to arrive; be became a supporter of the American military when the United States was fighting for control of the region; and he became a community leader when Vincennes became a government center under the Northwest and Indiana territories. Vigo's story shows that the conquest of the West was not an achievement of American frontiersmen alone. Without the supplies and support which Vigo provided, American control of the West would have been achieved only at a much higher cost.

[38] Vigo to John Abbott, July 9, 1802, Vigo Papers; Vigo to Askin, June 9, 1804, *Askin Papers*, 2:418–21.

[39] Vigo v. McIntosh file, 1805–1806, General Court Case Files for the Northwest Territory and the Indiana Territory, Indiana Commission for Public Records, Indianapolis; Knox County Deed Book B, p. 477, Knox County Court House, Vincennes; William McIntosh to Toussaint Dubois, 1806, Vigo Papers.

[40] Knox County Index of Deeds, Books A–H, Knox County Courthouse.

Count Andreani

A Forgotten Traveler

By G. Hubert Smith

PERHAPS FEW PERSONS NOWADAYS could give more than an approximate date for even the more important events in the history of science.[1] Nearly everyone has a general notion of the date on which the law of gravitation was announced, or would be able to connect this law with Sir Isaac Newton. But how many persons could tell when the exact shape of the earth was satisfactorily established? It is now known that the earth is not exactly round, but rather is an oblate spheroid—that is, the diameter from pole to pole is slightly shorter than that across the equator. It is somewhat surprising that this fact was not definitely established until the middle of the eighteenth century, some years after the death of Newton, and then only after the French Royal Academy of Sciences had sent expeditions under famous astronomers to Lapland and to Peru.

It may not at once be clear what this matter of the exact shape of the earth has to do with the history of the Northwest. The connection becomes clearer when it is said that in 1791 a titled Italian traveler, now nearly forgotten, could have been found on Lake Superior testing the French theory of the earth's true shape in the light of his own observations. Thus he was among the first of a long train of naturalists and scientists, including David Thompson, Joseph N. Nicollet, David Dale Owen, and many others, who were to visit the Northwest in search not of wealth or mere adventure, but of information on the geography and natural history of the region.

---

[1] A paper presented at the afternoon session of the eighty-ninth annual meeting of the Minnesota Historical Society in St. Paul on January 10, 1938. Ed.

In July 1790, the erudite president of Yale College in New Haven, Dr. Ezra Stiles, noted in his prodigious diary that he had been visited by one "Count Andreani a Nobleman of Milan," who was making a tour of America. In a letter of introduction to Stiles, the count is described as "a nobleman of character and consequence . . . and a friend of liberty whose zeal and curiosity have determined him to visit the United States."[2] This was Count Paolo Andreani, who, in March 1784, had made the first successful balloon ascension in Italy. The flight was so well known at the time that a medal was struck commemorating it. At a still earlier date Andreani appears to have traveled in the East Indies.

Count Andreani came to the United States carrying letters of introduction from several interesting persons of his day. A letter from Phillip Mazzei made him known to James Madison. Among his effects was an honorary ode by one of his countrymen, the dramatist, Vittorio Alfieri, which was to be presented to George Washington. In a letter to the president, John Paradise, another picturesque cosmopolitan and a friend of the great Doctor Johnson, described Andreani as "highly distinguished by every valuable endowment" and well deserving of the honor of being presented to Washington. He is said to have been thoroughly acquainted with affairs in Europe, and there is reason to suspect that he was a somewhat ardent political freethinker. An amusing and revealing allusion occurs in a letter of Richard Henry Lee to a nephew, who had probably met the count during a visit to Italy some years earlier. Lee had received from the nephew a letter for the visitor, and had searched for him several times, but in vain, and he finally left it with James Madison, who lodged in the same house. "Being as you state him an Agreeable," says Lee, "he is so sought after that there is no finding him."[3]

---

[2] Franklin B. Dexter, ed., *The Literary Diary of Ezra Stiles*, 3:398 (New York, 1901). Information concerning the letter of introduction from Dr. Richard Price, dated April 2, 1790, now in the Yale University Library, has kindly been furnished by Miss Anne S. Pratt, reference librarian.

[3] Richard C. Garlick, ed., *Phillip Mazzei, Friend of Jefferson: His Life and Letters*, 127 (Baltimore, 1933); Jared Sparks, ed., *Correspondence of the American Revolution*, 4:343 (Boston, 1853); James C. Ballagh, ed., *Letters of Richard Henry Lee*, 2:527, 533 (New York, 1914). See also Giuseppe Prezzolini, "American Travelers in Italy at the Beginning of the 18th Century," in *Italy and the Italians in Washington's Time*, 67 (New York, 1933), and Sylvia Harris, tr., "Search for Eden: An Eighteenth-Century Disaster; Memoirs of Count de Lezay-Marnesia," in *Franco-American Review*, 2: 50–60 (Summer, 1937). The latter source presents a charming reminiscence of Count Andreani.

Washington makes no mention of Andreani's visit, and although the reason for this is not known, it is not difficult to imagine. Perhaps he was displeased by the undoubtedly fulsome ode that Alfieri had written in his honor; what seems more likely is that he was offended by what he looked upon as mere democratic cant. It may perhaps be inferred that the reception accorded Andreani was somewhat cold, and that he came to think but lightly of the new United States. There appear to be few sources from which one can reconstruct the incident, but in October, Colonel David Humphreys, then on a special secret mission in Europe, wrote indignantly to the president to the effect that the Italian had written some things about the government of the United States which were "monstrously absurd and ill-founded." No such writings have been found, but the president, in a cold and haughty reply to Humphreys, suggested that the count's remarks did no credit to his judgment or his heart. "They are the superficial observations," says the president of the proud young republic, "of a few months' residence, and an insult to the inhabitants of a country, where he has received much more attention and civility than he seems to merit."[4]

The events of Andreani's travels in America are not easily traceable. It appears, however, that he traveled rather extensively during 1790 and 1791, and in the latter year, according to the Earl of Selkirk, he visited Grand Portage, then at the height of its importance in the fur trade. Selkirk's acquaintance with Andreani began in 1794, when they met in Switzerland, and it is possible that it was the count who first directed Selkirk's attention to the promise of the New World—an attention that was to be focused, some years later, on the formation of the famous Red River colony.[5] Andreani traveled "in the interior parts of America" in 1791, according to still another titled foreigner, François Alexandre Frederic, Duke de la Rochefoucauld Liancourt, who quotes from a journal kept by the count. From still other sources, it is known that Andreani made use of a birch canoe for the journey, large enough to hold ten or twelve men besides himself and his equipment. This canoe he seems to

---

[4] Worthington C. Ford, ed., *The Writings of George Washington*, 12:19 (New York, 1891). There is also a letter of July 17, 1790, from Dr. Benjamin Rush, discussing the count's remarks on America. See *Calendar of the Correspondence of James Madison*, 607 (Washington, 1894).

[5] Thomas Douglas, Earl of Selkirk, *A Sketch of the British Fur Trade in North America*, 36 (London, 1816); Chester Martin, *Lord Selkirk's Work in Canada*, 17 (Oxford, 1916).

have obtained from the firm of Forsyth and Richardson, Montreal merchants who at this time were trading south of the lakes, and later were partners, successively, of both the XY and Northwest companies.[6]

At least one person reports meeting Andreani on Lake Superior. John Johnston says that in September 1791, at La Pointe, he encountered Andreani, who was taking observations "to ascertain whether the earth was more elevated or depressed towards the poles."[7] A recent scholar has suggested that Andreani's interest in the shape of the earth was a bit naive; as has been seen, however, in his day the earth's shape was still a subject for discussion. Andreani's conclusion that the earth is more depressed toward the poles was based, Johnston infers, on the count's own calculation that La Pointe is only 690 feet above sea level. If Johnston did not misrepresent the reason for Andreani's belief in the oblateness of the earth—if the count actually thought that the earth was flattened at the poles because La Pointe, so far north of the equator, had only this slight elevation above the sea—his conclusion was certainly naive. It is difficult to see that the slight elevation of La Pointe has any bearing on the problem of the shape of the earth. It is, however, probable that Johnston did not understand the count's science—perhaps because he did not understand his English, or his French! Johnston concludes with the humorous reflection that "the subject was then much discussed amongst naturalists, but now is set at rest forever, for were the high aspiring parties to move towards each other in hostile array, the consequence would be rather disagreeable to us emmets occupying the intermediate mole hills."

Johnston related the circumstances of this meeting to another visitor to the lakes at a later date. An amusing paragraph in Thomas L. McKenney's *Sketches of a Tour to the Lakes* relates that Johnston recalled having seen, at La Pointe, "a scientific Frenchman, or Italian, with his instruments adjusted, taking observations; and endeavouring to ascertain the longitude."

---

[6] John J. Bigsby, *The Shoe and Canoe, or Pictures of Travel in the Canadas*, 2:228 (London, 1840); Patrick Campbell, *Travels in the Interior Inhabited Parts of North America in the Years 1791 and 1792*, 125 (Toronto, 1937). On the authority of Thompson, Bigsby states that the journey was made about 1800, but it is likely that Thompson's memory was at fault.

[7] Johnston to Henry R. Schoolcraft, June 10, 1828, in *Michigan Pioneer and Historical Collections*, 32:341 (Lansing, 1903).

He told him [*Johnston*] that he had visited the highest mountains, and among these Mont Blanc; and his ulterior object had relation to the question regarding the formation of the earth at the poles. His name was *Count Andriani*. Does anyone know anything of the result of the count's investigations? Few people would suppose that this extreme point, so far beyond the bounds of civilized life, and so far in the interior, had ever been the theatre of such investigations.[8]

Many persons have echoed McKenney's query, but it is still unanswered.

Andreani left La Pointe to continue his tour of the lake, and he may, as one reliable witness asserts, have circumnavigated Lake Superior, "occupying himself in astronomical observations, and admeasurements of heights, mingling also freely with the Indians."[9] One of his admeasurements, preserved by David Thompson, the geographer, was that of the height of Thunder Mountain on Black Bay, near the present city of Port Arthur. From this record, and the fact that he visited Grand Portage and La Pointe, it seems most probable that he actually did circumnavigate the lake. If such is the case, he is one of the first white persons of whom there is record to accomplish this feat.

How long Count Andreani was engaged in his travels in the Great Lakes region is not known. It may be supposed, however, that he spent the summer of 1791 there, for he had returned to Philadelphia by December of that year and early in the next was elected a member of the American Philosophical Society at that place.[10] Of his subsequent movements very little is known, and what meager information is available is contained in a single letter, written some years later to Madison, with whom he seems to have formed a lasting friendship. Andreani relates that he was in Europe during the closing years of the century. It would be interesting to know what part this "friend of liberty" played in the events of that troubled period, but he is silent on that point. For some years he had toyed with the idea of returning to America. In 1806 he found himself in a position to execute his design, but from the outset his venture was inauspicious. First of all, the ship in which he set sail for America

---

[8] Thomas L. McKenney, *Sketches of a Tour to the Lakes*, 263 (Baltimore, 1827).

[9] Bigsby, *Shoe and Canoe*, 2:228.

[10] Ernest A. Cruikshank, ed., *The Correspondence of Lieut. Governor John Graves Simcoe*, 1:94 (Toronto, 1923). Information concerning Andreani's membership in the American Philosophical Society has kindly been furnished by Miss Laura E. Hanson, librarian of the society.

was captured by pirates and taken to Jamaica. From Jamaica he eventually got to New Orleans. Scarcely had he been set down there when he contracted smallpox. As if this were not affliction enough for one of his years—he seems to have been rather well advanced in age by this time—he was seized with the gout. Such was his condition that he proposed, in his letter to Madison, to make the fashionable visit to the springs in New York or Virginia, in order to restore his shattered health.[11]

Whether the count's tour to the springs was accomplished is not known, nor is there further information now available on the career of this interesting traveler. He may have been the veriest dilettante, after the fashion of his day—one who was mildly interested in subjects as diverse as ballooning and the political fortunes of the new republics, who made a sentimental tour of the lakes, and who was vastly pleased by the wildness of the scenery and the primitive innocence of the Indian. It seems more likely to the writer that he was an earnest, if sometimes misunderstood, student of government, geography, and natural science. At any rate, he left an account of the fur trade, which is today of no little value. This account was preserved by La Rochefoucauld in his own *Travels* published in two ponderous quartos in 1799. Andreani's notes in this work are said to have been taken from his journal.[12]

These notes afford interesting information on the importance in the trade, at the time of Andreani's visit, of the various trading houses on the lakes. To the great carrying place, or Grand Portage, were taken annually fourteen hundred bundles of fine peltry—beaver, otter, marten, and wildcat—besides mixed furs of other sorts, an amount greater than the combined yield at Niagara, Lake Ontario, Detroit, Lake Erie, Michilimackinac, and Lake Huron, while the posts at Fond du Lac and at La Pointe yielded only twenty bundles of fine furs each. The finest furs were collected northwest of the lakes, in British dominions, the furs growing coarser in quality as one neared the lakes. Something of the enormous value of these furs is conveyed by Andreani's statement that at Montreal the bundles brought forty pounds sterling each. The por-

---

[11] The original letter from Andreani to Madison, dated at New Orleans, March 11, 1808, is in the Library of Congress; the Minnesota Historical Society has a photostatic copy.

[12] Duke de la Rochefoucauld Liancourt, *Travels through the United States of North America*, 1:325–35 (London, 1799). See also William R. Riddell, ed., *La Rochefoucauld-Liancourt's Travels in Canada, 1795*, 110–19 (Province of Ontario, Bureau of Archives, Thirteenth Report—Toronto, 1917).

tion taken to Grand Portage formed approximately half of all the yearly export of furs from Canada, exclusive of those from Labrador, the Bay
of Chaleurs, and Gaspé. In London the furs from Grand Portage would
bring as much as eighty-eight thousand pounds sterling.

The extensive trade described by Andreani was carried on by the
Northwest Company and two or three small companies. The success of
the Nor'westers he ascribes to the large capital available to them, the
"unanimity of the members," their untiring efforts, and their virtual
monopoly of the trade. Nevertheless, there were at the great carrying
place no fewer than three different companies, which "rivalled each other
in the purchase of furs with a degree of emulation, which could not but
prove highly detrimental to themselves and advantageous to the Indians." The powerful Nor'westers, more opulent than the others, used their
wealth to ruin their competitors—"no stone was left unturned"—by brib-
ing and seducing them from their own interests. The animosity among
the traders was so great as frequently to lead them to blows; their warfare cost several lives and large sums of money. All this finally caused
the traders to see the necessity of union, and to obtain this end the largest
company, which was most anxious for peace, made several sacrifices.

Andreani arrived at Grand Portage just after the period of the greatest congregations there. Formerly, he says, several thousand Indians took
their furs thither, but in 1791 the company agents were accustomed to go
as far as a thousand miles inland, where they frequently wintered before
returning. About two thousand men were thus employed in the interi-
or, and whatever articles of clothing or subsistence they required must
needs be brought from Montreal with considerable difficulty and at enormous expense. At this great meeting ground of the trade stood a fort,
kept in good repair, and garrisoned with fifty men, where at the time of
the "delivery of the skins" there was frequently a concourse of more than
two thousand persons. The merchandise imported for the trade consisted of woolen blankets, coarse cloths, thread and worsted ribands of
different colors, vermilion, porcelain bracelets, silver trinkets, firelocks
or flintlock guns, shot, gunpowder, "and especially rum." The prices of
these articles at Grand Portage, because of the expense of transportation, was eight times that at Montreal, and in the interior the chief traders
fixed the prices "at their will and pleasure." The employees were paid in
merchandise, and open accounts were kept with them. Extravagant as

these men were, in general, and given to drink and to excess, they were exactly the sort wanted by the company. In 1791 nine hundred employees owed the company more than the amount of fifteen years' pay.

Much time has been spent in an attempt to locate the original of Count Andreani's missing journal, used by La Rochefoucauld, but so far the search has been quite fruitless. If it could be found, it would doubtless afford other valuable items of information from his own observations on the Indian, the interesting persons he must have met at the various trading posts, and the geography of the great Lake Superior region, in that vast and then little-known area to the north and west of the new United States.

Giacomo Costantino Beltrami and the Indians of North America

By Luciano G. Rusich

S O MANY COMPREHENSIVE and authoritative biographies of Beltrami have been written that to repeat what has been said before would seem superfluous.[1] Yet, it is necessary to sketch an outline of his life, previous to his arrival in the United States, in order to clarify the circumstances which brought this enterprising and cultured man to brave the wilderness of America.

Giacomo Costantino Beltrami was born in Bergamo in 1779. Bred to the law, at the age of 28 he became chancellor of the Department of Justice at Parma and Udine. Later he was appointed judge of the civil and criminal court of Macerata. Because of his fine intellect, solid preparation, professional competence, and untiring zeal in carrying out his functions, his superiors proposed him for the presidency of the Court of Forlì. But the fall of Napoleon and of the Kingdom of Italy prevented his appointment. When the Austrians occupied the Marche, he resigned and retired to his estates at Filottrano. In 1821, accused of being implicated in the carbonarian plots in favor of a constitution, he had to choose

---

[1] Of these the most important are: Vertova Camozzi, *Costantino Beltrami da Bergamo-Notizie e lettere pubblicate per cura del Municipio di Bergamo e dedicate alla Società Storica del Minnesota* (Bergamo: Pagnoncelli, 1854). Eugenia Masi, *Giacomo Costantino Beltrami e le sue esplorazioni in America* (Firenze: Tipografia di G. Barbera, 1902). Augusto P. Miceli, *The Man with the Red Umbrella: Giacomo Costantino Beltrami in America* (Baton Rouge, La.: Claitofs Publishing Division, 1974).

between incarceration or exile. Although ill, and hardly able to stand upon his feet, he chose exile and fled from Italy. He went to France, Belgium, Germany, and England. There he resolved to visit the countries and the peoples of the far away but free American continent. He sailed for the United States from Liverpool and landed in Philadelphia on December 30, 1822, after a very difficult and trying voyage.[2]

From Philadelphia he went to Baltimore, Washington, Pittsburgh, Cincinnati, and Louisville. Then he stopped at the confluence of the Ohio and the Mississippi rivers. It is here that Costantino Beltrami made the decision which, for better or for worse, changed his whole life. Initially he had planned to take a steamboat down the Mississippi to New Orleans and from there to proceed to Mexico. But, while waiting for the steamboat *United States* to carry him there, it so happened that another ship, the *Calhoun*, bound for St. Louis, stopped at the junction. Among its passengers were General William Clark, superintendent of Indian affairs at St. Louis, and Major Lawrence Tagliaferro, the Indian agent at Fort St. Anthony (Fort Snelling). Beltrami met them, became their friend, and in the conversations that ensued, they re-awakened in him the interest in Indians and Indian lore he had had since adolescence. With that impulsiveness which was so characteristic of him, he decided to accompany them in order to learn as much as he could about Indian customs, habits, rituals, and daily life. Together they went to St. Louis where General Clark remained, while Beltrami and Major Tagliaferro continued the voyage to Fort St. Anthony on board the steamboat *Virginia*.

On May 10, nineteen days and 729 miles after leaving St. Louis, the *Virginia* arrived at Fort St. Anthony. The arrival of a steamboat, the first, to such an outpost of civilization as Fort St. Anthony had, in Beltrami's words, "marked a memorable epoch in this Indian territory, as well as in the history of navigation generally."[3] To the Indians who viewed with awe the "monster vomiting fire," the steamboat was an object of

---

[2] All information relative to Beltrami's life in the United States has been derived from his *A Pilgrimage in America, Leading to the Discovery of the Sources of the Mississippi and Bloody River; with a Description of the Whole Course of the Former, and of the Ohio* (Chicago: Quadrangle Books, Inc., 1962). This is a copy of the first edition in English, published in London in 1828). We shall refer to this book as *Pilgrimage*. For the chronology of the events, however, the author of this study has relied on A. P. Miceli's *The Man with the Red Umbrella*. . . .

[3] *Pilgrimage*, 199.

reverence and fear, and "all the persons on board were in their eyes some-thing more than human."[4]

Beltrami stayed about two months at Fort St. Anthony. He was made welcome and treated as a friend by the family of Colonel Josiah Snelling, commander of the fort, who gave him the opportunity to explore the surrounding territory and to go hunting. Most important, he was able to spend considerable time among the Indians, studying their ways and collecting their artifacts.

On July 2, an expedition led by Major Stephen H. Long arrived at Fort St. Anthony. The expedition had been organized by the govern-ment of the United States, ostensibly, with the purpose of exploring the St. Peter (Minnesota) River to its source and the Red River basin as far as Pembina (North Dakota), near the Canadian border. At the same time the expedition had the task of collecting all types of information, military and scientific, necessary for the defense and colonization of that sensitive and vaguely defined border area of the United States. Beltra-mi saw in the expedition a unique opportunity to push on to the north and asked Major Long to be allowed to join it, "simply in the character of a wanderer who had come thus far to see Indian lands and Indian people."[5] Grudgingly, Major Long gave his consent and Beltrami left Fort St. Anthony with the expedition on July 9, 1823. They remounted the St. Peter River and during the trip Beltrami never failed to take due note of its most important tributaries, to record for us their Indian names, and to describe anything Indian he came across. This became nearly a mania with him for the duration of his journey.

On July 22, the expedition reached Big Stone Lake, left the St. Peter River, and the next day arrived at Lake Traverse. After a few days' rest during which they were entertained by the Great Chief Wanotan of the Sioux, the expedition headed toward Pembina. Pembina had been for years the center of brutal competition between the Hudson's Bay and the Northwest companies for the monopoly of the fur trade. According to Beltrami, the real actors and victims of this competition had been the *bois-brûlés*—the result of the unions between French-Canadian colonists and Indian women—whom he describes as an "execrable race" because

---

[4] *Pilgrimage*, 200.
[5] *Pilgrimage*, 302.

of the atrocities they committed during the "war" between the two companies.[6]

In Pembina, on August 8, Major Long fulfilled one of the main purposes of the expedition by formally taking possession of the settlement on behalf of the United States. Beltrami witnessed the ceremony and dutifully reported that "The boundary which separates the territories of the two nations [the United States and Great Britain] was formally laid down, in the name of the Government and President of the United States."[7] The next day, following some differences with Major Long, Beltrami left the expedition and struck out on his own, plunging into the wilderness in search of the sources of the Mississippi, accompanied only by two Chippewas and a *bois-brûlé*.

The *bois-brûlé* who acted as an interpreter left him at the confluence of the Thief and the Red Lake rivers. Shortly afterwards, the two Chippewas abandoned him after a scuffle with a band of Sioux. All alone and without any experience on how to paddle a canoe, he capsized and then decided to reach Red Lake by towing his canoe up the river. Fortunately, after four days of this exhausting exercise, he met a party of friendly Indians, one of whom agreed to guide the canoe to the lake. At Red Lake, Beltrami had a chance to rest in the tent of the Chippewa who had guided him. Impatient to continue his journey, he pushed on with the help of another Chippewa and another *bois-brûlé* as guides. After a series of portages he reached a small lake which he called Lake Julia, in honor of his friend Countess Giulia Medici-Spada, and proclaimed it to be the northernmost source of the Mississippi. He continued south, encountering a number of small lakes that he named after friends, but unfortunately the names he gave them subsist only in his map. Finally he identified Bitch Lake—later named Itasca Lake by Schoolcraft—as the western sources of the Mississippi. Having completed the task he himself had chosen, he returned to Fort St. Anthony dressed in animal skins, sewed the Indian way, and with a hat made of two pieces of bark. He had lived in the wilderness for nearly three months unflinchingly meeting its challenge, and he had come back to civilization with a wealth of information concerning its geography and its Indian population.

---

[6] *Pilgrimage*, 350.
[7] *Pilgrimage*, 357.

The narration of Beltrami's explorations was published in English under the title of *A Pilgrimage in America Leading to the Discovery of the Sources of the Mississippi and Bloody River; with a Description of the Whole Course of the Former; and of the Ohio.*[8] The book takes the form of thirteen letters, addressed to Countess Geronima Compagnoni. The majority of these letters deal exclusively with the observations about the Indians he made while visiting Fort Armstrong, Fort Edward, and Fort St. Anthony, and while travelling with and among them in their territories. The first Indians with whom he came in contact were the Saukis. According to Beltrami the Saukis numbered only 4,800 members because of the endless little wars they would wage against their enemies, the Ottawa, the Winnebago, and the Potomawa who lived around the shores of the Erie, Michigan, and Huron lakes. Then he met with the Jacovas who lived on the shores of the Jacova River and with the Foxes who, at that time, were only 1,600 individuals divided into four tribes. Later, in the Prairie du Chien, he came across the Winnebago, a group of 1,700 people subdivided into seven tribes, and the Menomenees or Folle Avoine who consisted of only 1,200 people. Of all these groups of Indians, he described the physical and psychological characteristics; he related their history and legends; he explained their customs and ceremonies; he classified their languages. Not only that, but in passing from one group to another, he also observed and pointed out their differences in appearance, language, customs, dwellings, apparel, and artifacts.

Particularly detailed and interesting are his observations on the Sioux and Chippewas, the two most important and numerous Indian nations of the area who were always fighting each other over territory. According to the information Beltrami gathered from Wabiscihouwa, a Sioux chief, and Eskibugekogé, a Chippewa chief, this fighting had been going on for more than three thousand moons. So:

> Reckoning twelve moons to a year, as they do, more than three thousand moons, adding the complementary days, bring us pretty nearly to the time of the conquest of Mexico by the Spaniards.[9]

---

[8] See note 2. Before the English version of his travels, Beltrami had published another, more reduced account of his travels in French: *La Découverte des Sources du Mississippi et de la Rivière Sanglante: Description du Cours du Mississippi, etc.* (New Orleans, Impr. par Benj. Levy, 1824). We shall refer to this book as *Découverte*.

[9] *Pilgrimage*, 236.

Beltrami also speaks of the Assiniboins, brothers of the Sioux, and explains how the two peoples were originally one and they were known as Dakotas. But as he remarks:

> One finds Helens everywhere. The Dakotas had theirs, and she was the cause of as great evils as the beautiful Greek.
>
> Ozolapalda, wife of Winahoà-appà, was caried off by Ohatam-pà, who killed her husband and her two brothers, who came to reclaim her. Discord and vengeance arose between these two tribes, the most powerful of the nation. The relations, friends, and partisans of each, took up the quarrel; one act of revenge begat another, until the whole nation was drawn into a bloody civil war, which eventually divided it into two factions, under the names of Assiniboinà, the partisans of the offender's family, and Siowaé, those of the offended;—like the Bianchi and the Neri, the Uberti and the Buondelmonti, &c. &c.
>
> When they wanted greater extent of country they split into two nations, the Sioux and the Assiniboins; but separation and distance did not put an end to their wars, which continued for a long period of time; it is but lately that they have made peace. The event which gave birth to their divisions happened, according to their calculations, about two hundred years ago; and the identity of their language, manners, and habits, adds weight to their respective traditions. I can vouch for the authenticity of these details, though they are perfectly new and totally unknown even to the garrison of the fort.[10]

Continuing his descriptions of the Sioux, he notes that they are all united by a loose confederation of tribes. Each tribe makes war at its own discretion and manages its own tribal affairs. To decide on issues of interest to the whole Sioux nation, they convene a general council, usually in a forest. On such an occasion each tribe sends a deputy, and any resolution of the council which deserves to be transmitted to posterity is recorded on a tree by means of hieroglyphics (picture writings). Then, the deputy of each tribe carves the "armorial bearing" of the tribe he represents, to indicate his approval.[11] Beltrami is really puzzled, however, when it comes to explaining the religion of the Sioux. He confesses his inability to form any kind of judgement on the subject. The only thing he ventures to say is that they "have traditions without divinities,

---

[10] *Pilgrimage*, 209–10.
[11] *Pilgrimage*, 211.

Costantino Beltrami's search for the headwaters of the Mississippi River led to encounters with several Native American groups, some of whom, including the Sioux, he described in detail in his *Pilgrimage in America*. Portrayed in this sketch are several Sioux racing at Fort Pierre in 1833.

ceremonies without worship and superstitions without religion: the homage they pay to the sun and the moon, if it deserves the name of religious worship, is certainly the only one which exists among them."[12]

With respect to the population density of the Sioux nation, he relates the information obtained from the Great Chief Wanatá and gives a list of the bands that compose the nation and of the tribes which compose the bands. For each of these units, he indicates the name of the chiefs, their territories, and their numbers, which totalled 44,950 people. Then he continues describing their camps and their daily lives without forgetting even the most trivial detail. He enriches his own observations with the information obtained from the Indians themselves and from Mr. Renville, one of the guides of the Long expedition who was born and raised among the Sioux.

---

[12] *Pilgrimage*, 212.

Also the observations on the Chippewas, the Sioux's traditional enemies, take up quite a few pages of the *Pilgrimage*. This is so for two reasons. First, after the Sioux, the Chippewas were the most important
nation of the area, both in numbers and in territory. They were "scattered over those immense regions from Lake Ontario to Lake Winnipeg, near Hudson's Bay, a tract of about two thousand miles from east
south-east, to north-west."[13] Second, because he had been in closer and
more intimate contact with them than any other Indian tribe. During
his lonely search for the sources of the Mississippi, his guides had been
members of this nation. He had been received in their tents, had shared
their daily lives, and had been allowed to participate in their ceremonies.
Just to give an idea on how close he had become to the Chippewas, it
would be sufficient to note that they admitted him to their tribal council and asked his counsel on such an important matter as organizing a
punitive raid against the Sioux who had killed the chief's son-in-law.

Fortunately, he was wise enough to suggest that the only one who
could advise them was their agent at Fort St. Anthony, Major Tagliaferro. In spite of those who wanted immediate revenge, his suggestion
was accepted, but this personal involvement in their tribal life nearly
cost him his life. Twice he escaped assassination, thanks to the help of
Woascita, the beautiful daughter of Cloudy-Weather, the Chippewa
chief. Once he saved his own life and the chief's, only after a strenuous
hand-to-hand combat against two drunken Chippewas who had attacked
them.[14] This episode marked the end of Beltrami's life in the wilderness. The day after, accompanied by Cloudy-Weather, he started his
voyage to return to civilization.

In conclusion, even a cursory reading of the headings in which each
letter of the *Pilgrimage* is subdivided shows the wealth of information
gathered by this courageous Italian explorer. Nothing escapes his observant and keen eyes, especially for that which concerns the social organization, the daily life, and the culture of the tribes he visited. Everything
is taken into consideration: their origins, their social structure, their laws
and traditions, their religious beliefs and superstitions, their marriages
and their funerals, their dances and their medicine, their warfare tactics
and their peaceful pursuits, their sacrifices to appease the world of the

---

[13] *Pilgrimage*, 227.   [14] *Pilgrimage*, 449.

spirits and their sacred festivals to thank them, the leisurely life of the
summer months and the hard toil of the winter hunt, the prerogatives
of warriors and the unhappy conditions of women. In addition he gives
us an idea on how limited their scientific knowledge was. For instance,
he relates that they divide the year into twelve moons or months. He
lists the name of each moon in the Sioux and Chippewa languages and
observes that:

> The Indians have no division of the week. They reckon the days only
> by sleepings. They divide the day into halves and quarters, measuring the
> time by the course of the sun from its rising to its setting.
>
> Though the Indians are completely ignorant of geography, as well as
> of every other science, they have a method of denoting by hieroglyphics
> on the bark of certain papyriferous trees, all the countries with which they
> are acquainted. These maps want only the degrees of latitude and longi-
> tude to be more correct than those of some of our own visionary geogra-
> phers.[15]

He stresses that the course of the sun directs them by day and the north
star by night. When neither is visible, it is the color and the position of
the grass, of the tree tops, and of the moss that directs them when they
travel. Finally he informs us that their knowledge of arithmetic is so
rudimentary that in their languages there is no word for million and billion. Their largest number is one thousand.[16]

Another important source for the study of Indians in the American
continent is Beltrami's *Le Méxique* in two volumes.[17] Written in French,
the book has never been translated into Italian or English, and it may
be considered a continuation of the *Pilgrimage*. Like the *Pilgrimage*, it
takes the form of thirteen letters addressed to Countess Geronima Compagnoni and contains observations and impressions of his travels in
Mexico. The first letter is dated Tampico, May 28, 1824; the last one is
dated Alvarado, May 24, 1825. The book includes very interesting descriptions of the people, the geography, the climate, the vegetation of that
country. Most important for the historian, it tries to give an accurate
picture of the political and moral situation of the Mexican nation, in the
first years of its independence.

---

[15] *Pilgrimage*, 275.   [16] *Pilgrimage*, 276.
[17] Giacomo Costantino Beltrami, *Le Méxique*, 2 vols. (Paris: Crevot, 1830).

The book has a manifest political intention. Beltrami states that he has travelled to Mexico, moved by feelings of admiration for the Mexicans' strength of character, their love for freedom, their art, and their republican institutions.[18] And he concludes with a "good-bye" to the Mexicans expressing his hope that his work has helped to vindicate them from the calumnies with which the enemies of their independence have tried to smear their national character:

> Good-bye also to you, peoples for a long time slaves and always worthy of being free! Good-bye, Mexicans! May I have avenged you of the calumnies of your detractors, frivolous or malicious, by an impartial account of your customs, of your arts, of your new and old institutions! May I have joined to my best wishes and hopes, the expression of some useful truth![19]

As far as the Indians of Mexico are concerned, Beltrami was of the opinion that the history of ancient Mexico, written under Spanish domination, was full of inaccuracies because of ignorance and prejudice.[20] Therefore, he made it a point to look for original documents that could help him rectify them. He found an ancient record consisting of fourteen pictures surrounded by glyphs, painted on specially treated agave leaves, bound together to form a book. According to Beltrami, the fourteen pictures represented and the glyphs narrated the history of the fourteen kings of the Mexican nation—the Aztecs—who ruled before the conquest. They were made by the Indians under the supervision of Father Toribio de Benavente (Motolinia), in order to save from destruction a record of their ancient history. With the help of other documents researched in the Mexican archives and of the works of Fray Juan de Torquemada,[21] Beltrami tries to interpret these pictures and in so doing he devotes a whole long letter (Letter X) to the writing of a short history of the colonization of the Valley of Mexico by the various Indian peoples who settled there, up to the time of the Spanish conquest. This letter gives an excellent idea of their political organization, their religion, their art, and their traditions. As far as the glyphs are concerned, however, he confesses his ignorance and tells the reader that he leaves the glory of their interpretation to some scholar who has the patience and the talent to do it.[22]

---

[18] *Le Méxique*, I, ix–x.

[19] *Le Méxique*, II, 369. Translation by the author.

[20] *Le Méxique*, II, 88–89.

[21] *Le Méxique*, II, 88.

[22] *Le Méxique*, II, 87–88.

In *Le Méxique* he also mentions the finding of a copy of the *Comme-ntary on the Sunday Epistles and Gospels (Postila sobre las Epistolas y Evan-gelios Domenicales)* written by Fray Bernardino de Sahagún in Nahuatl and expresses his hope that this finding will greatly improve the under-standing of this language and help discover the origin of the people who spoke it.

> ... to conclude, I want only to notice, with Leibnitz, Vico, and others, that languages are the only monuments of the moral and civil history of primitive people; consequently, it is in the language, especially of the Mexicans [Aztecs], that philosophers may find a guide which may lead them to know, or at least to conjecture, their origins and their migra-tions. From the origins of the Mexicans will come forth, perhaps, some plausible inductions on the origin of the other American peoples.[23]

With the Louisiana Purchase (1803), the United States acquired an immense territory, still uncharted, inhabited by Indian tribes whose con-tacts with the white man had been minimal. For what concerns the northern Mississippi-Missouri area, attempts had been made to explore it by William Clark and Meriwether Lewis (1804) and by Lieutenant Zebulon M. Pike (1805). Further attempts were interrupted by the 1812 War, the last war in which Indians allied themselves with a foreign colo-nial power against the United States. After the war, the exploration of the upper part of the Mississippi River basin resumed with William Cass, who explored the wilderness of Minnesota and Wisconsin (1820). The exploration of these territories had been accompanied by efforts to deal with the Indian population who lived in it. In 1815 the United States signed the first treaty with the Sioux; in 1819 Congress, for the first time, appropriated a fund ($10,000) to civilize the Indians; and in 1824 the Bureau of Indian Affairs was established in the War Department of the United States government.[24]

This interest in the Indians was dictated by practical and moral rea-sons. Practically, the United States government aimed to safeguard the settlers, defend the Canadian border, quell intertribal warfare, and pro-tect the Indians from the ruthless practices of the fur traders that caused a state of constant tension between Indians and whites. Morally, the

---

[23] *Le Méxique*, II, 176–77.

[24] Harold E. Driver, *Indians of North America*, 2nd ed. (Chicago and London: The University of Chicago Press, 1975), 482.

American people, among a lot of controversy on how to solve the Indian problem, aimed to acquire "a more accurate knowledge of their actual condition, and devise the most suitable plan to advance their civilization
and happiness."[25] So, together with the foundations of forts, such as Fort
Howard at Green Bay, Fort Crawford at Prairie du Chien, Fort St.
Anthony at the junction of the Mississippi and Minnesota rivers, to
attain its practical goals; the government of the United States established Indian agents and sent missionaries like Jedidiah Morse to observe
and inspect the various Indian tribes, in order to fulfill its moral commitment.[26] This is the historical background in which the *Pilgrimage*
should be read and its great contribution to the knowledge of the Indians evaluated.

The very same reasons that made Beltrami's search for the sources of
the Mississippi an object of criticism, controversy, and discussion—such
as the fact that he did not have with him competent people to chart his
exploration, to witness his discovery, and to give its geographical coor-
dinates—helped him collect information about Indians. Because he was
alone, he was not considered a threat. Because he was an Italian, namely, one who did not belong to any of the white peoples they knew and
mistrusted, he did not arouse their suspicions. Because he was brave,
generous, and an excellent marksman, he aroused their admiration.
Because he approached them as human beings, he gained their friendship and trust. They called him Tonka-Wasci-cio-honska (the Great
Chief from a Far Country) and Kitci-Okiman (the Great Warrior) and
they did not hesitate to take him into their confidence.[27] On his part,
Beltrami did not betray this confidence and accurately and faithfully
reported what he heard and what he saw. He did not have any interest
to do otherwise. He did not belong to any of the nationalities or interest groups who, in those territories, were fighting for land, furs, commercial privileges, or souls. Furthermore, and even more remarkable, he

---

[25] Jedidiah Morse, *A Report to the Secretary of War of The United States on Indian Affairs, by Jedidiah Morse* (New York: A.M. Kelley, 1970), 11. Originally printed in New Haven in 1822.

[26] To solve the Indian problem, Mr. Morse, in his *Report*, advocated missionary action, intermar-
riage, and education, especially for Indian women (pp. 74–75). Beltrami, as a commentary to
Morse's *Report*, suggests that before any missionary action is undertaken the Indians should be
fed, first and foremost (*Pilgrimage*, 471–72).

[27] To the point of confessing to him that they often amuse themselves by "gulling the credulity" of
white traders with imaginary tales about Indian life (*Pilgrimage*, 418).

did not succumb to the romantic myth of the noble savage. Beltrami
sees and describes the North American Indians, objectively, as members of the family of man, with flaws and virtues, and in the context of
the history of mankind. Consequently, he constantly reminds the reader of the similarities—in attire, artifacts, customs, ceremonies, religious
practices, attitudes—which exist between them and the peoples of ancient
and modern times. He is not blind to their shortcomings, but makes us
aware that some of these shortcomings are not peculiar to the Indians,
indeed they are very common also to the white men.[28] As a matter of
fact, when compared with the white traders who cheated them, the Indians are definitely superior. And Beltrami cannot help accusing the white
men of having a corrupting influence over the Indians.

> . . . the Indians will revenge themselves, but will not descend to the office
> of accuser. There is great dignity and magnanimity in the silence they
> observe with regard to the traders, who are not ashamed to cheat them
> in every possible way. This is one powerful cause of their constant and
> increasing hostility to civilized people. The Red men, who are most in
> contact with the whites, are uniformly the worst. The Red women are
> completely corrupted by their intercourse with the white men. They have
> all the vices of both races; nor can they find a single virtue to imitate in
> men who come among them only to sate their sensuality and their avarice.[29]

Neither can he help lamenting the obtuseness of most of the whites
who do not recognize how many noble minds are concealed under the
rude exterior of the Indians, "notwithstanding the vices which their contact with civilized nations has already planted in their hearts."[30] Of course,
this does not mean that he is idealizing the Indian. While he expresses
his admiration for the pride, the dignity, the courage, the endurance they
display on many occasions, he condemns them for the cunning, unreli-
ability, cruelty they exhibit in others. He is especially critical of their
contempt of women. In his opinion, it is this contempt which retards
their civilization and increases their ferocity:

> The man who feels no moral sensibility, no moral attachment, towards
> that being whom heaven has destined to participate in our consolations
> and our difficulties, in our smiles and our best affections; towards the
> being by whom we are born in pain and reared with extreme tenderness

---

[28] *Pilgrimage*, 189.   [29] *Pilgrimage*, 224.   [30] *Pilgrimage*, 30.

and self-denial,—who enables a man to live again in his posterity, and whose graces, and love, and genuine friendship, constitute the very extract and essence of human happiness—such a man must inevitably be a barbarian or a brute, and his soul dead to every sentiment of virtue.[31]

In conclusion, however, he must confess that even though he has described the Indians and their culture exactly as they appeared to him, he cannot pass judgement on them. They are unique. They present the white observer with so many extreme contradictions that any fair judgement is impossible. In Beltrami's own words:

> In their manners, their customs, and their ceremonies, we see traces of the ancients, the moderns, all times, and all nations; but they resemble no other nation in the world. After such a contrast of sentiments and actions, of propensities and devotions, I leave it to those who can compress everything into a system, to decide on the character and the religion of the Indians. I hope they will be more fortunate than he who while attempting to catch the moon in a fountain was drowned in it himself.[32]

Concerning the Mexican Indians, in *Le Méxique* Beltrami aligned himself with the Mexican *indigenistas* who tried to rehabilitate the high Indian cultures as a worthy component of the glorious past of the Mexican nation.[33] In so doing, he followed the footsteps of two other Italians, Lorenzo Benaducci Boturini and Gian Rinaldo Carli. The former had demythicized pre-conquest Mexican history by applying Gian Battista Vico's theories to his *Idea de uno, nueva historia general de la America septentrional* (1746).[34] The latter, in his *Delle lettere americane* (1780), had already defended the Indians of the charges of natural inferiority levelled at them by the Abbé Corneille de Pauw in his *Recherches philosophique sur les Americains* (1768).

Like Boturini, even though to a much lesser extent and not as a professional historian, also Beltrami tried to contribute to the knowledge of the history of ancient Mexico by collecting documents. He offered to the attention of the scholars the codex he had found with the *Commen-*

---

[31] *Pilgrimage*, 245–46.

[32] *Pilgrimage*, 299.

[33] For example: Fray Benito Maria de Moxó, Servando Teresa de Mier, Carlos Maria de Bustamante, to cite only a few who were Beltrami's contemporaries.

[34] Benjamin Keen, *The Aztec Image in Western Thought* (New Brunswick, N.J.: Rutgers University Press, 1971), 234.

tary on the Sunday Epistles and Gospels.[35] He even made it available to the
members of the Academy of Sciences in Paris. In London he showed it
to Lord Kingsborough, a famous expert on Mexican history, so that he
could derive from it any type of information useful to his work.[36] Apparently, nobody paid attention to it. Nor did the Academy of Sciences pay
more attention to the other ancient manuscript containing the history
of the first fourteen Aztec rulers that Beltrami had sent them.[37] Unfortunately, the originals of both works were lost. What is left of them is
their descriptions in *Le Méxique*,[38] in the *Revue Encyclopédique*, and a
copy of the *Commentary*, printed in Milan in 1856 by the types of Bernar-
doni, under the title of *Evangelarium, Epistolarium et Lectionarium Axte-
cum*, with glossary and notes of Bernardo Biondelli.[39]

Like Gian Rinaldo Carli, he defended the intelligence of the Mexican Indians by citing the success of the College for Indians in Tiateloico,
under the wise and benevolent guidance of Fray Bernardino de Sahagún,[40]
and vindicated them from the unwarranted accusation of being malin-
gerers and lazy. Beltrami's argument was, how is it possible to consider
lazy and slothful a people who built a highly civilized nation and, without the help of work animals and metallic tools, created a thriving commerce, a flourishing industry, an intensive agriculture, and exquisite
works of art in stone and precious metals.[41]

From what has been said so far, it is obvious that Beltrami's work
should have constituted a valuable source of information on North American ethnology. Unfortunately it was not so, or perhaps it was so, but he
was given no credit. For instance, in the studies contained in the *Annual Reports of the Bureau of Ethnology to the Secretary of the Smithsonian
Institution*, which avail themselves also of information gathered from
travellers and explorers like Beltrami, he is mentioned only a few times.
Namely, concerning the funeral ceremonies of the Chippewas, in a study
of Harry Crécy Yarrow;[42] as regards the socio-political organization of

---

[35] Beltrami's letter to the President of the Academy of Sciences of Paris, dated April 25, 1830 (from
   Costantino Beltrami da Bergamo . . . , 100–2).   [36] *Le Méxique*, II, 88.
[37] Beltrami's letter to the President of the Academy of Sciences of Paris, dated May 10, 1830 (from
   Costantino Beltrami da Bergamo . . . , 103–4).   [38] *Le Méxique*, II, 175.
[39] *Costantino Beltrami da Bergamo . . .* , 35.   [40] *Le Méxique*, II, 120.
[41] *Le Méxique*, I, 227–8.
[42] "A Further Contribution to the Study of the Mortuary Customs of the North American Indians," in *First Annual Report of the Bureau of Ethnology to the Secretary of the Smithsonian Institution 1879–1880* (Washington: Government Printing Press), 190–91, 197.

the Sioux, in a study by Garrick Mallory;[43] and with reference to the
Indian names of months and rivers, and in respect to the population of
the Fox Indians, in a study by Albert Ernest Jenks.[44] In many other studies that deal with the ethnology of the tribes Beltrami had written so
much about, he is not even remembered. Of little consolation is the fact
that Hubert Howe Bancroft took into consideration also Beltrami's *Le
Méxique*, in the writing of his impressive *The Native Races of the Pacific
States of North America*,[45] and that the famous German anthropologist
Theodore Waitz, who knew Beltrami's work on Mexico listed it in the
bibliography of his monumental *Anthropologie der Naturvölker*.[46] The
fact remains that professional ethnographers nearly completely ignored
or were not aware of Beltrami's work. Yet the information it contained
is so varied and unique that even in more recent times some literates
found it useful. For instance, Professor William J. Peterson, of the University of Iowa, used the *Pilgrimage* as the main source for his article on
Minnesota history, which describes the momentous voyage of the *Virginia*, the first steamboat to navigate the waters of the upper Mississippi into Indian territory (1823).[47] Professor Allen E. Woodall, of Pittsburgh
University, refers to Beltrami to confirm the authenticity of the Indian
legends and tales that inspired some of the short stories of William
Joseph Snelling.[48] Professor Margaret Murray Gibb, in her important
study on the influence of Fenimore Cooper in France, cites Beltrami's
Découverte (Letter VII) to characterize the *coureurs de bois*.[49]

Naturally, this brings up the topic of the influence Beltrami's works
had in the literary field. In a letter he wrote from his villa near Heidel-
berg, he complained that without giving him any credit, James Feni-

---

[43] "Pictographs of the North American Indians—A Preliminary Paper by Garrick Mallory," in
Fourth Annual Report . . . , (1882–83), 104–5.

[44] "The Wild-Rice Gatherers of the Upper Lakes," in *Nineteenth Annual Report . . .* (1897–98), Part
2, pp. 1051, 1090, 1121, 1122.

[45] "Notizie di G.C. Beltrami sugli Indigeni Americani," in *Atti del XXII Congresso degli American-
isti* (Roma, 1926), 695.

[46] *Anthropologie der Naturvölker—Die Amerikaner, Ernste Hälfte, Dritter Theil* (Leipzig: Friedrich
Fleischer, 182), xx.

[47] "The 'Virginia,' the 'Clermont' of the Upper Mississippi," *Minnesota History* 9 (Dec. 1928): 347–62.

[48] "William Joseph Snelling and the Early North West," *Minnesota History* 10 (Dec. 1929): 367–85.

[49] *Le Roman de Bas-de-Cuir, Etude sur Fenimore Cooper et Son Influence en France* (Paris: Librarie
Ancienne Honoré Champion, 1927), 198.

more Cooper had used his descriptions of Indian life in his novels.[50]
Some of his American biographers state that Cooper acknowledged his
debt to him.[51] To the best of my knowledge, however, to this time, there
has not been any detailed study of the extent to which the American
novelist used Beltrami material, either directly or indirectly. Quite different is the case of René de Chateaubriand. As August P. Miceli, Beltrami's most recent American biographer, puts it: "Chateaubriand paid
Beltrami the double compliment of quoting from the *Découverte, etc.*,
with and without attribution."[52]

Referring to a study made by a scholar, Ernest Dick, who compared
the Chateaubriand and Beltrami books, paragraph by paragraph,[53] the
author of *The Man with the Red Umbrella* concludes that of 180 pages
of the *Voyage en Amérique* Chateaubriand borrowed almost 59 pages
from Beltrami's *La Découverte* and gave him credit only for a little more
than 2.[54]

> The appropriation from Beltrami covers a considerable part of the *Voy-
> age*, particularly the sections on animals (castors, bears, deer, buffaloes,
> reptiles), Indian customs (marriages, children, funerals, dances, hunting,
> war, calendars, medicine, language, religion), Indian tribes (the Natchez,
> Hurons, Iroquois, and other Indians of North America), and the itiner-
> ary along the Ohio and Mississippi.[55]

Nor was Chateaubriand's borrowing limited to his *Voyage en Amérique*,
also the *Mémoires d'Outre-Tombe* and his novel *Le Natchez* contain pages
and passages borrowed from Beltrami, without any credit given.[56]

At this point, one question arises: Why only literates took into consideration the writings of this intelligent, cultured, and versatile man,
while ethnographers nearly completely ignored them, in spite of the
wealth of ethnographical information they contained? Perhaps because
literates found in them excellent material suitable for further creative elab-

---

[50] Masi, *Giacomo Costantino Beltrami . . .* , 49.
[51] Giovanni Schiavo, *The Italians In America Before the Civil War* (New York-Chicago: The Vigo
Press, 1934), 97.
[52] Miceli, *The Man with the Red Umbrella*, 133.
[53] Ernest Dick, *Plagiats de Chateaubriand, le Voyage en Amérique* (Berne, 1905), 5–53.
[54] Miceli, *The Man with the Red Umbrella*, 134–35.
[55] Miceli, *The Man with the Red Umbrella*, 136.
[56] Ernest Dick, "Quelques Sources Ignorées du 'Voyage en Amérique' de Chateaubriand," *Revue
d'Histoire Littéraire de la France* 13 (1906): 228–45.

oration, while scholars considered them unreliable and amateurish. After all, Beltrami did not really belong to their community. Perhaps because the "experts" concentrated their attention and their criticism mainly on the geographical aspect of Beltrami's work, since his claim to fame rested principally on the exploration and discovery of the sources of the Mississippi. Very likely, however, the reason—or one of the reasons—may be that when the state of Minnesota in 1868 officially recognized the worth of his work as an explorer, by naming after him its largest county and an island, in a sense, it was too late to fully appreciate his contribution to ethnography. His observations and considerations on the Indians, disregarded up to that point, had lost their originality and had been superseded by the works of subsequent travellers and ethnologists. Furthermore, by that time, his books had become very scarce, especially in Italy, where Austria had ordered their sequestration, so very few people were able to verify and give him credit for the work he had done.[57]

In 1898, Albert E. Jenks, speaking of the Siouan names for September and October, in his study on the wild-rice gatherers, observed that "as early as 1828 Beltrami cited the names of these two months."[58] While Mr. Jenks' recognition is to be commended, Beltrami's work certainly deserves more credit than a mere acknowledgment. A careful reading of the articles which appeared, up to 1900, in the *Annual Reports of the Bureau of American Ethnology*, especially those dealing with the Sioux and the Chippewas, reveals that Beltrami had already said, as early as 1828, much more about Indians than the mere names of the months in Siouan. He had described and had tried to explain Indian cultures going back to their very origin. Some of his statements may seem obvious today; but their proper evaluation should take into due consideration some of the "fashionable" theories of his times. Then, just as important as the theory that the Indians had come from Asia through the Strait of Bering, was the theory that they were the survivors of the mythical Atlantis. Others saw in them the descendants of one of the Lost Tribes of Israel. The matter of their origin and of their civilization became even more complicated when the Mayan ruins of Yucatan and Guatemala began to astonish the world. Some ventured the theory that these ruins

---

[57] Masi, "Notizie di G.C. Beltrami . . . ," 692.
[58] "The Wild-Rice Gatherers," 1090.

had been the center from where all civilization had moved westward to China, Egypt, Greece, and Rome. For instance, in 1807, Guillermo Dupaix, the pioneer Mayan archeologist, maintained that the Maya Indians had come from Atlantis or from some other land to the east of it. The scholarly Brasseur de Bourbourg, translator into French of the *Popul-Vuh* (1861), the Mayan epic, also held the theory of Atlantis to be true.[59] The Viscount of Kingsborough lost his money and his freedom in publishing the nine volumes of the *Antiquities of Mexico* (1831–48) with the sole purpose of proving that the American Indians were the descendants of one of the Lost Tribes of Israel.[60] So, when Beltrami states that the Indians came from Asia through the Strait of Bering[61] and gives his reasons for this statement, he is doing much more than repeating a possible and known theory. He is making a considerate choice among equally important and, at the time, probable alternatives.

Similarly, when he correctly states that the mounds of St. Louis were the work of American Indians, he runs against the wild speculations of some of his contemporaries who considered them to be the work of a mythical super-race which supposedly flourished before the Indians came; or of the survivors of the sunken, and yet ever present, Atlantis; or, as others ventured, the work of Egyptians and Phoenicians wandering far from home. It took the magisterial work of the American archeologist Ephraim George Squier, *Ancient Monuments of the Mississippi Valley*, published in 1848, to silence these fantasies. Incidentally, Squier is the same archeologist who, in the Royal Library of Paris, in the autumn of 1855 found another copy of Sahagun's *Commentary on the Sunday Epistles and Gospels*, apparently similar to the one Beltrami had brought from Mexico and uselessly put at the disposal of the Academy of Sciences of Paris for examination, as early as 1830.[62]

In conclusion, Beltrami's *Pilgrimage* and *Le Méxique* are much more than simple narrations of things seen, heard, and done during a trip of exotic exploration. They contain more than enough ethnographic data to list them among the first works of ethnography written on the American Indians.

---

[59] Robert L. Brunhouse, *In Search of the Maya* (New York: Ballantine Books, 1976), 28, 127.
[60] Victor W. Von Hagen, *The Aztec, Man and Tribe* (New York: Mentor Books, 1961), 207 n48.
[61] *Pilgrimage*, 258–59.
[62] *Costantino Beltrami da Bergamo . . .* , 34–35.

Notes and Documents
The Middle West in 1837
Translations from the Notes of an Italian Count Francesco Arese

Edited by Lynn M. Case

I N THE YEAR 1836 Prince Louis Napoleon, later Napoleon III of
France, was exiled to America by the French Orleans monarchy
because of his unsuccessful *coup d'état* at Strassbourg. One of the
prince's pleasant consolations during this exile was the companionship
of Count Francesco Arese of Milan. Since the two had long been close
friends, the prince's mother, the former Queen Hortense of Holland,
had chosen Arese to go to America to help relieve her son's loneliness.
Although he had gladly accepted the mission and had remained loyally at Napoleon's side during his sojourn in New York, yet, when the
young prince hurriedly returned to Europe in 1837, Arese decided to
remain behind and make a tour of the United States. From New York
he went to Philadelphia, Baltimore, and Washington. Then he crossed
Virginia, passed down the Ohio to St. Louis, ascended the Missouri,
crossed the plains to Green Bay, Wisconsin, and returned to New York
by the way of the Great Lakes and Canada.

During all of this long journey, which lasted from June to about
November 1837, he wrote long, detailed notes in French on the geography and people of the regions through which he passed. These notes
were read after his death in the *Congresso geografico di Venezia* in 1881.

Later they were published in an appendix to Romualdo Bonfadini's biography of Arese.[1] But the copies of that book are so scarce in the United States, and so few students of American social history are able to learn of their existence because of their relegation to the appendix that it has been thought worthwhile not only to publish the more valuable extracts in more available form but also to translate them into English. William Roscoe Thayer translated and read the few paragraphs on Boston before the meeting of the Massachusetts Historical Society on which occasion he expressed the hope that all of the notes might eventually be translated and published.[2] Although Thayer's paragraphs on Boston were published in the Massachusetts Historical Society *Proceedings*, no further attempt was made to add this source to the many others of similar nature which had previously been made available for the study of American life in the early nineteenth century.

The present translation covers those parts of his notes dealing with the Ohio and Mississippi valleys and the Great Lakes. Because of their length his notes on the Atlantic seaboard and the Indians of the plains have not been included.

🙮 🙮 🙮

I LEFT GUYANDOTTE on a little steamboat which, although small, was typically American in its good construction, attractiveness, cleanliness, and comfort. From Guyandotte I went to Cincinnati. The earlier French colonizers of this region rightly called the Ohio "Beautiful River," for it is indeed very beautiful with well-cultivated hills, lovely farms, and growing towns lining its shores and offering the traveller a delightful scene of constant variety. In the distance a second row of higher hills covered with majestic forests could often be seen. Unfortunately the river's muddy water, caused by the heavy rains, detracted much from the beauty of the

---

[1] Romualdo Bonfadini, *Vita di Francesco Arese* (Turin, 1894).

[2] Massachusetts Historical Society *Proceedings* (Boston, 1791–), 43 (1909), 88–92. In this paper Thayer says: "The book, so far as I can discover, has never been read, or even mentioned over here. There is no reference to it in Mr. John Brooks's *As Others See Us* . . . nor have I seen it noted elsewhere. . . . [His notes] are also unique because no other highly cultivated, much travelled and observant Italian has left any similar account of our country as early as the thirties of the last century. Arese's notes, as he modestly calls them, might be worth translating and publishing entire."

scene. On our way down I saw the city of Portsmouth perched on a rather high part of the river's bank. I gained a rather exact impression of the extent of its commerce from the large shops, stores, and the activity which I noticed there. I saw Maysville only by moonlight, so I shall not say much about it. During this short trip I saw a large number of steamboats and flatboats going up and down the river, which indicated to me what progress was being made in this region.

Cincinnati is not only the largest city in Ohio but, I believe, also in the West. In a way it is the trading center (*entrepôt*) of this part of the Union. This city is well located, well built, and rather of the Philadelphia type (which is a very excellent one). It is surprising to learn that the city was founded in 1808, had a population of 16,000 in 1816, 26,000 by 1830, and now [1837] boasts of 40,000. A large number of Germans and Alsatians have settled here, amounting to about four-fifths of the population. The *"Ja, mein Herr"* heard in the streets, the number of cafes and breweries with their German signs, and the peasants dressed in black velvet with red vests and big silver buttons carried my fancy back to Mannheim. Indeed, even the construction of its streets added more realism to my dream. In all other respects Mannheim is a much more beautiful city than Cincinnati. I saw the exterior of the house built by Mrs. Trollope, the architecture of which is just as grotesque and fantastic as the writings of the above-mentioned. I took a short run into the neighboring hills from which a majestic view is had of the city and the river, the latter stretching in a meandering fashion between Ohio and Kentucky. From the outside the country houses which I saw resembled Swiss cottages.

To do something unusual I shall place a date here: it is the evening of the 16th of July at Cincinnati, and tomorrow I shall set out to cross Kentucky. I left Cincinnati for Lexington. On the Ohio shore opposite Cincinnati two pleasant little towns are seen, separated by the little Liking [*sic*] River. I cannot refrain from remarking about the striking contrast between the two towns located on the opposite shores of the Ohio. Cincinnati has only been in existence for about thirty years, already has 40,000 inhabitants, and is still growing. Newport, one of Kentucky's oldest towns with a history of 160 years [*sic*], and at the time of the War of Independence a recruiting center for the Republican army, has now a stationary population of only 1,600. The comparison which I have just made between the two cities can be extended, on a less absolute scale, to all Ohio and Kentucky. And what is the cause of it? *Slavery.* The people in Kentucky, who are enlightened enough to see it, admit it themselves and wish for an early abolition of the system which they find not only unnecessary but harmful to their state. I went through Kentucky by way of Georgetown, crossed Eagles Hill, passed through Frankfort, a charming little town very well located on the shores of the Kentucky, and finally arrived at the attractive city of Lexington. In fact it is rather rural in appearance since its houses are so scattered that, with the exception of the main street and one or two others, you would think you were viewing a group of several country houses rather than a regular [*proprement dite*] city.

I was to see Mr. Henry Clay for whom I had a letter of introduction. He was a famous man of this region who, as candidate, had a good chance of becoming president. Unfortunately I did not find him at his country home because he had gone to town for the court sessions or something of that nature. I inspected his estate and found his house well built, comfortable, and elegantly furnished, and the farm itself a perfect model for that kind of an establishment. They besought me to return next day to see Mr. Clay, but as that would have caused me to lose two days, I gave up the idea.

I admit that I have no mania to meet noted men, such as have Englishmen and Americans. They do not do it in order to appreciate their ability and qualities, but merely to be able to say: "I am very well acquainted with him." As a matter of fact, unless one is very indiscreet, there is never enough time during a first visit to enable a person to judge a man's merit. At the most he can only judge his patience. I think that the method of becoming acquainted with a man by making him a single visit is almost the same as the method some adopt for visiting libraries when they look only at the cartons and the bindings of the volumes.

I left Lexington for Louisville, which is a rather well built, very commercial town on the Ohio. In the evening I went to the theatre. It was not bad, and its audience was quite respectable in appearance.

The more honest and less boastful Americans call the countryside around Lexington [Louisville?] the garden of the United States; others call it the garden *of the world!* It is true that it has beauty, but a positive, numerical, monetary, quite American kind of beauty. It is a land rich in unsurpassed vegetation where fields are covered with wheat five feet high. It is a landscape flat enough to give you an extremely uniform and monotonous horizon: in fine it is a region which appeals to the purse rather than to the imagination.

Before I leave Ohio and Kentucky, allow me to make some general observations. The State of Ohio is very well cultivated, and the Germans, who make up the largest part of the population of this state, are the best settlers that could be desired. I cannot say very much about the interior of the state, having seen it only from the steamboat and being acquainted only with the cities and their surroundings. Kentucky is also a very rich region from an agricultural standpoint. I saw its fine fields and majestic forests, much more beautiful than those through which I travelled in Virginia. Virginia's virgin forests are, to tell the truth, a wall of foliage, trunks of trees, and vines so closely packed together that it is quite impossible to penetrate them without an axe. In addition there are many fallen, decaying tree trunks which have been either struck by lightning or blown down by the wind. In a forest like that most of the trees are not of a very large size because, being so close together, they hinder each other's growth. What few clearings there are, are marshy because the sun's rays have considerable difficulty in penetrating to the soil to dry it. In those forests you are likely to encounter snakes of all kinds and sizes. The rattlesnake is very common there, and you often hear its familiar music. To digress, I may say, of the various kinds of American music this is one of those which I least prefer. In Kentucky, on the other hand, the trees are so well spaced that they attain gigantic dimensions, and the eye can penetrate to a considerable distance into the forests where the ground is covered with the most delightful green grass. On first seeing such forests I thought that the hand of man had had something to do with them, and I began to lose faith in the superiority of good old virginity, especially as applied to forests. But I soon perceived that these too were virgin forests, which caused me to become somewhat more reconciled to them again.

The manners of the people in the Ohio Valley, especially those of the Kentuckians, are the opposite of those of Virginia. It is the reverse side of the medal, and if the ocean separated these states, the difference could not be greater. Out of love for the truth I must say that the people to whom I was recommended I found rather commendable. But as to the crowd travelling on steamboats and stages, the kind encountered in the hotels including all classes of society—for in America everybody travels and especially in the West—it must be admitted that this throng is very uncultivated, impolite, dishonest, disagreeable, filthy. In a word they are the worst conceivable beasts dressed as men. It must be added that Kentuckians have an unlimited egotism. If Americans themselves, who are more than sufficiently supplied with it, also criticize them for egotism, certainly this fault of the good people of Kentucky exceeds all limits. I really cannot refrain from copying here a notice which I read in the reading room of one of the best hotels in Louisville, perhaps the most important and most commercial city in Kentucky:

> Gentlemen are particularly requested not to deface or remove the files of newspapers from the Reading room: waste paper can be had on applying at the bar!!

In spite of such a positive and solemn sign, not a paper had been respected. It is to be remembered, too, that the season of fevers or other illnesses had not yet begun!!

I left Louisville to continue down the Ohio, a charming river although a little monotonous. Its waters, generally clear and green, unfortunately were rough during my trip. Since the Ohio was too low to allow us to go over the rapids, the steamboat went through a parallel canal dug for this purpose for a distance of two miles. It connects with the Ohio again by means of four large locks. Exactly thirty-two minutes are necessary to go through these large gates. It is about the same time as that needed to change coach horses. Unfortunate is he who has to travel in America by land; but on the contrary fortunate is he who can travel by water, whether it be on the sailing vessels of the sea, the river steamers, or even canal boats. On leaving the canal, you can see the beautiful shores of the Ohio for some one hundred miles, bordered by heights covered with forests. After that they become flat and monotonous. From time to time you see houses, cultivated fields, and little villages which are done the honor of being called towns [*villes*]. From the Ohio we enter the Mississippi at Trinity. At the mouth, both rivers being rough because of the rains, I could not enjoy the sight of their uniting without mixing, which can often be seen because one of them is usually clear and the other muddy. However, having seen several small rivers, whose waters were crystal clear, join the Mississippi and still keep their color as far as eye could reach, I could very well imagine it.

The Mississippi is an imposing river, one could almost call it a long, narrow lake. Its shores are generally flat and covered with poplars ,which reminded me of our Po. Its current is rather strong, sometimes going five or six miles an hour. A few hundred miles from St. Louis rocks begin to be seen and one especially, which is called the Tower because of its shape, is entirely isolated in the river. The constant erosion of its shores and the immense quantity of floating trees make the river seem like a perpetual flood. Amid the trees on the shores are seen plantations and small villages with whose names I have not the compunction to burden my memory, for often two or three log houses bore some illustrious historical name or one of some great European capital. Twelve miles from St. Louis, Jefferson Barracks are seen where the government has stationed a few regiments to protect the region from the Indians.

It is rather remarkable that from Louisville to St. Louis, a distance of five or six hundred miles, I saw at least twenty-five abandoned hulks. Having inquired of well informed people of the region, I was told that as a general rule forty or so ships every year strand themselves, burn, or blow up—an awful proportion of 10 percent out of the four or five hundred boats in the West. Most of them are stranded in shallows or pierced by what the Americans call snags—the French *chicots*. These are trees, dislodged by the current, whose roots sometimes get stuck in the mud bottoms. The tops, standing up, have their branches cut by the river ice in winter so that the end of the trunk remains just above the water. They are not dangerous to the descending traffic because they give way under the pressure of the boat; but since they are one or two feet below water, the pilot of the boats going up-stream cannot see them nor avoid them. When a boat strikes one of them it sinks immediately. More than once it has happened that snags have gone through to passengers' rooms—an agreeable surprise to be sure!

A false idea is entertained that the general cause of explosions of steamboats is the craze or mania for speeding. I can in no way share this opinion. When the boats are under way, the captain is on the bridge, the second officer at the helm, and the two engineers at the engine: with everybody at his place an accident is almost impossible. [To be sure] I have seen it happen more than once that just as soon as a ship is in sight and is recognized—especially if it is a fast one—it is as if a signal for attack had been given. But I believe that the following is more likely the cause of these disasters. Steamboats stop very frequently to take on and discharge passengers or cargo; they stop sometimes for a longer time than [the crews] realize. The steam condenses [*la vapeur se condense*] in the boiler and, diminishing in quantity, causes the upper part of the boiler to become red hot. Then when cold water is added, it causes the boiler to blow up at the first movement of the piston. The ship is thus put entirely out of order; the people are blown into the air, burned, wounded, or maimed; and what is left becomes food for the fish. But it all makes little difference to Americans provided they can go and go fast. Indeed in view of their negligence and carelessness it is almost inconceivable that more mishaps do not occur.

I was on board the *Tempest*, reading in the cabin, when I was urged to go up on deck to see a steamboat sink just as it was trying to get another one afloat. As we were going 16 knots an hour, I went on the roof of the upper deck instead of on the upper deck itself so as to be able to see it in the distance for a longer time. (Western steamboats have usually no uncovered decks; they have instead two decks and a roof.) The first thing which met my eye was a flame about three or four feet high on the roof [of our own ship]. I called out immediately, "Fire on board"— a terrible but magical shout for all on board ships. Everything became instantaneous confusion, and many came scrambling to the roof where I was, the captain first. Stewards had placed mattresses on the roof in order to sleep in the fresh air, and the sparks from the smokestack had set them on fire. They threw the mattresses in the river and all was order again. Five minutes later without that chanced good fortune and it would have been the end of the *Tempest*. Its roof was covered with a waxed or varnished cloth which would have aided the fire to spread quickly to the rest of the ship. I hoped that for the sake of the future passengers the captain might curse [the negligent stewards] a little or at least scold them severely and forbid them to put mattresses on the roof again, but not a word has been said.

One thing which shocked me much more on board this same boat was the following incident. A luckless German, whose only fortune was the sack on his back, was taken on board free provided he would haul wood. Fine. But it was not so fine when this poor man took sick in the night and was unable to haul the old wood [*ce coquin de bois*]. He was put off at the first stop the next morning and left to get out of his trouble as best he could. Unfortunately, since no one on board knew about it until we were again under way, it was impossible to be of the slightest aid to him.

A much more important incident, and one of a more serious and barbarous nature, took place on the Mississippi about two months before. During the night a fire broke out on a steamboat. If I am not mistaken, it was the *Bensherod*. Its crew, seeing that the fire was spreading rapidly, abandoned the ship in a rowboat without even sounding the alarm bell for the passengers who were awakened by the fire or by the water. About 180 people lost their lives, and only ten or twelve had the good fortune of being saved. The height of infamy and atrocity was the conduct of the captain of a steamboat that passed by the wreckage of the burned boat the next morning. He saw several survivors who had been lucky enough to get hold of pieces of wreckage, but instead of helping them he speeded his boat on and pitilessly submerged in the wake of his vessel those whom the fire and waves had spared. I should not have believed these horrors if I had not read the details of them in all the American newspapers.

The city of St. Louis is built on such an inclined plain that when you arrive there by the river, it appears like an amphitheatre. This city hardly existed six years ago, and now it has almost 18,000 inhabitants. On the day I arrived I counted forty-eight extremely large and luxurious steamboats docked at the quays. I visited the *St. Louis* which had eight boilers, two engines, one thousand tons displacement, and accommodations on board for four hundred passengers.

The most remarkable thing in St. Louis, which caused its rapid development in commerce and wealth, is the American Fur Company. It was founded by Mr. Astor, who is now the richest man in America—that is, in the United States. They say he has $30 million. This immense enterprise, which aims at the exploitation of the forests and prairies of the Far West, is divided into two sections: one, directed by Mr. Ramsay Crooks, exploits the Mississippi and the Great Lakes; the other, the country from the Missouri to the Rocky Mountains, is managed by Mr. Chouteau. I had the privilege of meeting these two very respectable individuals without whose support it would have been absolutely impossible for me to undertake the trip I counted on making. This enormous company has several steamboats and several thousand employees in its service. Mr. Crooks was one of those intrepid explorers who first crossed the American continent and the Rocky Mountains to found a post called Astoria on the shores of the Pacific. This was later destroyed for special reasons growing out of England's jealousy [*la jalousie de l'Angleterre*]—a frequent fate reserved for new colonies. This trade is very extensive and would be more so if the importation of American skins and furs were allowed in Europe.

There is a proverb which says that one cannot speak of the wolf without seeing his ears or his tail, and it is sometimes very true. Yesterday I wrote a line or two on steamboats blowing up, and an hour ago I was a witness of one such horrible sight. I was in the office of the American Fur Company, which is by the wharves, when I heard an explosion like that of a mine, accompanied by horrible cries. An immense mass of white smoke—or rather steam—human bodies, boxes, bales of merchandise, floating planks, all were hurled pell-mell, leaving no question in my mind as to the extent of damage and suffering caused. Seven men were killed and several severely wounded. I saw two whose flesh, having been torn from their chests by the boiling water, hung down almost to their thighs. It was a terrible sight to look upon. Immediately several canoes took to the water and sped down the river to pick up the victims who were being carried away by the current. The damage done to the boat was not as great as I thought. The explosion was forward and on both sides and only one board on the upper deck was torn off. Again this time the boiler had blown up just when they were starting up after a short stop. It was, as usual, the captain's fault, but on these catastrophes the law as well as public opinion is silent. In this region they are so frequent that no one pays any attention to them. I was speaking of this accident to the captain of another steamboat who blamed his fellow-navigator; and when I remarked that I was astonished that there was no law on the subject, he replied, "If there was a law, either it would be a dead letter, or no one would wish to be captain. Do captains beg the voyagers to go on board? If they go on board, it is at their own risk which, after all, is shared by the captain!" That, I hope, is very logical reasoning! One can imagine nothing comparable to the apathy and thoughtlessness of these men—an apathy which in a short time the uninitiated begin to share.

I asked the captain of a steamboat, which was to take me in a few days to Council Bluffs, how many days were needed to get there.

He replied, "Less than nine days, but we must figure on at least twelve days because of accidents."

"What do you call accidents?" I asked.

"Delays," he explained, "which come as the result of running aground. You must estimate the time needed to put the boat afloat."

"You are sure you are going to be stranded?"

"I am not sure about anything, but you must reckon on it [*il faudra passer par là*] because the water is low and the rapids are strong." "But why do you make the trip then?" "Because I have goods which I have to take up there." Convinced of the force and correctness of his reasoning, I got on board a few days later like any bale of merchandise which also might have to go up.[3]

☾   ☾   ☾

The theatre of St. Louis is one of the most beautiful in the United States. Certainly it had a more select audience than anywhere else in America. The drama plays a more important part in the life of St. Louis than it does in that of other cities where the people, being of English and Dutch extraction, care less for this kind of amusement than do the French Creoles. Here the plays were good, and there was even a little ballet. One certainly would not find such a fine and attractive theatre in a European city of 18,000. I like St. Louis too much to speak of its museum. But, on the other hand, I must be fair. What can be expected of a ten-year-old city? The people of St. Louis are very hospitable with a kindness and courtesy that were decidedly lacking among their Kentucky neighbors. The only really abominable things in St. Louis were her hotels, which are dirty and offensive—just the right kind to prepare travellers who are about to penetrate the Far West beyond the line of white settlements.

---

[3] This omission as well as that on pages 82, 83, 84, and 85, deals largely with Indian life.

Finally, when the boat was ready, I set out again. The deck of the boat indicated the kind of voyage we were undertaking. There were anchors, chains, piles of rope, immense poles, planks, axes, and a big beam to be used as a prop to keep the boat upright when it became stranded—a precaution which later proved to be wise. Everybody on board except myself belonged to the American Fur Company. Some were post directors, but most of them were hunters, trappers, and voyageurs of French origin—a very good sample assortment of all the shades of human skins, including Europeans, Creoles, negroes, different degrees of mulattoes, half-breeds, and what-not. A strict moralist or a Jesuit would call them lost souls, but judged less severely, they are good fellows full of life and energy, very agile, in very good spirits, very shrewd, especially more fond of whiskey than of the Good Lord, and no more fearful of the Devil than of the bullets and Indian arrows. Certainly the life which they lead for eleven months of the year, full of danger, fatigue, and privation, gives them the right to make up for it in the one remaining month when they feel called upon to spend all their yearly earnings. After all, why should they save when they are never sure of returning to enjoy their savings? In spite of the distance, the time, and the mixture of races, one sees some resemblance to the Paris vagabonds [*gamins*]: the same good humor in all circumstances, and the same physical and moral elasticity. Indeed, I was pleased, even amused, to see that rowdyism[4] was not unknown in the New World.

Although their costumes were as strange as their manners, they did not lack a certain regard for style, especially that of their hair. Some preferred it smooth and flat in Indian style; others chose to have it lie in curls down to their shoulders, for the use of curl papers was known even to these men of mountain and forest. Their farewells to their friends and acquaintances, who had come to see them depart and whom they might never see again, was much more comical than touching. It was similar to the conversations which take place in the Franconi Theatre between orchestra and upper gallery at carnival time.

𝕮   𝕮   𝕮

---

[4]*Rowdyism* is used as a translation of *la châute*, a word that does not seem to exist in French. Probably Arese meant *le chahut* which, indeed, seems to fit in with the sense of the passage.

IN MY CONVERSATIONS on board the Missouri steamboat I learned of two incidents which prove how insufficiently the laws of the United States are enforced, especially when public opinion is against them. A band of gamblers made a successful living on the steamboats on the Ohio and the Mississippi. They arrived at Pittsburgh or Vicksburg—I don't remember exactly which—where these poor fellows carried on a good business. It appears to have been even too good a business, for the people massacred them in the most pitiless manner. Only two or three of them escaped, thanks to their legs. No attempt was made to punish this crime which cost the lives of a dozen people. The second event occurred in St. Louis. A negro was accused of having tried to strike a constable, and another officer of justice arrested him. On his way to prison he assassinated both and got away. He was recaptured and sent to prison, but during his trial friends and relatives of the constable appeared and demanded of the warden the release of the negro to them. This poor fellow was thereupon given over to them and taken out of town where a bonfire was made. While they were lighting the fire, one of the older men remarked that the negro was about to be tried, condemned, and executed, and that consequently it was absolutely unnecessary for them to stain their hands with his blood since justice would take charge of inflicting on him the punishment which his crime deserved. The reply which he received was that if he did not leave at once, they would make him hang the negro himself. The good man was obliged to put his philanthropy in his pocket and take to his legs, or he would certainly have shared the same fate as that of the negro and would have been inhumanly burned over a slow fire without any attempt on the part of public opinion to stop it. Not even the slightest investigation was made to apprehend and punish, the guilty. This incident took place in 1836. I mention these two events, although I was not present, since they were told to me by very respectable and truthful people. If all such incidents were mentioned, there would be no end of them.

❧   ❧   ❧

MR. CASS, WHO WAS secretary of war and one of the heroes of the Temperance Society, had a law passed to stop the distribution of whiskey to the soldiers and sailors. This worked well for the sailors while at sea, but for the soldiers the effect was very bad. When the soldiers in their camp were contented with their ration of whiskey, it rarely happened that the men were imprisoned for drunkenness because it was difficult for them to become drunk. The soldiers of the American army, who are in the forts at the farthest Indian frontiers, had then no means of their own for procuring spirituous liquors. But as soon as this law went into effect, charitable souls, more interested in money than in the success of the Temperance Society, appeared in the neighborhood of the forts and sold the soldiers, not as much whiskey as they could drink, but as much as they could pay for. The result was that the troops became drunk and frequently did not come back in time for taps. They then had to be confined on their return, and, becoming angry at this treatment, they would desert. It often happened that there were not even enough to man the forts.[5]

𝕮   𝕮   𝕮

I ARRIVED AT GREEN BAY in the evening, and the next morning at ten o'clock I left for Chicago. A very few minutes was enough to visit this new village [Green Bay]. I did not bother to go to see the fort, for they are all alike: small encampments sometimes built of stone but more often of wood. A chance acquaintance of mine, who had visited the fort a few days before, told me that the garrison consisted of nine men (drummer and officer included), five of whom were in the camp jail.

I left on the steamboat *Packet Pennsylvania,* which is not a good boat. On the contrary, it is dirty and badly managed—more like the European steamboats which run either between London and Calais or between Dover and Ostend than the American steamboats, which are generally beautiful. There were 640 passengers, a veritable Tower of Babel in miniature. With the exception of a dozen respectable people among whom I venture to number myself—although perhaps my very variegated costume did not allow me that privilege—and perhaps another dozen who deluded themselves with the idea that they too were respectable—but most certainly they were not—the rest were nothing but a horrid mixture of Irish, Germans, and Kentuckians, or something

---

[5] The material here omitted covers in great detail his journey across the plains and his experiences with the Indians.

like them. To add to the discomfort there was a mob of little children who yelled and howled enough to tear off one's ears! Some women were nursing their babies. There was such a disgusting odor and atmosphere that it was enough to turn a stomach made of the hardest metal, and I said to myself several times how much better off I had been while sleeping on the plains or in the forest even in a pouring rain. In spite of all that I must admit that I was glad to be on board a steamboat. After so many misfortunes, annoyances, setbacks, and delays which I encountered, it seemed almost like home. The eventual pleasure which I felt later when I again boarded one of the more luxurious American steamboats was hardly surpassed.

☜ ☜ ☜

ON BOARD I HAD the good fortune to meet one of my New York friends, Mr. Shermerhom [*sic*], a pleasant, educated young man who shared his room with me. As everybody in America does something, Mr. Shermerhom builds towns not only on paper—which is quite the style—but also in real lasting masonry; and his business is very good. There was also on board a theatrical company on its way to Chicago. Two very striking members of it were the leading lady [*première actrice*] and the leading dancer, Mrs. or Miss Ingerson—I do not know exactly which. She was neither young nor pretty, indeed quite the contrary. As compensation, however, she strode over the boat's deck with as much importance as Semiramis or Cleopatra. The dancer, calling herself French—or to be exact, advertising herself as French—had apparently had her shoes badly damaged, for she wore a pair of her husband's boots. Considering the slenderness of her legs—which would have done honor to a game rooster—and considering the fullness of her dresses, you might have called her a butterfly in heavy boots.

On account of a strong wind we could not leave Green Bay the first day but spent the night at anchor. The next morning we went out by Death-Door [*sic*] which takes its name from a disaster in which 40 canoes with all their occupants perished. We saw Milwaukee and Racine, two young villages, both well located on the shores of rivers; and then we arrived at Chicago, a very pretty little town almost at the lower end of Lake Michigan and on the Chicago River.

Although [Chicago] is not yet 44 blocks long by 40 wide, as it is shown to be on the map, still it is an astonishing town. Four or five years ago it was nothing but an Indian village and now it is a very attractive little town of 6,000 people with fine stores, beautiful streets, sidewalks, wharves, an excellent hotel, a theatre, four churches of different denominations, and a large number of beautiful stone houses. Because of its strategic position Chicago is destined to become a great city. They are already engaged in digging a canal to connect the lake with the Mississippi, a work which would be gigantic in a well populated region but which is really unbelievable and supernatural in a region which is, in a sense, still in its wild state.

You can certainly tell many bad, even ridiculous, things about America. But if a person has just a bit of good faith, he must put his pride in his pocket and, although European, admit that this is an astonishing, magical, and miraculous country where many, many things must be seen before you begin to believe them. What in Europe we would not dream of, what would be thought absurd in spite of our resources, is in this country carried out, as soon as some one gets the idea, with means as limited as his courageous enterprise is unlimited—and by limited means I refer especially to the size of the population.

During the voyage we passed near enough to land to see the beautiful country that skirts the lake. It is mostly fertile, lightly wooded plains. A contrary wind and a heavy swell made the boat stay at Chicago one day more. [During this time] a scene took place between the mate and the passengers, which proves the truth of what I said above about the very strange mixture of people on board. The Irish in a somewhat heated discussion with the mate fell on him in a body. But this individual, powerfully built and aided by a member of the crew, knocked out five or six Irishmen before the two were overcome by numbers. As a result the officer was confined to his bed with his internal organs apparently quite badly upset, and the other member of the crew suffered from a broken head. At night they feared that the Irish, who had landed, might come back and attack the steamboat. Arms and ammunition were given to all the crew and passengers, and some men were selected to stand guard. Everybody was ready except the Irish who came back only as far as the wharf and returned quietly to their homes, as I suppose, to apply sops of vinegar water on their bruises received that morning. If the Irish had come on board, there would certainly have been a fight and many more would have suffered from injuries. But the local governmental authority, according to its usual habit, certainly would not have taken cognizance of it before, during, or after the affair.

Is it a good or bad condition to have the absence or complete silence of the forces of the law, which are supposed to protect, defend, and guarantee restitution in case of individual assaults? Another question which I asked myself, and to which I shall make reply later when I have more leisure and especially when I am in the mood for discussing economics and public law, is whether America would not prosper more under a stronger government, under a government which directs to one object all the separate efforts which now go to right and left without either rhyme or reason, creating from time to time local or general crises. Perhaps its progress would not be as rapid, but it certainly would be more firm and lasting and would give more guaranties for the future. For it must not be overlooked that the vaunted progress of the American Union depends on contingent causes which will have ceased to have any influence at a future day, which is nearer than is generally thought. Among these causes the most important are the immensity of the territory, the newness of political institutions, and the almost continuous increase of population the old strata of which, if you will allow me to use such a term, is always receiving new vigor from European immigration. When the territory will have become overcrowded by the settlements which will have been scattered over it, when the institutions will have aged and thereby come in conflict with the efforts at reforms which are forerunners of revolution, when the population formerly settled on the soil will have to dispute its rights and privileges with immigrants whom the American Union will no longer regard as auxiliaries but rather as harmful and annoying competitors; then indeed the Union will find itself in about the same position as our old European institutions. Then it will be necessary to gather up the reins of the government lest its citizens be constrained to exceed the powers granted by their constitution,[6] for only strong and firmly established governments are durable. History gives us

---

[6] "Au risque même de tomber à l'Arche Sainte de sa constitution."

many proofs for this statement which holds true as much for republics as for monarchies.

At Chicago we set down our theatrical troop and almost all our passengers while others in fewer numbers came on board. The bad weather, which continued, did not allow me a very complete inspection of the city. I saw there a foundry, a steam grist mill, a steam sawmill for making sashes, free schools, several printing shops, reading rooms with three daily newspapers, a post office, several stagecoach lines running through the wilderness, several steamboats, brig-schooners [*bricks seunners*], and so forth: all these in a city only five years old. How many European cities with centuries of history and twenty or thirty thousand souls still are shamefully backward in civilization in comparison with this small town! Shame, thrice shame, on governments which are motivated only by sordid greed and thirst for power. They not only do not foster but actually discourage with every means in their power the development and natural progress of nations. Instead of fostering wise and liberal institutions they inflict castes, nobility, and rabble on nations and employ police who violate, rather than protect, the rights of citizens. In the end they goad on [*pousser en avant*] what may be properly called the vermin of society.

The wind having finally subsided a little toward the evening of the third day, we left Chicago. There were at least a hundred passengers on board, most of whom did not leave their berths although we were on a lake which is almost as large as the Mediterranean. We passed near the Manitou, Fox, and Beaver islands, which would be remembered as great, high, sandy landmarks revealing nothing but sand and a few thin, scrubby bushes. The shores of Lake Michigan offered everywhere this same appearance.

We arrived at Mackinac Island which is at the other end of the lake, 300 miles from Chicago. This island is situated between Lakes Michigan and Huron almost opposite the St. Mary River, which serves as an outlet for the waters of Lake Superior. The island is very well located and looks fine at a distance. Its summit is crowned by a fort from which you can obtain a very charming view. The object of curiosity on the island is a natural arch carved in a rock. The remnants of the Octawa [*sic*] Indians are still on the island, and they make pretty rush mats and other objects from the bark of trees. I left the island at night, but because a storm came up suddenly, the boat was forced to tie up at Presque Isle where I saw a beautiful bay which offers excellent protection. When the storm subsided a little, we finished the Lake Huron part of our voyage, entered St. Clair River, crossed Lake St. Clair, and arrived finally at Detroit. This is a pretty, flourishing city which I found to be more beautiful than perhaps it really was because, after having been without any letter for more than three months, I found a whole bundle of them there. The next evening I left Detroit by another steamboat. Although I had changed rivers, boats, and lakes frequently, the weather had not changed at all: it was bad again two hours after our departure.

I was in my cabin reading and digesting my letters at leisure when a bad shock rudely interrupted my preoccupation. I said to myself, "We must be stranded," and although I was surprised that that should happen on a lake, I went on with my reading. I heard some men shout and complain, but it did not engage my attention very much. However, when I heard them shout that axes should be brought forward, my curiosity was excited enough so that I admit I left my letters to see what was the matter. It was nothing much, at least for me and my boat. They had neglected to light the lantern on the prow, and as the night was very dark and stormy, an unfortunate schooner [*seunner*] crossed our path, not discovering until too late the presence of the steamboat. The prow of the steamboat by catching itself in the rigging of the schooner broke its bowsprit mast as well as the schooner's. The broken masts, sails, and rigging of the two boats, mixed together in confusion, had motivated the command for the axes. In another moment all was in order again, somewhat like the order which reigned at Warsaw. The steamboat, damaged very little, had hardly disengaged itself when it started on its way again while the poor dismasted schooner, with some wounded on board and in very heavy weather, had to get along as best it could. I was convinced myself that it would get along all right.

As soon as the boat got under way again, I returned to my thirty-four letters which I had received. They brought me both good and bad news about which I shall spare my unfortunate reader my private feelings.

On Lake Erie we saw Cleveland, an attractive little city which in a short time will be a very important one. We also passed by Grand River,

Ashtabula, and Concat [*sic*]—other towns, or to be more exact, other places where there is everything necessary to make a town except houses and people. There are streets marked out with stakes, all christened with great names, the beginning of a railroad or a canal, a post-office, a church, a school, and one or two wooden huts.

This reminds me of an incident which happened to one of my friends. He was hunting snipe somewhere in northern New York state when he saw a half-dozen people shouting and waving papers in their hands. His curiosity having been aroused, he made a truce with the snipe in order to find out what it was all about. They told him that it was the auctioning of contracts for the construction of the city hall. "But of what city?" he asked. I do not remember with what resounding name they replied, but it was some name of antiquity such as Rome or Athens. My friend asked where the city was located. "Right here where you are, sir," they answered—and he was in the mud up to his hips. It is well to note that there are many towns of like nature in the United States.

After having crossed Lake Erie, I arrived in Buffalo which is not a town in the class with those I have just described, but a beautiful city, well built and already quite extensive. Here is found perhaps the best hotel in America. I confess, too, that after having fasted or eaten poor food for four or five months, I came to the conclusion that a good dinner had a charm and poetry all of its own.

I also had the opportunity on this trip to verify a kind of axiom that civilizations vary directly according to the number of tines on their forks. Hence among savages where there is no civilization, eating is done with the fingers. Here no forks are used. When civilization begins to appear, the knife is first used. This can be called a fork with one tine. Then come big forks with two iron tines, then with three. Finally when any one has the good fortune to pick up a silver fork with four tines, he can be sure he is in a highly civilized country.

From Buffalo I went to Niagara Falls. Any description of it is impossible. I stayed there five days and left only because everything in this world must have an end, else I should still be there perhaps. The longer this astonishing spectacle is viewed, the more astonishing it becomes, the more it pleases you, and the more it reveals its beauty. I visited it all with thoroughness and in detail from both sides, from above and below, in good and bad weather, in sunshine and moonlight, and ever and always it was sublime, magnificent. Everybody agrees that the finest view is obtained from Table Rock. At a certain place on the railroad from Lewistown the falls are seen at a certain distance, among the trees, like a magnificently framed miniature. The only disappointment comes when you go to see the grotto behind the small falls. They say that it is worth seeing and that you can go about sixty or eighty steps behind the large falls. The venturer, wearing a special coat of oiled cloth and clinging desperately to the rocks, encounters an incomparable rain and wind. He is obliged to hold one hand over his mouth in order to breathe, while with the other he grasps the rocks in order not to go plunging into the abyss below. After having bruised himself all over and taken his life in his hands at every step, he comes back without having seen a thing because of the blinding water and mist. To give you some idea of the size of the falls I shall say that they are a mile and three quarters wide and from 160 to 172 feet high. They estimate the thickness of the falling water at from 20 to 24 feet. It is the outlet of four of the Great Lakes whose overflow is on its way to Lake Ontario. I visited many other points of interest which are not worth a separate mention. I shall make one exception for the whirlpool of rapids below the falls, where the water has such an eruption that it seems to rise as much as eight or nine feet higher than the shore. I do not know whether there is really that difference or whether it is an optical illusion, but the natives tell me that it is not an exaggeration. The guide, who takes tourists to see the falls, has an album. Among the curious things which I read in it I can not refrain from copying what Captain Marryat [*sic*] wrote:

> Upon a patient and careful examination of the Falls called Niagara, I have come to the conclusion that if any person were to be taken down in them, he would be in considerable danger of receiving serious injoury [*sic*]!

One thing which sometimes amused me and at other times tried my patience excessively was to see the crude and stupid way some travellers visited this marvel of nature. They only chance to come to Niagara because it may happen to be the shortest route to their destination. They also come in haste, see in haste, and even speak hastily so as not to be late for dinner. Very often I would be sitting on a rock somewhere near the falls where I spent my time and I would be asked what there was to see. I would point out to them different points worth visiting, but they would often say that these were too far away. Sometimes after examining the falls for two minutes, they would ask me with a calm and coolness typically American: "Oh, is *that* Niagara Falls?" That was all!

With many regrets and much against my will I left Niagara for Upper Canada on board an English boat. "What a difference," a good American who was on board said to me in triumph, "between American and English steamboats!"

"Yes," I replied, "there is a big difference. Yours are beautiful, well built, and smoother running; but on the other hand you have here a clean table-cloth, a bed with two white sheets, individual towels, a well served table, plates changed with every course, a silver service, a captain and crew who are courteous and kind to the passengers, all of which are absolutely unknown on American steamboats."

The poor dismayed man turned on his heel and went off without another word. Indeed there was nothing for him to say.

PART TWO

The Missionaries

ELIGIOUS MISSIONARIES were integral to the earliest settlement
efforts in the New World, especially among the Spanish colonizers. As historian Lewis Hanke has observed, the crown and
the cross were inseparable aspects of Spanish policy during more than
three centuries of colonial rule. The religious emissaries were responsible for the conversion and for the acculturation of the subject people to
European patterns of behavior. To their credit, in critical confrontations
with secular authorities priests like Father Bartolomeo Las Casas were
fierce defenders of Indian rights, securing such recognition from the
Council of the Indies in the Laws of Burgos and the New Laws of 1542.

The task of proselytizing was assigned by geographic region to specific orders of priests and brothers, including the Franciscans, Dominicans,
and members of the Society of Jesus or Jesuits. The community of Jesuits
reflected the most cosmopolitan composition, including Bavarians,
Bohemians, Belgians, Frenchmen, and numerous residents of the as yet
not nationalized Italian peninsula.

Some of the missionaries within the viceroyalty of New Spain ventured north and west of present-day Mexico establishing missions on
behalf of Spain in Pimería Alta (northern Sonora and southern Arizona) and in Baja California. Among them was Father Eusebio Kino,
a native of Trento, known as the "Padre on Horseback" because of his
more than fifty expeditions of settlement and exploration as far as the
lower Gila and Colorado rivers. He rode weekly between various missions he was constructing, and made longer surveys of missions along
the Magdalena and Altar rivers to assure himself that they remained

self-sufficient outposts, supported by their farms, orchards, pastures and workshops.

Kino, an astronomer, as well as a trained cartographer who mapped much of the Southwest, was appointed royal cosmographer of an early government expedition to Baja California. In May 1702 he made a remarkable assertion based upon several geographic observations. First, he was given blue shells found only along the Pacific coast, suggesting Indians had access to an overland route to the ocean to acquire them. He then found he was able to easily raft to the California side of the Colorado and later discovered that he could traverse by land north of the junction of the Gila and Colorado rivers. As a result, he made the unprecedented observation that California was not an island but part of the North American land mass. In 1847 King Ferdinand VII of Spain officially concurred.

The essay by historian Herbert Eugene Bolton that follows focuses on Kino the explorer, but also on his other accomplishments as a mission builder, rancher, protector of frontier outposts, and a man of faith. Traveling on horseback Kino journeyed throughout the region, covering up to seventy-five miles a day. As Bolton writes, he was instrumental in establishing approximately twenty missions in the greater Southwest and, in the course of his invaluable service, introducing several strains of livestock, which provided the basis for the region's successful cattle economy. Nearly two dozen towns are associated with this intrepid missionary.

Kino served as part of the Jesuit community in Baja California under the direction of Father Giovanni Salvatierra, a native of Milan descended from the aristocratic Visconti family. Salvatierra served as provincial for the Jesuit Order in New Spain and created a network of mission outposts where Indians worshiped, worked, and became accustomed to the European culture which was inexorably encroaching upon them. To facilitate their economic transition from hunting and gathering to a herding and farming economy, the Jesuits introduced European grains and fruit along with farming methods.

Salvatierra was aided by an international corp of priests including two from Sicily, Father Francesco Maria Piccolo and Father Francesco Saverio Saetta. The latter lost his life to Pima Indians in 1705. Two other Italian priests had been slain in earlier uprisings. Father Jesus Lombardi was among the twenty-one missionaries killed in 1680; Father Antonio Carbonelli succumbed to violence in 1696.

The work of the Society of Jesus was abruptly terminated in 1767 when the Spanish crown, prompted by political considerations, temporarily expelled them from the empire. Some Jesuits, including Father Francesco Clavigero, lived in exile in Italy. Although born in New Spain, Clavigero became a resident of the Italian city of Cesena, where he wrote the respected four-volume history *Storia Antica del Messico* (1780) and *Storia della California* (1789). As a result of the expulsion, Jesuit missionaries like Fathers Francesco Piccolo, Geronimo Minutili, and Ignacio Napoli were replaced by a contingent of grey-habited Franciscans who soon extended the mission chain northward to Alta California.

A century later missionaries from the Jesuit Province headquartered in Naples were dispatched to Colorado where, beginning in 1858, mining rushes at Pike's Peak had attracted both American and migrant settlers along with Spanish Catholic arrivals migrating northward from New Mexico. Beginning in 1871 Father Salvatore Personé embarked upon his ministry to this unique mix of frontiersmen, by building churches and preaching to ever-growing congregations.

In the essay, "Neopolitan Jesuits on the Colorado Frontier, 1868–1919," Manuel Espinosa describes how Personé established mission stations and later parishes and schools throughout Colorado. In 1879 another Italian Jesuit, Father Giovanni Fuida, established the first parish in Denver. By the 1880s Personé organized Sacred Heart College, later Regis College, the first institution of higher learning in Colorado, under the direction of Father Dominic Pantanella. The Neapolitan province would carry on its work in Colorado until 1919, when the task was assigned to the Missouri Province of the Society of Jesus.

In the nineteenth century the roster of the Missouri Province included Father Paul Ponziglione who had instructed at the Jesuit College in Genoa until he was caught up in the revolutionary struggles of 1848. As an alternative he chose to live as a missionary among the Chippewas, Arapahoes, Cheyennes, and other tribes. He continued a tradition established by French members of the Society of Jesus more than a century earlier when Jesuit missionaries played a central role in French colonial settlement associated with the fur-trade economy thriving in the northern woodlands and around the Great Lakes. These missionaries, led by Father Isaac Jogues, were to meet a tragic fate resulting in their being canonized as the "North American Martyrs."

Though marked by martyrdom, the effects of the early Jesuits' ministry in French Canada were to be long lived. Nearly two centuries later a group of Iroquois, still faithful to the Biblical words from the "Great Book of Life" uttered by the black-robed missionaries, shared their belief in eternal life with their newly adopted brothers, the Flathead or Salish Indian inhabitants of the Interior Columbia Basin. During the seasonal buffalo hunts, the beleaguered Flatheads, like their neighboring Nez Perce and Coeur d'Alene, were being vanquished by fast-riding Blackfeet from the plains, armed with rifles supplied by white traders.

As protection the Iroquois offered the promise of eternal life made long ago by the black-robed Jesuits. Inspired by the prospect of invincibility in battle, when armed with the promised immortality found in the Black Robes' "Great Book of Life," the Flatheads sent several delegations as far as St. Louis where they requested these "Black Robes" from Bishop Joseph Rosati. Because of his position as bishop of the vast region stretching from Missouri to the Rockies, Rosati dispatched the Flathead request to Father Pierre Jean De Smet, leader of the Jesuit missionary efforts in the Rocky Mountains that would serve later as the epicenter for subsequent missionary ventures.

Bishop Rosati was a member of the Lazarist Order brought to the United States in 1816 by Father Felix de Andreis, a native of the region of Piedmont. Within a year the group had built the first seminary west of the Mississippi River at Perryville, less than one hundred miles south of St. Louis. In 1820 Rosati was named superior of the order in America and helped found what later became St. Mary's College, the first school for deaf mutes west of the one hundredth meridian, as well as St. Louis Hospital, along with orphanages, convents, schools, and thirty-five churches, including St. Louis Cathedral.

The Jesuit's positive response to the Flatheads' plea, conveyed by Bishop Rosati, resulted in the assignment of several missionaries including the young Roman Father Gregorio Mengarini, Father Giovanni Nobili, and later Fathers Antonio Ravalli, Giuseppe Cataldo, and Giuseppe Giorda. They soon established St. Mary's and St. Ignatius missions in the Bitterroot Valley in present-day Montana. Mengarini, a pious and gentle man, was a musician and a remarkable linguist, who, faced with necessity, also became a skillful medical practitioner. In his "Life in the Rocky Mountains" (Partoll 1938)[1] and his *Memorie* (Lothrop 1977) he described the colorful ceremonies he organized in the crude log church, the singular fervor of the recently baptized, the daunting discomforts of the Montana winters, and, to his distress, the continuing depredations by the Blackfoot Indians.

Mengarini was a keen student of the culture, customs, and linguistic patterns of the Salish or Flathead people. He published *A Salish or Flathead Grammar* (1861) and *A Dictionary of the Kalispel or Flathead Indian Language* (1877) to which Father Philip Canestrelli added *A Kootenai Grammar* (1894) and Father Anthony Morvillo published *A Dictionary of the Nez Perce Language* (1895). The studies continued with Father Alexander Diomedi's *Sketches of Modern Indian Life* (1894). Diomedi also wrote a book of scripture and a dictionary in the Kalispel language composed from 1876 to 1879.

The accomplishments of these Italian missionaries were made possible by the high caliber of Jesuit training. In *The Immigrant Upraised* (1968), Andrew Rolle notes that many had pursued higher education in Austria, France, and Belgium, as well as Italy. They were also experienced teachers. Canestrelli had taught at the Gregorian University in Rome. Father Nicholas Congiato had been vice president of the College of Nobles in Rome and of the University of Freibourg in Switzerland. He would eventually become president of St. Ignatius College, later the University of San Francisco.

But faith rather than academic preparation sustained these dedicated priests when the welcome and the fervor with which the supplicants greeted them became short-lived. The converts ruefully discovered they were still beset by continuing fatalities. The Black Robes' "medicine" had not endowed them with invincibility against the Blackfeet. Confronted by the Indians' widespread disaffection, the first Jesuits departed in the late 1840s. They headed first to the Oregon Territory where, William Bischoff in *Jesuits in Old Oregon* (1945) explains, between 1840

---

[1] "Life in the Rocky Mountains," Albert Partoll, ed., *Frontier and Midland* 18 (1938).

and 1900 some seventy Italian Jesuit priests, seminarians, and lay brothers labored, some like Father Nicholas Congiato, well into their nineties.

Fathers Mengarini and Nobili were dispatched to the gold camps of California, where Mengarini would continue his ethnographic work among the local Indians reported in numerous scholarly journals and in several entries in John Wesley Powell's *Contributions to North American Ethnology* (1877) while serving as both faculty member and administrator at Santa Clara College headed by Father Nobili as president. There he was visited by a Flathead delegation unsuccessfully pleading for his return to the Bitterroot Valley. In the rapidly growing city of San Francisco, Father Anthony Maraschi established St. Ignatius College, where one faculty member, Father Joseph Neri, won the admiration of the local townsfolk when in 1876 he used three arc lights to illuminate San Francisco's bustling Market Street for the first time.

The dedicated ministries of the Italian Jesuits in the Interior Columbia Basin, in the Oregon Territory, and also in California are abundantly documented in the missionaries' letters, in the official annual reports, and even in their necrologies on deposit at the Jesuit Provincial archives at Gonzaga University and the University of Santa Clara. The documents shed light on the lives of memorable figures like Father Anthony Ravalli, who arrived at Fort Vancouver in 1844 in the company of Father Michael Accolti. The next year he reached the Bitterroot Valley, where he soon distinguished himself as a physician and pharmacist, while also accomplishing much as a carpenter, blacksmith, and mason. He soon built a grist mill and a sawmill, while displaying skills as an artist and musician. As a result of his long ministry, interrupted only by a brief assignment at the College of Santa Clara, his name was attached to a Montana town, a railway stop, and a county.

Jesuits also settled in the wide-open Montana mining town of Virginia City where in 1865 Father Giovanni Giorda, a Piedmontese, celebrated Christmas eve midnight Mass in a hastily vacated variety theater. Grateful citizens soon built him a sturdy church and appointed him chaplain to the Montana territorial legislature. His ministry was also devoted to the Native Americans. A gifted linguist, Giorda could preach in half a dozen native languages and he too contributed several linguistic studies.

In *Westward the Immigrant* (1999) Andrew Rolle notes that the last phase of missionary activity in the Interior Columbia Basin was represented by Father Joseph Cataldo, a hearty Sicilian who was born in 1837 and lived until 1928. He would spend sixty-three years serving in the Rocky Mountain missions. Cotaldo's work extended to seven regions including Alaska, because from 1877 to 1893 he served as superior general of the Northwest Province of the Society of Jesus. This master of twenty European and Native American languages was beloved as a peacemaker among the tribes. He also founded Gonzaga University and added Cataldo Mission in Idaho to the chain of Jesuit missions in the Rocky Mountain region, where dedicated and capable Italian missionaries helped fashion a network not unlike the Franciscans' California mission system.

While the Jesuits were responding to the Flatheads' "Plea from the West," Father Samuel Charles Mazzuchelli, O.P., a Milanese Dominican, was dispatched to Iowa and Illinois following a decade of service to trappers and tribesmen in northeastern Wisconsin. By 1839 he was actively engaged in his ministry in the Midwest, building churches and schools and establishing a religious order of Dominican Sisters. Mazzuchelli's manner, which won the favor of Catholics and Protestants alike, was ecumenical. He was invited to address the first session of the Iowa state legislature and subsequently became its chaplain.

In her biographical essay author Flora Breidenbach explains that in 1844 the indefatigable Mazzuchelli established a college, St. Clara's School, which he not only headed but where he also served as professor of physics and astronomy. A firm believer in the value of real estate, he continued to acquire property and to implement his farsighted views on Indian education which boldly asserted traditional tribal rights. His memoirs reveal the breadth of his knowledge and experience, as well as the depth of his faith, his loyalty to Native Americans and his patriotism to his adopted land.

In the final decades of the nineteenth century the growing influx of Italian immigrants led to the formation of the Missionaries of Saint Charles by Bishop Giovanni Battista Scalabrini, who, in turn, urged a colleague to turn her attention from the mission fields of Asia to the Western Hemisphere to which Italian migrants were streaming. The seemingly frail Mother Frances Xavier Cabrini and her Missionary Sisters of the Sacred Heart responded audaciously, extending their ministry to South America and establishing four of their six United States centers in the West, including Denver, Seattle, Los Angeles, and Chicago, where Mother Cabrini died in 1917, having seen her order grow to 1,500 religious and her ministry to the migrants expand to include orphanages, hospitals, and schools. To this end, the unprepossessing master builder wielded maps and surveys like a general and firmly negotiated agreements with political administrations. Though beset by seasickness throughout her life, she crossed the Atlantic thirty-five times and defied heights by boldly crossing the Andes by mule train, in order to advance her sacred ministry. It is not surprising that in 1946, not even three decades after her death, she was canonized by the Roman Catholic Church. She was the first American citizen thus recognized.

Eusebio Francisco Kino

By *Herbert Eugene Bolton*

P EER OF ANY OF THESE NOBLE SPIRITS was Eusebio Francisco Kino, Apostle to the Pimas. Eusebio Chino[1] was born in Segno, a tiny village near the famous city of Trent in northern Italy. The exact date of his birth has not been determined, but we know that he was baptized on the tenth of August 1645. It is an interesting coincidence that his advent into the world was nearly contemporaneous with that of his intimate friend, fellow countryman, and co-worker, Juan Maria Salvatierra, the Apostle to Lower California. Kino's family, still numerous at Segno, now spell their surname Chini. In his early days our missionary signed himself Chino, or, in Latin, Chinus. When he came to America he wrote his name Kino, to retain its Italian pronunciation. Spaniards sometimes wrote it Quino.

Kino's cognomen was a troublesome one. In Spain Chino was the word for Chinamen: in Mexico it was also the name applied to certain mixed-bloods of low caste. Hence Father Chino changed his name to Kino. But this did not end the trouble. Kino is pronounced the same as Keno, the well-known gambling game, today popular on trans-Atlantic ocean liners. And now Kino is the German word for cinematograph, or "movie." Hence the recent appeal from Italy by a member of the missionary's family that I write the name Chini, "because Kino smacks too much of Hollywood." But the missionary himself determined the spelling of his name in America, and I shall respect his preference.

In point of nationality Kino was typical of a large number of the early Jesuit missionaries in Sonora, Arizona, and California. That is, although

---

[1]Pronounced Keeno.

Eusebio Kino, a native of Trento, Italy, prepared for life as a missionary with the Society of Jesus and in 1678 was dispatched for his first missionary field in Baja, California, where as the "Padre on Horseback" he explored, established missions, and introduced cattle ranching to the Southwest. Though only a pen and ink portrait survives, contemporary descriptions emphasizing his humility, modesty, and asceticism provide an understanding of the man himself.

he was in the service of Spain he was non-Spanish by blood and breeding. Among Kino's companions and successors, for example, we find Salvatierra, Picolo, Minutili, and Ripaldini, bearing in their names the marks of their Italian extraction; Steiger, Keler, Sedelmayr, and Grashofer, whose names disclose their German origin; and Januske and Hostinski, whose surnames stamp them as Bohemians.

Had he chosen to do so, Kino might have enjoyed scholarly reputation, and perhaps even won fame in Europe, for during his student career at Freiburg and Ingolstadt he greatly distinguished himself in mathematics. When the Duke of Bavaria and his father, the Elector, went in

1676 from the electoral court at Munich to Ingolstadt, they engaged Kino
in a discussion of mathematical sciences, with the result that the young
Jesuit was offered a professorship in the University of Ingolstadt. But
he preferred to become a missionary to heathen lands. To this calling
he was inclined by family tradition, for he was a relative of Father Martini, famous missionary in the East and author of many works on China.

Kino's decision to become a missionary was made when he was eighteen, as the result of a serious illness. In his *Favores Celestiales* he tells us
that "To the most glorious and most pious thaumaturgus and Apostle
of the Indies, San Francisco Xavier, we all owe very much. I owe him,
first, my life, of which I was caused to despair by the physicians in the
city of Hala, of Tirol, in the year 1663; second, my entry into the Company of Jesus;[2] and, third, my coming to these missions." Another mark
of Kino's gratitude for his recovery was the addition of Francisco to his
name.

Splendid Wayfaring

Kino had hoped to go to the Orient, to literally follow in the footsteps of his patron, but there came a call for missionaries in New Spain,
and thither he was sent instead. From his Jesuit college in Bavaria he set
forth in April 1678. On June 12 he and eighteen companions sailed from
Genoa for Spain, thence to embark for Mexico. Early in the voyage they
experienced a heavy storm, and later were becalmed for several days. On
the way they passed numerous vessels, and as each one hove in sight they
prepared to give it battle, but all proved to be friendly. Alicante was
reached on the twenty-fifth of June. Thence the companions went to
Cadiz, where they arrived too late to take passage in the fleet sailing to
the West Indies. So they were sent up to Seville to await an opportunity to sail. Their experiences before they finally reached America were
typical of missionary adventure, or of what Ortega called *Apostólicos
Afanes.*

Father Gerstl, one of Kino's companions, gives a very graphic account
of some phases of Seville life at this time. He was especially interested
in the monopoly of industry and commerce by the Dutch and the French,

---

[2]This took place two years later, in 1665, when he was twenty.

of the latter of whom forty thousand lived in Seville; in the amazing numbers of clergy and monastic houses there; in the prevalence of poverty and the multitude of beggars, of whom the archbishop regularly fed twenty-two thousand out of his income; in the crude skill of the bloodletters, at whose hands one of the nineteen, Father Fischer, succumbed; in the depreciation of silver on the arrival of a treasure fleet from America; in the crude methods of public execution, and the premature burials; and in the bullfights, in which the nobles participated and on which the Church frowned.

The delay in Spain was unexpectedly long. Some royal ships sailed for America, but as they went by the African coast to get slaves the Jesuits did not embark. Private vessels also sailed, but their charge for the passage was higher than the Father Procurator was willing to pay; consequently the Jesuits awaited the departure of the next royal fleet for the West Indies.

Late in March Kino and his companions returned to Cádiz, and on the eleventh of July the West Indian fleet sailed, convoyed by two armed galleons. But the vessel on which the Jesuits embarked foundered on a rock shortly after sailing, and they returned the same night on a small boat to Cádiz. The Father Procurator now bent every energy to get passage on the other vessels, and hurried back and forth between the port authorities and the admiral of the departing fleet. About two o'clock the next morning the sleeping band of Jesuits were awakened by the Procurator, put on board a boat, and taken to the fleet, already outside the harbor. The first vessel overhauled consented to take Fathers Calvanese and Borgia; the second refused to take any; on the third embarked Fathers Tilpe and Mancker; on the fourth Father Borango and Father Zarzosa, superior of the mission; on the fifth Fathers de Angelis and Ratkay; on the sixth Fathers Strobach and Neuman. Brother Poruhradiski, who had remained on the wrecked vessel with the Jesuits' baggage, also managed to find passage on the same ship with the superior. But twelve were left behind, among them being Gerstl and Kino. It was a hard blow.

Father Gerstl and seven companions now returned to Seville to wait, and to minister during an epidemic. Kino remained at Cádiz, where he observed the great comet which was visible there between December and February. The Father Procurator conducted a lawsuit to recover six thousand dollars paid in advance for passage in the wrecked vessel. Meanwhile Kino carried on a correspondence with the Duchess of Aveiro y Arcos, a patroness of missions in the Orient. Little did the young Jesuit dream that one day in the twentieth century these letters to a lady whom he had never seen would be sold to an American library at the rate of $235 a page. I have heard of a higher price being paid for letters to a lady, but not for letters by a missionary.

In January 1681, Father Gerstl and his companions rejoined Kino at Cádiz. On the twenty-ninth they at last set sail for America. In the West Indies the fleet divided, according to custom, and eight of the eighteen companions went to New Granada, the rest continuing to Vera Cruz, which they reached on May 3, after a rough voyage of over ninety days.

The band of devoted Jesuits who had set out from Genoa together were destined to scatter to the ends of the earth. The story of their personal experiences in America and the islands of the western seas occupies large space in the pages of Stöcklein's *Neue Welt-Bott*. Their travels over the face of the globe take rank with the wanderings of Ulysses.

As has been stated, eight of the splendid wayfarers were sent to New Granada. Ten came to Mexico, whence some went to the Orient. Fathers Borango, Tilpe, Strobach, de Angelis, and Cuculinus went to work among the heathen of the Marianas Islands. Mancker and Klein went to the Philippines and Gerstl to China. Ratkay worked in Sonora, Neuman in Nueva Vizcaya, Kino in California, Sonora, and Arizona. Of the four who went to Marianas Islands, three—Borango, Strobach, and De Angelis—won the martyr's crown.

Father Kino's mathematical knowledge brought him into prominence as soon as he arrived in Mexico, where he at once entered into a public discussion concerning the recent comet. One of the fruits of this episode was a pamphlet published by Kino in Mexico in 1681 under the title: "Astronomical explanation of the comet which was seen all over the world during the months of November and December, 1680, and in January and February in this year of 1681, and which was observed in the City of Cadiz by Father Francisco Kino, of the Company of Jesus." This little book is still one of the important historical sources of information regarding the movements of that notable comet.

STUBBORN CALIFORNIA

FATHER KINO'S FIRST MISSIONARY FIELD in America was Lower California. For two centuries and a half the Spaniards had made weak attempts to subdue and colonize that forbidding land. California had been discovered by one of Cortés's sailors in 1533. Two years later the great conquistador himself led a colony to the peninsula, then thought to be an island and called Santa Cruz. The enterprise failed, but Cortés continued his explorations, and Ulloa, sent out by him in 1539, rounded the cape and proved Santa Cruz to be a peninsula. Henceforth it was called California. Three years later Cabrillo, in quest of the Strait of Anian, that is, the northern passage to the Atlantic in which everybody believed, explored the outer coast of California beyond Cape Mendocino.

New interest in California followed the conquest of the Philippines by Legazpi (1565–71); indeed, in the later sixteenth century California was as much an appendage of Manila as of Mexico. Legazpi's men discovered a practicable return route to America, down the California coast, and thereupon trade, conducted in the Manila Galleon, was established between the Philippines and Acapulco. But the voyage was long, scurvy exacted heavy tribute of crews and passengers, and a port of call was sorely needed. English pirates, too, like Drake and Cavendish, infested the Pacific, and were followed by the Dutch freebooters, known as Pichilingues. California, therefore, must be explored, protected, and peopled.

It was with these needs in view that Cermeño made his disastrous voyage down the California coast; that Vizcaíno attempted the settlement of La Paz and explored the outer shore; and that the king ordered a settlement made at Monterey.

The Monterey project failed, but settlements and missions crept up the Sinaloa and Sonora mainland, and the pearl fisheries of California attracted attention, hence new attempts were made on the peninsula. Having little cash to spare, the monarchs tried to make pearl fishing rights pay the cost of settlement and defense. In the course of the seventeenth century, therefore, numerous contracts were made with private adventurers. By the terms the patentees agreed to people California in return for a monopoly of pearl gathering. With nearly every expedition went missionaries, to convert and help tame the heathen. In pursuance of these agreements several attempts were made to settle, especially at La Paz, where Cortés and Vizcaíno both had failed. Other expeditions were fitted out at royal expense. The names of Carbonel, Córdova, Ortega, Porter y Casante, Piñadero, and Lucenilla all stand for seventeenth-century failures to colonize California.

At first the natives of the peninsula had been docile, but they were enslaved and misused by the pearl hunters, against the royal will, and so became suspicious and hostile, as later pioneers learned. Through various misunderstandings and incomplete explorations, in the course of the century California had again come to be regarded and shown on maps as an island.

In spite of the repeated failures, another attempt at settlement was decided upon. By an agreement of December 1678, the enterprise was entrusted to Don Isidro Atondo y Antillón. This was to be primarily a missionary venture, and the costs were to be borne by the crown. Don Isidro was given the resounding title of Governor of Sinaloa and Admiral of the Kingdom of the Californias. The spiritual ministry was assigned to the Jesuits. Prophets now heralded a better day for the land of pearls. . . .

MISSION BUILDING

FROM HIS OUTPOST AT DOLORES, during the next quarter century, Kino and his companions pushed the frontier of missionary work and exploration across Pimería Alta to the Gila and Colorado rivers. By 1695 Kino had established a chain of missions up and down the Altar and the Magdalena. In April 1700 he founded, within the present state of Arizona, the mission of San Xavier del Bac, and within the next two years those of Tumacácori and Guebavi, likewise within the present state of Arizona. Kino's exploring tours were also itinerant missions, and in the course of them he baptized and taught in numerous villages, all up and down the Gila and the lower Colorado, and in all parts of northern Pimería.

Most of these missions, after being started by Kino, were turned over to others, or were attended by him at long range. Three of them, however, he built, nurtured, and administered personally. These temples stood in a north and south line, at Dolores, Remedios, and Cocóspora. First, last, and always Kino was a missionary. And between his long jaunts through the Pimería, his time and energy were given over to teaching his neophytes, building churches, and developing his fruitful ranches nearer home.

The story of progress in mission building occupies generous space in Kino's long reports. In these pages we can follow the church at Dolores from the day of its beginning to its completion and dedication. Kino arrived in the middle of March 1687. Before the end of April, with the aid of the willing natives, he had built a chapel for religious services and a humble house for himself. In June Dolores already presented a busy building scene, "where with very great pleasure and with all willingness," the natives were "making . . . adobes, doors, windows, etc., for a very good house and church to replace the temporary quarters." The bells had recently arrived from Mexico. Their coming was an event; "and now," wrote Kino, "they are placed on the little church which we built during the first days. The natives are very fond of listening to their peals, never before heard in these lands. And they are very much pleased also by the pictures and other ornaments." It was six years before the new church was ready for dedication, but when that time arrived the ceremony was a holiday for all the Pimería. To it came important Spaniards, Jesuits, and civilians, from all the country round. "Likewise, there came very many Pimas from the north and the west," cheering the anxious heart of the missionary, and lending a bright touch of color to the scene.

We have a precious description of Dolores that Kino wrote two years later. The establishment, under his magic management, had become temple, orchard, farm, stock ranch, and industrial plant, all combined in one.

This mission has its church adequately furnished with ornaments, chalices, . . . bells, choir chapel, etc.; likewise a great many large and small cattle, oxen, fields, a garden with various kinds of garden crops, Castilian fruit trees, grapes, peaches, quinces, figs, pomegranates, pears, and apricots. It has a forge for blacksmiths, a carpenter shop, a pack train, water mill, many kinds of grain, and provisions from rich and abundant harvests of wheat and maize, besides other things, including horse and mule herds, all of which serve and are greatly needed for the house, as well as for the expeditions and new conquests and conversions, and to purchase a few gifts and attractions, with which, together with the Word of God, it is customary to contrive to win the minds and souls of the natives.

To help him manage this vast establishment Kino had built up a well-organized corps of native functionaries, civil, educational, and industrial. He continues, "likewise in . . . Dolores, besides the justices, captain, governor, alcaldes, fiscal mayor, alguacil, topil . . . masters of chapel and school, and mayor domos of the house, there are . . . cowboys, ox-drivers, bakers, . . . gardeners, and painters."

The churches at Remedios and Cocóspora were of slower growth till 1702. Then Kino turned to completing them as a major interest. To carry on the work, he tells us, he assembled "maize, wheat, cattle, and clothing, or shop goods, such as cloth, . . . blankets, and other fabrics, which are the currency that best serves in these new lands for the laborers, master carpenters, constables, military commanders, captains, and fiscales."

For beams and framework for the churches, the tireless Kino had pine timber cut and hauled from the mountains near by. To obtain the necessary tools he went personally to purchase them in the towns of Sonora. To help with the building he invited Indians from all directions, and there came, he says, "far and away more than I had requested, especially from Bac." The hills of Remedios and Cocóspora now echoed the sounds of hammer and saw. Adobes were made, walls went up, roofs were tiled. Meanwhile Kino cut a deep trail riding back and forth to supervise all this activity. "I managed all the year (1703)," he writes, "to go nearly every week through the three pueblos, looking after both spiritual and temporal things, and the building of the two new churches." That is to say, each week he rode to Remedios, Cocóspora, and back to Dolores. The round trip was a good hundred miles.

The laborers had to be fed and clothed. During the work on these two churches, five hundred beeves and five hundred fanegas (over a thousand bushels) of wheat were eaten by the workmen. To cover their nakedness Kino spent three thousand pesos, a sum which now would be equivalent to many thousand dollars. His pack trains were all the while on the go, to and from the towns and mining camps of Sonora, carrying south pack loads of flour, maize, meat, lard, and tallow, and returning north with the precious merchandise needed for the church building.

Father Eusebio may be pardoned if he was a little vain of his two new temples. Father Leal had called Dolores the finest church in Sonora. But those of Remedios and Cocóspora were finer. "Each has a chapel of the most glorious apostle to the Indies, San Xavier," Kino tells us, "and each chapel would have cost ten thousand pesos were it not for the fertility of these new conversions."

TRAIL MAKING

KINO'S WORK AS MISSIONARY was paralleled by his achievement as explorer, and to him is due the credit for the first mapping of Pimería Alta on the basis of actual exploration. The region had been entered by Fray Marcos, by Melchior Díaz, and by the main Coronado party, in the period 1539–41. But these explorers had only passed along its eastern and western borders; for it is no longer believed that they went down the Santa Cruz. Oñate went from Moqui down the Colorado River and became acquainted with the Yumas and their neighbors in 1604–5. Since that time settlement had edged slowly north, and the Pimas had become well known on the Sonora border. Kino tells us that before his day New Mexico traders had visited the tribe. But of this contact no satisfactory information has come to us. So far as recorded history goes, therefore, the rediscovery and the detailed reconnoissance of Pimería Alta was the work of Father Kino.

Not to count the minor and unrecorded journeys among his widely separated missions, he made at least fourteen expeditions across the line into what is now Arizona. Six of them took him as far as Tumacácori, Fairbank, San Xavier del Bac, or Tucson. Six carried him to the Gila over five different routes. Twice he reached that stream by way of the Santa Cruz, returning once via Casa Grande, Sonóita, the Gulf of California, and Caborca. Once he went by way of the San Pedro, once from El Sáric across to the Gila below the Big Bend, and three times by way of Sonóita and the Camino del Diablo, along the Gila Range. Two of these expeditions carried him to Yuma and down the Colorado. Once he crossed that stream into California, and finally he reached its mouth.

East and west, between Sonóita and the eastern missions, he crossed southern Arizona several times and by various trails. In what is now Sonora he made at least half a dozen recorded journeys from Dolores to Caborca and the coast, three to the Santa Clara Mountain[3] to view the

---

[3]Sierra del Pinacate.

head of the California Gulf, and two to the coast by then-unknown routes south of the Altar River. This enumeration does not include his journey to Mexico, nor the numerous other trips to distant interior points in what is now Sonora, to see the superior mission authorities, or to drive cattle and purchase supplies.

CATTLE KING

THE WORK THAT FATHER KINO DID as ranchman, or stockman, would alone stamp him as an unusual businessman and make him worthy of remembrance. He was easily the cattle king of his day and region. From the small outfit supplied him from the older missions to the east and south, within fifteen years he established the beginnings of ranching in the valleys of the Magdalena, the Altar, the Santa Cruz, the San Pedro, and the Sonóita. The stock-raising industry of nearly twenty places on the modern map owes its beginnings on a considerable scale to this indefatigable man. And it must not be supposed that he did this for private gain, for he did not own a single animal. It was to furnish a food supply for the Indians of the missions established and to be established, and to give these missions a basis of economic prosperity and independence. It would be impossible to give a detailed statement of his work of this nature, but some of the exact facts are necessary to convey the impression. Most of the data, of course, were unrecorded, but from those available it is learned that stock ranches were established by him or directly under his supervision at Dolores, Caborca, Tubutama, San Ignacio, Imuris, Magdalena, Quiburi, Tumacácori, Cocóspora, San Xavier del Bac, Bacoancos, Guebavi, Síboda, Búsanic, Sonóita, San Lázaro, Sáric, Santa Bárbara, and Santa Eulalia.

Characteristic of Kino's economic efforts are those reflected in Father Saeta's letter thanking him for the present of 115 head of cattle and as many sheep for the beginnings of a ranch at Caborca. In 1699 a ranch was established at Sonóita for the triple purpose of supplying the little mission there, furnishing food for the missionaries of California, if perchance they should reach that point, and as a base of supplies for the explorations which Kino hoped to undertake and did undertake to the Yumas and Cocomaricopas, of whom he had heard while on the Gila.

In 1700, when the mission of San Xavier was founded, Kino rounded up the fourteen hundred head of cattle on the ranch of his own mission of Dolores, divided them into two equal droves, and sent one of them under his Indian overseer to Bac, where the necessary corrals were constructed.

Not only his own missions, but those of sterile California must be supplied; and in the year 1700 Kino took from his own ranches seven hundred cattle and sent them to Salvatierra, across the gulf at Loreto, a transaction similar to several others that are recorded.

And it must not be forgotten that Kino conducted this cattle industry with Indian labor, almost without the aid of a single white man. An illustration of his method and of his difficulties is found in the fact that the important ranch at Tumacácori, Arizona, was founded with cattle and sheep driven at Kino's orders one hundred miles across the country from Caborca by the very Indians who had murdered Father Saeta. There was always the danger that the mission Indians would revolt and run off the stock, as they did in 1695; and the danger, more imminent, that the hostile Apaches, Janos, and Jocomes would do this damage and add to it the destruction of human life.

STRONG OF HEART

Kino's physical courage is attested by his whole career in America, spent in exploring unknown wilds and laboring among untamed savages. But it is especially shown by several particular episodes in his life. In March and April 1695, the Pimas of the Altar Valley rose in revolt. At Caborca Father Saeta was killed and became the protomartyr of Pimería Alta. At Caborca and Tubutama seven servants of the missions were slain, and at Caborca, Tubutama, Imuris, San Ignacio, and Magdalena—the whole length of the Altar and Magdalena valleys—the mission churches and other buildings were burned and the stock killed or stampeded. The missionary of Tubutama fled over the mountains to Cucurpe. San Ignacio being attacked by three hundred warriors, Father Campos fled to the same refuge, guarded on each side by two soldiers. At Dolores Father Kino, Lieutenant Manje, and three citizens of Bacanuche awaited the onslaught. An Indian who had been stationed on the mountains, seeing the smoke at San Ignacio, fled to Dolores with the story that Father Campos and all the soldiers had been killed. Manje sped to Opodepe to get aid; the three citizens hurried home to Bacanuche, and Kino was left alone. When Manje returned next day, together they hid the treasures of the church in a cave, but in spite of the soldiers' entreaties that they should flee, Kino insisted on returning to the mission to await death, which they did. Fortunately they were not killed. It is indicative of the modesty of this great soul that in his own history this incident in his life is passed over in complete silence. But Manje, who was weak or wise enough to wish to flee, was also generous and brave enough to record the padre's heroism and his own fears.

In 1701 Kino made his first exploration down the Colorado below the Yuma junction—the first that had been made for almost a century. With him was one Spaniard, the only other white man in the party. As they left the Yuma country and entered that of the Quiquimas, the Spaniard, Kino tells us in his diary, "on seeing such a great number of new people," and such people—that is, they were giants in size—became frightened and fled, and was seen no more. But the missionary, thus deserted, instead of turning back, dispatched messages that he was safe, continued down the river two days, and crossed the Colorado, guided by tall Yumas of awe-inspiring mien, into territory never trod by white men since 1540. Perhaps he was in no danger, but the situation had proved too much for the nerve of his white companion, at least.

VELARDE'S EULOGY

AND WHAT KIND OF A MAN personally was Father Kino to those who knew him intimately? Was he rugged, coarse fibered, and adapted by nature to such a rough frontier life of exposure? I know of no portrait of him made by sunlight or the brush, but there is, fortunately, a picture drawn by the pen of his companion during the last eight years of his life, and his successor at Dolores. Father Luís Velarde tells us that Kino was a modest, humble, gentle ascetic, of medieval type, drilled by his religious training to complete self-effacement. I should not be surprised to find that, like Father Junípero Serra, he was slight of body as he was gentle of mind. Velarde says of him:

Permit me to add what I observed in the eight years during which I was his companion. His conversation was of the mellifluous names of Jesus and Mary, and of the heathen for whom he was ever offering prayers to God. In saying his breviary he always wept. He was edified by the lives of the saints, whose virtues he preached to us. When he publicly reprimanded a sinner he was choleric. But if anyone showed him personal disrespect he controlled his temper to such an extent that he made it a habit to exalt whomsoever mistreated him by word, deed, or in writing. . . . And if it was to his face that they were said, he embraced the one who spoke them, saying, "You are and ever will be my dearest master!" even though he did not like him. And then, perhaps, he would go and lay the insults at the feet of the Divine Master and the sorrowing Mother, into whose temple he went to pray a hundred times a day.

After supper, when he saw us already in bed, he would enter the church, and even though I sat up the whole night reading, I never heard him come out to get the sleep of which he was very sparing. One night I casually saw someone whipping him mercilessly [as a means of penance]. He always took his food without salt, and with mixtures of herbs which made it more distasteful. No one ever saw in him any vice whatsoever, for the discovery of lands and the conversion of souls had purified him.

These, then, are the virtues of Father Kino: he prayed much, and was considered as without vice. He neither smoked nor took snuff, nor wine, nor slept in a bed. He was so austere that he never used wine except to celebrate Mass, nor had any other bed than the sweat blankets of his horse for a mattress, and two Indian blankets [for a cover]. He never had more than two coarse shirts, because he gave everything as alms to the Indians. He was merciful to others, but cruel to himself. While violent fevers were lacerating his body, he tried no remedy for six days except to get up to celebrate Mass and to go to bed again. And by thus weakening and dismaying Nature he conquered the fevers.

Is there any wonder that such a man as this could endure the hardships of exploration?

Kino died at the age of sixty-six, at Magdalena, one of the missions he had founded. His companion when the end came was Father Agustín de Campos, for eighteen years his colaborer. Velarde thus describes his last moments:

Father Kino died in the year 1711, having spent twenty-four years in glorious labors in this Pimería, which he entirely covered in forty expeditions, made as best they could be made by two or three zealous workers. When he died he was almost seventy years old. He died as he had lived, with extreme humility and poverty. In token of this, during his last illness he did not undress. His deathbed, as his bed had always been, consisted of two calfskins for a mattress, two blankets such as the Indians use for covers, and a pack-saddle for a pillow. Nor did the entreaties of Father Agustín move him to anything else. He died in the house of the Father where he had gone to dedicate a finely made chapel in his pueblo of Santa Magdalena, consecrated to San Francisco Xavier. . . . When he was singing the Mass of the dedication he felt indisposed, and it seems that the Holy Apostle, to whom he was ever devoted, was calling him, in order that, being buried in his chapel, he might accompany him, as we believe, in glory.

The words of that eloquent writer, John Fiske, in reference to Las Casas, Protector of the Indians, are not inapplicable to Father Kino. He says:

In contemplating such a life, all words of eulogy seem weak and frivolous. The historian can only bow in reverent awe before . . . [such] a figure. When now and then in the course of centuries God's providence brings such a life into this world, the memory of it must be cherished by mankind as one of its most precious and sacred possessions. For the thoughts, the words, the deeds of such a man, there is no death. The sphere of their influence goes on widening forever. They bud, they blossom, they bear fruit, from age to age.

Samuel Charles Mazzuchelli
GIFTED PIONEER OF THE MIDWEST

By Flora Breidenbach

IN 1843, A STATUE OF MARY, the mother of Jesus, was shipped from Paris, France, addressed simply to "M. Mazzuchelli, United States of America."[1] Though the population of the United States was about sixteen million people and its territory vast, it found its way to the correct person, Father Samuel Charles Mazzuchelli in Galena, Illinois. In the mid-nineteenth century, Mazzuchelli was well-known in the United States, yet today very few people in the Midwest, and even fewer elsewhere, know who he was.

The purpose of this essay is to bring to the attention of others the magnitude of the work of Father Mazzuchelli, thereby contributing to the cultural history of the Midwest and of Italians in America.

Carlo Gaetano Samuele Mazzuchelli was born in Milan, Italy, on November 4, 1806, to a family famous in banking, business, and the arts. Given a private education by tutors as was befitting the child of a well-to-do family, Samuel was later sent to Switzerland to continue his studies when the political situation changed as the movement for independence and unification began.

Hoping Samuel would eventually enter politics, his family was disappointed when, at the age of 17, he asked for his father's permission to enter the Dominican Order to study for the priesthood. Opposed at first, his father eventually consented, and the young man went to Rome

---

[1] Archives of Sinsinawa Mound.

to begin his studies. Five years later, Samuel Mazzuchelli left Italy. He spent several months in France improving his French, then emigrated to the United States. After a long voyage by ship, stagecoach, and steamboat, he arrived in Cincinnati. Shortly thereafter, he was sent to Kentucky to study English.

The trip from Cincinnati to Kentucky was a rugged introduction to life on the American frontier. After a long train ride, the cultured young man from Italy mounted a horse; he had never been on a horse before, and, after an exhausting thirty-eight-mile non-stop trip, which put him to bed for two days, Mazzuchelli "prayed earnestly that he would never see a horse again."[2] Little did he know at the time that horseback would become his primary means of transportation!

After an intensive study of English, Mazzuchelli was able to continue his theological studies, and in September 1830 he was ordained a priest. A month later, at the age of twenty-four, the tolerant, gentle, mild-mannered young priest set out for his first assignment, Mackinac Island. There were no other priests in the area at the time and his parish covered 200,000 square miles. It was removed by thousands of miles and hundreds of years from the refined culture of Milan which he had known.

Years before Mazzuchelli's arrival in Mackinac, French Jesuit priests, including Father Marquette, had built a church there. It was the only place where Mazzuchelli ever found a church "already built and waiting for him."[3]

After some time, Mazzuchelli moved on to northeastern Wisconsin. There he ministered to fur trappers, traders, and several tribes of Native Americans: the Winnebago, Menominee, Ottawa, and Chippewa. Mazzuchelli was well-liked by the Native Americans. In 1833, Whirling Thunder, representing the Winnebago tribe, presented a petition to the United States government agent for Indian Affairs. It stated, "We wish to know more of our great Father above. We want Mr. Mazzuchelli to remain with us."[4] Mazzuchelli remained with the Native Americans of

[2] Dorcy, S. M. J., *Saint Dominic's Family* (Washington, D.C.: Dominicana Publications, 1983), 522.
[3] Bartels, J., and Alderson, J. M., *The Man Mazzuchelli: Pioneer Priest* (Madison: Wisconsin House, Ltd., 1974), Chapter 2, n.p.
[4] Mazzuchelli, S. C. *The Memoirs of Father Samuel Mazzuchelli, O. P.* (Chicago: Priory Press, 1967), 84.

Wisconsin until 1835, when he was requested to minister to the people of the lead-mining area around Galena, Illinois, and Dubuque, Iowa, because he was the only available priest who could preach well in English. Though not the first priest in the area, he was the first to remain there. Those who had preceded him had either died in one of the frequent cholera epidemics, or had left, "unable to stomach the ugliness of the hard-drinking mining area."[5] Deeply moved by the number of orphans left by the cholera epidemics, Mazzuchelli became the foster parent of two of them, John Cavanaugh and Frank Mealiff.

The Irish had an especially difficult time with the name of Mazzuchelli and, because of this, he was known variously as Father Samuel, Father Mathew Kelly, Father Kelly, and Father Massy Kelly. As a result, it is believed that many of his accomplishments have been lost; it has made it difficult to trace them.[6]

By 1839, Mazzuchelli's parish of 3,500 Catholics spanned an area that extended two hundred miles long by thirty to fifty miles wide. In an area without developed roads or bridges, many of his parishioners lived in cabins without windows or floors, though an occasional wealthy soul had a piano.

Mazzuchelli revealed an open-minded attitude. His ideas were modern for his time, and he was criticized by those more conservative than he. For example, he said Mass wherever it was possible to do so, not hesitating to use a table, a dresser, or even a piano for an altar. When ministering to the Native Americans he used the vernacular in the liturgy rather than Latin as was the custom, or he said one verse in Latin and one in the Native American language. He won respect from the Protestants in the area because of his strong and simple lifestyle. They admired him so much that they did not hesitate to contribute money for the construction of Catholic churches. On the other hand, when a Protestant church was destroyed by an arsonist's fire, Mazzuchelli donated money to help rebuild it. He did not object to non-Catholics attending Catholic religious services; he did not care whether they attended out of mere curiosity or out of a real desire to learn about Catholicism. In fact, he always welcomed them, even allowing for a non-Catholic Native Amer-

---

[5] Alderson, *The Man Mazzuchelli: Pioneer Priest*, Chapter 7.
[6] Alderson, *The Man Mazzuchelli: Pioneer Priest*, Chapter 16.

ican chief to carry the cross at the funeral of a woman of his tribe. Today this act would be called "ecumenical."

In 1847, Mazzuchelli made a long-lasting contribution to the church in the New World. This was the year in which, under his direction, four women became the first Dominican Sisters of Sinsinawa, Wisconsin, a congregation which today numbers over one thousand members who minister in a variety of fields throughout the United States, Trinidad, and Bolivia. Mattias Hannon, a contemporary of his, described Mazzuchelli as a missionary "in the order of Marquette. . . . He was the grand missionary of the Northwest."[7]

This apostle of midwestern America was more than a simple missionary, however. He possessed an astonishingly wide range of interests and abilities, and he generously shared his talents with others.

One of his salient talents was that of educator, coupled with a strong sense of social justice. A modernist in his approach to learning, he believed that education was necessary for women as well as men, for minorities, in this case Native Americans, as well as whites, and for adults as well as children.

Mazzuchelli developed a plan to educate adults and children of the Menominee nation. He wanted to: 1) establish a school located in the center of the village so it would be easily accessible; 2) hold classes in the Menominee language in order to preserve the native culture; 3) introduce a broad curriculum that included arithmetic, spelling, singing, musical instruments, geography, history of the United States, patriotism, carpentry, agriculture, and needlework; and 4) establish lodging for those students who lived far from the village. The Indian agent in Green Bay, Colonel Stambaugh, a non-Catholic, approved Mazzuchelli's plan and recommended it to the secretary of war. However, the government granted only two hundred dollars to Mazzuchelli. Distressed over the paucity of funds, he nevertheless continued his work to achieve his goals.

Proficient in the languages of the Native Americans among whom he worked, Mazzuchelli, while visiting Detroit, had an eighteen-page book printed in the Winnebago language, one of the Sioux dialects. The book, *Ocangra Aramee Wawakakara*, containing a pronunciation key according to the English language, the Ten Commandants, and various

---

[7] Alderson, *The Man Mazzuchelli: Pioneer Priest*, Chapter 16.

prayers, is the first known publication in one of the Sioux dialects. The following year, Mazzuchelli published a Chippewa almanac at Green Bay, the first known printing job done in Wisconsin. The only known copy of the almanac is in the rare-book room collection of the Library of Congress.

Mazzuchelli never lost sight of the needs of Native Americans and he never tired of making them known to government officials. He continued to be their advocate after leaving the Native American missions. He lobbied hard to procure funds to establish schools for Native Americans, though he met with little success in this endeavor. Depressed, he later wrote prophetically in his *Memoirs*:

> the education of the tribes, even to a moderate degree, is practically impossible under the present conditions and these appear to be so permanent as to foretell the future destiny of the Indians who will have to continue in their . . . roving . . . state until the day when the . . . population of European origin will have filled the entire continent. Then the Indian will have left scarcely a trace of his existence in the land.[8]

In the Galena-Dubuque area, Mazzuchelli met George Wallace Jones, the congressional delegate from Prairie du Chien. In 1844, for $6,500 Mazzuchelli purchased eight hundred acres in southwest Wisconsin from Jones to establish a college for the young people of the area. The following year, a school for boys and young men, from eight to twenty years of age, opened at the site known as Sinsinawa Mound. At the beginning, the students lived in a log cabin, but in 1846 the cornerstone was laid for a large stone building for the school. That stone building still stands and remains in use to this day. In March 1848 the college was incorporated by one of the first acts of the new Wisconsin state legislature. By the fall of that year, the school, which charged twelve dollars per month for tuition, advertised in the eastern and southern press in the promotional language of the day:

> The system of education embraces the various arts and sciences usually taught in colleges. A complete knowledge of the Greek and Latin languages and literatures, of Mathematics, Natural Philosophy, Geography, Rhetoric, History, and English Composition is indispensable for graduation.[9]

---

[8] Alderson, *The Man Mazzuchelli: Pioneer Priest*, Chapter 5.
[9] S. Mary Nona McCreal, *Samuel Mazzuchelli, O.P.: A Kaleidoscope of Scenes From His Life* (n.p., n.d.), 44.

Father Mazzuchelli headed the college as its president and also served as one of its instructors.

At about the same time that the college was being developed, Mazzuchelli had established his community of Dominican Sisters. He personally prepared them, teaching them to be intellectually objective but at the same time sensitive. He always "respected their intelligence and treated them as men's equals," a concept not popular historically.[10]

Eventually the college at Sinsinawa Mound became a girls' school, St. Clara. Mazzuchelli loved teaching and he gained the reputation of being an excellent teacher. The curriculum at the girls' school included Moral Theology, Sacred History, Latin, French, German, Rhetoric, English Literature, Mathematics, Bookkeeping, Geography, Astronomy, and Physics. Mazzuchelli purchased pianos and encouraged singing. He directed plays and designed costumes for the students. He himself taught "Human Affairs" using newspapers and magazines as textbooks. He became the first teacher of Physics, then called Natural Philosophy, in the state of Wisconsin. He introduced the laboratory method in Wisconsin and is considered to be "the father of science" in that state.[11] The scientific instruments he used were considered to be superior to what the University of Wisconsin had. Among other equipment, Mazzuchelli had a galvanic battery, a mini Morse telegraph, revolving globes of both the earth and the heavens, Magdeburg spheres, an electric motor, apparatus to show the center of gravity, and a gadget which was a precursor of the neon light.

Mazzuchelli was also the Astronomy instructor at the school. On clear nights he took students out to look through the telescope, even in midwinter. He had slides which he projected by using a miner's lantern. Some of the slides which he used came from a company in New York, but others were apparently made by Mazzuchelli because they were made of materials differing from those used in commercial slides of the day, albeit of equal quality. Many of his slides are displayed at Sinsinawa Mound, to this day the motherhouse of the congregation of Dominican women which he founded.

When Samuel Mazzuchelli first began his ministry among Native Americans, he used temporary churches constructed of Indian mats that

---

[10] Alderson, *The Man Mazzuchelli: Pioneer Priest*, Chapter 13.
[11] Archives of Sinsinawa Mound.

could easily be dismantled, but he soon realized that makeshift churches were not enough and that permanent church buildings were needed. Having an accurate vision of the future development of the United States, Mazzuchelli purchased land for churches, schools, and cemeteries. He believed in the security of what is today called "real estate." In a letter dated January 1, 1863, he wrote: "Gold pays no interest and greenbacks are doubtful stuff. Land and minerals never fail."[12]

On the land he purchased, Mazzuchelli began to organize parishes, often serving as architect, master craftsman, and builder of the church. He cut timber, quarried stone, and carved the ornamentation. In 1831, he acquired land for the first Catholic church in Green Bay. Between then and 1852, he built more than thirty churches in Wisconsin, Illinois, and Iowa. He designed and supervised the construction of St. Augustine's in New Diggings, Wisconsin, in 1844, probably the only church that has survived unaltered. It is listed in the National Register of Historic Places. This church has an elegance of grace which is surprising in a frontier church. Much of the charm of the church is due to its altar, which Mazzuchelli carved with a pocket knife, modeling it after an altar in Rome sculpted by Bramante. Mazzuchelli also chiseled grooves in the wood siding of the building to make it look like blocks of stone. St. Michael's in Galena, Illinois, is another important church built by Mazzuchelli. It features a trussed roof, a type of construction which eliminated the need for pillars, thereby creating a large, magnificent open space on the inside. Mazzuchelli was the architect of many other Galena buildings, including the old market-house, various private homes, and the stone portion of the County Courthouse.

As Mazzuchelli's fame as a builder grew, he was asked to design buildings for pay. The new Iowa Territory Legislature decided to lay out a new capital and call it Iowa City. Mazzuchelli has been credited with planning the entire community. The *Iowa Historical Record*, among other publications of the time, listed Mazzuchelli as designer of the state capitol itself, a building 120 feet long and 60 feet wide. Built of stone, consisting of three stories, it is an example of classic architecture, containing a hanging stairway that features a two-story-high spiral that appears to be without support. The work Mazzuchelli accomplished in Iowa City

---

[12] Archives of Sinsinawa Mound.

and the churches he built make him worthy of the title given to him, "Builder of the West."[13]

Mazzuchelli's labors as priest, educator, and builder should be sufficient for him to be important in the history of the United States, as well as Italian American ethnicity. But this dynamic individual accomplished even more. He started temperance societies, directed the Galena Town Choir, belonged to the Shakespeare Coffee Club of Dubuque, and organized the festivities conducted in Dubuque on July 4, 1836, to celebrate the nation's birthday, creation of Wisconsin Territory, and inauguration of Henry Dodge as the territory's first governor. Aware of Mazzuchelli's interest in government, the members of the legislature elected him to address them at the first session on October 25, 1836. In a learned, instructive, and humorous speech Mazzuchelli spoke to the legislators about the responsibilities of their fiduciary mandate and gave them a brief history of the forms of governments from absolute monarchy to modern democracy. He remained as chaplain to the legislature. Humbly awed at having been chosen chaplain, he wrote in his *Memoirs*: "It would be difficult to find in the history of any country whatsoever a legislative assembly where Protestants outnumbering Catholics eighteen to one have nevertheless conferred the office of chaplain on a priest."[14]

In a ceremony in Burlington, Iowa, in 1841, Mazzuchelli made official his love for his adopted country: he became a United States citizen.

Traveling through the vast area where he ministered, occasionally accompanied by Native American guides, but often alone, Mazzuchelli further distinguished himself as a trail blazer. More important, however, is the fact that as he traveled he recorded his findings in little drawings with comments and names in both English and Italian. Out of his drawings he created maps. Indeed, he was one of the first map-makers to detail the central region of the United States. In the introduction to the 1915 edition of Mazzuchelli's *Memoirs*, Archbishop Ireland of St. Paul wrote:

> Mazzuchelli understood with singular clearness the principles of American law and life, and conformed himself to them in heartfelt loyalty. There lay one of the chief causes of the influence allowed him by his fel-

---

[13] Dorcy, *Saint Dominic's Family*, 524.
[14] Mazzuchelli, *The Memoirs of Father Samuel Mazzuchelli, O.P.*, 166.

low-citizens of all classes, and of the remarkable success with which his ministry was rewarded. He was a foreigner by birth and education; situations in his native Italy were much the antipodes of those in the country of his adoption. Yet he was American to the core of his heart, to the tip of his finger. He understood America. He loved America.[15]

Mazzuchelli's *Memoirs* were written precisely out of his love for America and out of his desire to acquaint the Italians of his time with the New World. They provide a vivid picture of the era in which he worked in the Midwest.

Mazzuchelli formulated a topic of keen interest about the Native Americans' culture and their exploitation at the hands of whites. In his *Memoirs*, he compared and contrasted various tribes. Upset, he described how Native Americans lost their lands and how they were forced to move to new areas. He commented that this moving is "always accompanied by dissipation, by disease, and by various calamities which . . . lessen the numbers of the Indians."[16] Always interested in the causes of events, Mazzuchelli described how lands taken from Native Americans were settled, how the land was divided among the settlers, the order in which merchants established their businesses, and how cities came to be.

The variety of topics which he presented in his *Memoirs* illustrated his keen powers of observation and the broad spectrum of his interests. He provided accurate descriptions of nature, means of transportation, differences between a territory and a state, making of syrup, construction of log and frame houses, various religious denominations, electoral system, principles of American democracy, and many other elements of significance on the frontier. Mazzuchelli's understanding of the times in which he lived is evident from a remark he made the night after John Brown's attack at Harper's Ferry in 1859: "This is the beginning of the end of human slavery in the United States. It is but a premonition of the approaching storm that is destined to break over this happy land with a violence that will shock the world."[17] Indeed, slavery was the one thing that Mazzuchelli disliked about the United States.

Mazzuchelli's comments are valuable for the light they shed on many

---

[15] Mazzuchelli, *The Memoirs of Father Samuel Mazzuchelli, O.P.*, 327.
[16] Mazzuchelli, *The Memoirs of Father Samuel Mazzuchelli, O.P.*, 205.
[17] Alderson, *The Man Mazzuchelli: Pioneer Priest*, Chapter 14.

aspects of early life in the Midwest. Archbishop Ireland reflected on Mazzuchelli's *Memoirs*:

> As a historical document the *Memoirs* is of exceptional value. It tells of a wide region of territory—from the waters of Huron to those of the Mississippi and to Des Moines—exactly as it was in the days of its wilderness and its first entrance into civilization. The populations that tenanted its forests and prairies—the Ottawa, the Menominee, and the Winnebago, the fur-gatherer and the trader, the incoming land seeker and the town builder—rise from its pages in full native vividness. The reader is brought into immediate touch with them, made to mingle in their daily doings and manners of life. It is precise and exact in descriptions. . . . The writer was a keen observer of incidents of every nature, and a faithful narrator of what he saw and heard. . . . No fervent student of American history will be without a copy of the *Memoirs* on the shelves of his library room.[18]

One of Mazzuchelli's duties as priest was to anoint the sick. Riding his faithful horse, Napoleon, he would leave his house at any time of day or night in good or bad weather to minister to a person's spiritual need. On February 15, 1864, during a blizzard, he was called to minister to a dying person. In haste, Mazzuchelli left without putting on his overcoat. He became ill with double pneumonia and died on February 23, 1864. After a funeral attended by hundreds of people, both Catholic and Protestant, some of whom traveled great distances, Father Mazzuchelli was buried in Benton, Wisconsin, close to St. Patrick's Church, which contains a painting thought to be his work. Mazzuchelli's obituary appeared in many newspapers throughout the country, including the *San Francisco Monitor* and the *Metropolitan Record of New York*. The latter newspaper commented:

> There he is high up on the scaffold of the church, with coat off and sleeves tucked up, industriously at work in brick and mortar. In the evening you see him in the pulpit discoursing on some abstruse questions of Christian philosophy and tomorrow he lectures before the governor, judges and legislators on the science of political economy but he is always and everywhere present when the sacred duties of the ministry require.[19]

---

[18] Mazzuchelli, *The Memoirs of Father Samuel Mazzuchelli, O.P.*, 329.
[19] McCreal, *Samuel Mazzuchelli, O.P.: A Kaleidoscope of Scenes From His Life*, 38.

At the time of his death, Mazzuchelli was known from New York to California. Why is it, then, that so few Americans today are aware of the man and his achievements? At one point, he had written to the bishop of Dubuque: "To live retired not known to the world is great happiness. . . . If the Lord is not very much displeased with me He will permit me to sink into oblivion before the world."[20] This wish of his seems to have been fulfilled, but it is a "shame that America, who honors her heroes so magnanimously, should have overlooked this man who brought to our New World the finest gifts of the old."[21] Samuel Charles Mazzuchelli, O.P., was indeed a pioneer of the Midwest and the fact that he was born in Italy and became an Italian American attests to the rich ethnic tapestry of American civilization. His story is central to the development of the American Midwest.

---

[20] John C. Piquette, *Providence Did Provide* (Galena, 1989), Tape.

[21] Dorcy, *Saint Dominic's Family*, 524.

The Neapolitan Jesuits on the Colorado Frontier, 1868–1919

By J. Manuel Espinosa

COLORADO'S PIONEER DAYS were relatively recent, for the region was not permanently settled by Europeans till after the turn of the middle of the nineteenth century. But the obstacles that faced the pioneers here were very much the same as those that faced pioneers on every new frontier, and the early Catholic missionaries who labored here recall to mind the sixteenth-century ideal that brought to the American Far West its first pioneers of civilization, the grey-robed Franciscan and the black-robed Jesuit.

Before the coming of the first permanent Jesuit missionaries to Colorado in 1871, the secular Catholic clergy had already been laboring for eighteen years in the Spanish-speaking settlements of the San Luís Valley. The first settlers here, who were in fact the first permanent settlers in what is now Colorado, were from the older Catholic Spanish settlements of New Mexico, of which southern Colorado was in effect the last northern frontier.

The San Luís Valley settlements being of Catholic Spanish origin, the New Mexico secular clergy virtually came in with the first settlers. By 1854 there were several villages established along the Conejos and Costilla rivers, and on some scattered ranches, about one hundred families in all. The idyllic villages of the fertile San Luís Valley, predominantly Spanish-speaking in population, with a few Americans among them, most of whom had also come up from New Mexico, were not to remain in isolation for long.

The discovery of gold in the Pike's Peak country in 1858 started a mad rush of Anglo-American immigrants into the hills and valleys of the eastern slope of the Colorado Rockies. This opened a new chapter in Colorado church history. The older Catholic Spanish frontier was met on its northern and eastern fringes by a new Anglo-American mining frontier. This was to have far-reaching reactions, different but equal in significance to those that had already been felt in the New Mexico settlements ten years earlier. To the Catholic Church these new frontier developments opened a new and challenging field of missionary endeavor.

The decade of the fifties had witnessed the coming of the first permanent Catholic missionaries into Colorado. The following decade was the formative period for the Catholic Church in Colorado. During that time its original elements were brought together and organized into regular groups. The first permanent missionaries in Colorado who came from New Mexico had been under the jurisdiction of Archbishop John B. Lamy of Santa Fe. In 1866, however, the Vicariate Apostolic of Colorado and Utah was established under the jurisdiction of the Rt. Rev. Joseph P. Machebeuf, who later, in 1887, became bishop of Denver. Machebeuf, who began his missionary activities in Colorado in 1858, was destined to be perhaps the most conspicuous Catholic clergyman in Colorado history. He was the guiding spirit behind all Catholic Church activities in Colorado in the early period.

While these significant changes were taking place in the Colorado Rockies, other events were taking place in far-off Italy that were to result in the coming of the first Jesuits to the Colorado frontier. Italy was in the midst of revolution and the Jesuits were being dispersed. During this time of great anxiety, in the year 1867, Archbishop Lamy of Santa Fe, in need of more missionaries for his diocese, asked the father general of the Jesuits, Father P. J. Beckx, for Jesuit missionaries. At the moment the provincial of Naples was looking for a foreign mission in which to place part of the dispersed Neapolitan Province of the Society of Jesus, so by the direction of the father general he accepted the mission of Colorado and New Mexico. Thus through a turn of events in Italy, missionaries of the Neapolitan Province of the Society of Jesus were to play a significant role in the history of the New Mexico–Colorado frontier.[1] The first little band of five Jesuits reached Santa Fe, New Mexico, on the fifteenth of August 1867. Thus began the New Mexico–Colorado Mission of the Neapolitan Province of the Society of Jesus. A half century later, in 1919, when the mission was divided and transferred to the Missouri and New Orleans provinces, there were 122 Jesuits active in the field, and the scene of their activities had expanded to embrace the vast area from Montana to Old Mexico and from Arizona to Oklahoma.

Among the first Jesuits who came to Santa Fe in 1867 was Father De Blieck, a Belgian, who had been temporarily loaned to the Neapolitan mission by the Missouri Province. He was the first Jesuit in Colorado of whom we have definite record. In a letter dated April 14, 1868, Father Machebeuf wrote:

> The celebrated missionary, Father De Blieck came to Denver over a month ago from Santa Fe. . . . He gave a mission in our principal mountain parish where I was with him for a week, and he began one here in Denver on Friday of Passion Week. Unfortunately he was taken very sick on the third day of the mission . . . the work of finishing the mission fell upon me.[2]

Father De Blieck also took Father Machebeuf's place in charge of the Denver parish for a short time in the spring of 1868, during the temporary absence of the latter.

The first permanent missionary work of the Jesuits in Colorado, however, dates from the establishment of the Conejos mission in 1871. Although there had been permanent settlements in the San Luís Valley since 1851, and although Mass had been said in the Conejos Valley from

---

[1] The only detailed accounts of the Jesuits in Colorado are the manuscript records, the bulk of which are preserved in the archives of Regis College, Denver. The present article is based on these materials, especially F. M. Troy, S.J., *Historia Societatis Jesu in Novo Mexico et Colorado*, Ms., n.d., 140 pp., Regis College Archives, and Vito M. Tromby, S.J., *Historia, Missionis Novi Mexico et Coloradi et Elogia Nostrorum qui in ea Missione defuncti sunt*, Ms., n.d., 136 pp., ibid.; and also Rev. W. J. Howlett, *History of the Diocese of Denver*, Ms., n.d., Chancery Office, Denver. See also the commemorative booklet entitled *The Jesuit Fathers in Denver* (Denver, 1924), commemorating the dedication of St. Ignatius Loyola Church, and the little booklet *A la parroquia de Conejos en sus bodas de diamante* (Antonito, 1934).

[2] Rev. W. J. Howlett, *Life of the Right Reverend Joseph P. Machebeuf, D.D.* (Pueblo, 1908), 337.

about 1853 by priests from Abiquiu, New Mexico, there was no resident
priest in Conejos until June 10, 1857, when Our Lady of Guadalupe parish
was established by Bishop Lamy. From that time on there was a resident secular priest at Conejos. But the secular clergy were apparently
apathetic. Governor Gilpin decided to try to obtain Jesuits to administer the parish, and he wrote to Father Pierre De Smet in St. Louis in
that regard. De Smet immediately forwarded the letter to Father Gasparri, at Albuquerque, which had become the central headquarters for
the New Mexico–Colorado Mission. Gasparri wrote to the governor
asking for a map of the parish and the San Luís Valley. A short time
later Machebeuf, Vicar Apostolic of Colorado, asked the Jesuits to take
over the parish, and Father Salvatore Personé and Brother Cherubin
Anzalone were assigned to the Conejos mission, where they arrived
December 9, 1871.

Father Personé, the first Jesuit to take up permanent work in Colorado, was destined to spend almost fifty years of his missionary life on
Colorado soil. Two months later, February 1, 1872, he was joined by
Father Alejandro Leone and another brother. Personé immediately began
to restore the church, and there began a period of religious revival the
like of which had never before been seen in the San Luís Valley. They
made a visitation of their mission and found about three thousand souls
in the twenty-five different villages extending north as far as Saguache
and San Luís, some 115 miles, south to Los Pinos, about 6 miles, east as
far as Los Sauces, some 25 miles, and west as far as Las Mesitas, some
7 miles. To quote from the original parish diary describing the remarkable religious activity of the Jesuits during their first months at Conejos, the Lenten season of 1872:

> Considering the lamentable state in which the people lived, the Fathers
> sought a means of urging and getting them to fulfill their religious oblig-
> ations. The time was very favorable, for it was the Lenten Season, and
> much more so because it was winter, when the people live shut up in their
> houses and in their huts, while in the summer they are so scattered that
> it is impossible to gather them together. Hence the two Fathers began
> to visit the villages and the ranches, going from house to house, and con-
> fessing almost everyone in his own home. To be sure, almost the whole
> night went in hearing confessions, which at times were continued until

time for Mass, especially since there were boys and girls and also adults who had not yet made their First Communion. But God lightened this work with almost 2,000 confessions, with eight persons who left the bad life, with the removal of other less public scandals, and the destruction of many Protestant books. . . . The fact is that since the Fathers arrived the people come to Mass, go to confession, abuses and scandals are being removed, and the people live in peace and without fear of being attacked and killed.[3]

The next parish to be established by the Jesuits in Colorado was that of St. Ignatius in Pueblo, where Father Charles Pinto took charge on October 20, 1872. He first made his home in a little room in the house of Captain J. J. Lambert, but in 1873 he erected a two story building, the upper story being used for a church, and the lower for a residence. The parish of the Seven Dolors had been established in 1869 for the Mexican settlers on the Cucharas and Huerfano rivers, but between there and Denver, a distance of 175 miles, there was no priest until Father Pinto took charge of the lower half of the territory with headquarters at Pueblo. In 1875 Father Pinto succeeded in obtaining the Sisters of Loretto to teach in the parochial school of St. Ignatius.

The next mission to which the Jesuits were called was Trinidad. Father Munnecum, the pastor there, did not understand the people and had alienated many from the church. And so the Jesuits were asked to give a mission there, which was conducted by Fathers D'Aponte and Salvatore Personé, beginning on December 13, 1874. The parish was in such a disgraceful condition that in the following year Bishop Machebeuf turned it over to the Jesuits.

Fathers Pinto and Leone were ordered to Trinidad on November 20, 1875. The first thing they did was to restore the church, which was nothing but a hall, without floor, without ornament, without light, and with a very poor altar. In this work they were aided by the Sisters of Charity, who had been conducting the school there since 1871. The new parish comprised the whole of Las Animas County, a territory 150 miles long and 50 miles wide.

---

[3] This quotation is taken from volume one of the *Diario de la residencia de la Compañía de Jesus de Nuestra Señora de Guadalupe, Conejos, Colorado, 1871–1920,* 9 vols., Ms. in Regis College Archives, Denver. It may also be found in the author's translated and edited excerpts from the same in *Mid-America* 28 (October, 1936), 274–75.

During these years Bishop Machebeuf worked unceasingly in his efforts to bring other Catholic religious orders to those places in Colorado where Catholic settlers lacked the ministrations of their clergy. Meanwhile the Jesuits worked unceasingly. From September 4 to October 14, 1876, they were temporarily in control at Walsenburg, due to the death of the pastor. From their headquarters at Conejos, Pueblo, and Trinidad, missions were being given in the surrounding territory to revive the faith of the Catholic people. The mission conducted by Fathers Gasparri and Minasi at Conejos in April 1876 was most successful. At the close of the mission Father Gasparri suggested that the citizens erect a more commodious building for a convent, and as a result a fairly decent building was set up. And in the following year the school was improved and the Sisters of Loretto took charge; they were to remain there until 1918. The educational activity sponsored by the Jesuits was notable, and until the end of the Jesuit regime in Conejos in 1919, one or another of the Jesuits was a member of the school board. In 1879 Bishop Machebeuf established a parish at Carnero and placed Father John Brinker in charge, because the Jesuits did not have enough men to administer the whole valley. In 1888 the Jesuits were again given charge of the entire valley, and in 1899 Father Francis X. Tommasini built at Del Norte the first church to be consecrated in Colorado.

Meanwhile Bishop Machebeuf was agitating for a Jesuit parish in Denver. He had written to Father Baldassarre, superior of the mission, asking for men to open a house in Denver, but the superior replied that he had no men. But when the bishop heard that Father Camillus Mazzella had been appointed visitor to the mission and was in Pueblo he immediately went to see him. He asked the visitor to accept two more missions and found either a residence or college in Denver. Father Mazzella realized that Denver was fast becoming the principal city of the region and after much deliberation decided to grant the bishop's request, although it could be done only at great sacrifice and inconvenience.

In 1879 three Jesuits came to Colorado, and with Father Guida as pastor established Sacred Heart parish in the eastern part of Denver, opening a temporary chapel on September 12 in the parlors of their own residence recently purchased. This was the third Catholic parish established in Denver. On the sixteenth of September Father Guida began construction of a new church. The cornerstone was laid October 16 and the new edifice was opened to the public on April 25, 1880. During the summer months the basement was divided into rooms and fitted and furnished for school purposes, and in the beginning of September the School of the Sacred Heart was formally opened. It was the second Catholic parochial school in Denver. The pupils came from all parts of the city. Father Guida organized a "Free School Society," which, however, was short lived. In the summer of 1882 he arranged for the Sisters of Charity of Cincinnati to take charge of the school.

The parish was so large that it was necessary for the Fathers to open a chapel in the eastern part of it in order to accommodate the parishioners. The new church was called Loyola Chapel and served the parish until replaced by the present Loyola Church in 1924. At first the back part of the building was used as a residence. After the present rectory was built, the partition was torn out and the church extended to the rear of the building. Although Denver may have been proud of her new church, Dr. Edward J. Nolan was a bit critical when he wrote in 1894:

> Our first Sunday was spent in Denver. We were fortunate enough to be directed to the Jesuit Church, which we found to be poor, small and dingy, unworthy alike of the great Order and the growing city. We were assured, however, that it was the best Catholic church in Denver, which is the more surprising as our dissenting brethren have kept pace with the progress of the city, fine Episcopalian, Presbyterian, Methodist, and Unitarian churches have been erected. In fact there was apparent truth in the remark of the hotel clerk of whom we asked guidance.—"The Catholic Church in Denver is slow;" the more to be regretted as it appears to be the only slow thing in the place. The congregation, however, was large and devout, with a gratifying proportion of the male element. The beauty of the sermon, however, consoled us in a measure for the short-coming of the building and its adornment.[4]

While the Jesuits were opening a church and school in Denver, they were also organizing a new parish at Pueblo–St. Patrick's. On the 11th of October of that same year, 1882, the residence and church of St. Patrick's were destroyed by fire. Other misfortunes were to dog the steps of the

---

[4] Edward ,T. Nolan, M.D., "Certain Churches in the West," *Records of the American Catholic Historical Society of Philadelphia*, 5 (1894): 89.

Jesuits in Pueblo, but success in their religious work was not to be denied. Their field of activity embraced a wide area. Father Pinto originally served three counties, Pueblo, Fremont, and Bent. Later Father Francis X. Tommasini served from St. Patrick's sixteen mission stations in the six counties of Pueblo, Otero, Crowley, Bent, Prowers, and Baca. In 1885 Father Tommasini built the parochial school at St. Patrick's which, to his credit, was paid for as soon as it was finished.

Meanwhile a new church was being built by the Jesuits at Trinidad. The cornerstone was laid on October 14, 1883, and the edifice was dedicated on the Feast of the Most Holy Trinity, May 31, 1885. It was then described as the most beautiful if not the largest church in all Colorado. At Pueblo the Jesuits were not very popular, due mostly to the rise of a local Italian race prejudice and the fact that nearly all of them were Italians. In 1887 it was decided to abandon work there, but after consultation they gave up only St. Ignatius. Years later, Father S. Giglio finished the building of Mount Carmel Church there.

The Jesuits played a significant part in the coal mining areas near Trinidad. In the early nineties there was much radical agitation among the Italian coal miners in that region, a trend in evidence at that time among the laboring classes all over the United States. It frightened the conservative mine operators, and so they encouraged the Jesuits to work among the miners, financing the building of Catholic chapels in the mining settlements, and asking the Jesuits to put good books in the hands of the people so as to counteract the influence of radical and destructive doctrines.

In the 1880s the Jesuits established the first Catholic institution of higher learning in Colorado, Sacred Heart College. Since the seventies Bishop Machebeuf had hopes of establishing a Jesuit college in Colorado. Originally the idea had been to build it in the San Luís Valley, where a rich English company had offered land for that purpose. Twice efforts were made in this direction that did not materialize. Finally in 1883 a third and successful effort saw the emergence of the sixth oldest institution of higher learning in Colorado.

The Jesuits were having trouble maintaining their college at Las Vegas, New Mexico, founded in 1876, and besides it drew most of its student-body from New Mexico, and that section could be cared for by the

Christian Brothers at Santa Fe. So Bishop Machebeuf induced the Jesuits to move their college to Colorado. Permission was obtained from Rome to make the move, and on September 15, 1883, Sacred Heart College was opened at Morrison, sixteen miles from Denver, in the large building known as Evergreen Hotel, which had been secured by the bishop. The college at Morrison co-existed with Las Vegas College until both were combined and removed to Denver under the name of The College of the Sacred Heart in 1887. The school at Morrison had a large attendance from the beginning. At the opening of the scholastic year 1884 there were seventy pupils present. They came from northern Mexico and Texas, as well as Colorado—some even came from as far as Philadelphia.

The College of the Sacred Heart was built on a forty-acre tract in what was then known as the Highlands, near Denver, the land having been obtained through an English corporation. There, Father Dominic Pantanella, father of the institution, erected the present administration building and opened the school for classes in the fall of 1888. The institution was empowered to grant degrees in 1889, and the first class of three was graduated in 1890. In 1921 the name was changed to Regis College.

After the opening of Sacred Heart College in Denver the Catholics of the neighborhood found it much more convenient to attend Mass in the college chapel than to walk several miles to the nearest church. As a result Bishop Matz established the parish of the Holy Family in 1891, and the college chapel served as the parish church until Father Fede organized the parish in 1902 and erected the present Holy Family Church in 1904. He also built a residence and left a surplus in the bank for the founding of a parochial school.

Another important work carried on by the Jesuits from their principal centers of activity in Denver, Trinidad, Pueblo, and Conejos, was the conducting of missions in outlying settlements. And "their efforts resulted in a great revival of zeal and devotion." They visited almost every Spanish-speaking section of southern Colorado, undergoing all the hardships of pioneer life. They traveled from Colorado to give missions in Montana, Oklahoma, New Mexico, Arizona, and the states of northern Mexico.

On August 15, 1919, the letter of the father general of the Society of Jesus dissolving the New Mexico–Colorado Mission of the Neapolitan Province was read in the refectory of Sacred Heart College in Denver.

New Mexico and Texas were given to the New Orleans Province, and Colorado to the Missouri Province. Thus came to a close an interesting and romantic chapter in the history of the Jesuits in North America. These pioneer Jesuits of the Neapolitan Province were an important force in the religious and cultural life of Colorado that cannot be overlooked. And apart from their actual spiritual and material accomplishments, the vast number of contemporary records left by the pioneer Jesuits on the Colorado frontier, along with those of other Catholic missionaries, in the form of diaries, journals, church records, and the like, constitute a rich source for the study of the social and economic history of the region as well as for church history proper.

Frances Xavier Cabrini, Foundress of the Queen of Heaven Institute

By Sister M. Lilliana Owens

OTHER FRANCES XAVIER CABRINI,[1] foundress of the Queen
of Heaven Mother Cabrini Memorial School in Denver, was
born at Sant' Angelo di Lodi (Lombardy), Italy, on July 15,
1850. While still a child she longed to be a missionary. At the age of thirteen she revealed this desire to her sister Rose, fifteen years her senior, who said, "You are too small and not yet educated. How can you dare to dream of becoming a missionary?" The young girl said no more, but kept her radiant dream in her heart. At the age of eighteen she obtained her teacher's certificate. At this time she made two attempts to enter different religious communities, but was rejected on the basis of ill health and for other reasons. She was not dismayed by these rejections, but devoted her leisure time to the performance of works of charity. At the request of her parish priest, she taught catechism to neglected children and visited the sick. In 1872, at the age of twenty-two, she distinguished herself by assisting the victims of a smallpox epidemic. From 1872 until 1874 she taught in the public schools of Vidardo and gained a reputa-

---

[1] For detailed information regarding the life of Blessed Frances Xavier Cabrini see "Blessed Frances Xavier Cabrini," translated from the Italian of Very Reverend Monsignor John Della Cioppa by the Missionary Sisters of the Sacred Heart, Blessed Cabrini High School, 701 Fort Washington Avenue, New York, N. Y., p. 3 *et seq.*; also, *Sanctity in America*, "Blessed Frances Xavier Cabrini," by the Most Reverend Amleto Giovanni Cicognani, D.D., Apostolic Delegate to the United States (Paterson, N. J.: St. Anthony Guild Press).

tion among the civil authorities for ability, patience, and kindness. She accepted a position of directress of a school for orphans at Codogno in 1874—never, however, forgetting her desire for missionary work.

The Most Reverend Dominic Gelmini, bishop of Lodi, learned of her zeal and of her extraordinary intellectual and moral qualities. He summoned her and told her the time was ripe for her to found a community of sisters who would be entirely devoted to missionary work. Her obedience was complete. On November 14, 1880, she and her first companions took up their residence in the abandoned monastery which had formerly been the property of the Franciscans of Codogno. She soon placed a statue of the Sacred Heart over the house and on the door was placed this inscription, which has since become known throughout the world—"Institute of the Missionary Sisters of the Sacred Heart."

At the time large numbers of Italians were emigrating to the United States, where, without religious instruction in their own language, they were in danger of losing their faith in God. Appeals were made to her for help. In her prudence she exposed her plans to the then reigning pontiff, Pope Leo XIII.[2] She had previously told him of her great desire to work among the infidels of China. The pope, mindful of the great needs of the Italians in the New World, especially in New York, considered her plan and gave her the following answer: "Not to the Orient but to the Occident. There you will find a great field of labor."[3] Thus guided by the hand of Divine Providence, Mother Frances Xavier Cabrini arrived in New York on March 31, 1889. Her spirit of faith and the knowledge that she was fulfilling a mission entrusted to her by Pope Leo XIII gave her the courage she needed to surmount the difficulties that were awaiting her in New York. She had previously been assured that she would find in New York an orphanage for Italian children; instead she found *nothing* prepared, not even the quarters for her and her six missionary companions. The archbishop who had asked her aid had changed his mind and went so far as to tell her to return to Italy. But full of faith in the words of the great Pope Leo XIII, she rose to her full height and replied: "Here the Holy Father has sent me and here I will stay."[4] She took for herself the motto of the great Apostle Paul, *"Omnia possum in eo qui me confortat"*[5]—"I can do all

[2] See *Extension*, May 1944, for a picture of Blessed Frances Xavier Cabrini before Leo XIII. This picture is the work of Martin Gulzer.
[3] Cioppa, "Blessed Frances Xavier Cabrini," 12.   [4] Ibid., 13.   [5] Phil. 4:13.

Saint Frances Xavier Cabrini, the first United States citizen saint, with her congregation, the Missionary Sisters of the Sacred Heart, established in 1886, pursued her ministry to Italian immigrants in the Western Hemisphere. With the assistance of four thousand sisters who had joined her order by 1905, Mother Cabrini established hospitals, schools, and orphanages throughout the Americas, including six centers in the United States. *Missionary Sisters of the Sacred Heart.*

things in Him who strengtheneth me." When she died twenty-eight years
later she had founded in Europe and the two Americas sixty-seven houses—one for each year of her life. These included convents, schools, hospitals and orphanages. Igino Giordani said of her:

> She constructed islands of rest, havens against germs, cold, hunger and
> death; restful houses of prayer and schools ventilated with fresh air . . .
> and by all those buildings she put in circulation the wealth of the rich for
> the benefit of the poor. Mother Cabrini placed the education of the learned
> at the disposal of the uneducated, turned kindness to the relief of mis-
> ery, and brought fresh air and sunlight for the destruction of typhoid and
> tuberculosis. She was a swift and determined agent for the Sacred Heart.[6]

Don Guiseppe De Luca said that in the midst of her feverish activity
"she seemed a portrait of peace."[7]

Mother Frances Xavier Cabrini studied carefully and inquired where
the greater number of the Italians in the United States were settling. As
soon as this information was an established fact with her, she followed
in their wake to bring them the consolation of the word of God in their
own mother tongue and the counsel and help of one who understood
their sorrow and felt their humiliations.

In the summer of 1902 she sent Mother Umilia Campietta and Sister
Clemenza Boldrina to Denver, Colorado, to investigate the Italian situation there.[8] Father LePore was the pastor of the Italian parish at this
time. The two sisters found a pitiable condition existing here[9]—boys and
girls of fifteen to twenty years of age, who because of their bilingual difficulties were growing up without a knowledge of the existence of God.
It is true that Father LePore was making a brave effort, but the burden
was too much for him. He had hoped and prayed that God would send
him help when he heard that two missionary sisters were visiting his
parishioners. He hastened to them and requested them to come to his
aid. His Excellency, Most Reverend Nicholas C. Matz, the bishop of
Denver at this time,[10] was consulted and was overjoyed that these reli-

---

[6] *L'Osservatore Romano*, "La Madre Cabrini in America," Nov. 13, 1938, p. 3.
[7] *Parole Sparse della Beata Cabrini* (Roma: Instituti Grafico Tiberino, 1938), p. xlvi.
[8] Cioppa, "Blessed Frances Xavier Cabrini," 13.
[9] "Foundations of the Mission in Denver, Colorado," unpublished manuscript in the archives of
   the Queen of Heaven, Mother Cabrini Memorial Institute, Denver, Colorado. This manuscript will hereinafter be cited as the A.Q.H.M.I.
[10] Denver has since then been raised to the dignity of an Archepiscopal See.

gious women were willing and eager to undertake the care of these neglected people. He showed his appreciation of this in a letter to the Foundress,
Mother Frances Xavier Cabrini, which began with these words:

Con Gaude magna.[11]

After mature consideration Mother Frances Xavier Cabrini accepted the Denver Mission. Preparations for the new foundation were begun
at once, as it was deemed wise to have the Sisters for the beginning of
the school year. A two-story house at the corner of Palmer Street and
34th Avenue was leased at forty-five dollars a month. This is a small sum
today, but at that time Mother Cabrini and her Sisters wondered how
they could secure so large an amount. Besides this there was furniture
and the necessities to be provided. The parish priest was unable to give
them any financial aid, as there was a debt on the parish building and
his parishioners were direly poor. Some of the parents of these children
promised to pay twenty-five cents a month for school tuition and that
was all the support they could give. From the offing it looked like an
impossible undertaking, and the Sisters advised Mother Cabrini of the
financial predicament of the place. She sent them all she could spare and
told them to place their trust in Divine Providence and carry on.

By September 1902, the first floor of the rented house was ready for
use. Mother Cabrini was at this time engaged at the Novitiate House,
but she was ever with them in spirit and kept in touch with them by frequent and encouraging correspondence, promising to come to Denver
as soon as she could leave New York. The first community of the Missionary Sisters of the Sacred Heart to work in Denver were those who
opened Our Lady of Mt. Carmel grade school and they were as follows:
Mother Maddalena Martinelli, first superior, Sister Lucida Nocera,
Sister Raphael Dazzini, Sister J. Berckmans Bogan, Sister Filomena
Locantro, Sister Mercedes De Lorenzo, Sister Taresia Casonato, Sister
Orsolina Bauer, and Mother Luigina Albertini, who succeeded Moth-
er Maddalena as superior. Later on, Sister Imelda Manale and Sister
Rosario Colombo were missioned to Denver.[12]

Mother Frances Xavier came to Denver in October as she had

---

[11] Manuscript account, A.Q.H.M.I., Denver, Colorado.
[12] Letter from Sister Mary Domitilla, M.S.S.H., Oct. 14, 1944, in the Machebeuf History files at
St. Mary Academy, Denver, Colorado.

promised she would do. She wished to share the privations of the Sisters in this new foundation, thus making them realize that she was back of them in every great movement they would make. Her first visit was to his Excellency, Most Reverend Nicholas C. Matz,[13] who showed her every deference; next she visited the Jesuit Fathers, Pantanella and Gubitosi, who were such a great aid in the work of the foundation of the Denver Mission; after this she called to see the Italian consul and prominent Italian families who had helped and befriended the Sisters. After these visits she donned her apron and set to work to improve conditions wherever improvements were necessary. In the meantime she studied the situation more closely. Through the medium of the press and conversation with the friends whom the Sisters had made, she heard of the needs of the mining camps and of the widows and orphans left without aid. Her heart was moved, her decision made. She would open an orphanage in Denver for the poor and the destitute. To decide was to act. The attic of the school was immediately fixed up and beds were either purchased or begged, and when the first poor mother came bringing her hungry, ragged little girls they found refuge there.[14] That night the Sisters took some of their own petticoats and made dresses for their new charges. Soon others came, until the Sisters were forced to restrict their own lodgings to make room for them.

In the meantime the school at Our Lady of Mt. Carmel, which was dedicated on November 17, 1902,[15] was progressing. Bishop Matz had taken a warm interest in it. He visited the school periodically and, realizing the poverty of the house and school, gave Mother Cabrini a letter of recommendation with permission to solicit aid from friends.

By 1904 Mother Cabrini was aware that the attic was entirely too small, and she realized that this house was not large enough to take care of the parish school, convent, and her newly founded orphanage. She began at once to look around for a more suitable site and for a larger house. This search was not rewarded until 1905, when she decided to purchase the grounds at 4825 Federal Boulevard, where now stands the beautiful Queen of Heaven Mother Cabrini Memorial School.[16]

---

[13] See *Annals*, A.Q.H.M.I., Denver, Colorado.

[14] See *Annals of the Queen of Heaven Institute* in the A.Q.H.M.I., Denver, Colorado.

[15] *Travels of Mother Cabrini*, copyright 1944, chap. 14, "On the Occasion of the Inauguration of the House in Denver," 229.   [16] At time of publication of essay in 1945.

Mother Cabrini remained in Denver and Colorado during the summer of 1905. From 1905 to 1912 she worked hard to buy other pieces of land adjacent to the one previously purchased. She wanted the orphans to have plenty of room and much fresh air. Her innate sense of business told her that this mission undertaken purely for charity would succeed and expand. She was also busy selecting a site for what she planned to be a sanatorium for the convalescents of the Cabrini Hospital in Chicago. In 1910 she purchased a part of the site of Mt. St. Francis, the sanatorium of which she dreamed. In 1911 and 1912 she purchased the ground adjacent to this, and in 1912 she chose the spot where the house now stands. This was started in 1913 and completed in 1914. It was built with rock gathered from the mountainside. Her dream of a sanatorium did not materialize, but Mt. St. Francis did, and perhaps in a way that was dearer to her heart. Today Mt. St. Francis is a summer camp for the orphans at the Queen of Heaven Mother Cabrini Memorial Institute.

In 1906 the number of orphans had increased to such an extent that Mother Cabrini advised that a frame house be erected. This was to have a chapel, classrooms, and dormitories for the children. The original house was to remain for the use of the Sisters. By September 8, 1906, this new structure was ready for occupancy. Six years later, this also became too small and Mother Cabrini began in 1912 to plan for the present large brick structure. She had learned to love Colorado and looked with especial fondness upon the Queen City of the Plains.[17] She wanted the Denver institution to be one of the best schools. The plans for the new building were laid by her, but World War I broke out and for this reason the work on the building progressed very slowly. In the meantime, on December 22, 1917, at the age of sixty-seven, the "Saint of the Immigrants" died in a small room in the Columbus Hospital in Chicago. At the time of her death the Queen of Heaven Memorial Institute[18] was as far as the second story. She never saw it except in blueprint form; but nevertheless it stands in her memory, a monument of her achievements, a remembrance of her holiness.

The remains of this valiant woman rest beneath the high altar of the chapel in the Mother Cabrini High School, 701 Fort Washington Avenue,

---

[17] See *Travels of Mother Cabrini*, 233 *et seq.* for her description of Denver in a letter written to the Sisters under date of November 18, 1902.

[18] This title was later changed to the Queen of Heaven, Mother Cabrini Memorial Institute in honor of its foundress.

New York City.[19] The study of the Cause of Beatification began soon after her death. The ordinary process was opened on August 3, 1919, at Chicago, Illinois, and closed at Lodi, Italy, on April 5, 1929. The apostolic process began at Lodi on April 3, 1933, and was terminated in Chicago on September 27, 1933. The recognition of the body took place at West Park, New York, on October 3, 1933, in the presence of the Apostolic Delegate, and was then transported to the Chapel of the Mother Cabrini High School in the city of New York.

There was a difficulty in the process of the beatification of Mother Frances Xavier Cabrini. She died only sixteen years before and Canon law prescribes that fifty years must elapse after the death of a servant of God before the examination into the heroism of his virtues is begun.[20] On May 8, 1935, the Most Reverend Amletto Giovanni Cicognani, apostolic delegate of the United States, petitioned the supreme pontiff, Pius XI, to dispense from the prescription of Canon 2101 for the cause of Mother Cabrini. The august pontiff, who had known Mother Cabrini personally, summoned Monsignor Natucci, promoter of the general faith, granted the dispensation and expressed the desire that the process of her canonization proceed rapidly "in view," as he said, "of the need of great spiritual currents."[21]

Frances Xavier Cabrini was declared Blessed on November 13, 1938. She is the first citizen of the United States officially pronounced Blessed in Heaven. The Pontifical Mass was celebrated in the Vatican Basilica by His Eminence, George Cardinal Mundelein, the late archbishop of Chicago, who had celebrated Mother Cabrini's funeral Mass twenty-one years before. On June 20, 1939, the Sacred Congregation of Rites issued a decree providing for that Cause of Canonization of Mother Frances Xavier Cabrini that was signed on February 27, 1944.[22]

On July 7, 1946, Frances Xavier Cabrini was canonized, the first American citizen to achieve sainthood.

---

[19] See Cicognani, "Blessed Frances Xavier Cabrini," *Sanctity in America.*
[20] *Canon,* 2101.   [21] *Travels of Mother Cabrini,* p. xi.
[22] The six centers Mother Cabrini established in the United States include New Orleans, Los Angeles, and Seattle, in addition to those cited.

PART THREE

The Settlers

HE ONLY PLACE IN IRELAND where a man can make a fortune
is America!" declared a transplanted son of the sod. Another
recent immigrant to the United States glowingly confided, "One
with few pennies can become prosperous in the West." Thus did the
newly arrived extol the economic opportunity to be found west of the
Mississippi River, an area that lay beyond the geographic line of demar-
cation of one hundred degrees west longitude. Their "America Letters"
were laced with such confident assertions as "I have 140 acres of land
fenced and nearly 30 under a good state of improvement." Reports of
livestock acquired and savings carefully husbanded were conveyed with
pride. Correspondents not infrequently observed with satisfaction that
in the West they tipped their hat to no man. Indeed, in their folk song
"Jolly Oleanna," Scandinavians sang of dining on meat three times a day
and gloried in the fact that they were free!

Such vaunted egalitarianism could be perceived quite differently by
some. An Italian visitor, the aristocratic journalist Francesco Varvaro
Pontero, was dismayed by the single class of travel available on railroad
cars. While he singled out for admiration such policies as the swiftness
of American justice, he looked askance upon the seeming absence of
courtesy and deference among Americans, particularly in the West.

Until the United States Census of 1890, the expanse of sparsely settled arable western land constituted the region commonly referred to as
the American frontier. The area actually reflected great geographic variety, ranging from treeless prairie lands to the richly forested Northwest,
from the Rocky Mountains and the headwaters of the continental river
system, to the region of the Southwest highlighted by the Grand Canyon,

and the Pacific region where slopes of the Sierra nearly reached the ocean's shore.

Amidst this unparalleled geographic variety, there were several common factors that attracted migrants westward and shaped them in a variety of ways. The first was the abundance and availability of land. To Italians motivated by the aphorism *"Chi ha prato ha tutto"* (Who owns pastures has everything), the promise of land ownership was particularly appealing. This prospect lured the adventurous ever westward. Secondly, the environment yielded an abundance of resources — from beaver pelts to precious metals, from dense stands of timber to fruitful harvests. This abundance led adventurers to venture expectantly from one horizon to the next. These unique aspects of settlement of the West reinforced distinctive characteristics that were gradually associated with the western settlers' personality.

As early as the mid-eighteenth century Italians joined in the initial phases of the westward migrations by fur trappers and traders like Francesco Vigo. They bartered with Native Americans for the precious peltries eagerly sought by Europeans. They were also part of early European missionary efforts that established permanent religious settlements in the Rockies, the Interior Columbia Basin, and the Northwest. Those were followed in the 1840s by the first waves of pioneer settlers and traders making their way along river routes and rediscovering old trappers' trails, which they transformed into the Santa Fe Trail and the Great Platte River route, which was later known as the Oregon Trail.

In the wake of the trappers, missionaries, and pioneer travelers on the overland trails, by 1848 a very different procession hastened westward. The advance, dominated by relatively young men, launched the mining frontier, first in the Mother Lode of California, followed by subsequent mineral strikes in Nevada, Colorado, Arizona, and elsewhere. This high-stakes, relatively short-lived phase of the westward movement was to permanently affect the West as a result of the rapid infusion of both miners and mineral wealth. The dramatic changes necessitated increased food production, expanded commercial and financial services, and extended rail and shipping networks to serve them.

While the frenzied pursuit of mining fortunes sometimes ended in disappointment, the transportation system it had necessitated remained to support yet another economic frontier, this one funded in part by profits garnered from the nation's recent Civil War. In war's wake, the breeding of hybrid cattle on ranges extending from Texas to southern Canada and shipped to urban centers along the recently constructed railroad lines, contributed to the emergence of this fifth frontier—the cattle economy, which thrived until the late 1880s. This cowboy's frontier attracted its share of hardworking Italian wranglers, whose way of life was colorfully captured by Italian American cowboy-turned-detective, Johnny Siringo, in a string of stories beginning with his autobiographical adventure, *Texas Cowboy or Fifteen Years on the Hurricane Deck of a Spanish Cow Pony.*

The ever-moving cattle frontier came into direct conflict with the sixth and final group of frontier settlers, the farmers, who by the 1870s had learned to cultivate the extensive prairie lands of the American Midwest and to protect their crops from roaming cattle and sheep by erecting the newly patented barbed wire. Some Italians joined Germans and Scandinavians on what has been called "the farmers' last frontier," which produced wheat and corn harvests using dry-land farming techniques and costly mechanized farm equipment.

While each phase of the six separate waves of frontier settlement was economically and geographically distinctive, each successfully lured migrants westward. Between 1783 and 1860 the United States government acquired 465 million acres of land. The generous provisions of the Homestead Act of 1862 designed to distribute 160 acres of surveyed public land after five years residence or in six months for $1.25 per acre, attracted 9 million settlers by the end of the century. Their letters to their families and neighbors resulted in continuing chain migrations of newcomers eager to share in the opportunities their correspondents enthusiastically described.

Despite the repeated reports of success, in much of the West prosperity—in fact, survival—rested upon the availability of water, described in the words of one historian as "the arithmetic of rainfall." Response to that challenge and the vastness of the settlement enterprise itself demanded close-knit community cooperation. Italian migrants found themselves part of larger groups of settlers engaged in common cause. This shared enterprise, often essential for their immediate economic survival, weakened the migrants' allegiance to inherited traditions. Furthermore, the arduous challenges of western settlement blurred cultural differences between migrants. Instead, the shared pioneer experience of settling the West was forging a new American identity.

The migrants' predisposition to new ways was further reinforced by the influence of the American common school. The education it provided not only assured English proficiency for migrant children, it also transmitted the American cultural canon and standardized the new arrivals' response to their adopted communities.

A sense of community was not the only effect arising from interaction with this new-found homeland, which was to distinguish the migrants in the West. The most compelling lure, the availability of land, contributed to the demise of the idea of an aristocratic land-holding society. Western migrants discovered that the available land was the ultimate leveler of class. Having a farm of one's own implied a body of legal rights, and for many decades was the license for entry into the rough and tumble of the political process. It was, as a result, a validation of the democratic creed that had lured many to America to begin with.

The fruitful abundance of the land, its forests, and the minerals it yielded, continued to expand the panorama of opportunities. It was firmly believed that upward mobility awaited all those who applied sufficient energy and ingenuity. The Protestant work ethic and the vision of inevitable progress of a people chosen and uniquely blessed by their Creator evolved into the doctrine of Manifest Destiny, which shaped the national vision and will.

Inspired by hero images of Davy Crockett, Sam Houston, and Kit Carson, Americans began to shape a new national culture energized by the West. Their new iconography gradually supplanted inherited foreign traditions. Faced with the countless tasks to be accomplished, a premium was placed not upon birth, but upon innate practical skills and the ability to adapt and innovate in the face of necessity. Rather than theoretical suppositions or abstractions, migrants on the move valued inquisitiveness and the sharpness of intellect that could solve an immediate problem.

Admittedly, the westering experience also engendered wasteful and destructive tendencies. The very wealth of the resources encouraged a profligate disregard. The abundance of opportunity led to the ruthless pursuit of the next bonanza with little commitment or sense of responsibility to place. For Italian migrants this resulted in a dissolution of ethnic settlements and a weakening of any sense of *campanilismo* or provincial loyalty. The greater diffusion into the dominant culture further contributed to the loss of their native language and culture. The rapid acculturation to emerging American ways also led to a social disorientation and detachment between the generations.

By 1920 a significant portion of the 88,504 first-generation Italians in the United States had headed west. Lured by competitively priced rail transportation and such promotional literature as Peter Remondino's *Mediterranean Shores of America* (1892), plus the relative ease of travel from Italian ports to points of debarkation along the Gulf of Mexico, they fanned out, ranging from the Deep South to the Northwest.

As early as 1827 a brig captained by the Italian John Dominis reconnoitered the Pacific Northwest coast and initiated eastern investors' interest in the potential of a salmon-fishing industry in Oregon Territory. Dominis became a pioneer trader in the region, while members of his family became key players in the Hawaiian trade. His son would soon be the husband of Queen Lilioukalani.

In 1850 there were only six Italian settlers in the area, three of whom were priests, including the Jesuit Father Giovanni Nobili, who was soon dispatched to a ministry in Gold Rush San Francisco and would become one of the founders of the College of Santa Clara. By 1910 the vastly increased population of the region included 13,000 Italian immigrants who had been attracted by the majesty and wealth of the Pacific Northwest's natural resources. They formed a community large enough to support several newspapers, churches, and fraternal organizations. Italian settlers fished salmon, halibut, and cod, and by the turn of the century they were canning and shipping across the nation.

A scant three decades after Dominis' landfall in the Northwest, the Mormon community in Utah, which actively recruited converts abroad, welcomed a group of Piedmontese Mormons, half of whom were former Waldensians, who had trekked across the Great Plains. Their arrival resulted from much earlier events. While Brigham Young's Church of Jesus Christ of the Latter-day Saints was still headquartered in Illinois, a Sicilian migrant, Giuseppe Taranto, had donated his personal savings for the construction of a Mormon tabernacle in Nauvoo, Illinois. As a result of that early association, in 1850 four Mormon elders, disembarking in Genoa, declared Italy to be a missionary field. Within two years the *Book of Mormon* had been translated into Italian, and conversions in the Piedmont region were soon being reported. Many of the converts soon departed for the American Mormon community of Deseret in Utah. Among them marched Rosa Cardon, who, in a case hanging from her neck, carried the silkworms that provided the basis of the Mormons' flourishing siriculture industry.

While the largest number of Italian migrants settled in California— by 1920 constituting 11 percent of the total foreign-born population— the next most desirable destination was Louisiana. Many of the settlers came from Calabria and Sicily, sailing directly from Naples to New Orleans. Those settling in the southern part of the state cultivated sugar cane and cotton, working a few acres on a share cropper basis; others were vegetable farmers. Each year their numbers increased when sojourn-ers arrived to join in the seasonal harvests.

After 1860 an expanding rail network diverted Italian settlement from the South. In addition, by the first decades of the twentieth century the Italian government actively discouraged migration to the Deep South fearing that the scarcity of employment and the persistence of a ram-pant boll weevil infestation, which deeply reduced cotton production, would jeopardize the success of any Italian settlement efforts.

In 1870 migrants paying fares of $21.35 per person, traveled by train from eastern ports of entry to Kansas, where they settled on unfamiliar prairie lands. They were attracted by the reasonably priced parcels, some-times costing no more than $2.00 per acre. Often unable to cultivate the vast prairie acreage, the recent arrivals became truck farmers or settled in centers like Kansas City, where Italians soon became the third largest group of foreigners.

By 1890 railroads had laid 166,000 miles of track, enabling the Great Northern to reach the Pacific, while its major competitor, the Southern Pacific, crossed the continent to California. Those rails carried Italian migrants westward, drawn by a deep love for the soil. Upon arrival in the Upper Midwest they laboriously cleared timber from seemingly useless land, allowing them to begin harvesting grains in parts of Illinois and Wisconsin overlooked by others.

During the same decade, in 1898, in the Ozarks of northwest Arkansas, bordering Oklahoma and Kansas, Father Pietro Bandini established the colony of Tontitown, named in honor of Enrico Tonti, who was gener-ally referred to as the "Father of Arkansas." The Italian government pro-vided seeds and tools to cultivate the land so similar to the homeland, while appointments for the local church were presented as gifts from Italy's Queen Margerita. Undeterred by the overt hostility they experienced, the new settlers developed the colony into a model agricultural community. Until his death in 1917, Bandini continued to promote the idea of western settlement to Italian government officials.

Some Italians made their way west from ports along the gulf coast, while some chose to remain in Texas. By 1900 more than 8,000 Italian migrants had settled there. Arriving as early as 1800, the first several thousand future Texans included a Corsican who is remembered today in the town of Corsicana. A group of Sicilians established a settlement on the banks of the Brazos River where they attentively tended their crops. Others established truck farms supplying Galveston, where 10 percent of the population was Italian-born. As with their compatriots throughout the West, ownership of the land was paramount. By 1900 one successful colonization society had acquired 25,000 acres, which it distributed to its members in 50-acre parcels.

The vagaries of cattle ranching and the presence of large numbers of Cherokees, Chickasaws, and Seminoles, displaced by Oklahoma "land boomers" who began arriving in April 1889, made that area less appealing to Italian settlers. They were also disinclined to settle in Indian Territory, where alcoholic beverages, including wine, were prohibited by federal law. Nevertheless, a few Italians worked in coal mines, and later, the growing number of oil fields, always claiming a plot of land where, in their pursuit of self-sufficiency, they cultivated their closely planted vegetable gardens.

Because of its distinct Latin heritage, New Mexico offered a unique welcome to Italian settlers. Their arrival had been presaged as early as the sixteenth century by the pioneering visits of Fray Marco da Nizza, and later by the ministry of Jesuits like Father Eusebio Kino. The long tradition also included the much later missionary work of Daughter of Charity Sister Blandina Segale, dedicated to building schools and hospitals, and ministering to both Native American and white settlers on the mesas and in the valleys of New Mexico. Here, Italians who came to mine and herd sheep tripled their presence each decade.

At one time lightly settled, Arizona was listed as another county of New Mexico. Its sparse Italian population did, however, include an army bandmaster's son, Fiorello La Guardia, destined to become the mayor of New York City. In recalling his youth growing up in an adobe house in Prescott, La Guardia described the land as "a paradise for a little boy."

A comparative population boom suddenly occurred in neighboring Nevada in 1859 when "yonder siders" from the California gold fields scrambled across the eastern Sierra's Washoe district, which sheltered the fabled Comstock Lode. Italians who were part of this stream of reverse migration labored as quartz millers, charcoal burners, ore smelters, and even mule packers. Some of these enterprises are described by Albin J. Cofone in the essay "Reno's Little Italy: Italian Entrepreneurship and Culture in Northern Nevada."

In California the population influx first attracted by the lure of gold continued even after the great rush of 1849–52. Recent arrivals wrote to others about the rich lands of the Sacramento delta and the sprawling San Joaquin valley, and of the variety of California landscapes including the Mediterranean environment so familiar to them. The resulting migration was facilitated by the completion of the transcontinental railroad line in 1869 and the completion of the southern route connecting California to the Gulf of Mexico in 1882. It was further aided by the decline of mining strikes in the intermountain states and the diminishing stock of quality public lands in the Midwest. Consequently, by 1920 80,000 Italians had settled across the expanse of California.

In all these distinct geographic areas and differing frontier economies, settlers, including Italian migrants, were permanently shaped by their experiences. If westering Italian migrants underwent a greater degree of assimilation than their counterparts settling along America's eastern seaboard, it was a phenomenon nourished in part by tragedy. A xenophobic impulse was present in each of the six phases of the frontier advance. It was directed primarily toward the Native American, but also manifested its antagonism toward Blacks, the Mexican population of the Southwest and California, and Asians first lured by California's gold. As a result of this western antipathy toward people of color, Italian migrants were accepted as a numerically essential component of the white majority rather than being viewed as foreign intruders.

Along with the foregoing, several other factors explain the sharp distinction between the Italian migrants' experience in the urban East and the West. In addition to the sociographic phenomenon of joint community building and co-option by the dominant community of whites,

Italian settlers were affected by at least two other forces. The Italian migrants to the West were self-selected independent spirits confident enough to have journeyed abroad to an unfamiliar environment, usually without the cohesive community support enjoyed by their counterparts in the urban East. Secondly, the significant cost of extended travel to the West precluded all but the economically advantaged or enterprising. The very difficulty and cost of transit discouraging return also lessened the sojourner mentality, with its keen attachment to the homeland. Thirdly, the enterprising migrants to the West, while stopping to earn additional funds to continue the next leg of their journey, underwent an ongoing process of acculturation as they were exposed to Americans' language and culture. Each settlement and employment experience increased familiarity with English and with American ways. At the point of final western settlement the Italian migrant had less need for the mutual support represented by fraternal networks, permitting him to range more widely in pursuit of opportunity.

Many of these factors appear as interpretive elements in the ensuing five essays. In "Italian Immigrant Women in the Southwest," Phylis Cancilla Martinelli examines the support networks women developed in the West, specifically comparing the communities of Denver, Phoenix, and Albuquerque. She concludes that Denver, with its significantly larger Italian migrant population, developed a community most similar to its eastern counterparts. She notes several differences, however. For example, the predominantly male Italian migration preceded settlement on the eastern seaboard, which shaped later familial relationships. In addition, communities like Phoenix became home to migrants from different regions, including Piedmont, Toscana, Liguria, Campania, and Sicily. The many dialects made communication difficult, presenting English as a useful alternative.

Other differences distinguishing these communities from the urban settlements in the East, Martinelli explains, included the fact that the relative prosperity enjoyed by Italians in the Southwest permitted women to remain in the home instead of working for wages. At the same time, the West was far more tolerant of women entering the public sphere. Hence Italian women, if they chose, joined and even organized women's clubs and established businesses ranging from boarding houses and restaurants to silk manufacturing industries.

Westerners were particularly appreciative of the uplifting influence of women, not only giving them wide latitude but the vote as early as 1869 in Wyoming Territory. Women were valued as essential helpmates and as welcome arbiters of social discipline. In a frontier sparsely populated by women as late as the turn of the century, women were seen as symbols of genteel culture. Where settlements often emerged in haste, women were designated the city builders, assigned the tasks of teaching, ministering to the needy, and generally supporting the higher cultural aspirations of the community.

Italian women shared in these opportunities for public involvement and civic betterment. Where so much was to be done they also engaged in a myriad of occupations. A significant proportion of their employment was professional, for while in 1890 the West reported only 5 percent of the population, it claimed 15 percent of the women professionals including lawyers, teachers, and doctors. Martinelli notes that the relative affluence of the Italians of the Southwest afforded their daughters the education necessary to join these ranks.

The varied fortunes of Italian settlers in Colorado are described by Janet Worrall in "Adjustment and Integration: The Italian Experience in Colorado," which provides a demographic profile and a survey of employment history, which unfortunately includes several major labor disputes, one ending in the Ludlow massacre of 1914, in which 24 lives were lost, including 2 Italian women and 11 children.

Worrall highlights personalities ranging from newspaperman Angelo Noce, who successfully crusaded for the establishment of Columbus Day, to Saint Frances Xavier Cabrini, who upon arriving in Denver in 1902, accompanied by several of her Missionary Sisters of the Sacred Heart, established a school and what was to become the largest orphanage in Denver.

The essay includes a description of the "Arata affair," one of the rare expressions of nativist hostility toward Italian migrants in any frontier settlement. Nevertheless, the mob lynching of "the Dago" in 1893 is a reality that blighted the Italian migration experience in the West. This essay, along with the others in this section reveals the formative influence of the West upon the Italian migrants as they daringly negotiated their futures and their fortunes with the uniquely powerful reality of the American West.

Italian Immigrant Women
in the Southwest

By Phylis Cancilla Martinelli

G LANCING OUT of her kitchen window one summer evening as dusk was settling over Phoenix, Teresa Grosso saw the face of an Indian peering in. Grabbing a butcher knife, she shouted, "Nobody better come in here!"[1] The figure vanished and Teresa remained friendly with the Indians who regularly visited her. This scene was not one that an Italian woman living on Mulberry Street in New York would have encountered. Alone or combined with similar tales it could make the lives of Italian women in the West sound like a dime cowboy novel by Charles Siringo, vastly different from their sisters' lives in the East.

While colourful, such stories do not give the total picture of the experience of Italian women in the West. Researchers are now beginning to fill the large gaps in the history of Italians who ventured west of the Mississippi. Most of their work deals only with the lives of Italian men. Consequently this essay must be seen as an effort to sketch an outline of the lives of Italian women who forsook the East for the West. Future research will be necessary to add the more subtle strokes and finer lines to the picture.

Italian men depicted in Andrew Rolle's book, *The Immigrant Upraised*,[2] were cattle barons riding herd along the Rio Grande, missionaries pacifying Indians, homesteaders on the Great Plains, miners, fur traders, businessmen—living lives far different from their counterparts in the East.

---

[1] Mrs. Mary Grosso Stokley, taped interview by Phylis Martinelli (Phoenix, August 1, 1977). Cited hereafter as Stokley interview.

[2] Andrew F. Rolle, *The Immigrant Upraised* (Norman: University of Oklahoma Press, 1970).

Were Italian women riding the range beside their men, working with Indians, exploring, and homesteading, or were their lives in the more traditional Italian mode? Were they withdrawn from the larger world, letting their husbands, children, and relatives form the scope of their lives? The answer is complex. To explore these complexities this essay will concentrate on the Southwest, namely, the states of Colorado, Utah, New Mexico, and Arizona.[3] The lives of the women within the home in traditional roles, and outside of the home in less typical roles, will be considered.

Generally speaking, the Italians who came to this area were few in number and arrived earlier than the great wave of their compatriots who migrated to the East Coast. The overall figures tell of an overwhelmingly male population arriving from Italy, especially in the early years. However, the women who did arrive become more interesting because of their scarcity.

Some of the earliest Italian women in the Southwest came for religious purposes. Appearing in the area as early as the 1850s, their lives were those of pioneers, difficult and full of hardship. The first women were converts to Mormonism from the high alpine valleys of Piedmont. The women were descended from the Vaudois or Waldense, a heretical sect that fled persecution in France by migrating to Italy. In 1849 Lorenzo Snow and others began actively to seek converts to the Mormon Church among these people. Women from the Stalle, Cardone,[4] Goudin, Combe, and Malan families joined other converts in the journey across the plains to Utah. Harassed by hostile Indians, often dirty, hungry, wet, and fearing the great herds of buffalo that thundered across the plains, these Italian women finally arrived in Zion by 1855.

The promised land was less than perfect for the new arrivals, who found themselves living through difficult winters in crude dugouts with scarce food supplies. Sometimes women would have to walk miles to find work. Forced to abandon many of their fine Italian silks on the journey west, the women were often without sufficient clothing.[5] Several of these early Italian women were soon part of polygamous marriages. Rolle notes that polygamy had an appeal for certain Italian males.[6] However,

---

[3] The four states included in the definition of the Southwest represent only one of several different definitions of the area.
[4] These names often appear as Cardon and Stale. The Italian spelling has been used in this paper.
[5] Roberta F. Clayton, *Pioneer Women of Arizona* (Mesa, n.d.), 69.
[6] Rolle, *The Immigrant Upraised*, 205.

the feelings of the women about plural marriages are difficult to judge. Once married, the lives of these women revolved around their families and the constant chores of preserving food, spinning wool, knitting clothing, and raising fruits and vegetables.[7]

It was for the Catholic religion that other early Italian women ventured West. One of the best known women was Sister Blandina Segale. Born Rosa Maria Segale in 1854, near Genoa, she arrived in America as a child. The family lived in Cincinnati, Ohio where Rosa and her older sister, Maria Maddalena, entered the Sisters of Charity Order. In 1872 Rosa, now Sister Blandina, was sent to Trinidad, Colorado. Her first school in the rough frontier town was a crude adobe building, but, before she left Trinidad, the townspeople had been coerced into rebuilding it for her. Her next move was to Santa Fe, New Mexico, where she taught and helped establish an orphanage. A few years later she was reassigned to Albuquerque, New Mexico, where a plaque to her memory stands in Old Town. After twenty-one years she left the Southwest to begin work among the Italian immigrants of Cincinnati.

Many adventures during those twenty-one years fill the pages of her book, *At the End of the Santa Fe Trail*.[8] Although exactly when she met Billy the Kid is not agreed on, she is credited with preventing Trinidad's four physicians from being killed by the bandit. The doctors, violating their Hippocratic Oath, refused to tend one of Billy's wounded men. Billy vowed to scalp them until Sister Segale stepped in and cared for the man.[9]

As Italian migration to the Southwest began to grow in the 1880s, more women came, not for religious purposes but seeking a better life. The primary attraction was the mining activities, especially in Colorado, and business opportunities in the growing towns and cities. A frequent pattern was for a wife and husband to leave Italy and move from one location to another. One couple, for example, left Torino in 1903 and settled in Cripple Creek, Colorado. Better opportunities caused them to move to a frontier camp near Deadwood, South Dakota, then to Denver. Finally the couple tried life in the copper-mining town of Miami, Arizona. Their descendants are still in the area.[10]

---

[7] Clayton, *Pioneer Women of Arizona*, 71.

[8] Blandina Segale, *At the End of the Same Fe Trail* (Milwaukee, 1948).

[9] Sytha Motto, *No Banners Waving* (New York, 1966), 72.

[10] *Honor the Past . . . Mold the Future* (Gila Centennials, Inc., 1976), 77.

Another common pattern was for one member of the family to come
first, usually a male, sending for the others when he was successful. Carlo
Perazzo, for example, arrived in Arizona in 1875 seeking gold in the Vul-
ture Mine near Wickenburg. He soon turned his attention to a small
desert town further south, Phoenix. Sensing that the area would begin
to grow and prosper, he sent for his daughters, Louisa, Fredrica, and
Virginia, and sons Paolo and Henry.[11]

Women were often active in influencing the decision to emigrate.
Their decisions were usually based on the desire to be reunited with family members, a chance to improve their standard of living, or both. In
1888 Angelina Giomi heard of high wages in New Mexico—she could
earn a dollar for sewing on a button. She encouraged her husband Girolamo to leave Lucca and join Angelina's sister in Albuquerque. The couple took advantage of business opportunities, prospered, and remained
in New Mexico.[12]

Besides establishing that there were Italian women in the Southwest,
it is important to look at the types of communities in which they lived.
Such an examination can determine the influence of community on the
roles of women. The lives of the Italian immigrant women traditionally focused on their homes and families.[13] At first appraisal the Italian
family system is strictly patriarchal. The role of the woman seems totally subservient in relation to the male. However, the mother is the center of the family in a society where family relationships assume primary
importance.[14] The woman in the home should not be seen as without
influence in the family but as the symbolic center of the family.[15]

---

[11] Judge Francis Donofrio, taped interview by Phylis Martinelli (Hereafter as P. M.) (Phoenix, July 1, 1976).

[12] Ioli Giomi, ed., *Il Giornalino* 4: 6 (Albuquerque: Club Culturale Italiano, July, 1977): 10.

[13] The Italian family usually discussed in American literature is the Southern Italian family. Since there were many Northern Italians in the Southwest as well as Southerners, the question aris-es, can we speak of one family institution, or must we discuss two different family institutions, one North, the other South Italian? For the purposes of this paper, while not trying to gloss over differences that do exist, Barzini's assessment indicates that we can speak of one family institution in Italy. He notes that the family is the only fundamental institution in Italy. He sees Southern Italians as preserving the traditional family almost intact. However, he consid-ers deviations among Northern Italian as superficial. See Luigi Barzini, *The Italians* (New York: Bantam Books, 1964), 201.

[14] Francis X. Femminella and Jill S. Quadagno, "The Italian American Family," in *Ethnic Fami-lies in America*, ed. Charles Mindel and Robert Habenstein (New York, 1976), 65.

[15] Richard Gambino, *Blood of My Blood* (New York, 1974), 147.

Of major importance to a woman in her management of the household were her female relatives, who were frequently her companions.[16] In the Italian neighborhoods of the East, women lived lives of daily routines, patterned by constant interaction with other women, both relatives and neighbors. Judith Smith notes that in Providence, Rhode Island, residential proximity made it easy for women to exchange social information, child care, goods and services, gossip, and mutual aid.[17] Research is showing such networks are not exclusively Italian but important to women of many societies.[18] In the frontier environment of the Southwest was it possible for women to establish these important supportive networks? The answer lies in an examination of the different types of communities that developed. Denver, Phoenix, and Albuquerque are representative of these types.

Of the three, Denver represents a community most like the Little Italies of the East. Louisa and Gian Cuneo were the first Italians settling in Denver in 1872.[19] They were soon followed by other families who moved into the cheap housing near St. Patrick's Church in North Denver. The location was close to the railroad tracks and fertile land near the Platte River.

As the community grew, so did the number of social institutions to ease the transition from Italy to America. An Italian national church, named Mount Carmel Italian Church, was organized in 1894. Everyone in North Denver could enjoy the parades in honor of favorite saints, especially the feast of San Rocco. There were four Italian language newspapers, several mutual-aid societies, and many other Italian businesses, including the Italian American Bank.

Of special importance to women were the imported Italian food stores that opened. Women could easily buy the flour to bake bread in their outside globular ovens or pick dandelion greens for salads. However, until Italians started their own businesses the women had difficulty in buying olive oil, ricotta cheese, and other ingredients not typically stocked in American stores.

---

[16] Femminella, "The Italian American Family."

[17] Judith Smith, "Work and Family Patterns of Southern Italian Immigrant Women in Providence, Rhode Island, 1915" (unpublished ms., June, 1976), 7.

[18] Louise Lamphere, "Strategies, Cooperation and Conflict Among Women in Domestic Groups," in *Woman, Culture and Society*, ed., Michelle Zimbalist Rosaldo and Louise Lamphere (Stanford: Stanford University Press, 1974), 111.

[19] Dr. Giovanni Perilli, *Colorado and the Italians in Colorado* (Denver, 1922), 181.

Although there was poverty among the Denver Italians, the overall picture was one of success. The Southern Italians often became truck farmers, selling their goods in the city market and the streets of North Denver. Northern Italians were often skilled laborers, so many found work in the booming building trade. Italian-owned restaurants, grocery stores, and mercantile companies attested to the ambition of both Italian groups.[20]

Denver, then, was the type of community where daily communication with other Italian women would be easy. Strong supportive networks could develop and the difficulty of acculturation would be eased.

While there were not so many Italians in New Mexico as there were in Colorado, as Table I illustrates, the community in Albuquerque had some features of an Italian enclave:

TABLE I. COMPILED FROM CENSUS
OF THE UNITED STATES[21]

	1870	1880	1890	1900	1910	1920
Arizona	12	104	207	699	1,531	1,261
Colorado	16	335	3,882	6,818	14,375	12,580
New Mexico	25	73	355	661	1,959	1,678
Utah	74	138	347	1,062	3,117	3,225

The Albuquerque community was composed largely of Tuscans hailing from the town of Lucca, thus referring to themselves as *Lucchese*. In the 1880s the handful of Italians in the city were railroad laborers and gardeners. Before long the new arrivals began to branch out into a variety of occupations and were generally successful financially. The *Lucchesi* formed a fairly close-knit group with many families intermarrying. However, as a group they were not socially visible, generally being accepted by the larger community. A descendant of pioneer Italians noted that after many years in Albuquerque, "The only sign of Tuscans to be found is in the telephone book: there are no stores with the sign '*Il Cupolone*,' '*La Pantera*' or such."[22]

---

[20] Ruth Eloise Wiberg, *Rediscovering Northwest Denver* (Denver, 1976), 40–44.
[21] Rolle, *The Immigrant Upraised*, 350.
[22] Giomi, *Il Giornalino* (April 1977), 10.

According to Phylis Martinelli, Italian women gradually settled in the Southwest, where as wives and mothers
they were at the center of the family where traditionally they were accorded great respect. They were also active
in a variety of social institutions which facilitated the
transition from the home land to their new land. Pictured is the Salvatore Fallico family of Denver, Colorado.
Author's collection.

While few archival materials document the experiences of Italian immigrant women in the western settlement, photographs record some of the more celebratory events like the wedding of Nellie Rietta and Anthony Bucola in 1908. Following their first dance at the reception held in the newly constructed Italian Hall, the bride and groom continued an Italian tradition, distributing almond-filled *confetti* to the 150 guests. *Historic Italian Hall Archives.*

Neapolitan Jesuits served the religious needs of the Albuquerque Italians from 1868 until 1924. The missionaries originally purchased the San Felipe de Neri Church. As more missionary priests and brothers came, the Immaculate Conception Church was built in 1883 with the help of Italian immigrants.[23] Further cohesion in the Italian community came from the Associazione Italiana di Mutua Protezione Cristoforo Colombo. Such societies provided a sense of security for immigrants far from their homeland.[24]

---

[23] Giomi, *Il Giornalino* (May 1977), 16.   [24] Giomi, *Il Giornalino* (June 1977), 16.

Women emerged as active members of the community. While not living in a Little Italy, they did have a supportive network of female relatives who could be counted on to give assistance. Some social institutions, for example, the church, eased the transition to a new society. There were numerous grocery stores where Italian foods could be purchased. The ties of kinship and bond of shared regional origin were important in this type of community.

Phoenix presents a distinct contrast to Denver. The Italian community that was established in Phoenix was a small one, lacking many of the features of the Italian communities in other parts of the country. In Phoenix the group was loosely knit; there were no Italian neighborhoods with stores and restaurants to remind the immigrant of Italy. There was no Italian church or priests to serve their religious needs. No Italian newspaper brought news of their friends in the Valley of the Sun or their homeland. In times of trouble there were no Italian mutual-aid societies to help.[25] The first Italian club was not formed until 1938.

Italians did interact for business purposes, however. A few examples show that in the 1880s Alexander Barsanti bought land from Carlo Perazzo and Francisco Ceschetti; in the 1890s Mary Bardone sold land to Oduardo Magniani; in 1900 Genevieve Bardone bought land from Charles and Rebecca Salari.[26]

For those willing or able to make the effort there was communication between members of the loosely knit community. There were some hotels that catered to Italian bachelors, also serving as meeting places. However, for women, who were often in the home, these contacts were limited. The type of supportive network so important for Italian women did not exist.

There are several factors that contributed to the scattered Italian community in Phoenix. Italians were scarce in Arizona, so the community was small. An early absence of prejudice[27] and the relative affluence of the early arrivals meant that no ghetto areas formed. Most Phoenix Italians had skilled occupations and often some money to invest in businesses. Finally, the Italians in Phoenix came from many different regions in Italy. There were Italians from Ticino, Piedmont, Liguria, and Tusca-

[25] Phylis Martinelli, "Italy in Phoenix," *Journal of Arizona History* (1979).
[26] Grantee records, microfilm Box 13, Maricopa County Recorder Office.
[27] Evidence shows prejudice developed later.

ny in North Italy. From South Italy there were people from Sicily, Campania, and Potenza. The different dialects made communication difficult unless English or Italian spoken.

While to date no diaries or letters have been uncovered to tell of the feelings and experiences of women in the loosely knit Italian community in Phoenix, we do have glimpses from their children's view of their mother's lives.

Giusseppa Benenato arrived in the hot, dusty little town in 1893 with her husband Frank and their small children. It was the end of a journey that had started in Messina, Sicily, when she left home as a bride. The couple's early years together in America had been a series of moves from Boston to California, then to Texas, and finally Arizona.

The early years in Phoenix were hard on Giusseppa. Two of her children died from drinking contaminated water. The climate helped her husband's health, but she found it hard to adjust to the heat and dust.

Her only contact with other Italian women was a neighbor. She corresponded with relatives in Sicily for a while, but eventually the letters stopped. She kept no Italian customs with the exception of some traditional foods. Most other time was spent tending her family. One of her few outlets was Mass at St. Mary's Church.

While Giusseppa maintained a traditional role in the home, she actively encouraged the Americanization of her children. She spoke Sicilian to her husband, but she insisted the children speak English.[28]

Ellen Girot arrived in the mining town of Jerome in 1903 with her brother to join relatives already there. She was courted by Felix Bertino, who was also from the Canavesu area in Piedmont. Married in Jerome, they soon moved to Globe, where there was another Piemontese community. Felix tired of mining and the couple sought a new life of farming in Phoenix.

Unlike Giuseppa, Ellen taught her children to speak her local dialect as well as Italian. The dialect was reserved for relatives' visits; "real" Italian was spoken when other Italians visited. The children normally spoke English, while Ellen and Felix continued to speak their dialect to each other.

Ellen's female support system was small and diffuse. She knew one

---

[28] Miss Cora Benenato, taped interview by P. M. (Phoenix, August 1, 1977). Cited hereafter as Benenato interview.

woman on a neighboring farm who was Italian. Her sister and aunt might visit from Jerome, or other friends might come to see Ellen from Glendale, Scottsdale, or other parts of Phoenix.

She continued few Italian customs. However, polenta and risotto were staples for cooking, served with sauces made from the tomatoes, onions, and peppers grown on the farm. Ellen was especially known for her molded cheeses—soft, creamy, yellow cheese reminiscent of Fontina cheese. She and her husband also made wine, which they sold to the mining camps.[29]

Teresa Grosso came to Phoenix in 1907 at the urging of her brother, Charles Donofrio. Charles had become well established in Arizona after he left Basilicata. He brought his brothers over from Italy and encouraged his brother-in-law Michael to give up mining in nearby Philadelphia.

Life in Phoenix was different for Teresa in several ways. She missed the Italian neighborhood she had left, where she had not needed to master English. Her eleven children did not learn Italian because their parents had to learn English after their move. In Philadelphia, Teresa had contributed to the family income by doing sewing at home and managing the savings. With her family growing she had no time in Phoenix to earn outside wages. Her days were filled with cooking, cleaning, and washing. She did continue to be the financial expert in the family, however, through money management and good business deals.

While Teresa did not speak Italian to her children, they were exposed to other aspects of Italian culture. There were Italian meals despite the difficulty she had in getting proper ingredients. She had to rely on monthly visits from the grocer in Prescott, Arizona, for spaghetti, olive oil, sausage, cheese, and tomato sauce. The children grew up with stories of the big celebrations in Italy for the feast of Our Lady of Mt. Carmel. Letter writing to her family in Italy was an important event. Once a month she chased all the children out so she could concentrate on composing a letter.

Except for her visits with Giusseppa and her brothers, none of whom married Italian women, Teresa spent most other time with Americans. She is remembered as a strong, independent woman who made every minute count.[30] These insights give some idea of how different women

---

[29] Miss Elsie Bertino and Mr. Felix Bertino, taped interview by P. M. (Phoenix, September 15, 1976).

[30] Stokley interview.

adjusted to the diffuse Italian community in Phoenix. All three maintained traditional roles rather than moving rapidly into the mainstream of Phoenix society.

While the ideal in Italian culture was for women to remain in the home, reality often dictated a different pattern. Especially in Northern Italy, women often worked outside the home. America offered a chance for some immigrant women to break with more traditional roles. Some of the women worked, while others became involved in clubs or societies within the Italian community.

Many Italian women in the Southwest, like immigrant women in other parts of the country, operated boarding houses to take care of the many single men who migrated. The boarding house was not a total break with the traditional role, for it was really keeping house for a large and sometimes troublesome family. Rose Basile Green states that "The universal characteristic of this institution was that the boarding house resembled a large, boisterous, vivacious family."[31] Rolle notes that the boarding house environment was a transplanted bit of home, providing a safe place for lonely immigrants to share their confidences, enjoy a glass of wine, a smoke, and a game of *briscole* or *morra*.[32]

For the woman running a boarding house it meant unending cleaning and cooking for a sometimes fussy clientele. In some cases women took in boarders to supplement their husband's wages. Often the women were widows struggling to make a living. For example, Kate Bigando and Angelina Bairo, who operated boarding houses in Globe, were both widows.[33]

Women worked in other areas, too. Miss Farnese taught vocal culture to Phoenix residents,[34] while Mrs. Rodolfo Albi was the first Italian midwife in Denver.[35] Maria Bachechi of Albuquerque became known as a woman with an excellent business sense. She operated a dry-goods store and hotel independent of her husband's business ventures, which she took over when he died.[36]

---

[31] Rose Basile Green, *The Italian-American Novel* (Cranbury, 1974), 44.
[32] Rolle, *The Immigrant Upraised*, 140–41.
[33] *Honor the Past*, 75.
[34] Phoenix City Directory (Phoenix, 1905), 142.
[35] Perilli, *Colorado and the Italians in Colorado*, 47.
[36] Giomi, *Il Giornalino* (June), 16.

Susanna Cardone is credited with bringing the silk industry to Utah. As a young girl in Northern Italy she had learned to care for silkworms and reel silk. The experience was useful, for Susanna and her husband Paul saw the similarity between the Cache Valley in Utah and the silk-growing area of Piedmont. The mulberry trees they started from seed grew well, as did the silkworms. The silk that she reeled was of such high quality that she was called by Brigham Young to Salt Lake City to teach her craft to others. In 1876 she went to Logan, Utah, to teach women there to care for the worms and sell the silk. She continued producing silk in her own home for about fifteen years after that.[37]

Tomasi, in noting some of the differences between the Italian family in Italy and the first generation in America, points out that in addition to working for wages, women started to have a social life outside the home. They began to join some clubs in America.[38] This pattern can be observed in the Southwest. An Italian fair was held in Denver in 1889 by a society of Italian women to raise money for charitable purposes. Both La Società Sant' Anna and La Società Santa Margherita in Denver had women presidents. Women in that city were also active in Il Circolo Filodrammatico and the Dante Alighieri Society.[39] Pueblo, Colorado, had two women's clubs, La Nuova Italia and the Principessa Jolanda.[40] In Gallup, New Mexico, the local women formed the Società Regina Elena, Sorelle di Colombo in 1912.[41] By 1921 Albuquerque women had formed the Italian Women's Club.[42] Most of these clubs were organized to promote social events, to preserve the Italian culture, or to raise funds for charitable purposes.

Considering this preliminary look at Italian women in the Southwest, what conclusions can be made about differences between the East and West? The lives of many of the women in the Southwest appear to have been similar in many ways to those of their counterparts in the East. No matter what the setting there was hard work, much of it in the home, and a dedication to their children and family.

---

[37] Kate B. Carter, ed., *Heart Throbs of the West*, vol. 3 (Salt Lake City, 1948): 131.

[38] Lydio Tomasi, *The Italian American Family* (New York, 1972).

[39] Perilli, *Colorado and the Italians in Colorado*, 34.

[40] Perilli, *Colorado and the Italians in Colorado*, 148.

[41] Ellis Arthur Davis, ed., *The Historical Encyclopedia of New Mexico*, vol. 2 (Albuquerque, 1945): 236.   [42] Giomi, *Il Giornalino*.

However, there emerge at this point two factors which do lead to differences. One obviously varies by location, and it is the amount of support a woman was able to receive from other Italian women. The Little Italies of the East and cities in the West like Denver allowed the immigrant to function in an environment which was not totally alien, offering an amount of protection from the larger, not always accepting society. In areas such as Phoenix, the lack of an ethnic enclave was likely to be more strongly felt by women who were traditionally more housebound than men and relied on neighbors, friends, and relatives for their social life. There are many Italian settlements in the Southwest yet to be studied to find the amount of cohesiveness within the community, the geographic patterns of settlement, and the ways this influenced the lives of immigrant women and their children.

The other major difference from the East is the general picture which emerges of the economic success of men. Andrew Rolle contends that the West offered the Italian immigrant "opportunities not available in the mills and factories of the eastern city. Instead of becoming a bootblack, barber, or fish-peddler, the Italian who deserted his first American home on New York's crowded Mulberry Street might, thus, move toward more rewarding pursuits."[43] The story of hard work and prosperity rings true for Phoenix and Albuquerque, but a different picture may emerge from a close study of Denver. Little is currently known about other towns and cities in the Southwest.

Given a general picture of prosperity, this success affects the position of women in two ways. First, it allowed women to retain their position in the home more than their counterparts in the East. It was economic hardship that forced so many Italian women to work outside their homes in the East. Many of them, and certainly their husbands, would have preferred that they stay in the home. Yet Italian women did work in great numbers, doing a wide variety of jobs to add to the family income.[44] They worked because their husbands were unemployed or paid low wages and because the immigrants wanted to save for a better life.

Another factor in the Southwest that might have contributed to the women's staying in the home was that western cities did not offer the

[43] Rolle, *The Immigrant Upraised*, 6.
[44] Robert Foerster, *The Italian Emigration of Our Times* (New York: Russell & Russell, 1968), 345–49.

same amount of factory labor and home manufacturing jobs as cities in the East. What has not been explored yet is the question of what other kinds of acceptable work existed for Italian women which may not have existed in the East.

The second way in which the economic success of the men affected women is the rapidity with which their daughters began to complete their education. One of the goals of immigrant women was to see their children living a secure life. In describing his mother, who migrated to Colorado from Italy as a young woman, Jo Pagano notes that "She had a mind and a will of her own, a mind and will which seemed directed to only one object—the gaining of greater advantages for her children."[45]

In the East the desire of women to see their children advance was often blunted by harsh economic realities. In New York research has shown that where poverty and opportunities for work were both present, Italian girls attended school only until they were old enough to qualify for work papers. They began to work officially when they were fourteen or fifteen years old. High truancy rates meant that younger girls who were officially enrolled in school often did not really attend. This situation did not begin to change until the 1940s when attendance became more regular and was likely to last until high school.[46]

In Denver, Italian children were educated at Mount Carmel School or at the public schools. The girls who were trained at the Queen of Heaven Orphanage, established in 1902 by Mother Francis Xavier Cabrini, were trained for work in business offices, as nurses, and as teachers.[47] In Phoenix the daughters of Giusseppa, Ellen, Teresa, and other immigrant women were able to finish high school. They became teachers, nurses, stenographers, cashiers, and clerical workers. For the Southwest, then, mothers were able to see their daughters establish themselves in white-collar jobs as early as 1914.[48]

Of course going to school did not ensure that a woman would enter a career or break away from traditional roles. Maria Scarpi, a character modeled on John Fame's mother, went to the Sisters' school in early

[45] Jo Pagano, *Golden Wedding* (New York, 1943), 37.
[46] Miriam Cohen, "Italian-American Women in New York City, 1900–1950: Work and School" (unpublished ms., San Antonio, November, 1975), 10.
[47] Perilli, *Colorado and the Italians in Colorado*, 31.
[48] Phoenix City Directory (1914).

Denver, then to a public school. She ended up "in the kitchen . . . ,
imprisoned behind pots and pans."[49] The Benenato sisters had good jobs
and their first paychecks were turned over to the family to build a house.
It was money for the family, not the individual woman.[50]

The picture that emerges at this time for Italian immigrant women
in the Southwest is of a life economically less harsh, in an environment
more alien than that of their sisters in the East. What research does not
show is Carmella riding the range with Giovanni. Instead, Carmella is
in the kitchen in a role familiar to Italian women in all parts of America. The tradition-free atmosphere that the Italian man found which
allowed him to develop new attitudes about his role and future in America[51] was apparently not as liberating for woman.

---

[49] John Fante, *Dago Red* (New York, 1940), 6.
[50] Benenato interview.
[51] Rolle, *The Immigrant Upraised.*

Adjustment and Integration
THE ITALIAN EXPERIENCE
IN COLORADO

By Janet E. Worrall

C OLORADO IN THE NINETEENTH CENTURY is often characterized as a frontier society. Recent scholarship portrays it more
accurately as an area of rapid change where mining towns were
"industrial islands" dominated by large corporations.[1] Cities like Denver
reflected this industrialization brought on by the mining economy. By
1887, Denver had four smelters, several manufacturing companies producing mining equipment, three large railroad shops, stockyards, and
several textile factories. Immigrants, attracted to these industries, flocked
to Denver after the Civil War. British (including Welsh and Scots), Irish,
Germans, and Scandinavians (especially Swedes) dominated the labor
scene, bringing their churches, newspapers, ethnic celebrations, and
immigrant societies. Gradually Italians began to trickle in, showing a
dramatic increase between 1900 and 1920 (along with the German-Russi-
ans). Denver as well as mining towns experienced the growing pains of
industrialization—low wages, crowded living conditions, poverty, and
exploitation of an immigrant working class. The traditional, Protestant-
based population of Denver was challenged and alarmed by the growing number of Catholics, first Irish and Germans, and then Italians.

---

[1] David Thomas Brundage, "The Making of Working-Class Radicalism in the Mountain West:
Denver, Colorado, 1880–1903" (Ph.D. dissertation., University of California, Los Angeles, 1982),
4; see Lyle W. Dorsett, *The Queen City: A History of Denver* (Boulder: Pruett Publishing Company, 1977) for overview of Denver.

Their fears were reflected in the rapid growth of the American Protective Association (APA) in the 1890s and domination of Colorado's government by the KKK by 1926.[2]

The Italian immigrant population in Colorado grew steadily from 3,882 in 1890 to 12,580 in 1920. Mines provided work for many of the Italians, with the inevitable result that they became involved in labor of that time. While some immigrants found jobs in the precious metal mines of Central City, Georgetown, Empire, Leadville, Creede, and Cripple Creek, the majority worked in the coal mines in southeastern Colorado. Prior to 1890, northern Europeans, Mexicans, and Americans provided labor in the southern Colorado coalfields; after 1890, Italians and Slavic immigrants entered the mines in growing numbers. In 1900 (when the first statistics are available for individual counties), 44 percent of Colorado's Italians (2,986 of 6,818) lived in the four southeastern counties where coal mining dominated the economy (Las Animas, Pueblo, Huerfano, and Fremont). That number grew in 1910 to 69 percent of Colorado's Italian population, then dropped to 46 percent in 1920. Not surprisingly, Italians participated in numerous labor strikes as the miners tried to organize the Rockefeller-controlled coalfields of the Colorado Fuel and Iron Company (CF&I). (CF&I used the coal to provide coke for its steel mills—coal mining was secondary to the company's steel mills.) Among the most memorable strikes were those of 1903–4 and that of 1913 ending in the Ludlow massacre of 1914.[3]

The United Mine Workers of America (UMW) led the struggle to organize workers in the southern Colorado coal fields. Miners sought to achieve recognition of an eight-hour day; a 10-percent increase in wages; an end to the use of scrip; improved health and safety regulations; and better company housing. In 1903, when company representatives refused to meet with UMW representatives, 90 percent of the coal miners in Las Animas and Huerfano walked out. When company officials responded

---

[2] S. Brundage, ibid., Chap. 1.
[3] U.S. Census Office, *Twelfth Census, 1900*, vol. 1, pt. 1, Table 34, pp. 739–41; *Thirteenth Census, 1910 Supplement for Colorado*, Table 1, pp. 594–606; *Fourteenth Census, 1920 State Compendium for Colorado*, Table 12, pp. 39–40; U.S. Congress, Senate, *Reports of the Immigration Commission*, S. Doc. 633, 61st Cong., 2nd sess., pt. 25, 1911, p. 259; H. M. Gitelman, *Legacy of the Ludlow Massacre: A Chapter in American Industrial Relations* (Philadelphia: Univ. of Pennsylvania Press, 1988), 4.

by evicting workers from company housing at Hastings, where many workers lived, violence followed. Gov. James H. Peabody called out the national guard and as many as ninety-eight workers (including many Italians) were escorted across the border into New Mexico. As Philip Notarianni points out in his perceptive study of this strike, Governor Peabody's actions reflected his hatred of unions as well as Italians.[4]

Numerous other labor conflicts in the coalfields culminated in the tragic Ludlow massacre several years later. For years the UMW had been trying to organize workers in the northern and southern coalfields. In September 1913, southern miners voted to strike demanding higher wages, an eight-hour day, and recognition of their union, but the Colorado Fuel and Iron Company was intransigent. Miners at the Ludlow coal camp, fifteen miles north of Trinidad, joined the general strike. In the following months, struggles broke out between miners and strikebreakers, including Mexicans and Japanese brought in by the mine owners. Miners and their families had moved to tent colonies near the mines and were supported by union funds. The inevitable confrontation broke out with firing between the militia and miners at 10:00 A.M., April 20, 1914. No one knows who fired the first shot; gunfire continued throughout the day and claimed the lives of 10 men and one child. Even worse, when the temporary tent colony housing 900 men, women, and children caught fire, 2 Italian women and 11 children who had dug under a tent to escape the gunfire died of suffocation. In all, 24 lives were lost. Armed miners invaded the coalfields and town of Trinidad—gunfire continued and mine buildings were set on fire. Only when federal troops were called in was order restored by the end of the month.[5]

Northern Europeans also dominated coal fields in northern Colorado until the 1890s, when increasing numbers of Italians, Slovenians, and Poles entered. The 1903–4 strike had little impact in the northern part of the state. No strikebreakers were called in, and the UMW negotiated an

---

[4] Philip P. Notarianni. "Italian Involvement in the 1903–04 Coal Miners' Strike in Southern Colorado and Utah," in George E. Pozzetta (ed.), *Pane E Lavoro: The Italian American Working Class, Proceedings of the Eleventh Annual Conference of the American Italian Historical Association* (Toronto: The Multicultural History Society of Ontario, 1980); Luciano J. Iorizzo and Salvatore Mondello (eds.), *The Italian Americans* (Boston, 1985), 93–94.

[5] Gitelman, 17–20; see Manfred F. Boemke, "The Wilson Administration, Organized Labor, and the Colorado Strike, 1913–1914," Ph.D. dissertation, Princeton Univ., 1983. for full account of Ludlow Massacre; Reports of the Immigration Commission, pt. 25, p. 260.

176   JANET E. WORRALL

agreement with the northern mine operators. Because of greater labor peace in the northern fields, there was less worker turnover and racial lines seemed clearly drawn. Supervisory jobs went to native born and Northern Europeans, while miners and general laborers were Southern Europeans.

Discrimination by employers as well as the workers was shown toward Chinese, Japanese, and Blacks. In short, they were never offered jobs in the northern fields. Greeks were marginally acceptable, in times of labor scarcity, which rarely occurred in the northern fields.[6]

While the majority of Italians outside Denver worked in some aspect of the mining industry, many others found employment with railroad companies which recruited them and often paid their passage to Colorado. In 1881, Adolfo Rossi was one of seventy Italians brought by the Denver, South Park and Pacific Railroad (later the Union Pacific). Believing that they would be employed as timekeepers, cooks, and carpenters, Italian immigrants instead were sent to a railroad camp at 11,000 feet, where they cleared a forested area to make way for new track. The work was far harder than anticipated for a paltry salary of $2.50 per day with room and board. They made the best of their situation, spending leisure time with their musical instruments, which they had fortuitously brought along, much to the amusement of their Irish working partners.[7]

Not so fortunate was another Italian railroad worker near Gunnison. In a confrontation with a contractor named Hoblitzell, the Italian shot and killed him. The Italian escaped, but was later caught and confined in the courthouse in Gunnison. Through a ruse, the prisoner was abducted and hanged. Gunnison residents feared retaliation by the Italian community, but nothing came of the incident, which probably reflected a mining town mentality more than anti-Italian sentiment.[8]

The railroad companies and the padrone system both exploited Italian workers. The Union Pacific left several hundred jobless in 1884 and when Denver residents raised money to help them, natives objected to charity, which they feared would encourage joblessness.

[6] Reports of the Immigration Commission, pt. 25, pp. 241–56.
[7] Andrew F. Rolle. *The Immigrant Upraised: Italian Adventurers and Colonists in an Expanding America* (Norman, Ok., 1968), 171.
[8] George A. Root, "Gunnison in the Early 'Eighties'," *Colorado Magazine* 9, no. 6 (November 1932): 201–13.

Through their work in mines and on railroads, Italians contributed much to the growth of Colorado. Unfortunately, due to the nature of those industries, workers became embroiled in labor strife and violence, which often reflected negatively on them and in the worst cases led to loss of life. We have presented merely an overview of Italians in mining and railroad camps. Much research remains to be done on the local level to fully understand role of Italians in these industries, as well as their interaction with other immigrants.

Many immigrants eventually settled in the growing southern towns of Trinidad and Pueblo where they found work in steel mills. Newspapers testify to their numbers. In Trinidad, *Corriere de Trinidad* served the Italian colony with articles in both English and Italian. Starting around 1900 and continuing into the 1940s, the paper carried mainly international news. In Pueblo the best-known and longest-published Italian paper was *L'Unione*, starting in 1907. Vincent Massari, a leader of Pueblo's Italian community, was its editor and publisher from 1921 until publication ceased in 1947. Massari, born in Italy in 1898, came to the U.S. in 1915, joining his parents in Pueblo. His father was a coal miner and union organizer who served as secretary/treasurer of the Pueblo Smeltermen's Union and helped reorganize the miners after the Ludlow massacre. Vincent Massari became a U.S. citizen in 1923. He was a leader of Pueblo's Italian community and an active member of the city's mutual-aid society. A vocal Democrat, Massari served in both the Colorado House of Representatives and Senate for over twenty years.[9]

According to census reports, the Italian population in Denver nearly tripled between 1900 and 1920, increasing from 1,000 to 2,872. These figures are probably on the low side as many Italian workers who had migrated to Denver due to poor working conditions and a decline in jobs in railroad and mining camps were missed by census takers. The actual size of the Italian American population is difficult to determine. In 1907, an Italian newspaper in Denver claimed that there were 15,000 Italians in Denver and 60,000 in the state.[10]

The Zarlengo family is an example of a migrating family that eventually settled in Denver. Charles (Gaetano), aged 13, came to Colorado

<hr>

[9] Vincent Massari Collection, Univ. of Minnesota Immigration History Research Center, see description for file.   [10] *Il Guido del Popolo*, Denver, Colorado, October 2, 1907.

with his father, Francesco, in June 1890. His five brothers migrated later from their rocky family farm in Campobasso. Charles worked as a water-boy for a railroad section gang. Francesco disliked subjecting his son to the dangers of blasting and earth-moving, and they moved to the mining area of Silver Plume, Colorado, where a second brother, George, fourteen years old, joined them in 1895. There the family contracted to supply wood as fuel for the silver and gold mines and eventually hauled ore from the mines to the railroad. During snowbound winters, they learned English from another Italian immigrant who had picked up the rudiments over the years.

In 1910, when the mines declined, the family moved to Denver. Having the language and some knowledge of business operations, they took advantage of the numerous opportunities offered by the growing city and started the Zarlengo Brothers Contracting Company. Their firm expanded from unloading coal and ore at the smelters to operating their own coal and lumber enterprise. In turn they hired hundreds of newly arriving immigrants, in many cases paying for their passage over.

George married Elizabeth Fabrizio while his brother, Charles, returned to Italy in 1905 to bring his childhood sweetheart back to Denver. Each couple had nine children who attended Catholic schools in Denver and eventually entered the professions of law, teaching, and medicine.[11]

Many Italians in Denver followed their agricultural inclinations by settling along the South Platte River. Railroads owned the land, but tracks occupied only part of it. Most of the immigrants came from southern Italy, especially Potenza and Naples, but a few were from Genoa and Milan in the north. Denver was a place of mixed blessings for immigrants. Land was cheap, but the hazards of poor sanitation, the smell of garbage treatment plant, and the refuse carrying diphtheria and typhoid fever made it a less than desirable place to live. Homes were often one-room cottages or tents.

Poverty conditions of the inhabitants evoked little sympathy from Denverites. Children gathered watercress along the banks and sold it uptown, where they picked up cigar butts to sell back in the Bottoms. As one local said, "The majority of the children belong to these dagoes,

---

[11] Massari file, unidentified newspaper clipping.

who would probably follow the same thing if they had thousands of dollars."[12] Young boys often landed in jail for stealing pieces of wood or coal from railroad cars as a desperate effort to keep the family from freezing in the cold winter.

Yet immigrants quickly turned the fertile land into vegetable and flower gardens, giving Italians a monopoly on supplying Denver's population with fresh fruits and vegetables. Farmers took their produce to the City Market (Colfax and Speer) by 4:00 A.M. in horse-drawn wagons often accompanied by women and children. Mothers put hot bricks in the wagon to keep the children's feet warm. For many this was a social event. Sometimes women did the selling as Sam Santangelo recalls, "husbands came to town all dressed up and went to the bars." Retailers, often Italian peddlers, sold produce door-to-door throughout Denver or out of their wagon on street corners. So good was the reputation of Italian growers that grocers came up from Colorado Springs twice a week for fresh produce.[13]

John Figliolino, a native of Italy, was one of the peddlers who regularly bought his produce at City Market. His son, Tom, followed the trade, and had peddled fruits and vegetables in Denver for fifty-five years until 1978, when he finally cut back on his schedule. He rose at 4:00 A.M. and drove his 1950 green Chevrolet pickup truck, with a cornucopia painted on the side, to the Denargo Market. There he loaded his truck and was home by 5:30 A.M. to have breakfast with his wife and daughter. Then he traversed the neighborhoods where his customers waited. Some he had served for three generations. Those who could not be home would leave their orders. Knowing where keys were placed, Tom would fill the order, place it inside, and lock the house again. Many remembered Tom from Depression days when he would give fruit to children. He was so well regarded that some of his customers remembered him in their wills.[14]

The Garramone family came from central Italy in 1901, settling on a farm on the outskirts of Denver. Sons Mike and Tony subsequently bought thirty acres in the river bottoms, then known as Frog Hollow, in 1916 for the rather high price of $2,000 an acre. Their specialty was bedding plants, petunias, snapdragons, and a few vegetable items, main-

---

[12] Stephen J. Leonard, "Denver's Foreign Born Immigrants 1859–1900" (Ph.D. dissertation, Claremont Graduate University, 1971), 189.   [13] *Denver Post, Empire Magazine*, December 17, 1978.
[14] Ibid.

ly lettuce. They sold products to grocery stores, first the Piggly Wiggley chain and then Safeway. Mike's wife, Elvira, from Denver's Italian colony, worked side by side with him in the field in addition to raising a family and keeping an immaculate house. As an Italian co-worker said, "Women did a tremendous amount of work . . . up at 3:00 o'clock in the morning to make coffee for the men to go out into the fields. Then shortly afterward, they'd be out there themselves. You don't find this breed of people anymore."[15]

The rise of Italian newspapers reflected the growing Italian community in Denver. Angelo Noce, born in Genoa and having emigrated to America in 1850, published the first one in 1885, *La Stella*, an Italian weekly. However, this was somewhat premature, given the limited Italian population in the city, and the paper ceased publication in 1889.[16]

Probably the most influential and best patronized Italian weekly at beginning of the century was *Il Grido del Popolo*, published by Frank Mancini. It encouraged Italians to become U.S. citizens and even carried the questions and answers for a citizenship test in a 1907 issue. In a push to Americanize Italians, the paper stated that it would begin publishing articles in English, "so that the American people may read them and when they see that the Italian people want to become not only a part of the Great American Republic, but a necessary part, they cannot but help respecting them for the interest and service and they render to the Land of their Adoption. [sic]"[17]

In an effort to increase readership the paper lowered its price from $1.50 to $1.00 per year. Touting the virtues of Italians, *Il Grido* stated that an American dealer in the Italian district said that "he had never yet lost a bill owed by an Italian creditor; and this speaks well for the Italians."[18]

Several other Italian newspapers were published in Denver in the first decades of the twentieth century, some continuing into the 1940s. These included *Il Risveglio*, directed by Frank Mancini for a time, *La Capitale*, *La Frusta*, and *La Roma*, the last published by one of Denver's leading business men, Peter Albi.

---

[15] *Denver Post*, Section C. May 9, 1976.
[16] Giovanni Perilli, *Colorado and the Italians in Colorado* (Denver: n.p., 1922), 14.
[17] *Il Guido del Popolo*, October 2, 1907.
[18] Ibid.

Catholic churches and schools were vital to Denver's Italian community. The first permanent Catholic Italian priests were two Jesuits who came in 1879 and started the Sacred Heart Church at 28th and Larimer streets. They laid the cornerstone within two months of their arrival. The following year a school opened and in 1888 Regis College was started, then known as Sacred Heart.[19]

In the 1890s, the Italian community gradually moved from the bottomlands to nearby north Denver, forming the city's "Little Italy." There in 1893, newly appointed Jesuit Father Mariano LePore initiated construction of Our Lady of Mount Carmel, the Italian national church at Navajo and West 36th streets. LePore, a handsome, dynamic young man, lived in the Italian community and quickly won the support and affection of his flock. But LePore soon reflected and exacerbated the growing dissension in the Italian community. Some members objected to LePore's involvement in secular activities. He published his own newspaper, *La Nazione*, and encouraged his congregation to join the Democratic Party. Others questioned his morality around the opposite sex and some men prohibited their wives, sisters, and daughters from speaking to him. So strong was antagonism to Father LePore that leaders of the Italian community tried to have him dismissed from the parish.[20]

Matters worsened in 1898 when Mount Carmel caught fire and burned by what firemen suggested was a deliberately set fire. Father LePore had left the church unlocked after Mass, as was the custom. He heard about the fire when he was downtown; he rushed back to find the wooden building completely destroyed. The anti-LePore faction, led by Frank Damascio, then built a chapel nearby on the corner of Osage and West 36th streets. The bishop, however, refused to appoint a priest, and the building became the Mount Carmel Grade School. Meanwhile, Mt. Carmel Church was rebuilt and dedicated on December 18, 1904.[21]

The end of the dissension came tragically with the murder of Father LePore in 1903. The assassin, a laborer, Giuseppe Sorice, also died in the confrontation, leaving motives and details unanswered.[22]

---

[19] Perilli, 31.
[20] Leonard, 194; Christine A. Derose, "Inside 'Little Italy': Italian Immigrants in Denver," *Colorado Magazine* 54, no. 3 (Summer 1977): 284–86; Ruth Eloise Wiberg, *Rediscovering Northwest Denver, Its History, Its People, Its Landmarks* (Denver, 1976), 40.
[21] Ibid.   [22] Leonard, 195.

Without doubt the most famous of the Catholic leaders in Colorado was Mother Cabrini. In 1902, she led the first group of the Sisters of the Sacred Heart to Denver, where they established the Mt. Carmel School on Navajo and West 34th streets. Three years later, Mother Cabrini opened the Queen of Heaven Orphanage nearby. Apparently two Sisters of the Sacred Heart Order happened upon two weeping little girls, who had no place to go as their mother was dead and their father worked. They were afraid to stay home alone. At the time of its founding, the orphanage was the largest in Denver.[23]

Italians loved processions, feast days, and societies. One of the most important for the Denver colony was the feast of San Rocco, named after one of the most beloved saints, patron of the sick and plague-stricken. Denver had its first San Rocco celebration on August 16, 1892, in the chapel of what now is Regis University. Two years later, a special San Rocco chapel was completed there, which added to the festiveness of the occasion.[24]

With the opening of Mt. Carmel Church and the friction in the Italian community, each parish had its own San Rocco celebration. The two parishes tried to outdo each other and attract the most followers with raffles, fireworks, flowers, and music.[25] Once the factionalism subsided, the religious nature of the day dominated again. Italian societies bid for the honor of carrying San Rocco in the procession ending in the San Rocco Chapel—all joined in the celebration.[26]

The major festival for Mt. Carmel Church was the celebration of La Madonna del Carmine (Our Lady of Mt. Carmel), first held July 16, 1896. People came from all over the state to participate in the daylong activities of processions, Mass, and the final carnival-like celebration with fireworks, brass bands, and flower-covered booths.[27]

Columbus Day generated nearly as much excitement in the Italian colony as religious holidays. In 1892 a committee of Denver's leading Italians planned a celebration for the fourth centenary of Columbus's landing. Later they tried to take credit from the printer, Angelo Noce, who led the campaign for constructing a statue to Columbus and for

---

[23] Pirelli, 32.
[24] "Colorado Festivals—Pt. II," *Colorado Magazine* 29, no. 3 (July 1952): 189.
[25] Ibid., 188–89.   [26] Ibid.   [27] Ibid.

As Janet Worrall notes, Italians were enthusiastic supporters of societies, traditional holiday celebrations, and religious observances. They celebrated familiar
religious holidays like St. Joseph's Day and seasonal holidays like *vendemia*, the
traditional fall grape harvest festival and picnics on the Monday after Easter attended by scores as pictured in the photo of Italian migrants on an outing at Rancho
Cucamonga in Southern California. *Al Vignolo Collection, Naples, California.*

recognizing October 12 as a legal holiday. Noce persuaded Gov. Jesse
McDonald to designate the date as Columbus Day and wrote the bill
that was introduced in the Colorado House and Senate in 1905. It failed,
but was reintroduced and passed two years later. Colorado became the
first state to recognize Columbus Day, October 12, as a legal holiday. As
tribute to Noce for his efforts, he led the parade as grand marshal on
October 12, 1907.[28] To many first-generation Italians, Columbus sym-
bolized hope and pride, and the parade unified the Italian community.

The incidents surrounding Father LePore and Angelo Noce raise the
issue of factionalism and perhaps regionalism. Leaders of the Italian
community were wealthy businessmen, including Agostino Roncaglia,
banker and businessman; Frank Mazza, a wealthy merchant; Frank Damascio, designer and donor of San Rocco Chapel and one of the richest Italians in Denver; Luigi Mosconi, restaurant owner; and A. Abiati,
an artist. These were the leaders in Denver's first Italian organizations.
They were uncomfortable with Father LePore and resented his outside
activities, especially promotion of the Democratic Party among his congregation. Later they shunned Noce and took the credit for promoting
Columbus Day. Noce lived in east Denver rather than the Little Italy
of northwest Denver where Damascio resided. No doubt other issues
also caused hostility between Noce and the Italian leaders. There was
obviously a wealthy, educated group who came in the 1880s and seem to
have provided leadership well into the twentieth century. Still to be determined, however, is whether regionalism, status, politics, or other factors
accounted for a person gaining status in the Italian community. However important in their own colony, Italians had not earned acceptance
in Denver "society" as had wealthy Germans and English. For example,
no Italians could join the prestigious Denver Club or the exclusive Denver Athletic Club.[29]

Colorado was the center of nativism in the West in the late nineteenth and early twentieth centuries. Denver was white, Protestant, and
conservative with a reputation for intolerance. Indicative was the increase
in membership of the American Protective Association, which rose from
3,000 in 1893 to 10,000 in 1894, as older residents became alarmed at the
increasing number of Catholic immigrants. The 35,000 first- and sec-

---

[28] Perilli, 14; DeRose, 280–81.   [29] Leonard, 192–95; Derose, 278, 286.

ond-generation Catholics in Denver in 1920 frightened nativists more than the usual nativist causes of white supremacy and anti-Semitism, and led to the Ku Klux Klan's dominance of government in Colorado by 1924. While historians have yet to assess how nativism directly affected the Italian community, the incident surrounding the lynching of Daniel Arata in Denver in 1893 has manifestations of nativism.[30]

On Tuesday night, July 25, B. C. Lightfoot, a sixty-three-year-old Civil War veteran, went to Daniel Arata's saloon, the Hotel Italia, for a beer. After finishing it, Arata asked Lightfoot if he wanted another, he replied, yes. Upon finishing the second Lightfoot began to leave, Arata asked him for payment for the second. As Lightfoot had no money and thought the second drink was free, he refused to pay. Arata, in a drunken state, attacked Lightfoot first with his fist and then struck him on the head repeatedly with a heavy chair. As Lightfoot seemed ready to fall off the chair, Arata shot him in the chest, then dragged him out of the saloon into a narrow courtyard. A crowd gathered, the police came and arrested Arata, who was described in the newspaper as a native of Italy, twenty-eight years old, and with a very bad reputation having been engaged in several shooting episodes.[31]

Wednesday night, July 26, a mob of 10,000 broke into the Denver jail and dragged out Arata. The mob action appeared to start when a half-dozen Grand Army of the Republic (GAR) men, led by a Colonel C. F. Brennan, urged a group of just-dispersed men who had gathered to discuss the hard times to "Follow me." (Brennan maintained that he was of the Forty-eighth Pennsylvania regiment during the war and wore a GAR medal prominently on his breast.) A mob temperament quickly took over and they let out a yell to "Hang the Dago! Hang Arata!" Their number grew as they approached the jail.[32]

The sheriff and police were helpless in their efforts to halt the mob of 10,000, who eventually found Arata and dragged him out to a nearby cottonwood tree. There they lynched him and filled his body with bullets. His body was cut down and dragged through the streets—then strung up on a telephone pole—a grisly sight.[33]

---

[30] Kenneth T. Jackson, *The Ku Klux Klan in the City, 1915–1930* (New York, 1967), 215, 219.
[31] *Rocky Mountain News*, July 26, 1893.
[32] Ibid., July 27, 1893.
[33] Ibid.

While there was no question over Arata's guilt, the lynching was a mob reaction tinged with nativism that was reflected in the frequent cries of "Hang the Dago" and in the reverence shown to the GAR. On July 28, the *Rocky Mountain News* carried a story on the event labeling lynchings as outrageous and unacceptable in a civilized country. The article explained the action as resulting from an atrocious act by a "member of an organization so venerated by the country and in which sentiment plays so strong a part, the criminal, being of a nativity against which a deep and exaggerated prejudice exist."[34]

In the following days, attention was focused on culpability—did it lie with the sheriff's office or police? Both took considerable criticism. Stories in the *Rocky Mountain News* indicated that citizens of Denver should be shocked and ashamed that such barbarous actions could take place in their city.

Some feared that the Italian colony would retaliate, and there were rumors that "the Italians were concocting dreadful schemes in the bottoms as a revenge for the bloody execution of their fellow countryman."[35] Further research will show whether this was an isolated event or had the overtones of nativism reflected in the growth of the APA and KKK in Denver. Careful examination must be made of incidents which on the surface appear to be racist, but may be the result of mob reaction. As the *Colorado Catholic* editorialized, "No one will contend that Arata would have met the same fate had he been of a nationality other than Italian."[36]

This essay has been a preliminary study of Italians in Colorado. While the Italian population was never very large in Colorado or Denver, if compared to that of eastern states in 1920, Italians were the second-largest immigrant group in the state, after the Germans from Russia. Now it is time for more probing, detailed studies on nativism, residential patterns, associational life, regionalism, newspapers, voting patterns, community leadership, and generational changes. Ultimately, this will allow for comparative studies of the Italian experience in the less urbanized West and the more industrialized, urbanized East.

---

[34] Ibid., July 28, 1893.
[35] Ibid.
[36] Leonard, 209.

Reno's Little Italy
ITALIAN ENTREPRENEURSHIP
AND CULTURE
IN NORTHERN NEVADA

By Albin J. Cofone

T HE DEVELOPMENT of a "Little Italy" in Reno was an outgrowth of the small but steady population gains that distinguished Reno from other Nevada communities during the late nineteenth and early twentieth centuries. This growth provided Reno with a level of economic stability, which, when combined with the ability of Italians to save discretionary income, made the city headquarters for the acquisition of Italian capital and investment.

Complementing this concentration of Italian wealth was an active and informed Italian press that reflected the needs of the community.[1] Much of what Italians did and thought is revealed in this press, and it provides a unique opportunity to see how they perceived their presence in the region. Ethnic groups in America have frequently viewed themselves differently than the dominant group that surrounds them. Sometimes their perceptions of events differ dramatically, at other times subtly. Consequently, the use of the ethnic press can prove a valuable tool in

---

[1] Three Italian language newspapers were published in Nevada between 1907 and 1944. In Reno, there was John Granata's *Bollettino del Nevada* and F. Moracci's *Italian-French Colony News*. In Sparks, M. Paggi published the *Corriere Di Nevada*. The *Corriere* apparently only went through a few editions in 1907. No copies have been located. By far, the *Bollettino* was the most enduring, lasting almost to the end of World War II.

assessing both areas of agreement and disagreement between the immigrant group and the host society. In the case of Reno's Italian newspapers, there were constant expressions of pride that Italians were now new Americans, and satisfaction with life in Nevada. The press consistently extolled business, cultural, and personal events associated with Italians, and it was frequently unrestrained in its endorsements of the fine lives Italians had achieved in the Reno area.

A brief review of Italian involvement in other communities and areas will add perspective to the discussion of Reno. It seems clear that in Nevada, the region's overall climate and dry farming requirements to some extent matched past experiences, and led to an Italian proclivity to save and invest in Nevada, rather than merely taking quick profits and moving on. There were not only significant Italian businesses, farms, and ranches in Reno, but also in Virginia City, Carson City, Austin, Eureka, and Paradise Valley, among others. In Sparks, for example, although not one of the first settlers in the area was Italian, by 1924 many of the Italians who had originally come to the community as laborers had saved enough to have purchased ranches, farms, shops, and homes. A review of the history of Sparks shows that of the twenty-three properties owned by the first settlers, by 1924 eleven had ended up being owned by Italians.[2]

A similar pattern can be seen in the settlement of Dayton. Although in 1880 there were only three Italian-owned ranches along the Carson River in the vicinity of Dayton, by 1900 twenty-seven of the twenty-eight ranches in the area were Italian-owned. (The one non-Italian ranch was owned by a former resident of Maine.) There were also two saloons in Dayton owned and operated by Italians.[3]

---

[2] F. B. Kingsbury, "Pioneer Days in Sparks and Vicinity. Earlier Settlers and Points of Interest," *Nevada Historical Society Papers* 5 (1925–26): 309–17.

[3] Manuscript Census of 1880, Dayton, Lyon County, Nevada, Census Population Schedules, Washington, D.C., microfilm number C235–57; Manuscript Census of 1900, Dayton, Lyon County, Nevada, Census Population Schedules, Washington, D.C., microfilm number C235–91. See also the *Census of the Inhabitants of the State of Nevada*, Vol. 2, Lyon County (Carson City, 1875). At that time, the estimated value of real property in Lyon County was $924,454. Of that amount, the Italian share was only $900. Personal property for the county was estimated at $587,743. The Italian share of personal property amounted to $525. The state figures of 1875 support the state figures of 1880, in showing that only three Italians had enough funds to own land. Although there are no comparable figures for 1900, the amount of thrift required to become the dominant ranch-holding faction in the Dayton area within twenty years suggests that Italians were quite adept at managing their finances.

During the 1860s and 1870s, the Comstock boom in Virginia City attracted many Italians eager to work on the lode. Having come to Nevada with few financial resources, this was one way to earn a stake. Once having saved up enough money, the majority went into ranching, farming, and business, but at least one group of Italians went back to the mines as capitalist investors. Founded in 1874, the Roman Capitol Mine was an entirely Italian operation.[4] Unfortunately the company was mired in conflict, with two shareholder factions vying for control. By April 1874 relations between the two groups had reached the boiling point, when two slates of officers, all Italian, were elected at separate meetings. Noting that extreme tension existed between the two groups, the *Territorial Enterprise* observed: "Which party owns the mine we really cannot say. Shotguns and pistols will probably prove the potent arguments which will make the title clear."[5] In fact, the eventual outcome is not clear. In June 1881 litigation was still in progress.[6]

Other areas of the state also were impacted by the presence of Italian entrepreneurship. In Austin, Samuel Crescenzo, described in Thomas Wren's *A History of the State of Nevada* as "the well known retired capitalist," lived in the community for forty years, and at one time ran both the International Hotel and a general merchandise store.[7] Further to the east, in Elko, Emilio Dotta, born in Switzerland but of Italian ethnicity, started out as a freight hauler only to become, through thrift and shrewd business sense, the largest supplier of milk and dairy products to the community.[8] While in Eureka, Frank Pastorino, who arrived from Italy in 1875 to work in the mines, saved enough to buy the prosperous Hay Ranch. He did well with the ranch, selling it in 1937 to become city assessor. In addition, he owned and managed the Eureka Theatre.[9]

In Paradise Valley, Batista Recanzone and Angelo Forgnone, who arrived in Nevada in 1863 (they were among the first Italians in the state), became the wealthiest entrepreneurs in Humboldt County.[10] Prior to

---

[4] *The Territorial Enterprise*, April 7, 1874.

[5] Ibid., April 9, 1874.

[6] Ibid., June 13, 1881.

[7] Thomas A. Wren, *A History of the State of Nevada* (New York, 1904), 333.

[8] Ibid., 620.

[9] Although Pastorino's achievements were primarily in Eureka County, in later years some of his family members moved to Reno. As a result, a record of his activities is to be found in the Nevada Historical Society's *Early Nevada Families Collection. Washoe County.*

arriving in Paradise Valley, they had spent time in North Africa work-ing as masonry contractors. The construction skills developed in North Africa apparently served them well in Nevada, where they were able to find employment working on canals near Winnemucca and in stone-mason work at Fort Scott. Eventually they acquired vast amounts of land in Paradise Valley, built up their possessions, and invested in the com-munity. By the end of their lives they had owned several ranches, a num-ber of homes and commercial buildings, and a flour mill. The mill, known as the Silver State Flour Mill, was built in 1866 and purchased by the Recanzone family in 1890.[11] The flour ground at the mill was of such quality that it was awarded the gold medal at both the Saint Louis Expo-sition of 1904 and the San Francisco Exposition of 1915. Capacity at the mill was about two tons a day; it remained in operation until 1945.

By the turn of the century, Reno was still the premier choice of all the state's communities for Italian investment, and this reflected both a favorable economic location and the continuing enthusiasm of Italians for Nevada real estate. In part, this loyalty to Reno and Nevada can be understood in terms of the poverty experienced in Italy and the con-trasting success that could be achieved along the banks of the Truckee. John Gottardi, a prominent member of the Reno community, wrote in his University of Nevada thesis in 1926:

> Speaking particularly of the Italians in Reno, the community is well organized with an excellent element. The people are daring, have initia-tive, honest, good, and respected by the American population.
>
> Fifty years ago they helped Reno develop into a great city. Not many of the original miners are left, but their children have settled, dedicated to commerce, business, mining, agriculture, and fellowship. Some min-ers that originally settled in Reno became hoteliers, restauranteurs, store owners, and before the Volstead Act, liquor store operators.[12]

Italians stayed in Nevada, not thinking they had arrived in El Dora-do, but because they formed a successful and valued part of the com-munity.

---

[10] See Nevada Historical Society, *Early Nevada Families Collection, Humboldt County.*
[11] *Nevada State Journal,* January 6, 1957.
[12] John R. Gottardi, "Gl'Italiani Di Nevada" (M.A. thesis, Department of Modern Languages, University of Nevada, Reno, 1926).

Some years later, agreement with Gottardi's view of local Italians was expressed by another resident of Reno. Amy Gulling, who lived in Reno from 1911 to 1965, was an astute observer of the mores and social trends of the city. Although her comments regarding Italians are somewhat condescending, they accurately reflect the genuinely high rate of social mobility achieved by Italians:

> Our Italian people have become such fine citizens, and in two generations they have become complete Americans. They have married girls of other blood sources and have become complete Americans. Some of our finest citizens are the Italian people. They are a very fine looking people; in every way just the finest kind of citizen.[13]

Indeed by the late 1940s the success of the Italian community in Reno was a matter of record throughout the state.[14] The president of the First National Bank of Nevada was Edward Questa.[15] Until his death in a plane crash on February 10, 1962, Questa was one of Reno's, and Nevada's, leading citizens. He was the son of Italian pioneers, Fred and Camella Questa, and was born in Reno in 1899, and he worked his way up the First National Bank hierarchy and contributed greatly to the bank's economic profile in the state. His contributions to Nevada were recognized beyond the state's boundaries when the Italian government appointed him vice counselor of Italy in Nevada. He was again recognized by Italy when he was awarded the Order of Merit for his achievements in America, the Italian government's highest award for noncitizens. Newspaper accounts of Questa at the time of his death reflect on both his importance to Nevada's economy and how well liked he was as an individual. The First National Bank also provided an avenue of mobility for other Italians in the state. Among the bank's officers in the late 1940s from Italian backgrounds were Hugo Quilici of Reno and Harry Menante of Las Vegas as vice presidents, and William Cassinella, the manager of the Carson City branch.[16] Italian economic success in the immediate area is evident when one notes the many successful Italian farmers and

---

[13] Amy Culling, "An Interview with Amy Gulling" (Reno: University of Nevada, Oral History, 1966), 40–41.

[14] *Nevada State Journal*, July 6, 1952.

[15] *Reno Evening Gazette*, February 11, 1962.

[16] *Nevada State Journal*, July 6, 1952.

ranchers in Washoe County, among them the Garaventas, Ghiglieris, Avansinos, Pecettis, Raffetos, Gardellas, Raggios, and Pirettos.[17] The "Grand Old Man" of the successful Italian community in Reno was acknowledged by the *Nevada State Journal* to be Manuel Cafferata.[18] Cafferata's father, James, was born in Italy in the 1830s, and had previously worked in Australia before coming to California. Upon arriving in America, he was joined by his wife. Manuel, who was born July 16, 1862, was quite possibly the first European child born in Amador County, California. When he was six months old, his family crossed the Sierra Nevada and relocated in Virginia City, where they eventually prospered. In later years, Manuel's achievements in the region were generally acknowledged by his peers, as was his extensive knowledge of Nevada real estate.

By 1910, the growing concentration of Italians in Reno had resulted in an Italian district centered around Lake Street in the vicinity of Second and Commercial Row. Although a number of Italian stores were scattered throughout downtown, this was the heart of the community, the "Little Italy."[19]

As an ethnic area, the Lake Street district rested heavily upon the perceptions of local Italians. Compared to the large Little Italies of the West End of Boston, South Philadelphia, or Mulberry Street in New York, where the presence of Italian-oriented commercial services overwhelmed all other business activities, Reno's Little Italy, which had shops run by Basques, Chinese, and French within its boundaries, might appear to be too ill defined. However, even the sizeable Little Italies of the East and Midwest were often not as homogeneous as popularly imagined. While neighborhoods with large numbers of Italians in the East are culturally visible by the presence of Italian shops, statues of saints on front lawns, and the occasional fig tree wrapped in cloth to protect branches against

---

[17] Ibid., July 6, 1952.

[18] *Nevada State Journal*, December 23, 1939.

[19] This high concentration of Italians in the Reno-Sparks area is also revealed in street names. At least twenty-three streets in Reno and Sparks are named after Italians who were involved in the development of the Truckee Meadows region. In Reno: Anelli Lane, Aquila Avenue, Aquila Way, Bigotti Way, Carano Lane, Casazza Drive, De Lucchi Lane, Depaoli Street, Ferrari Street, Ferretto Lane, Mastroianni Drive, and Raffetto Drive. In Sparks: Capurro Way, Cassinelli Lane, Figoni Ranch Road, Galletti Way, Lagomarsino Court, Lagomarsino Drive, Martini Road, Parlanti Lane, Puccinelli Drive, Rizzo Drive, and Rossi Lane.

cold winters, non-Italian residents are not always unknown. These neighborhoods have historically proven attractive to a wide variety of people, since they are considered stable and well-kept. Loyalty to a church (if only at times on the part of the women), strong family bonds, and pride of home ownership are usually cited as factors in the desirability of an Italian neighborhood. In Herbert Gans's *The Urban Villagers*, a study of the West End of Boston, it is argued that non-Italian bohemians found the West End desirable because the Italian residents did not interfere with their unorthodox lifestyle.[20] As Gans points out, as long as the bohemians did not threaten Italian family values, they were free to live in their own way. Similarly, in San Francisco, a large bohemian population has for years lived side by side with an Italian population along Columbus Avenue in the city's North Beach neighborhood.[21]

In essence, ethnic and social differences in Reno's Little Italy were more a matter of scale than of substance. The greater interaction of different ethnic groups along Lake Street reflected the sociological dynamics of a small western city, as opposed to an eastern metropolitan center. The important point is that the Italian population's mental, or cognitive, map considered the Lake Street area to be the commercial center of their community, and by extension the cultural hub as well.[22]

The Lake Street district served the marketing needs of the substantial Italian population in Reno and surrounding Washoe County.[23] Included at different times in the area were grocery stores, liquor stores, insurance agencies, a travel agency, and a significant number of hotels. Bilingual merchants facilitated the shopping patterns of Italians still learning English, while also providing a level of camaraderie tradition-

[20] Herbert Gans, *The Urban Villagers* (New York: Macmillan, 1962).
[21] For a comprehensive look at San Francisco's Italian community, see Paul Radios, *The Italians of San Francisco, Their Adjustment and Acculturation* (San Francisco: R and E Associates, 1935).
[22] For a discussion of mental maps and their application to an ethnic group's understanding, see Peter Could and Rodney White, *Mental Maps* (Baltimore: Penguin Books, 1974).
[23] *Thirteenth Census of the United States*, vol. 3, 1910 (Washington. D.C, 1913), p. 145. *Fifteenth Census of the United States*, vol. 3, 1930 (Washington, D.C., 1933), p. 92. In 1910, Italians, with 372 members, were the largest single foreign-born ethnic group in Reno. By 1930, they were still the largest foreign-born group with a population of 637. At that time, Italians were also the largest group, numbering 733, of native-born who had parents born in a foreign country. In addition, the 1930 census shows that the Italian position as both the largest single foreign-born ethnic group and largest single group of foreign-born parentage in Reno was also true in the rest of Washoe County, as well as in nearby Storey and Lyon counties, and in distant Eureka County.

TABLE I: RENO'S ITALIAN HOTELS	
1. The Depot	130 East Commercial Row.
2. Europa Hotel	244 Lake Street.
3. Firenze Hotel	B Street, Sparks.
4. Hotel Europa	Sparks.
5. Italia Hotel	120 East Commercial Row.
6. Italia Hotel Annex	128 East Commercial Row.
7. Mizpah (Pincolini)	248 Lake Street.
8. Piemonte	37 Plaza.
9. Saint Francis	Virginia, between Fourth and East Plaza.
10. Senator Hotel	West at Second.
11. Toscano	238 Lake Street.
12. The New Toscano	246 Lake Street.
13. Travatore Hotel	222 Lake Street.
14. The New Travatore Hotel	210 Lake Street.

ally associated with American Little Italies. The hotels in the area provided similar services in the realm of accommodations, catering to ranch hands, farmers, miners, railroad men, and merchants in town from outlying communities. According to the local Italian press, accommodations ranged from the superior to the basic and appealed to both a business and an ethnic trade.

There are today only faded remnants of these hotels. A walk down Lake Street shows that the Pincolini (Mizpah), Toscano, and Colombo are still standing, although by no means in their former state. The Lake Street and Commercial Row area was a district where deviance and respectability existed side by side; the hotels, at least in their newspaper ads, did not take notice of the negative side of their location. Ads for the hotels appeared regularly in the Italian language press for the first three decades of the twentieth century, and were usually unabashedly glowing in the assessment of amenities offered. While a level of boosterism is to be expected, the persistence of the ads over time suggests that if the hotels were not in fact first class, they were at least respectable enough for the city's Italian trade. In a number of cases, the hotels appear to have been making their pitch directly to the Italian market by emphasizing in their advertisements Italian cooking, cigars, and wines.

The Pincolini was built by the Aldevado Pincolini family, which migrated to Nevada from Palma, Italy, in the last decade of the nineteenth century.[24] Having achieved financial security by working and investing in the western Nevada region, the family decided to build a first-class hotel in Reno. In 1927, the *Bollettino del Nevada* observed that the Pincolini was "the most unique modern hotel in the state of Nevada."[25] Over the years the family continued its involvement with the local hotel scene; in 1967, Bruno and Guido Pincolini bought and refurbished another downtown hotel, the El Cortez.[26]

North of the Pincolini, the Toscano was a respected rival, and claimed to have an excellent Italian restaurant. In 1915, the management proudly ran an ad stating:

> Cooking is strictly Italian. The maximum in cleanliness with well furnished and airy rooms. Wine and liquor served. Famous brand cigars. The best beers.[27]

Next door to the Toscano, the Colombo also sought to provide its patrons with a fine environment. Affirming its carriage-trade aspirations, the management advised in its publicity that the Colombo was "a first class and elegant establishment featuring an Italian restaurant."[28] The Colombo's food and entertainment were also endorsed by local mystery writer Greer Gay in *The Case of the Well Dressed Corpse*.[29] Caught in a tale of murder and intrigue involving the citizens of Newlands Heights, the heroine of the story, Julie Barclay, suggests to her fiancé, Curt Terry, that they escape their present problems and enjoy a pleasant evening at the hotel: "Could you enjoy Italian food tonight? The floor show at the Colombo is super."[30]

---

[24] *Nevada State Journal*, January 27, 1974.
[25] *Bollettino del Nevada, Annual Edition*, October, 1927.
[26] *Nevada State Journal*, biographical questionnaires, February 1, 1969, January 27, 1970.
[27] *Bollettino del Nevada*, November 13, 1915.   [28] *Bollettino del Nevada*, January 19, 1929.
[29] Gay Greer, *The Case of the Well Dressed Corpse* (New York, 1953).
[30] Ibid., 57.

Two other hotels with Italian roots in the vicinity of Lake Street that
are still standing are the Saint Francis on Virginia between Fourth and
East Plaza, and the Senator, on the corner of Second at West Street. The
Saint Francis (the Piazza Building) was built by Santino Piazza in 1925.
Piazza left a small town near Genoa in 1905, and with his wife migrated
to Nevada. He first worked as a ranch hand, then prospered in Reno after
opening a successful produce transportation business. Funds from this
venture assisted in the construction and operation of the hotel property.[31]

The Senator was built by Leopoldo (Pete) and Teresa Saturno, founders
of one of Reno's most prominent Italian families.[32] Leopoldo was born
in San Marco, Italy, and Teresa in Genoa. They were married in Reno
in 1885, and embarked on a life that would earn them a fortune in western Nevada real estate. The Saturnos first built up their equity through
the purchase of large farming and ranching parcels in the Truckee Meadows and Mason Valley. In later years, they parlayed this into additional
ranch holdings around Stockton and Oakdale, California, and into commercial real estate in Reno. Besides the Senator, at one time they also
owned the property on Virginia Street where Harrah's Club stands, and
another parcel near the corner of Virginia and First Street. Although
Leopoldo died in 1919, Teresa lived until 1958; during those years she continued to reside in Reno and was especially helpful to new Italian immigrants arriving in the community.[33]

The rest of the extensive Italian hotel business in Reno is no longer
visible, but impressions can still be gained from the newspaper record.
Italian newspapers of the period carried ads for most of the commercial
hotels in the area, usually indicating the segment of the market that each
establishment sought to serve. While the Travatore and the Europa both
prided themselves as "first class establishments," the more modest Depot
Hotel, run by the Dormio family, restricted its ego to "modest rooms."[34]

---

[31] *Nevada State Journal*, biographical questionnaire file.
[32] *Nevada State Journal*, November 6, 1959, and *Reno Evening Gazette*, August 18, 1960. The Saturno name became world famous in 1959 when two of Leopoldo's and Teresa's children, Joseph
and Victor, gave away $1,200 of Bank of America stock to every resident of their fathers' native
Italian village of San Marco. This generous act was based on a desire to share with the people
of that village some of the riches that their father had found in Nevada.
[33] *Nevada State Journal*, January 27, 1958.
[34] *Bollettino del Nevada*, December 2, 1916, October 13, 1917, and *Italian French Colony News*, December 19, 1908.

In neighboring Sparks, two hotels, the local Europa and the Piemonte, simply provided an address in newspaper advertisements.[35] Of the existing Italian hotels in Reno, only one is the recipient of an endorsement as a lodging place.[36]

In spite of the hoopla contained in many hotel ads regarding superior accommodations, there were of course still unsatisfied customers. In 1907, Frank Guscetti came to Reno to spend a few days and checked into C. Ramelli's (Italian) Swiss American House.[37] In a letter to his brother Louis, he observed that the room cost twenty-five cents and was not very good.

Besides the hotels, a variety of stores met the needs of the Italian shopper. In 1908 Lake Street had an Italian grocery, the Grosseria Italiana Di Zolezzi, which in later years continued to cater to the same clientele as Joe Brunetti's Lake Grocery.[38] During the 1930s a more extensive supermarket-style grocery, The Italian Chain Store Company, opened at Fifth and Virginia. Although a flyer announced that the owners were "direct importers of foreign products and delicacies," the grand-opening sale was decidedly non-ethnic, featuring instead bargains on Heinz's 57 Varieties.[39] Also on Lake, the Nevada Fish Market specialized in a wide variety of fish especially attractive to the Italian palate.[40] Not unaware that money was to be made from the extensive Italian commerce downtown, in 1929 the Reno National Bank ran an ad noting that "Italian is spoken."[41]

John Granata was a major voice of the Italian community during the first four decades of the twentieth century. Granata was born in Torre, Italy, in 1881, and ran an insurance and travel business on Lake Street. In 1911 he made local history when he opened the first car wash in the

[35] *Italian French Colony News*, November 14, 1908.

[36] A review of contemporary American travel guides indicates that of the existing hotels in Reno with Italian roots only the Senator receives any sort of recommendation. In Arthur Fromer's *Where to Stay U.S.A.* (New York, 1982), the Senator is suggested as a budget hotel when staying in Reno. It is compared to the popular Motel 6 chain.

[37] Jacqueline and JoEllen Hall, *Italian-Swiss Settlement in Plumas County* (Chico: Association for Northern California Records and Research, 1973), 25.

[38] *Italian French Colony News*, November 21, 1908, and *Bollettino del Nevada*, December 6, 1916. Both stores were located at 252 Lake Street.

[39] Advertising flyer, Nevada Historical Society collection.

[40] *Bollettino del Nevada*, June 3, 1930. The store was located at 233 Lake Street.

[41] *Bollettino del Nevada*, January 12. 1929.

state on the corner of Lake and Second.[42] While his skill as an entrepreneur and the assistance that he gave to other Italians still hoping to
come to America made him a respected member of the community, it
was in his role as publisher and editor of the *Bollettino del Nevada*, the
largest-circulation Italian-language newspaper in the state, that his influence on the politics of Reno was most keenly felt. As publisher of the
Bollettino, Granata often played a role as the conscience of the Italian
community. He greatly wanted Reno's Italians to remember that they
were *Italian*, and was alarmed at the ease with which members of the
group assimilated into local society. Fearful that as a result of business
success Reno's Italian heritage was on the verge of extinction, he ran an
editorial in the *Bollettino* entitled "What We Want to See in Reno." The
editorial expressed his dismay with the Italian status quo in Reno, and
exhorted his countrymen to consider the folly of their ways:

> We want the Italians of Reno to be the best in Nevada. The Italian com-
> munity of Reno is weak because it lacks cohesion and harmony. We want
> to see our community strong and compact; together. Consider the mer-
> its. We want the Italian family to speak Italian, for there are children of
> Italian families that cannot speak one word of the language. This is a
> great error, a great shortcoming of the parents, taking away from their
> children the advantage of knowing another language and thinking in Ital-
> ian. They should know Italy—the greatness past and present, for they
> will be proud of the country of their origin. It is so important that they
> understand the language. We want to stress that the thoughts and minds
> of Italians are developed along a special line that cannot be changed. The
> majority of Italians cannot think like Anglo-Saxons (those who try do
> not realize the consequences). Our ideal should not be the dollar; one
> does not live by bread alone. Do not forget Italy. Therefore, read Italian
> books, Italian magazines, and play Italian sports. Always hold high the
> name of Italy and her leader.[43]

In the same issue, Sam Platt, "the perennial Republican" candidate
for the Senate and political rival of Key Pittman, wrote a laudatory essay
entitled "Mussolini: Italy's Mighty Man."[44] Platt was no doubt aware of

---

[42] *Nevada State Journal*, November 16, 1962.

[43] *Bollettino del Nevada, Annual Edition, 1927*.

[44] The reference to Platt is found in Russell Elliot, *History of Nevada* (Lincoln, Nebr., 1973), 272.

Italian migrants brought their homeland's traditional vintners' skills to places in the Pacific West endowed with a similar Mediterranean climate. By 1866 annual shipments from the De Mateis Winery in southern California amounted to 66,000 cases. In nearby Guasti, wine entrepreneur Secondo Guasti operated what he described as "the world's largest winery." *Historic Italian Hall Archives.*

Italian political clout, for the article unabashedly praised all things Italian. Written in English, the essay was based on a trip that Platt had made to Italy: "I wished sincerely to see the man (Mussolini) who from every rational point of observation or contact had done so much for Italy."[45]

Governor Fred Balzar, another politician who was well aware of Italian political power, and who was himself of Italian descent, wrote an article that proclaimed a bright future for all the state's citizens. Writing in Italian, Balzar observed that an industrious citizenry, of which Italians were very much a part, was the key to Nevada's progress.[46]

The Dante Club was an important local Italian social organization that stressed some ideas similar to Granata's.[47] Located on Sierra between First and Second, the purpose of the club was to keep alive the interest of Italians in their heritage. It sought to achieve this through an emphasis on sports, rather than just lectures and readings. Organized on the principle of good fellowship, Dante members believed that sports built good character and contributed to an informed citizenry. The club offered its members a full line of sporting activities including baseball, boxing, bowling, football, and bocci. At different times during the year, competitions were held between the branch in Reno and branches in Sacramento and San Francisco. Sporting activities may have been the hook, but the statement of the club's philosophy emphasized the ethnic tradition from which they were descended:

> The Italian people lived under circumstances that encouraged their bringing into flower some of the finest products of the human mind. The spread of that civilization is at least one of the goals of the Dante Club.[50]

An appreciation of the art, music, and literature of Italy was for the members of the Dante Club the needed tonic to calm the mercantile passions of Reno's Italians.

In the end, however, the exhortations of both Granata's *Bollettino* and the Dante Club proved to be of little avail. Italian cultural pursuits in Reno continued to decline. During the period from 1910 to 1930, Ital-

---

[45] *Bollettino del Nevada, Annual Edition, 1927.*
[46] Ibid.
[47] Promotional supplement to the *Bollettino del Nevada 1927 Annual Edition*. The Dante Club was located at 133 Sierra. The building still stands and has several tenants, including the Reno-Tahoe Visitor Center.

ians were well established in business and community activities, and had they wished the old ethnic roots could have prevailed. But that was not their choice. The ethnic past that originally defined Italians as different was quickly lost because of the success and local acceptance of group members as Nevadans, rather than Italians. Italians were not viewed as unique in Nevada, but rather as one of the many European ethnic groups that dotted the citiscapes of the state. Too, there was nothing special to the majority of Italians about being Italian. Both Granata and the Dante Club appear to have ignored the fact that most Italians left Italy with few regrets. Many came to America hoping to forget the bitter memories of life in poverty-stricken mountain towns, and to get a fresh start in a new land. As Hubert S. Nelli reported in a study of Chicago's Italians, once even a modest success was achieved, Italians tended to pick up and move away from old ethnic enclaves. A Little Italy might provide a cultural beachhead for new immigrants to get their bearings in a strange country, but once a course was set upon, the primary objective was to move out and get on with life. While the wish of both Granata's *Bollettino* and the Dante Club that Italian culture would flourish in Reno was noble, there was little desire for it among the majority of their countrymen. Italian culture in Reno was doomed by the success of its own practitioners. The West in general, and Reno in particular, had provided Italians who were willing to take a risk with more opportunity than the East. As Erik Amfitheatorf noted in *The Children of Columbus*:

> The Italians who did manage to cross the Mississippi and settle in the West usually had a far better chance of rising economically and socially. They were newcomers in an opportunistic, if frequently dangerous, world of newcomers.

The economic achievements of the hoteliers, store owners, and investors meant that they could afford a better life. Reno's Little Italy, as well as the tightly knit ethnic bonds that existed in Italian communities throughout the state, were of a time and place. The images and values that allowed Italians to perceive their social space in Reno as a Little Italy were transitory. Once having gained acceptance, there was little economic incentive to hold on to the past.

As in Reno's "Little Italy," immigrants who came to western communities as laborers soon saved enough to purchase ranches, homes, and businesses. Enterprises included general merchandise stores, hotels, and theaters. Piedmontese Giovanni Piuma, who settled in El Monte in 1884, operated Piuma's Italian Pharmacy, which also included a grocery store that operated for nearly a century. The facility also served as Piuma's offices as Italian consular agent to Los Angeles. *Courtesy of the editor.*

PART FOUR

The Laborers

I TALIAN MIGRANTS who settled in the West often experienced greater economic opportunity and upward social mobility than did their counterparts along the eastern seaboard. They learned the language and customs and frequently became active members of their communities. The unfamiliar conditions they encountered in this new land rarely resembled their Old World environment. As a result, those inherited practices and traditional customs that did not provide useful solutions were soon replaced. In the West the diminished influence of traditional folkways and beliefs was further weakened by the fluidity of the cultural conditions in rapidly growing settlements inhabited by a cross section of newcomers. In that setting Italians became co-workers in newly settled communities extending from New Orleans to Montana—from Kansas to Colorado.

The migrants were drawn to the great adventure of the frontier by hope as well as by the memory of scarcity. Whether they were Sicilian settlers in Texas or Calabrian farmers in the corn fields of Kansas, memories of their past compelled them westward. As late as 1900 agricultural workers in the southern part of Italy earned less that thirty-five cents a day. An unskilled worker earned little more, and a trained artisan was given approximately a dollar and a half each day. As a result, workers in the southernmost provinces of Basilicata, Calabria, and Puglia consumed no more than ten pounds of meat per year, a small amount when compared to a British worker's annual ration of fifty-seven pounds per year. But the impoverished land often held by absentee landlords yielded nothing more.

It is not surprising, therefore, that in the nineteenth century 80 percent of the migration to the United States emanated from the south. At
the same time, Italians from the more northern provinces of Piedmont
and Lombardia were being driven from their vineyards by the blight of
phyloxera and continually diminishing agricultural yields. But urban
centers like Turin and Milan had not yet developed sufficient employment opportunities for them in the manufacturing sector. Consequently, by the latter part of the nineteenth century a general exodus severely
diminished the population of towns like Asti and Bosco Nero. Many of
the emigrants departed for North or South America from the Ligurian
port of Genoa. In 1850 the Genoese ship *La Democrazia* was, in fact, the
first Italian vessel to sail into San Francisco bay.

Among the trans-Atlantic voyagers was a scattering of political exiles
fleeing the partisan tumult surrounding Italian unification efforts. Some
were supporters of the king of Savoy. Others were Mazzini republicans.
Many came to avoid political retribution when their regimes fell from
power, while others came to avoid military service mandated by a suc-
cession of political administrations. Among them was Alessandro Garbi,
a Florentine hero of *Il Risorgimento,* who later served as the first sur-
veyor of San Mateo County, California.

While western settlements were not as densely populated with Italians as New York or Boston, Italian migrants were distributed throughout a wide range of western communities. As early as 1800 they had
begun cultivating the lands of southeast Texas. By 1819 migrants from
Sicily and Calabria were draining the boggy marshlands of Louisiana
to plant vegetables and berries. Elsewhere they cultivated cotton, corn,
and cane sugar. In the city of New Orleans Italians soon dominated the
French Market and were successful importers of produce from Central
America. They established local truck farms and dominated the fish and
oyster trades. Others operated ferry services, manufactured barometers,
and participated in the city's musical and theatrical life. It was in New
Orleans that the gifted soprano, Adelina Patti, made her professional
debut in 1855.

By 1885 Italians had established an agricultural colony near the banks
of the mighty Mississippi which drained the heartland of the continent.
Concentrated in Coahoma, Washington, and Bolivar counties, they out-
numbered all other foreign groups. In *The Immigrant Upraised* Andrew

Rolle adds that during that same decade large numbers of Italians settled in Arkansas to work on the Mississippi levees. Others were brought
by Austin Corbin under special agreement with the mayor of Rome, to
cultivate cotton at his colony, Sunnyside, Arkansas. The new settlers,
mostly urban traders and craftsmen ill-equipped for agricultural life,
arrived aboard Corbin's own Anchor steamship line. Proving that their
strength was in their self-sufficiency, the newcomers survived harsh conditions by raising okra, beans, peppers, and greens to supplement their
scarce rations of meat. After Corbin's death, the community, which by
then had built its own church and school, faltered as malaria began to
claim the residents.

The economic and environmental challenges posed by the South, as
well as outbursts of nativist hostility in which sixteen Italian migrants
were lynched in 1891 and 1899, forced the migrants, at the urging of the
Italian government, to move farther north and west. In some instances,
Italian settlers transmigrated from Kentucky and Arkansas to the more
heavily populated European settlements in Missouri, especially St. Louis.
Others like a group of Waldensians from northern Italy had journeyed
first to Uruguay. Lured by railroad lands offered for fifteen dollars per
acre in 40-acre parcels, families sometimes joined together to make pur-
chases in common. Others availed themselves of the several homestead
laws which offered quarter sections (160 acres) to both citizens and future
citizens who agreed to improve the land over a five-year period. By 1920
there were almost 15,000 Italians in Missouri, three-fifths located in the
cosmopolitan western gateway city of St. Louis where they organized
fraternal groups and published several newspapers.

In southeastern Kansas they worked as coal miners. At first, hired
to break labor strikes, they developed into an important segment of the
Kansas labor force. Italians from Missouri journeyed as far away as Illinois to work in the coal mines. Migrants also mined coal in Indiana and
worked the mineral resources of the Vermillion and Mesabi ranges in
Minnesota. In Nebraska Italian migrants clustered around Omaha. As
a result, they were more cohesive there than in most western communities. By the turn of the century they had effectively cultivated a political presence there.

In Iowa, the heartland of the continent where Father Samuel Charles
Mazzuchelli had served so successfully as priest, educator, and builder,

Italians settled most frequently in northern sections. There they cultivated small parcels of land or worked in towns with names like Verona, Genoa, and Parma, gradually amassing enough to purchase parcels of the highly productive Iowa acreage where, in addition to the crops, they raised chickens, pigs, goats, and, when affordable, a horse to aid in tedious farming tasks.

Like other westering pioneers, Italian settlers were forced westward by dust, drought, and erratic business cycles, which depreciated their savings. The frontier could as easily break as make a man's fortune. In the course of their wanderings these transmigrants avoided the Dakotas, located in the north central prairies. In fact, few immigrants except Scandinavians attempted to farm the vast expanses located in that generally inhospitable climate. Consequently, by 1920 both states reported a total of 589 residents who had been born in Italy.

In contrast, in neighboring Montana in the 1870s Italians responded positively to the appeals of local leaders looking for settlers to develop their territory. A decade later a group of Italian Swiss settled in Billings. Since passage from Chicago cost only fifty dollars and land sold for three dollars an acre, Italians soon settled in Meaderville and became employees of the Anaconda Copper Mining Company. There were comparatively few, however, attracted by what they perceived as treeless plateaus of buffalo grass in neighboring Wyoming. A handful of settlers from the northern provinces of Italy worked on rail lines, herded, or operated truck farms supplying Cheyenne and Laramie. By the 1930s no more than 2,000 Italians had settled there.

Some Italians mined the mineral resources of the Northwest, as evidenced when a massive underground explosion in Diamond, Washington, killed eighteen, thirteen of whom were Italians. But the majority of the local Italian migrants were loggers. As early as 1907 some timber men had been organized by Joseph Ettor of the Industrial Workers of the World. The strike that ensued spread throughout the logging camps of the Northwest. On the eve of World War I the IWW expanded its organizing efforts among loggers encouraging labor protests in 1916 and again in 1917.

The arid land drained by the Colorado River, commonly referred to as the Southwest, held little appeal for Italian migrants. Its vast unwatered terrain demanded dry farming skills unfamiliar to them. Instead the scattered settlers worked on the construction of railroads, dams, and harbors. Others mined coal and minerals including zinc, lead, and copper. In neighboring New Mexico they herded sheep and mined coal, while Jesuit priests from the Neapolitan Province ministered, building churches and schools for fifty-two years, from 1867 to 1919. Although few, the number of Italian migrants trebled between 1870 and 1880, a rate that continued until 1910.

The promise of striking another Comstock Lode attracted some Italians, but a significant portion pursued the more entrepreneurial side of mining life, operating hotels, restaurants, and boarding houses, which provided temporary homes to many single male migrants. Italians were also grocers, distillers, shoemakers, tailors, watchmakers, and itinerant peddlers.

The Italians employed as miners were often caught up in disputes with local laborers who feared the immigrants would drive wages down and also with owners who feared the immigrants would be more inclined to go on strike. The fact that anarchism, a traditional tool of Italian political activists, had become a weapon of the United States labor movement raised citizens' concerns about migrants' participation in union issues. Northern Italians, who had an established tradition of organized labor activism, were the most supportive of labor causes. As a result, when many of them were excluded from the craft-based American Federation of Labor, they joined more radical groups like the Industrial Workers of the World.

In 1882 five hundred disgruntled migrant miners descended on Denver to protest unfair working conditions. The result was the formation of the Italian Protective and Benevolent Association.

Anti-foreign sentiments were particularly volatile in mining districts when a surplus of workers occurred. In Colorado, where Italians worked as coal miners as well as granite and field-stone quarriers, cutters and dressers, their presence in 1905 exceeded 5½ percent of the population, resulting in a rash of minor confrontations along the mining frontier. These were soon sensationalized by the local press, further raising tensions.

Despite labor tensions, the mineral resources and the rich agricultural lands of Colorado attracted Italians from the mountainous regions in the north of Italy who found the Alpine setting particularly hospitable. Many had been recruited by promoters who were located in Italy but represented Colorado labor bosses. They were such a sought-after labor group that in 1910 the Colorado State Board of Immigration made a concerted effort to attract additional Italians experienced in dairying and fruit-growing.

In Utah the Mormon economy quickly capitalized on the Italian migrants' deeply ingrained work ethic and their many artisanal skills. They labored as miners and farmers and also served as church functionaries. By 1920 first-generation Italians constituted 5 percent of Utah's foreign-born population of 59,200.

In contrast with their relatively sparse settlement in the Southwest, large numbers of Italians displayed a pronounced affinity for California. In the eighteenth century Italian Jesuits had established outposts in Baja California. In ensuing years Italians, including Captain Alessandro Malaspina and ship's doctor Paolo Emilio Botta, made landfall in California. The latter's account, published in 1841, generated considerable interest in Europe.

Italian merchants and ranchers first appeared in Los Angeles, Monterey, and San Diego as early as the 1820s. Beginning in 1849, the Gold Rush attracted a considerable number of migrants from Piedmont, Liguria, and Tuscany to northern California. Participating in what they perceived to be a great frontier adventure, they searched for loose placer gold, especially along the concave bends of river banks, eventually resorting to sluices and long toms. Unfortunately, the average daily yield soon fell from sixteen dollars a day in 1849 to barely enough to pay the inflated price of an apple or a canister of corn in 1852.

The more adventurous moved to Amador, Tuolomne, and Calaveras counties, where they searched for the richer veins of quartz in the Mother Lode region at sites like Italian Bar or La Fortuna Bar in Nevada City. In some shaft mines they worked alongside Cornish and Alsatian hardrock miners or as muckers scooping out ore and discarding the tailings for four dollars a day. Others turned to farming in the lightly populated gold country areas where, unaffected by intruders, they preserved their traditions over the generations.

Liberato Del Vecchio of Lucca used his savings from fourteen years as a mining foreman to launch a successful grocery store in Los Angeles. Others left the gold fields to become loggers, dairymen, boat builders, or purveyors of fishing supplies. Two hundred from the Gulf of Genoa settled around San Francisco Bay and became fishermen. Some had truck farms outside San Francisco. Others were scavengers or proprietors of hotels, boarding houses, and restaurants which crowded the Latin Quarter in North Beach. Some of San Francisco's many Lucchesi may have been *figurinae* noted for their skills in casting and decorating plaster figures which were successfully traded along the streets of most major American cities during the latter part of the nineteenth century.

Many former Italian argonauts became business people around Sacramento and the Bay Area, including confectioner Domenico Ghirardelli, a mining-camp peddler who became a successful manufacturer of liqueurs and chocolates and one of the founders of the Italian Hospital Association in San Francisco. Another San Franciscan, Nicola Larco, became a prosperous importer of foodstuffs, an owner of a silkworm operation, and served as the local representative of the Chilean government. To the benefit of the community Larco provided the financial support for *L'Eco della Colonia*, the first Italian newspaper published west of the Mississippi River. Larco also served as the president of the Italian Benevolent Society, the oldest continuing Italian institution in the United States today. A biographer was inspired to refer to him as *"l'astro maggiore della nostra colonia"* (the major star of our community).

By 1850 the community of Italian migrants was large enough for King Victor Emmanuel II of Sardinia, of whom Ligurians and Piedmontese were subjects, to authorize a consular office in San Francisco It was headed briefly by Count Leonetto Cipriani, and later by Federico Biesta. In his official report submitted to Prime Minister Count Camillo Cavour, Biesta listed sixteen Sardinian businessmen in the region offering coffee, spice, hardware, and musical instruments. Two owned a steam-operated macaroni and vermicelli factory. Another manufactured imitation marble.

Biesta estimated that by the 1850s the Italian population had reached at least six thousand throughout California, six hundred alone in burgeoning San Francisco. Of these Biesta declared, "the Italian population is one of the best, most active and hardworking in California."

Despite the large numbers of Italian migrants, reports of discrimination and abuse, aside from the Foreign Miners Tax passed in 1850, were rare. Among the few was a formal protest lodged with the California governor by San Francisco consul general Salvatore Rocca objecting to the treatment of Italian workers in the state's lumber industry. The relative absence of strife was, in part, a reflection of the wide dispersal of Italian settlers. Fertile land was available and the migrants, attracted by the opportunity to cultivate the soil, largely avoided concentrated settlements.

Several other forces, at work even before their arrival in California, accelerated the process of assimilation into the host culture. Most Italian arrivals were transmigrants who had been exposed to the language and culture of Americans over a period of time. In addition, the migrants' attainment of their immediate goal of reaching California added to their confidence and lessened the need to look back to the Old World traditions for reassurance and support. Finally, many of the recent arrivals now shared a unique westering experience with other California settlers. This bound the migrants as closely to their neighbors as to their past.

As elsewhere, the new arrivals welcomed the opportunity to settle on their own land. Juan Bandini, who arrived in San Diego via Argentina around 1819; Giovanni Batista Leandri, who arrived in Los Angeles in 1823; and Alessandro Repetto, who came a decade later, all raised herds of cattle on the Mexican land grants. Migrants settling farther north farmed the rich lands of the Central Valley and the Sacramento delta. Marco Fontana and Rosario Di Giorgio both developed agricultural empires which included growing, harvesting, processing, and transporting their produce to market. Their abundant harvests introduced Americans to the artichoke, bell pepper, eggplant, and broccoli, among others. The canning of these foods for shipment and sale sometimes led to bitter labor disputes, as Elizabeth Reis describes in "The AFL, the IWW and Bay Area Cannery Workers."

In several coastal areas Italian Swiss from the region of Ticino successfully pursued dairying and cheese-making. Other Italian Swiss established a thriving cooperative at Asti in northern California, which by 1900 had become the second-largest winery in California. Even earlier, in 1869, the forty-three wineries located in Los Angeles, many owned by Italian vintners, were producing four million gallons of wine. By the turn of the century Secondo Guasti, a Piedmontese, created a self-contained village at Rancho Cucamonga on the outskirts of Los Angeles that he

described as "the globe's largest vineyard." By 1900 California was producing table grapes, raisins, fortified spirits and thirty million gallons of
wine, which as early as 1889 had begun to garner awards worldwide.

Soon after arriving in gold-rush San Francisco, Genoese and other
northern Italians returned to their traditional occupation as fishermen.
When they later turned to refuse hauling, Sicilians replaced them at sea.
With the advantage of their traditional Italian boats, the *paranzellas* and
feluccas, and using the very efficient purse seiner nets, they were processing thirty-five million pounds of fish by 1911. Italian fishermen were
equally successful in Monterey, San Diego, and Santa Barbara, where
the catch yielded halibut, barracuda, bonita, bass, and smelt.

The San Pedro/Long Beach fishing fleet, which also attracted Japanese
and Yugoslavs, was dominated by settlers from Sicily and Ischia. San
Pedro's high-volume operations, which included canneries like Marca
Genova, focused on the substantial sardine catch. A three-month strike
at the onset of the sardine season in 1936 led to a policy of ongoing negotiations between the owners, the representatives of the local fish-packing
industry, and the Italian Fishermen's Protective Association. However,
even this effective means of heading off potential labor disputes could not
offset the inevitable economic decline resulting from the shifting migratory pattern of the sardine. It was an economic decline made worse by
increased federal regulation of fishing and increased foreign competition.

In his article, "California's Fishermen's Festivals," Carlo Speroni looks
at the fishermen's celebrations patterned after old-world customs. In
San Francisco the October event included the blessing of the fleet followed by a *festa*. At the time of the full moon in September Monterey
fishermen participated in religious services culminating in a procession
with a statue of the Sicilian patron saint of fishermen, Santa Rosalia,
followed by a parade of decorated boats and festivities. The best known
celebration was the San Pedro Fishermen's Fiesta, begun in 1938. By 1952
the televised event featured floats aboard a flotilla of nearly a hundred
boats, contests, dances, a wholesale fish market, and other events attended by 150,000. In contrast, the San Diego fishermen's festival in late
spring was a largely religious festival dedicated to the Holy Spirit, reflecting the traditions of the Portuguese who constituted the majority of San
Diego fishermen.

Italians from the earliest days of settlement in California earned their livelihood as entertainers and artists. San Francisco's cosmopolitan population provided a congenial audience for visiting performers like Adelina Patti, Eliza Biscacianti, and Luisa Tetrazzini and were loyal patrons of the second-oldest opera group in the United States. At the Apollo Theatre Italian actors transformed Stenterello, a stock eighteenth-century harlequin, into Farfariello, a comic interpretation of the Italian migrant himself.

In addition to a host of Italian impersonators and ventriloquists, trained Italian artisans made a lasting impression on California art and architecture. There were craftsmen who were masters of terrazzo, *sgrafitto*, and *scagliola*, a process which simulates marbleized surfaces. At the Gladding McBean factory in Lincoln, California, Tuscan craftsmen from the town of Pietra Santa guided the manufacture of artistic terra cotta tile, which today graces buildings nationwide. They are also graced by frescoes, murals, and statuary created by the numerous Italian migrant artists who have chosen to make America their home.

Perhaps the most familiar art form to which Italians contributed from the outset was the motion picture. The thriving Italian cinema efforts in the earliest decades of the twentieth century were dealt a calamitous blow by World War I. As a result, an experienced cadre of film directors like Roberto Vignolo, musicians like Nicola Donatelli, and set designers like Carlo Romanelli were available to travel west to Hollywood, where film pioneers like David W. Griffith and William Ince engaged their services to help nurture the fledgling domestic cinema industry emerging in southern California.

Clearly, Italian migrants embraced the myriad opportunities available to them in the lands west of the Mississippi. Ironically, one of the opportunities was provided by the sand lots of San Francisco where informal baseball games would lead some to major league stardom far from home, as Lawrence Baldassaro explains in "Go East Paesani: Early Italian Major Leaguers from the West Coast."

While they found some settings more hospitable and inviting than others, the migrants invariably discovered a variety of economic opportunities, shared in the infectious optimism, and thrived in an atmosphere that encouraged individuality and experimentation as they traversed the lands of the Trans-Mississippi West.

California
Fishermen's Festivals

By Charles Speroni

I T IS A WELL-KNOWN FACT that almost all occupations have their patron saints. Since bakers have St. Nicholas of Myra, cab drivers St. Fiacre, carpenters St. Joseph, shoemakers St. Crispin, etc., it is to be expected that fishermen, who lead an especially dangerous life, should also have their patron saint. In many parts of Europe St. Andrew—who is also the patron saint of Scotland and of Russia—is the generally recognized protector of fishermen; but, in various parts of the Christian world, other saints share with the apostle-fisherman of New Testament fame the prayers and vows of the fishing folk. Saint Peter, for instance, brother of St. Andrew, and like him an apostle-fisherman, became a maritime saint, and was often invoked in storms. It is said that Hernán Cortes chose St. Andrew as his patron saint.[1] St. Anthony, who once preached a sermon to the fishes, is another favorite patron saint of fishermen;[2] Saint Nicholas of Myra, who resuscitated a dead sailor, is also

---

[1] Cf. F. S. Bassett, *Sea Phantoms or Legends and Superstitions of the Sea and of Sailors* (Chicago: Morril, Higgins, 1892), 81. The reader will find many other saints mentioned by Bassett. St. Peter is honored also in Sicily. On the eve of his *festa* day, June 29, a yearly festival is held in a section of Palermo inhabited by fishermen. In the evening, decorated and illuminated boats ply through the old harbor. Cf. G. Pitrè, *Biblioteca delle tradizioni popolari siciliane*, vol. 12 (*Spettacoli e feste*), 325, and also Saverio La Sorsa, "Marinai e pescatori siciliani," *Lares* (Organo del Comitato per le Tradizioni Popolari [Florence]), 6, no. 1–2 (1935): 81.

[2] Cf. this interesting passage in Longfellow's *The Golden Legend*, toward the end of Part 5:

> She is a galley of the Gran Duca,
> That, through the fear of the Algerines,
> Convoys those lazy brigantines,　　　　　　　　*(continued, next page)*

much honored, especially by South Italian, Greek, and Russian sailors. At one time there were 370 chapels in England alone dedicated to this saint.[3] Saint James, who traveled from Palestine to Spain on a marble boat without oars, sails, or rudder, is the protector of Spanish seamen. Saint Mark, the presence of whose lifeless body stilled a storm while it was being brought from Egypt to Venice, is the patron of Venetian mariners.[4] Needless to say, the Virgin Mary occupies a very special place in the hearts of all Catholic fishermen, and countless are the shrines erected to her by seafaring folk in all parts of the world.[5] I hardly need to call to mind that Columbus's flagship was named in her honor. But patron saints vary from country to country and often from town to town; in general, seafaring people in the Mediterranean venerate the saints of their own town or district, and pay homage at their shrine.[6] In this connection it is interesting to note that just as the ancient Greeks carved on the prows of their ships the image of the divinity under whose tutelage they had placed the craft, the fishermen of southern Italy paint on their boats likenesses of the Virgin Mary or of their favorite patron saints and name the vessels themselves in their honor.[7]

In various parts of the Christian world, closely connected with the religious fervor of seafaring people, there is the custom of blessing the sea and the ships. Although little is known about this custom in non-Christian countries, it is known that throughout the ages people from many parts of the globe have tried with various ceremonies to propitiate the favor of the gods of the sea. The ancient Greeks and Romans, for example, did this with libations and sacrifices of animals and even

---

Laden with wine and oil from Lucca.
Now all is ready, high and low;
Blow, blow, good Saint Antonio!

. . . .
With the breeze behind us, on we go;
Not too much, good Saint Antonio!

[3] Cf. Bassett, *Sea Phantoms*, 79.
[4] Cf. Ettore Bravetta, *Le Leggende del mare e le superstizioni dei marinai* (Milan, 1908), 29.
[5] Pious legends indicate that the Virgin Mary began protecting seamen as early as the year 200. Cf. Bravetta, *Le Leggende*, 26.
[6] Cf. Bassett, *Sea Phantoms*, 84. See also Paul Sébillot, *Le folklore des pêcheurs* (Paris, 1901), 88 ff.
[7] Cf. S. La Sorsa, "Folklore Marinaro di Puglia," *Lares* 1, no. 1 (1930): 29.

of human beings.[8] Boats are, and have been in the past, blessed or, at least, wished well on various occasions: upon being launched, before setting out on a fishing trip, before sailing forth to battle, and before departing for distant seas. Momentous indeed were the public blessings of the ill-fated Spanish Armada and of the more peaceful ships of Christopher Columbus and of Vasco de Gama.[9] According to Sébillot, the blessing of the sea and of vessels was more general once than it is now. Festivities in European countries were fairly simple and religious in nature: an occasional boat parade, processions with the clergy, the cross, and holy images, recital of litanies for the repose of the dead, etc.[10] In certain localities the blessing was given at the beginning of the fishing season; in others the boats were blessed more than once a year.[11] In southern Italy and in Sicily, where folk customs and festivals have not changed as much as in many other parts of Italy and of Europe, fishermen's festivals still thrive. In Sicily, for instance, to ensure a good fishing season the holy image of the local patron saint, varying from town to town, is brought to the seashore so that the sea and the boats may be blessed in his name.[12] Similar ceremonies are held throughout southern Italy. In certain localities festivities are very elaborate and last from one to two days. In Apulia, for example, besides the numerous religious ceremonies that take place within and without the church, on the date of the feast of the patron saint fishermen do not work; they don their best clothes and refrain from saying or doing anything likely to incur disfavor. They participate in the procession that accompanies the image of the saint to the seashore. Amid an air of gaiety and music, the holy image is placed in a colorfully decorated boat, and a regular boat excursion takes place. Some of the fishermen, in their religious fervor, jump into the sea and swim for awhile alongside the boats.[13] Finally the procession returns to the church, and later there is dancing, singing, and merrymaking.

---

[8] Cf. Bravetta, *Le Leggende*, 23.

[9] Cf. Bassett, *Sea Phantoms*, 402. Cf. also Angelo S. Rappoport, *Superstitions of Sailors* (London, 1928), 270.   [10] Cf. P. Sébillot, *Le folklore*, 104 ff.

[11] Ibid., 113.

[12] Cf. G. Pitrè, *Biblioteca delle tradizioni popolari siciliane*, Vol. 25 (*La famiglia, la casa, la vita del popolo siciliano*), 398. An excellent article on Sicilian fishermen was published by S. La Sorsa in *Lares* 6, nos. 1–2 (1935): 75–83, and 7, no. 4 (1936): 253–65.

[13] Cf. S. La Sorsa, "Folklore Marinaro di Puglia," in *Lares* 1 nos. 2–3 (1930): 30–31. In this article, the author describes also other interesting activities and festivals of Apulian fishermen.

Fishermen's festivals have been held at most major ports along the Pacific coast. Most of the coastal fishing fleet is operated by Italians, Slavonians, and Portuguese. The ceremonies are essentially religious, are dedicated to a patron saint and include the blessing of the fleet, followed by a variety of social activities. *Courtesy Mr. J. J. Savant.*

It is not within the limits of this article to survey the vast field of fishermen's festivals and lore; it should be pointed out, however, that these festivals are not confined to the Mediterranean basin or even to Europe. Information scattered in the few works I have quoted and in others not cited here clearly indicates that such maritime folkways are known in many parts of the world.

In the United States, fishermen's celebrations similar to those treated above are held on both the Atlantic and Pacific shores. This is not surprising if we bear in mind that a large percentage of the fishing folk of America are European immigrants who have brought with them many of their cherished customs and traditions.

In California, fishermen's festivals are held at the more important fishing centers of the coast: from north to south, they are held at San Francisco, Monterey, San Pedro, and Point Loma (San Diego). In San Francisco the fiesta is sponsored by Italian (mainly Sicilian) fishermen; in Monterey also by the Sicilian fishermen; in San Pedro mainly by the Italian and Slavonian fishermen; and at Point Loma by the Portuguese. The first three festivals are very similar to each other, and also are patterned after the respective old-world customs and usages. At all four ports mentioned the ceremonies are essentially religious in nature; but at the conclusion of the religious ceremonies, the "fiesta" spirit holds sway, and the carnival aspect of the observance dominates for the balance of the day (or days). Let us look at the four festivals individually.

San Francisco

ALTHOUGH THERE HAVE BEEN a few irregularities—for instance, in 1947, when the festival was observed on Sunday, September 28[14]—San Francisco's Italians gather to pay homage to their protectress, Maria Santissima del Lume (Our Lady Mary of Light), on the first Sunday in October. Festivities are well attended and impressive but are not on the same grandiose scale as at San Pedro, and in recent years at Monterey. This more modest display is undoubtedly assignable to two reasons: in San Pedro and in Monterey the chambers of commerce and other civic and religious organizations have taken a keen interest in the promotion of the festival, whereas in San Francisco this ancient observance has remained strictly a traditional fishermen's affair; also, in San Francisco the fishermen's festival comes at the same time of year when San Francisco is busy staging the colossal, nationally known Columbus Day celebration.[15]

The preparation of the *festa* is in the hands of the Society of Maria Santissima del Lume. This religious society was founded in 1937[16] to do

---

[14] Cf. the description of this festival in the San Francisco *Chronicle* of Monday, September 29, 1947.

[15] For the history and description of the Columbian festivities in San Francisco, cf. Charles Speroni, "The Development of the Columbus Day Pageant of San Francisco," *Western Folklore*, 7 (1948): 325–35.

[16] The society was founded by Mrs. Rosa Tarantino, who has been the president of it every year since 1937. Mrs. Tarantino, in her Sicilian dialect, gave me a great deal of information not to be found in the local newspapers. She was also kind enough to give me two large photographs of the procession.

honor to Mary, Mother of Light, protectress of the fishermen of Porticello, a village near Palermo in Sicily. According to a legend, untold years ago, some Porticello fishermen found washed ashore a white marble statue with the inscription, *Maria Santissima del Lume*. The statue, of incredible beauty, was taken to the church and placed upon the altar, only to be found again the next day on the beach. When this happened twice more, the fishermen brought the church to the statue. Thus, Our Lady of Light became their patroness. In San Francisco the Sicilian fishermen have a large painting of Maria Santissima del Lume, which is kept in the Church of SS. Peter and Paul at North Beach, the heart of the Italian colony.

Ceremonies have varied slightly from year to year, but basically they are as follows: a solemn Mass in the Church of SS. Peter and Paul; procession of a few hundred people, with the clergy, members of the Madonna del Lume Society dressed in white gowns and blue satin capes (the colors of Our Lady of Light), pupils of SS. Peter and Paul parochial school, a flower-decorated float carrying the image of Our Lady of Light, a few children dressed like angels, and a band. Although in a couple of "election" years there has been a "Queen" of the *festa*, it is not customary to have one, for the Queen is Maria Santissima del Lume. The procession goes from Washington Square, where the church is located, to the famous Fishermen's Wharf. Here, in the presence of several thousands of people, after a few appropriate speeches by religious dignitaries and civic leaders, the pastor of the Church of SS. Peter and Paul blesses the sea and also the fishing boats, which, on several occasions, have been colorfully decorated. Then the procession forms again and returns to Washington Square, where additional speeches are made and prayers recited. The religious rites are concluded with a rosary and solemn benediction. Later a bazaar is held for the rest of the day and evening, but the spirit of the *festa* is evident in all parts of North Beach, down to the cafes on the pier.

In recent years, because of repeated poor fishing seasons, the spirit of the festival has not been as ardent as usual. Many of the boats were forced to sail south to San Pedro, and the boats at the wharf lay unadorned. I was told that in Porticello also the celebration of Maria Santissima del Lume takes place on the first Sunday of October.

MONTEREY

IN MONTEREY the two-day fishermen's festival is celebrated in September, and at present the date is set to coincide with the full moon, for, at full moon, sardine fishing is poor, and the fishing folk are in port and can participate in the ceremonies.

Although at Monterey there are fishermen of many nationalities, it is the large and religious Sicilian group that is responsible for the colorful festival.[17] Since 1934, it seems, the Sicilians of Monterey have carried the statue of Santa Rosalia, their patron saint, through the streets of Monterey to the side of the bay, where churchmen have asked in her name that all fishermen be protected while at sea, and that their catch of fish be abundant.[18] Santa Rosalia is the favorite saint of Sicilians from Palermo and vicinity. Santa Rosalia, 1130–60, died unknown in a mountain cave near the city of Palermo, where she had spent a lifetime of prayer and penance. It was not until four hundred years later, when a plague ravaged Palermo, that a poor soapmaker went to the cave to ask for divine guidance. Santa Rosalia appeared before him and requested that she be given a Christian burial in return for putting an end to the plague. Her bones were paraded through the streets of Palermo and the plague ceased. She became a saint by popular acclaim, and the cave, overlooking Palermo, is now a shrine. (It has been visited and loved by many great people; especially famous is the visit paid by the German poet Goethe.) When the Sicilian fishermen came to Monterey to fish for sardines, they brought their veneration for Santa Rosalia with them.[19]

---

[17] The fact that the fishermen of a certain nationality dominate the festivities of a port, does not necessarily indicate that they form the majority of the fishermen of that port. At Gloucester (Massachusetts), for instance, where the Portuguese hold a yearly blessing of the fishing fleet, they are not as numerous as the Italians. In June 1953, of 202 vessels, only 32 were Portuguese; no fewer than 100 were Italian. Cf. the brief but interesting article illustrated with full color kodachromes by Luis Marden, "Gloucester Blesses its Portuguese Fleet," *National Geographic Magazine* 104, no. 1 (July 1953): 75–84. The first blessing at Gloucester occurred in 1945. The Portuguese fleet that goes every year from Portugal to Newfoundland and Greenland fishing for cod is also blessed. Cf. Alan Villiers, "I Sailed with Portugal's Captains Courageous," *National Geographic Magazine* 101, no. 5 (May 1952): 565 ff.

[18] The Reverend Father John J. Ryan of San Carlo Church informed me that although the statue of Santa Rosalia was acquired in 1934, the religious festival proper was inaugurated a few years before that date.

[19] On the feast of Santa Rosalia in Sicily (September 4), cf. G. Pitrè: *Biblioteca delle tradizioni popolari siciliane*, vol. 12 (*Spettacoli e feste*), 365–77.

At Monterey the statue of the saint is kept in the right wing of the transept of San Carlos Church. The early processions with the statue to fishermen's wharf were not recorded by the local newspapers, but they were identical with those held right after World War II. There were no festivities during the war years. The traditional festival of Santa Rosalia was resumed on September 8, 1946, and that year there was a Mass at San Carlos Church, a breakfast, and at 2:00 P.M. the procession from the church to the wharf, followed by the blessing of the fleet. At the conclusion of the religious ceremonies (sermon, rosary, and blessing), the statue of Santa Rosalia was carried back to the church, where the closing religious services were conducted. In the evening there was a dance at the parochial hall.[20] Similar celebrations were observed annually between 1947 and 1950.

In 1951 the Monterey fishermen's festival was celebrated on a much larger scale. Whereas—as it is also customary in Sicily—the Santa Rosalia festival was observed either on September 4, if it fell on a Sunday, or on the Sunday following that date, in 1951 it was decided to hold the festival on a Sunday of full moon. In September 1951 the moon was full about the middle of the month, and so on September 2 and 3 (Sunday and Monday, respectively), a combination Labor Day and Santa Rosalia Fishermen's Festival variety show was held to raise funds for the big event of September 15–16. There was also a "Queen Contest," and more than two thousand people participated in the double holiday.[21] On the weekend of the 15th and 16th brilliantly colored fish enmeshed in nets were strung across the downtown streets of Monterey. There were parades, water events, fireworks, etc.—a lighthearted spectacle of fun that contrasted with the solemn religious rites of the Santa Rosalia feast. Sicilian fishermen's stocking caps were the official costume of the fiesta and they were distributed gratis by the Chamber of Commerce. In order to give the reader a better idea of the entire spectacle I shall list here some of the numerous events: on Saturday there was an exhibition of the works of the Monterey Peninsula artists, the crowning of the Queen of the Wharf, a parade, skiff races, greased-pole-climbing contests over water and on land, tugs-of-war, pie- and watermelon-eating contests, sack

---

[20] Cf. the Monterey *Peninsula Herald* of September 9, 1946.
[21] Cf. the Monterey *Peninsula Herald* of Tuesday, September 4, 1951.

races, Sicilian dances in costume, an illuminated boat parade held at night, fireworks, and street dancing. On Sunday festivities began with an open-air Mass. Then there was the traditional procession to the wharf, the blessing of the fishing fleet in the name of Santa Rosalia, and band music. In the afternoon there was dancing, and then the parade of decorated boats over the course from Pacific Grove to Monterey. In the evening at a grand ball, prizes were awarded to the best decorated boats.[22]

The festivities held in 1951 were practically duplicated in 1952 and 1953.[23] In 1953 there was no boat parade; instead, there was a land parade of many floats through gaily decorated streets. Last year (1954), I was informed, because of the ever poorer fishing off the Monterey shores, festivities were of an exclusively religious nature, being limited to the procession of Santa Rosalia.[24]

SAN PEDRO

THE SAN PEDRO FISHERMEN'S FESTIVAL is the best known of California's maritime festivals, and its fame has reached many parts of the United States.[25] It has been televised since 1949. Furthermore, three full-color kodachrome pictures taken during the 1953 festival were recently printed in the *National Geographic Magazine*.[26] Because of this, and also because it is a truly grandiose spectacle with an interesting history, I decided to describe this festival in greater detail than the other festivals of the California coast. Also, with its numerous facets, the San Pedro fiesta indirectly reflects some of the details that I chose to omit in connection with the San Francisco and the Monterey celebrations.

The Los Angeles newspapers tell their readers every year that San Pedro has the largest fishing industry in the world, and that the town is the gate-

---

[22] Cf. the Monterey *Peninsula Herald* of Saturday. September 15, 1951.

[23] The recent festivals have been written up also in the daily Salinas *Californian* (September 18, 1951; September 8, 1952; September 14, 1953).

[24] I wish to thank for the courtesies extended to me during a visit to Monterey by Mr. V. Fratangelo, past president of the Italian Catholic Federation. This religious organization was especially active in the staging of the festivals for 1951–53.

[25] Notices may be read in many newspapers throughout the country, usually accurate, but at times not. The Buffalo *Courier Express*, for instance, wrongly stated (September 13, 1953) that it is the only celebration of its type held in America.

[26] They appear in the issue devoted entirely to the State of California, 105 (June 1954): 772 ff.

way to one of the fastest-growing centers of world trade. The vast and
complicated commerce of the Port of Los Angeles grew from humble
beginnings. We are told that the first commercial transaction in the harbor took place in 1805 when the ship *Lelia Byrd* of Boston dropped anchor
in San Pedro Bay to trade cloth, sugar, and household goods, for hides
and tallow from the Missions. As is well known, the port had been first
visited in October 1542, by Juan Rodriguez Cabrillo, a Portuguese navigator sailing under the Spanish flag. He named it *Bahía de los Fumos* (Bay
of Smokes) because of the presence of smoke from brush the Indians were
burning on the hillside. Today, with its 2,362 boats, manned by approximately 6,000 fishermen, San Pedro plays the leading role in California's
fourth-largest industry, fishing. The fishing fleet of San Pedro brings in
about one billion pounds of fish annually. It has been estimated that Los
Angeles Harbor produces more fish than Boston, Gloucester, and New
Bedford combined, and that it has also surpassed San Francisco.

With such a large fishing population, it is not surprising to find that
the fishing folk have been holding a yearly Fishermen's Day on which
to rejoice and also to pray in the Church of Mary Star of the Sea, where
fishing families have worshiped for sixty-five years. Indeed, their festival is at present so well organized and celebrated on such a grand scale
that it commands the attention of countless newspapers throughout the
country. Newspapers are somewhat in error in referring to the date of
origin of San Pedro's festival. The first one was actually held in 1938,
when, to celebrate a good season, fishermen decorated their boats with
flags and bunting, and took their families and friends for a cruise. It
must have been quite a spectacle even on that first occurrence (March
26), for we read in the files of the San Pedro *News Pilot* that no fewer
than 73 boats participated in the parade. That these beginnings were to
be notably expanded was confirmed in 1945 when on October 21, after
seven years of inactivity brought about by World War II, another parade
was held in celebration of the return to peacetime activities. The event
was planned by the Fishermen's Cooperative Association, and 96 fishing vessels decorated with flags and streamers, expressive of U.S. Navy
and South Sea motifs, sailed a twenty-mile course past anchored war-
ships. There participated in this boat parade also several minesweepers
that had returned from distant theaters of war. At a dance, in the evening,
prizes were awarded to the winning boats. The dance netted $850 for

Christmas food and clothing to be sent to Yugoslavia. This was fitting, for the majority of the numerous San Pedro fishermen are immigrants and children of immigrants from Yugoslavia and Italy. Appropriately enough, Victory was the theme for that year. The first of the prizes awarded at the evening dance went to the *City of Naples*, which had decided to depict the recent but already historical flag-raising on Mount Suribachi on bloody Iwo Jima.[27] At the dinner that followed the parade it was suggested that an annual tournament of boats be established. Indeed, another celebration, highlighted by a boat parade, was held on October 6, 1946. The first prize was awarded again to the *City of Naples*: four platforms had been raised above the deck of the boat and, on them, four living groups depicted the major wars in which the United States had participated. One hundred and twenty boats took part in the tournament, which was watched by about 42,000 spectators. It is interesting to note that that year there was also a "Queen" who ruled over the festivities. There is no indication that there was a queen for the preceding years. It is significant to point out that officially, 1946 is referred to as the year of the first fiesta. It was in that year that the San Pedro Chamber of Commerce assumed the sponsorship of the event, and this body has been largely responsible for turning the festival into the glorious spectacle that it is today. It was in 1946 also that the mayor of Los Angeles first participated in the festivities. And, finally, it was in that year that a comical incident almost marred the day. It had been decided that the signal for the beginning of festivities should be given by a parachutist who was to leap from a blimp with a forty-pound tuna and a scroll of greeting, and upon landing, deliver them to His Honor the Mayor of Los Angeles. The parachutist and his friend the tuna jumped off the blimp very neatly, but before they could reach the ground the parachutist became entangled in the wires of a telephone pole on the bluff overlooking the wharf and everything came to a standstill until the parachutist and the tuna were cut down.[28] The scroll, alas, was lost, and only the tuna was presented to the mayor. Also, in 1946 the queen of the San

---

[27] The Los Angeles *Times* of October 22, 1945, has a picture of the decorated prize-winning purse seiner.

[28] Cf. the files of the San Pedro *News Pilot*, and also the Los Angeles *Times*. The latter (October 7, 1946) carried three pictures: one of the winning boat, one of the parachutist on the telephone pole, and one of Mayor Bowron and the Queen of the fiesta.

Francisco fishermen's fiesta went to San Pedro, and conveyed the greet-
ings of the mayor of the northern city.

There were no festivities in 1947 or 1948, and no reliable information
is available to explain this lapse. In 1949 the celebration was held once
again, September 8–11,[29] with even greater enthusiasm than before, and
from that date the fishermen of San Pedro have tried every year to put
on a "bigger and better show." Festivities that year lasted four days. Of
special interest were the coronation of a "King Fisherman" and the dedication of the newly built fishermen's dock, which was christened with
sample waters brought to San Pedro from the "Seven Seas": the Aegean,
the Caspian, the Adriatic, the Black Sea, the Yellow Sea, the Mediterranean, and the Caribbean. The feat of bringing water from these far-
flung places was accomplished as follows: a stewardess of the Compañia
Mexicana de Aviación left from Los Angeles with seven small glass fish-
net floats, and later she passed them on to other stewardesses at junction points on the World Airways, and they relayed them until all seven
containers were filled. That year there were also fishermen's contests in
skills connected with their industry, such as rope splicing, rope tying,
net making and mending, etc. On Sunday, September 11, a High Mass
was celebrated at Mary Star of the Sea Church, and later, the fleet of
fishing boats was blessed by the archbishop of Los Angeles. Then followed the gay parade of the beautifully decorated purse seiners. First
prize was awarded to the *Veteran,* depicting "Red Sails in Sunset." The
sails of the front of the boat were red, while those to the stern were gold-
en, and heralded the California Centennial. Second prize went to the
Oakland, which represented "Sea Miners" and carried on the stern a real
live burro, a prospector, a waterfall, and simulated golden nuggets. There
was no special theme in 1949, but, naturally, a sort of a "Golden Theme"
was chosen to tie in with the California Centennial, and thus the Honorary Skipper—who is chosen every year—was called the "Skipper of
the Golden Fleet." That year fiesta buttons were sold representing a tuna
wearing a sombrero; a Big Top tent covering one whole acre was set up
to house displays of marine art and industry; besides a King Fisherman,
instead of the customary Queen, they also had a mermaid, La Sirena,
of the Port. King Fisherman was given a court of nine San Pedro girls,

---

[29] It was written up in various newspapers; cf., for instance, the Los Angeles *Times* of Monday,
September 12. The festival has since been featured every year in the leading local newspapers.

all daughters of fishermen. The religious blessing was given in English, Italian, and Slavonian. A wreath of flowers was tossed into the sea in commemoration of the dead.

In order to avoid unnecessary repetition I shall mention only a few points of interest for the years 1950, 1951, and 1952, and then I shall describe in detail the 1953 festival.

In 1950 (September 23–24) the fiesta opened with the dedication of a large wholesale fish market; a young lady who had been elected "Mermaid of the Port" assisted in the christening of the market with water flown from the distant Adriatic Sea, the sea that bathes the shores of Italy and Yugoslavia. In that year the festivities were highlighted by the presence of Cardinal Eugene Tisserant from Vatican City, and the sermon to the fishermen was delivered in Italian and in French. (Apparently the cardinal was not fluent in Slavonian or in English.) The "skipperette" of the fiesta was crowned by a fisherman impersonating Father Neptune. In 1950 the first prize awarded to the winning boat was a trophy to be inscribed with the boat's name. It was donated by the San Pedro Chamber of Commerce, and it was not to be kept in possession of the winner. It was a retroactive trophy, so to speak, and on it were inscribed also the names of the three previous winning boats. The fiesta theme that year was "The Golden Year," and the first prize was won by the *Endeavor* decked with red and white roses.

In 1951 (September 21–23) the theme was "American Holidays." As official symbol of the fiesta, Capri caps were sold, fashioned of light-green anchovy netting with a white tassel. The night before the parade 10,000 square dancers from all over southern California participated in more than one thousand squares. Fishermen's Fiesta stamps were issued to help publicize the three-day festivities; the stamps depicted the fiesta's famous trademark, a galloping tuna in a sombrero. These stamps were designed for use on outgoing mail; they were gold in color, with the tuna's picture in blue and white. Sixty-eight gaily decorated boats participated in the parade. The first prize was won again by the *Endeavor*, decorated in black and orange with a broomstick-riding witch floating in the rigging, to represent the Hallowe'en season. Another purse seiner, the *Maria*, carried a huge white statue of Christ to portray the religious significance of Christmas. Also, in 1951 San Pedro sent a float depicting a purse seiner to the famous Pasadena New Year's Day Rose Parade.

In 1952 over 150,000 people witnessed the celebration held on Sunday, September 21. On Saturday festivities were climaxed by a parade in which there were eighty equestrian, musical, and marching units. Again, there was a mammoth square dance. On Sunday the boats were, as always, spic and span for the occasion, and decorated with countless flowers and blossoms. They were competing under the fiesta theme "Musical Memories." There were so many spectators on the pleasure craft that the Navy loaned three thousand life preservers to permit craft owners to come up to Coast Guard safety requirements. The winner of the sweepstakes award was the *Western Explorer*, which represented "I'll See You in My Dreams." Other winners had chosen the following songs: "April Showers," "The Circus Waltz," "I'm Forever Blowing Bubbles," etc.

In 1953 the San Pedro festival lasted two days, and culminated with the festivities held on Sunday, September 20.[30] The fiesta opened officially at noon on Saturday on Fishermen's Dock with a carnival, fish fries, international food settlement, and excursion boat rides. These activities, along with outdoor movies, "open house" aboard the cruiser *Manchester*, and exhibitions of fishermen's skill in mending nets, rope splicing, etc., continued on Sunday as well. On Sunday morning the very important religious ceremonies began with the customary High Mass celebrated by Cardinal James Francis McIntyre in the quaint old Church of Mary Star of the Sea. The church was lavishly decorated inside and out with beautiful flowers: red gladioli and yellow chrysanthemums. Over the altar stood out the words: *Maria Stella Maris Ora Pro Nobis* (Mary Star of the Sea, pray for us). In the front pews sat the Knights of Columbus with their black and red robes and their white-plumed hats. It was a beautiful spectacle, and thousands of people were able to enjoy it on television. The sermon delivered at mid-Mass stressed the fact that fishermen are beloved by Jesus. Saint Peter was depicted as the greatest of fishermen. Fishermen were urged to thank God for the good catch of the past year, and to pray to him for the future. A choir sang the lovely and appropriate *Ave Maris Stella* (Hail Star of the Sea). After Mass the cardinal led a procession to the fishermen's dock for

---

[30] The 1953 festival was announced in an interesting article by Mary Nugent: "Prayers and Pageantry to Mark Fishermen's Thanksgiving" in the Long Beach *Sunday Independent Press Telegram* of September 13, 1953. Miss Nugent was publicity director of the festival for six years.

the blessing of the fishing fleet. It was a gay spectacle: the dock was decorated with flags, pennants, and large cardboard tunas, and was dotted with various kinds of concessions. All along the canal were anchored the lavishly decorated purse seiners, which later took part in the parade before the eyes of over 100,000 spectators. The Holy Image of Mary Star of the Sea was carried in the procession by four fishermen. After the orators of the day had delivered the customary speeches, the cardinal blessed the fleet of fishing vessels, and twelve girls from the Mary Star of the Sea parish cast garlands of roses into the waters in memory of the fishermen buried at sea, while the touching prayer *De profundis* (Out of the depths)" was recited. Then, at a signal given by the fiesta Queen, the lengthy and colorful parade of boats began, amid the almost constant blowing of sirens and the laughter and shouting of the happy crowds on board and on shore. The fiesta theme was "Beloved Stories," and so the spectators saw floating before their eyes many of the dreams of their childhood: Cinderella, Hansel and Gretel, Raggedy Ann, Treasure Island, etc. The first prize was awarded to the boat depicting Cinderella. On shore, visitors were entertained by Mexican musicians, Japanese dancers and judo exhibitionists, Polish and Castilian dances, Norwegian dances, and also a Gypsy pantomime dance. In the evening festivities came to a close with an outdoor movie.

Besides participating in the yearly fiesta, the Italian fishermen of San Pedro hold every year, during the last days of August, a Triduum, or three days of prayer. Their prayers are directed to their patron saint, San Giovan Giuseppe della Croce (John Joseph of the Cross), who was an eighteenth-century priest of Ischia, the island off the coast of Naples from which many of the elders came to San Pedro. It is believed that this annual festival was first held in San Pedro in 1908 with a picture of the saint placed on the altar during the Triduum. In 1912, after a house-to-house collection, a statue of San Giovan Giuseppe was purchased and still stands in the Church of Mary Star of the Sea beside the Sacred Heart Altar.[31] It is interesting to note too that many of the approximately 1,100 Italian fishing boats carry a shrine and statue of Saint John Joseph.

---

[31] *Sixty Years in Our Parish* (1889–1949) [*Commemorative Booklet on the Occasion of California's Centennial*], Mary Star of the Sea Church, San Pedro, California, 33.

In San Pedro, since 1949, the fishermen's fiesta has regularly been
held in September. The reason is a practical one: the fiesta is planned
for the interval between the tuna-fishing season and the sardine fishing
season. At that time the fishermen change the fishing gear, and the fleet
is at anchor in the port. The exact date is also determined by the phases of the moon, for, since sardines give forth a phosphorescent light, they
can best be detected on a dark, moonless night. Thus, a full moon forces
sardine fishermen ashore, and this is a good time to hold the fiesta. If,
as it happened in 1954, the September full moon falls too early, since at
that time many fishermen are still at sea, the fiesta is held in October.[32]

The families of the fishermen competing in the parade are very proud
and jealous of their work. Not only do they begin making plans for the
decoration of their boats months in advance, but when fiesta time
approaches, they work secretly with flowers, flags, pennants, wood, cardboard, etc. Some purse seiners have been decorated far away in the hidden coves of Santa Catalina Island! And it is little wonder. Besides the
understandable pride of the fishermen's families in their boats, one must
not forget that the prizes are greatly coveted too. In 1953 cash prizes
amounted to no less than $12,500!

POINT LOMA

AT SAN DIEGO'S POINT LOMA the fishermen's festival is entirely different from those described above. Actually, the fishermen's festival is
the festival of the entire Portuguese colony of Point Loma, which, it is
true, is made up essentially of fishing folk.

Point Loma's fishermen are justly proud of the fact that a Portuguese
navigator, Juan Rodriguez Cabrillo, was the first European to sail a ship
past Point Loma and into San Diego Bay. A statue of Cabrillo now
stands like a sentinel at the tip of the point and watches over the tuna
clippers as they sail for hundreds of miles into the sunset and return
loaded with fish for the San Diego canneries. In the early days there
were no canneries in the vicinity, and the catch was preserved by slit-
ting the fish, salting and drying them. Then the fish were tied into bales

[32] In 1954 the festival was held, after this article was finished, on October 10. As one would expect,
festivities were very similar to those held in 1953. Cf. the Los Angeles *Times*, October 11, 1954.

and shipped, largely, to the San Joaquin farming areas, where they were consumed by the Portuguese and Italian colonists.[33]

The patron saint of the Portuguese fishermen at Point Loma is the Holy Ghost, one of the three persons of the Holy Trinity. But they have another patron saint also, Saint Isabel of Portugal. Saint Isabel was born in 1271 in Sarragosa, Spain, and she was the daughter of Don Pedro, king of Aragon. While she was still in her teens, she became the wife of Dom Dinis, king of Portugal. That country, which had already rid itself of the Moors, was still torn by civil wars. Don Alfonso, brother of King Dinis, laid claim to the crown of Portugal and backed his claim with an army. Young Isabel, so the legend goes, succeeded in establishing peace between the brothers. She was also successful on other similar occasions, and she became known as the Angel of Peace. Isabel was a very pious and saintly person, and in her constant prayers she sought guidance especially of the Holy Ghost. She died in the odor of sanctity and, on May 25, 1625, she was canonized by Pope Urban VIII. The most memorable incident of Saint Isabel as a peacemaker took place in 1323. In that year civil war was rampant again: the followers of the king of Portugal and those of the Infante were battling at Alvalade. When Isabel was informed of the battle, she rode into the thick of the combatants and with tears in her eyes she succeeded in convincing husband and son to cease hostilities. The following night the Holy Ghost appeared to her in a vision and instructed her to have a church built in His honor as a permanent memorial to peace and brotherly love. The church was erected at the little town of Alemquer. The day of its consecration was declared a national festival. Isabel made this consecration the occasion of special almsgiving. For a week before the festival the poor were invited to Alemquer and given meat and bread. It was the queen's wish that this festival be repeated every year at Pentecost, the seventh Sunday after Easter. Thus, the confraternity of the Holy Ghost was founded, and throughout the centuries they have seen to it that the festival be repeated. With a few variations, this Pentecostal festival has been observed by the Portuguese also in their colonies and in foreign countries. Wherever the Portuguese have settled, every year a committee is appointed to collect funds and make the necessary preparations for the proper celebration of the feast. The two

---

[33] Cf. Hepsy A. Adams, "Pilgrims from Portugal," *Westways* (May 1953): 5.

keynotes of the festival have not changed: honor to the Holy Ghost and charity to the needy.

At Point Loma, where almost all Portuguese are fishermen, every year one of the fishing boats is selected and its captain is made president of the Feast of the Holy Ghost, and he has the usual duties that fall upon such office. A prominent role in the festivities is played by a silver crown and scepter. The crown represents both the supreme power of the Holy Ghost and the royalty of Saint Isabel. The scepter is surmounted by a dove, symbolic of the Holy Spirit. During the seven weeks preceding Pentecost—symbolic of the seven gifts of the Holy Ghost—each Sunday the crown is taken to church and placed on the altar. For each of these seven weeks a family and their friends recite the rosary. The Sunday before Pentecost the crown is taken to the house of the president of the feast, and it is offered there for seven nights. Finally Pentecost Sunday arrives. The tuna clippers in the harbor are decorated with bunting. A young girl selected by the president and representing Queen Isabel carries the crown from Portuguese Hall to Saint Agnes' Church. She is accompanied by her regal attendants, by various groups of children and adults, dressed in the clothes or uniforms typical of their religious or patriotic societies. There are also bands and drill teams. Upon the arrival of the procession in church, Holy Mass is celebrated. Before the beginning of Mass, the crown is placed upon the high altar, where it remains until the end of the service. After the last Gospel, the Queen and her maids of honor ascend the altar steps and kneel. Then the celebrant of the Mass blesses the crown and places it upon the head of the Queen while, accompanied by the choir, he intones the hymn "Veni, Creator Spiritus."

At the conclusion of the religious ceremony the procession forms again and escorts the Queen to Portuguese Hall, where a banquet is served. Fireworks and dancing follow the banquet, and an ample supply of food is brought to the poor of the neighborhood and to those who were unable to be present at the feast.[34]

The *Festa do Espirito Santo* has been written up, more or less uninterruptedly, in the San Diego *Union* newspaper since 1930. Apparently

---

[34] Most of the above information can be found in the little pamphlet *Special Devotion to the Holy Ghost, As Practiced by the Portuguese People* prepared by Rev. Laurence Forristai of Saint Agnes Church (May 1939), and distributed by the Ryan Mortuary of San Diego, California.

the festival first attracted the attention of the local newspapers in 1918 (May 20). The San Diego *Union* describes the festival of 1918 and says that it was held as early as 1910, but the newspapers of 1910–12 make no reference to it.[35]

As was pointed out above, the four festivals I described are by necessity of rather recent importation on our California coast, and they were started and kept alive mainly by the fishermen who have come from other countries to make their new homes in our midst. It is difficult to say how long these festivals will continue to thrive. This, it seems to me, will depend largely on whether new immigrants will join their former compatriots, and whether their children, born in this country, will continue to uphold the customs, traditions, and faith of their fathers. Also, in certain localities it will depend on fishing conditions. Because of repeated poor seasons many of the fishing boats that used to fish off the Golden Gate and Monterey have moved down to San Pedro. Should the yearly catch continue to become worse, it is possible that the small number of fishermen left will continue to observe the religious part of their festival, but will discontinue the expensive pomp and gaiety of the social and civic spectacle.

---

[35] I wish to thank Mrs. Zelma Locker of the California Room of the San Diego Public Library for placing at my disposal several newspaper clippings.

ITALIANI!

Una grande battaglia si sta com-
battendo a Lawrence, Massach., da
25,000 lavoratori, fra cui moltissimi
italiani.

Lunedi 19 Corr., alle ore 8 p.m.

NELLA

Jefferson Square Hall

925 GOLDEN GATE AVE.

si terra' un GRANDE COMIZIO
INTERNAZIONALE nel quale,
fra gli altri oratori, parlera' anche
il compagno

Edmondo ROSSONI

il noto propagandista italiano.
Intervenite in massa.

Viva la solidarieta' del proletariato internazionale!

Il Branch Latino I. W. W.

 1660 Stockton St.

The Bay Area cannery strike in the summer of 1917 disproved the
common stereotype of Italian immigrants as strikebreakers rather
than organized union loyalists. Convinced of their cause, immigrant men and women cannery workers in San Francisco, San
Jose, and Oakland walked off the job to protest wages and hours
and to demand union recognition. *California Historical Society.*

Cannery Row
The afl, the iww,
and Bay Area
Italian Cannery Workers

By Elizabeth Reis

A T THE HEIGHT of the canning season in late July 1917, hundreds of Italian workers did not report to their jobs at several San Francisco Bay Area fruit and vegetable canneries. Just four months after the United States had entered World War I, the production of canned foods had become a vital part of the war effort, and the industry was expanding its production to meet the needs of soldiers in the field. The strike was a protest against low wages and long hours and an effort to secure recognition for the cannery workers' recently formed union, the Toilers of the World. As the workers mounted picket lines and demonstrations at their own and neighboring canneries—the first such episode in the history of the California canning industry—the federal government reacted with alarm, calling out troops and charging that the strike was an act of sabotage masterminded by the radical Industrial Workers of the World (iww). One government official claimed that it was "perhaps the most acute situation" the Federal Food Administration had encountered in gearing up for the war effort.[1] Volunteer crews of housewives and students moved to keep the canneries going, while men joined "pickhandle brigades" to frighten the strikers back to work.

---

[1] *San Francisco Examiner*, July 28, 1917.

The main drama was over in a week as arbitration replaced picket-line confrontations and most of the workers returned to their jobs. But the strike had exposed significant tensions between radical and conservative forces in the San Francisco labor movement as well as parallel strains between militancy and respectability within the Italian community. The tension in the labor movement centered on the conflict between the radical IWW, committed to organizing the entire working class into "one big union" under a revolutionary program, and the more conservative, craft-oriented American Federation of Labor (AFL), which had only marginal interest in unskilled workers. Although the Toilers of the World was a federally chartered AFL union of unskilled workers, the strong presence of the IWW in San Francisco makes it likely that the IWW was also involved. While no individual names have survived to link the Toilers directly to the IWW, the name of the cannery-workers union certainly hints at IWW influence. Moreover, AFL support of the strike was little more than token, and the AFL cooperated in an arbitration process which ultimately undermined its own union.

Similarly, the Italian press expressed contradictory aspirations in the ambiguous support it gave the striking workers. The press wanted them to be seen as patriotic members of the working class, simply demanding higher wages, shorter hours, and better conditions. The press also wanted the cannery workers to win the respect of Labor and to shake off the stigma of docility often attributed to Italian workers. But to do so, they had to take actions that could discredit their reputation as loyal and patriotic Americans. Sensitive to accusations of disloyalty, the press would not encourage the workers' strike unequivocally.

Historians have frequently characterized Italians in the American labor movement as either "padrone slaves" or "primitive rebels,"[2] depicting them as unorganizable, docile strikebreakers or as politically naive radicals, and their reputation in the San Francisco labor movement was similarly dubious. Employed primarily in agriculture, fishing, and mining, the Italians did not appear to contribute to the emerging city-wide union campaigns. In fact, of course, they have been both strikebreakers

---

[2] Rudolph J. Vecoli, "Italian American Workers, 1880–1920: Padrone Slaves or Primitive Rebels?" in *Perspectives in Italian Immigration and Ethnicity*, ed. S. M. Tomase (New York, 1977), 26–43.

and radicals.[3] For the workers, the choice between the two was never so straightforward. In the Bay Area, indeed, the struggles between the IWW and the AFL complicated their alternatives.

World War I heightened these tensions. To the patriotic American public, little could be more dishonorable than striking during a time of war, particularly in an industry that was essential to the war effort. Association with the IWW, prosecuted during the war for sedition and disloyalty, was extremely damaging to the image the Italian press sought to portray. The press wanted the workers to think of themselves as patriotic members of the working class, simply demanding higher wages, shorter working hours, and better working conditions. Struggling to be seen as conscientious workers in the eyes of labor, the Italians had to take actions that would discredit their reputation as loyal and patriotic Americans. The workers were in a bind. The canning strike revealed the conflicts between radicalism and conservatism in the San Francisco labor movement in general and in the Italian community in particular.

America's entrance into the war meant more business for the canning industry as the United States increased shipments of food and munitions to the Allies. In 1917 American canners expected to produce nearly 2 billion cans of fruits and vegetables, of which the government and the Allies would require at least 200 million.[4] In 1918 the Del Monte Company management employees' magazine published a poem entitled "The Tin Can in War":

> We can march without shoes,
> We can fight without guns,
> We can fly without wings
> To flap over the Huns.
> We can sing without bands,
> Parade without banners,
> But no modern army
> Can eat without canners.[5]

---

[3] Ettore Patrizi, *Gli Italiani in California* (San Francisco, 1910), 7; Joseph Preston Giovinco, "The California Career of Anthony Caminetti, Italian-American Politician" (Ph.D. Dissertation, University of California, Berkeley, 1973), passim.
[4] *San Francisco Examiner*, July 28, 1917.
[5] *Del Monte Activities*, July 1918, Del Monte Archives, San Francisco.

The expanding industry needed markets as much as the armies needed canned foods. Already, in 1914 a manufacturer of canned goods had
touted his product in terms that would have seemed quite appropriate
in the spring of 1917:

> The world could not dispense with canned foods and live; for without
> them progress would be halted, effort hobbled, if not extinguished, navies
> dismantled, armies dispersed, the great progress of the world stayed and
> thrown back upon itself shattered. Deprived of canned foods, all nations
> would fall into greater depths of depravity than heretofore known.[6]

By 1916 the leading California canning corporations had consolidat-
ed to form the California Packing Corporation, or Del Monte, in a merger of the four corporations that dominated the market and controlled
most of the canning industry in the state. By far the largest contributor
to the merger was the California Fruit Canners Association (CFCA), a
canning syndicate owned by Marco Fontana, an Italian immigrant. CFCA
had dominated the market since the 1890s and at the time of the merger owned thirty of the forty-two canneries in California.[7] By 1913 CFCA
operated the world's largest cannery with an annual capacity of 24 million cans, one-seventh of the state's total output.[8] All of the Fontana
canneries were located in the San Francisco area. The Santa Clara Valley provided the produce, while the North Beach Italian neighborhoods
in San Francisco and similar Italian communities in San Jose and Oakland supplied the labor. In total, the four separate canning organizations
included seventy-one canneries and fruit-packing plants throughout
California, Washington, Oregon, Idaho, and the territories of Alaska
and Hawaii.[9]

Several factors contributed to the consolidation of the canning industry at the turn of the century. Only an extremely large-scale enterprise

---

[6] Arthur I. Judge, ed., *A History of the Canning Industry by its Most Prominent Men* (Baltimore, 1914),
5.
[7] Hans Christian Palmer, "Italian Immigration and the Development of California Agriculture"
(Ph.D. Dissertation, University of California, Berkeley, 1965), 243. The four companies were:
J.K. Armsby Company, Griffin and Skelley, Central California Canneries, and The California Fruit Canners Association.
[8] *San Francisco Call*, May 5, 1913.
[9] William Braznell, ed., *California's Finest: The History of the Del Monte Corporation and the Del
Monte Brand* (San Francisco, 1982), 42.

could afford to incorporate the technological changes in the processes of production and distribution that were becoming necessary to remain competitive. The Del Monte merger typified the emerging modern American business enterprise, requiring among other things a professional managerial hierarchy and coordination of the decision-making processes.[10] Before the merger each canning plant had its own management, its own processing equipment, and its own variety of product grades and sizes. The consolidation of all seventy-one plants was an enormous task, entailing an actual merger of all the administrative and marketing functions in one building under the Del Monte brand label.

In 1917 the corporation launched its first major national advertising campaign to take advantage of the new market for consumer and household goods that catered to homemakers. The corporation advertised its products as the finest fruits, "famous for their goodness and purity . . . packed on the very day they are picked, in clean, sunlit canneries." One full-page color advertisement in leading women's magazines and the *Saturday Evening Post* assured consumers that if they ever visited one of the Del Monte canneries they would marvel at "the rigid system of inspection which guards every detail of the work." Never again would women have to "put up" their own fruit or vegetables when it was so easy to have the golden sunshine of California brought right to the dining table.[11]

If American homemakers had taken Del Monte up on the invitation to visit the "clean sunlit canneries," they would have been shocked. In 1890 a Bureau of Labor Statistics report asserted that "The effluvia arising from the drains and waste vegetable matter is not inducive to the health of the employees."[12] In 1913 the Labor Bureau reported that adequate ventilation, lighting, draining, and toilet facilities were sorely lacking in most of the canneries. The workrooms were humid because of the steam from the cooking process, and the floors were often made of an absorbent material that soaked up the excess water and fruit and vegetable juice. The toilet and wash-rooms were neither ventilated proper-

---

[10] For an analysis of this type of industrial consolidation see Alfred D. Chandler Jr., *The Visible Hand: The Managerial Revolution in American Business* (Cambridge, 1977).

[11] Del Monte Archives, Del Monte Corporation, San Francisco.

[12] *Unsanitary Conditions of Canneries*, 4th Biennial Report, Bureau of Labor Statistics, State of California, 1890, p. 7.

ly nor closed off from the workroom, and the general area in which the
preparation of the food took place was filthy.[13]

The health and safety conditions in the canneries were no better in
the 1920s. Before receiving his Ph.D. degree in 1928, historian Donald
Anthony spent eight years working in canneries in the Santa Clara Valley. He reported that bandaged hands were a common characteristic of
women cannery workers and that infections and blood poisoning were
frequent.[14] In 1929 the situation had not changed significantly. One
woman worker in an Oakland cannery reported:

> The work in the canneries on the Pacific Coast is hard to learn and is
> hard work. The hands of the workers are stained and from holding the
> knife, the fingers blister and the workers' palms get raw. The fruit acid
> eats right into the sores. . . . Many of the time slips of the knife cut the
> hands very severely. But we must stand it in order to make a living.[15]

And in 1937 the cannery workers were still struggling to improve their
conditions. One protesting worker complained, "The first thing you
notice is how wet you get—and stay—from the waist both ways. I changed
my shoes every day and still didn't have a dry pair on my feet for three
months."[16]

Women cannery workers experienced these poor conditions most
acutely because of the nature of the gender-specific tasks. On the
"women's side" the workers peeled, cored, and cut the product. The men
carried heavy boxes of fruit to and from the women's work tables and
inspected the produce for defects. Donald Anthony's description of the
preparation of cherries illustrates the general process of cannery work.
First, the cutters removed the cherry stems and sorted the different types
of cherries by placing them in boxes laid out in front of them. Then they
had to wait for a male checker to replace a full box of fruit with an empty
one. Since the women were paid on a piece-rate for each box stemmed,
their wages were a function both of their own speed and efficiency and

---

[13] *Labor Conditions in the Canning Industry*, Bureau of Labor Statistics, State of California, 1913,
pp. 31–33.

[14] Donald Anthony, "Labor Conditions in the Canning Industry in the Santa Clara Valley of the
State of California" (Ph.D. Dissertation, Stanford University, 1928), 34.

[15] Ann Alden, "Industry Gets Poverty," *Daily Worker*, August 24, 1929, in Federal Writers Project
on Migratory Labor, Bancroft Library, University of California, Berkeley.

[16] "Look at a Cannery," *Labor Herald* 1:2 (June 15, 1937), 2, in Federal Writers Project on Migratory Labor, Bancroft Library, University of California, Berkeley.

of the efficiency of the male checker. Anthony reported that the male checker often had too many stations to handle or was uninterested in performing the task properly, forcing the women to sit idle and lose money while waiting for work to be brought to them.

Once the cherries were stemmed and inspected, the male checkers brought them to the canning tables, where other women placed them in the proper cans. The mechanics of this step depended on whether or not the cannery was automated. In the old-fashioned canneries the women graded the cherries by hand. In automated canneries the cherries were placed on an automatic grader that sorted the cherries according to size and fed them down a chute to the appropriate can. In either case, the women were responsible for getting the fruit into the correct cans and affixing the proper grade labels. This task was also on the piece-rate system, and again the women were dependent upon a steady supply of work brought to them by the male carriers.

Peaches, pears, tomatoes, and other fruits were processed in much the same way, although some fruits were more difficult to prepare and can than others. Peaches, particularly cling peaches, required special attention, because the cutters had to extract the pit while preserving the shape of the fruit.[17] Del Monte standards meant that consumers could count on consistent quality. The consumer should never know that peaches, pears, or apricots came any way other than sliced, pitted, cooked, and canned.

Most of the cannery workers during the peak seasons were women. In 1912 the Bureau of Labor Statistics compiled data on the California canning seasons in each district. Ten establishments were surveyed in the San Francisco Bay Area. At the beginning of the season, the last week of March, there were 190 employees of whom 152 were women. At the height of the season, the last week in July, there were 3,480 workers, and 2,363 of them were women.[18] Surviving photographs suggest that many of the women were over thirty-five years old, but otherwise the records do not indicate such things as whether they were generally married or single or whether they held other jobs during the off season.

In the city canneries, which ran a slightly longer term than the rural ones, the season ran from eighteen to thirty-four weeks. Most of the women did not work for the entire duration. Turnover was high, with

---

[17] Anthony, 33–44.
[18] *Labor Conditions in the Canning Industry*, 7.

new recruits constantly available, at least in the cities. After three weeks at a job a woman was considered an experienced worker and entitled to a raise of 3 cents an hour—from 13 to 16 cents—if she was paid by the day. However, the average span of work in the city canneries was only 7.7 weeks. Twenty percent of the women stayed at their jobs less than a week, and 40 percent worked less than four weeks in a season.[19]

City cannery workers in California straddled a line between factory workers and agricultural laborers. They resembled agricultural workers because their work was seasonal, but like factory workers, they were non-migratory and usually worked in urban areas. Because of their uncertain status, labor organizers were slow to approach them. The AFL had made a half-hearted effort to organize farmworkers between 1909 and 1916, but lack of funds and interest had condemned the campaign to failure. Even this modest attempt had been motivated by a desire to blunt the IWW's successful drive among agricultural workers, and it had not extend-ed to the cannery workers. Not only were the cannery workers season-al and unskilled, but most of them were women, and the AFL discouraged the organization of women, insisting that a woman's primary function rested in the home. In 1905 an AFL official exclaimed, "The great prin-ciple for which we fight is opposed to taking . . . the women from their homes to put them in the factory and the sweatshop."[20] The AFL's aver-sion to women in the paid labor force derived largely from the pragmatic realization that they might supplant unionized male workers.

Industry representatives recognized the benefits of female labor, how-ever. Cannery executives perceived the Italian women workers as pas-sive and uncomplaining. One cannery worker remarked that "cannery bosses are claiming that the young girls make the best workers because they have the courage not to complain much of the sore hands."[21] Accord-

[19] *The Regulation of the Fruit and Vegetables in the Canning Industry of California*, California Indus-trial Welfare Commission Report, (Sacramento: California State Printing Office, 1917), 63.

[20] Alice Kessler-Harris, *Out to Work: A History of Wage-Earning Women in the United States* (New York, 1982), 153.

[21] Ann Alden, "Slavery at the Belt," *Daily Worker*, August 26, 1929, in Federal Writers Project on Migratory Labor, Bancroft Library. An article in the *Chautauquan* about the garment industry in New York City stated that the Italians were willing to accept low wages because they were "accustomed to starvation wages." For an analysis of the Italian's image in contemporary jour-nals see, Salvatore Mondello, "The Italian Immigrant in Urban America, 1880–1920, As Report-ed in the Contemporary Periodical Press" (Ph.D. dissertation, New York University, 1960).

ing to Anthony, it was generally assumed that "most of the workers . . .
being of the typical casual laborer type, are not themselves particularly
interested in either their future in the canning industry or their future
in life. They live in the present, or in their dreams of the future not in
any way connected with the canning industry."[22] The industry's image
of the typical cannery worker mirrored the AFL's attitude toward agricultural workers in general. Unable to develop their own sense of col-
lectivity, cannery workers would have to rely on government legislation
rather than trade unionism for protection.

In 1913 the Industrial Welfare Commission (IWC) created by the California Commission of Immigration and Housing (CCIH) attempted to
establish uniform standards of wages, hours, and working conditions in
all California canneries. California's progressive reformers originally
conceived of the CCIH as a social welfare agency to improve the economic position and aid the social assimilation of the state's immigrants.
After the Wheatland Riot in 1913 called attention to the exploitation of
migratory labor in the state's agricultural sector, Gov. Hiram Johnson
expanded the IWC's initial mandate to include a statewide campaign to
improve working conditions in the agricultural labor camps. The commission recommended but did not require minimum standards to which
most farm employers agreed, perhaps to head off further uprisings. Such
voluntary compliance was precisely what the commission's progressive
leadership wanted: its members believed that mutual understanding
between employers and workers would make trade unionism unnecessary.[23] Growing out of CCIH's reformist impulses and its aversion to trade
unionism, the IWC sought to improve labor relations in the canning
industry to make canning "one of the most desirable occupations for
women."[24]

From 1916 to 1920 the IWC embarked on a program to elevate canning conditions to "American" standards.[25] Working closely with cannery owners, the commission established a series of minimum wage
standards for women that significantly improved their earning power.
Since over 90 percent of the women worked on the piece-rate system,
the IWC raised the minimum rate a few cents per box. In addition, can-

---

[22] Anthony, 19.   [23] Daniel, 91.
[24] *The Regulation of the Fruit and Vegetables*, 7.   [25] Ibid., 63.

neries were required to conform to commission rulings on specific improvements in the work environment.[26]

The Industrial Welfare Commission worked in conjunction with the industry, and by taking the struggles between labor and management to the state bureaucracy, it hindered the development of trade unionism. The commission's work made it easier for the AFL to ignore the demands of women workers because this state organization was already the "legitimate" voice of the women workers.[27]

While the AFL relied on state legislation to replace trade unionism among agricultural workers, the Industrial Workers of the World was ready to organize these workers and to address their economic and political needs. Founded in 1905 by groups of industrial workers who had left the craft-controlled AFL, the IWW reached its peak in California between 1910 and 1924. Its largest local was in San Francisco, and it devoted the majority of its efforts to free-speech issues and to the problems of agricultural workers in the state.[28] Unlike the AFL, the IWW eagerly organized women workers, asserting that women "cannot be driven back to the home. . . . They are a part of the army of labor. . . . [We must] organize them with the men, just as they work with the men."[29]

By the end of 1916, the IWW's Agricultural Workers' Organization had 20,000 members, and total IWW membership had risen from 500 in 1910 to 5,000 in the spring of 1916 to 70,000 at its peak in 1917.[30] This dramatic increase in numbers, accompanied by a powerful image of the IWW as a revolutionary and dangerous group, was a result of the 1913 Wheatland Riot in which 2,800 workers protested horrendous living conditions at a hops ranch in the Sacramento Valley. Many of the riot-

---

[26] Ibid., 67. Regulation of the industry was becoming more feasible as new technology made large, concentrated labor pools necessary, putting small rural canneries scattered around the countryside out of business. For a discussion of the new technologies, see Peter Philips, "Towards a New Theory of Wage Structure: The Evolution of Wages in the California Canneries, 1870 to the Present" (Ph.D. dissertation, Stanford University, 1979), 151.

[27] Martin Brown, "A Historical Economics Analysis of the Wage Structure of the California Fruit and Vegetable Canning Industry" (Ph.D. dissertation, University of California, Berkeley, 1981), 376. Brown's analysis of the role of the Industrial Welfare Commission has influenced the direction of my paper.

[28] Ralph Edward Shatter, "Radicalism in California, 1869–1929" (Ph.D. dissertation, University of California, Berkeley, 1962), 221.

[29] Philip S. Foner, *The Industrial Workers of the World, 1905–1917* (New York, 1965), 127.

[30] Linda Lewis Toomi, *Farm Labor Organizing, 1905–1967* (New York, 1967), 14.

ers were card-carrying Wobblies, although estimates of the actual number vary considerably. Federal troops were called in, strikers arrested, and some convicted of murder. Radical coalitions in California rallied to raise money for the strikers, and the IWW's militancy won growing support for industrial unionism from the Left in the state.[31]

Given the influence of the IWW in California, it is hard to imagine that the Wobblies were not in some way involved in the organization of the cannery workers' union. Yet in the spring of 1917, it was the AFL that granted a charter to the Federal Labor Union, also known as the Toilers of the World, headquartered in San Jose. By July of that year the union boasted 1,000 members. But "federal" unions—groups of workers unrelated by skill—had little power and received little support in the AFL.[32] There was constant tension between the state AFL officials and the Toilers' leadership, perhaps reflecting suspicion within the conservative AFL that the radical IWW was involved. Indeed, the Toilers echoed the IWW's all-inclusive policies, recruiting male and female unskilled workers sixteen years or older, and the union proclaimed itself "willing to assist any working class movement regardless of race or creed."[33]

The canning and field fruit workers began meeting in March 1917, organizing primarily to address economic issues. The cost of living skyrocketed after the United States entered the war, rising over 20 percent from 1916 to 1917.[34] The Italian women workers complained of the increased price of basic necessities, particularly macaroni and olives.[35] A union representative claimed that some cannery owners were cutting wages below the standards set by the Industrial Welfare Commission, and the workers believed that their pay was not commensurate with the enormous profits that the cannery owners were receiving as a result of the increased war production.[36]

---

[31] Shaffer, 220–35. See Melvyn Dubofsky, *We Shall Be All: A History of the IWW* (New York, 1969) for a complete treatment of the IWW. Other interesting works include Joyce L. Kornblug, ed., *Rebel Voices, An IWW Anthology* (Ann Arbor, Mich., 1965), and Carleton Parker, *The Casual Laborer and Other Essays* (New York, 1920). Parker was the executive secretary of the California Commission of Immigration and Housing in 1914 and investigated IWW activities in the state. He was also a sociologist and wrote a psychological interpretation of the IWW.
[32] Kessler-Harris, 155.
[33] *San Jose Mercury Herald*, July 17, 1917.
[34] *The World*, August 3, 1917.
[35] Brown, 375.
[36] *San Francisco Examiner*, August 1, 1917.

On May 6, 1917, 1,000 workers, mostly Italian men and women, participated in a mass meeting. Following a parade to the meeting hall, the workers were addressed by local clergy, a representative of the Italian Benevolent Society, the business agent for the union, and the local attorney for the AFL. The speakers at the meeting outlined the strategies for the union. The Toilers would try to gain union recognition first and then discuss wages and hours, demanding a 25-percent wage increase. For the men this meant an increase from 25 cents to 31¼ cents per hour, or $2.50 per eight-hour day. The women's demands were not specified.[37] Wage rates for both organized and unorganized workers were increasing in most industries as a result of wartime inflation, and most unions were able to secure pay increases without striking.[38] But some of the canning companies refused even to negotiate with the Toilers, much less recognize the union, claiming that the Industrial Workers of the World was involved.

During the busiest season of the year the Toilers decided to strike this crucial wartime industry. On Monday, July 23, 1917, 600 workers at the California Fruit Canners Association in San Jose set up pickets surrounding the cannery. On the same day 175 men and 125 women walked off their jobs at the Bisceglia Brothers cannery in San Jose. Both companies were forced to close and several hundred sympathizers joined the strikers outside the plants. At the Bisceglia plant a striker was shot and wounded as he tried to prevent a car from driving up to the plant. At the Pratt-Low cannery in Santa Clara, where over 900 workers went out on strike, an incident between a foreman and the strikers left one striker dead and two others wounded.[39]

The next day workers at the DiFiore Company went out on strike, joined in sympathy by the Kartschoke-Peterson brickyard employees. Two days later, on July 26, approximately 450 workers at several San Francisco canneries struck in support of the San Jose strikers. Later that day, 150 workers, 50 of them women, traveled to the Griffin-Skelley plant in Oak-

---

[34] Robert Knight, *Industrial Relations in the San Francisco Bay Area, 1900–1918* (Berkeley: University of California Press, 1960), 335.   [35] *San Francisco Examiner*, July 29, 1917.
[36] *La Voce del Popolo*, August 3, 1917.   [37] *San Francisco Examiner*, July 23, 1917.
[38] Knight, 334.
[39] *San Francisco Examiner*, July 24, 1917. Some of these canneries had recently merged into the California Packing Corporation, Del Monte, but their names had not changed.

land to urge the workers to join them in the strike. The Oakland police met them at the train station and sent them all back to San Francisco. A day later the workers made a second attempt and managed to arrive at the cannery before police rounded most of them up and brought them back to the ferry landing. Some of them succeeded in creating a blockade around the cannery and, amidst cheers from their fellow workers, the women scrambled over the fence that enclosed the cannery cook-room.[40]

The San Jose *Mercury Herald* described the militancy of the women workers:

> Yesterday, some 50 Italian girls and women riding in autos from the west side of the city, stopped at 7th and Jackson at 6:30 A.M. and made a concerted rush for the doors of the Central California Canning Plant. They discovered the plant locked and started away on a run for the Golden Gate Company's plant, three blocks away. A dozen patrol-men . . . started in pursuit. The crowd of women took to the railroad tracks of the Niles line to make a short cut to the plant. They were immediately hemmed in by the police. . . .
>
> The majority of the women were armed with cutting knives and, as soon as they realized the possibility of arrest, began throwing them in ditches. After the women threw the knives away, a patrol wagon was sent for. At the sight of it, the prisoners tried to break past the patrolmen. The rout became a panic. . . . The women were threatened with arrest as they congregated around the plants again.[41]

Both of the Bay Area Italian newspapers covered the strike in San Francisco, Oakland, and San Jose extensively. *L'Italia* and *La Voce del Popolo* (The Voice of the People) supported the strikers and encouraged them to continue the strike until they received their demands. Yet they tempered their exhortations with advice to remain calm and non-violent, urging the workers not to be carried away by their emotions. The political differences between the two major Italian newspapers had long been an indication of the internal divisions within the Italian community. The older of the two papers, *La Voce del Popolo*, generally supported labor and the Democratic party, whereas the more conservative paper, *L'Italia*, represented local business leadership. However, when the Ital-

---

[40] Ibid., July 25, 1917; *L'Italia*, July 28, 1917.
[41] *San Jose Mercury Herald*, July 28, 1917.

ians became the victims of nativist prejudice and immigration restriction, even *L'Italia* came to their defense.[42] Both newspapers sent mixed messages to their Italian readers. They advocated their participation in the strike, but worried about their reputation as respectable Americans. The press praised the working-class consciousness exhibited in the conflict, yet tried to guide the workers cautiously in a more moderate direction. The labor-oriented paper, *La Voce del Popolo*, was impressed by the solidarity of the workers. One article remarked, "Very few times have crowds of people all been in unison on an issue with all the simplicity and brotherhood . . . their souls have been raised to a perfect unity and an ineffable serenity."[43] The editors thanked the workers for their determination, reflecting that their solidarity was nothing but the "faithful mirror of their misery." They urged them to persevere and sacrifice to attain victory for themselves and the entire working-class: "Calloused hands have the right to well-being and happiness since the capitalists live in luxury and abundance, squeezing the strength of their muscles."[44]

Although it warned the strikers of possible repercussions from unpopular actions. *L'Italia* supported "their legal strike for the improvement of working conditions."[45] The editors of this paper were convinced that the strikers could not fail to elicit the support and sympathy of the public if they remembered that they were striking for decent conditions and nothing more. The editors urged the Italians to prove their seriousness and discipline by "avoiding nasty demonstrations that only result in discrediting the working class."[46]

The Italian press had reacted similarly on other occasions when Italians were involved in labor struggles. In 1903 Italian miners from the Western Federation of Miners joined with non-union sympathizers to demand an eight-hour day and union recognition. *L'Italia* urged the Italian workers to cooperate with their American brothers to attain their demands. The Italians were to be involved but not to be too committed and certainly not to assume leadership positions. The editors feared the vindictive wrath of employers years down the line. In the lumber indus-

---

[42] Samuel F. Vitone, "Community, Identity, and Schools: Educational Experiences of Italians in San Francisco from the Gold Rush to the Second World War" (Ph.D. dissertation, University of California, Berkeley, 1981), 142.   [43] *La Voce del Popolo*, August 3, 1917.
[44] Ibid., July 31, 1917.   [45] *L'Italia*, July 28, 1917.
[46] Ibid., July 27, 1917.

try in 1909, Italians took collective action in what the editor of *L'Italia* termed a "justified" strike. He wrote, "That demonstration made it clear to the big jobbers in this country that Italians know how to feel personal and national dignity; that they are no longer a flock of sheep . . . but that they know how to be treated, finally as human beings equal to their brothers of other nationalities."[47]

The government responded immediately to the canning strike. The day after it began, on July 24, federal troops from nearby Camp Fremont reached San Jose. One hundred Coast Artillery men serving as infantry went into the Pratt-Low cannery in Santa Clara prepared to take action against what was described in local papers as rioting and mob demonstrations. The message from the Santa Clara county officials to the War Board urged the temporary location of federal troops in San Jose to "protect the food industry from violent intimidation by agitators and large groups of disaffected migratory labor. . . . [They] assemble in large numbers and by threats and violence intimidate women workers in food packing plants."[48] The editor of *La Voce del Popolo* expressed outrage at the government's overreaction, pointing out that San Francisco had had industrial fights "a hundred times more difficult than this" that had been solved without the intervention of federal troops.[49]

Many middle-class Americans shared the government's alarm. The cannery owners gathered San Jose Rotary Club members, prominent doctors, lawyers, and businessmen; posses of citizens were formed and ninety Home Guards were trained. This vigilante activity was neither unique nor spontaneous. Local organizations such as the Liberty League, Knights of Liberty, the Boy Spies of America, and the Sedition Slammers appeared in every western community where there was labor conflict, particularly where there was IWW involvement. These groups frequently took the law into their own hands to suppress "wartime disloyalty."[50] The federal troops left after two days, but the employers joined with community members to form a pickhandle brigade, which went to the factories to intimidate the striking workers. One worker submitted the following poem satirizing this action to the Oakland socialist newspaper:

---

[47] Ibid., April 20, 1903; June 19, 1909. [48] *San Francisco Examiner*, July 27, 1917.
[49] *La Voce del Popolo*, July 28, 1917.
[50] Paul L. Murphy, *World War I and the Origins of Civil Liberties in the United States* (New York, 1979), 87.

> They are men both strong and valiant;
> They are trusted, tried and true;
> They are guarding our fair city;
> They are shielding me and you
> From these terrorizing strikers—
> On strike; though overpaid—
> Who would kill us all, if it were not for
> "The Pick-handle Brigade."[51]

The government made an effort to suppress information about the strike, fearing the disruption would spread to other industries throughout California. Officials were determined to keep the strike activities quiet. A telegram from Attorney General Thomas Gregory to the executive officer of the California Commission of Immigration and Housing stated that the department would do its best to see that no publicity was given to the strike. A coded telegram to the director of the CCIH from the head of the Industrial Welfare Commission pleaded, "Whatever you do, don't hold a public hearing down there."[52]

In a telegram to President Wilson, the Canners League of California suggested that the conflict might be more than a simple controversy over wages:

> This is not a strike but a conspiracy to stop fruit and vegetable packing resulting in destruction to large quantities of food products necessary for use for our army and navy, our allies and the country at large. Imperative that the National Government take action to control this desperate movement of the enemies of our country which is sweeping over many Western States.[53]

In the canning executives' nightmare, the "enemy" was an IWW-German alliance.

The Italian press vigorously denied that there was any IWW influence in the strike. *L'Italia* asserted that charges from the government that the Germans were using the IWW to manipulate the workers were merely a

---

[51] *The World*, August 10, 1917. The poem was entitled "A Tribute Dedicated to San Jose Merchants, Canners and Society Dames," and had three other stanzas.

[52] Simon Lubin Papers, Boxes on Commission of Immigration and Housing (hereafter cited as CCIH) and Western Governors, Bancroft Library. In Gregory's telegram it is unclear to which "Department" he is referring.

[53] Simon Lubin Papers, CCIH, Bancroft Library.

ploy to avoid confronting the demands of the strikers. Fearing a link between the radical IWW and the cannery workers that might discredit the strike, the press maintained that the Italians only wanted the best relationship between workers and capitalists.[54]

Cannery owners also worried that fruit under government contract for war supplies would spoil, although both the Italian press and the San Jose *Mercury Herald* reported that there was no real danger to the fruit crop. If the strike had continued, some of the fruit that was not canned could have been dried. In addition, some of the canners affected by the strike owned other canneries in the Bay Area, and others had connections to different plants as a result of the recent merger, making it possible to transfer fruit.[55] These alternatives were not discussed, however, during mediation of the strike.

The Italian press supported mediation, contending that arbitration was the "American" way, as long as it "adjust[s] things in the best possible way for the good of the working-class." But the press was not concerned only with working-class interests. *La Voce del Popolo* conceded, "Maybe the workers acted too fast, and not in the way they were supposed to act, yet their behavior after the strike has been correct and not threatening."[56] The desire to be seen as respectable American citizens was equally important.

Four days after the strike began, Harrison Weinstock, state market inspector, and Ralph Merritt of the Food Control Department, directed by Herbert Hoover met at the Labor Temple in San Jose to begin arbitration. These representatives were joined by AFL officials and the leadership of the Toilers. All of the discussions were translated into Italian. A general meeting of the union membership at the Labor Temple followed. Merritt urged the workers to go back to work if there was fruit to be processed and assured them that the arbitration council would settle the differences as soon as possible. Angry workers rose to leave the meeting while the AFL official threatened to expel the Toilers from the AFL if the strikers did not listen to the mediators, again indicating the marginal support provided by the AFL for the Toilers' cause. (*L'Italia*

---

[54] *L'Italia*, July 28, 1917.
[55] *San Jose Mercury Herald*, August 8, 1917; *La Voce del Popolo*, July 28,1917.
[56] *La Voce del Popolo*, July 31, 1917.

reported that the AFL speaker did not speak Italian and no one translated his speech.)[57] Speaker after speaker was interrupted with catcalls and hisses from the audience. The workers did not intend to go back to work until they were assured that their demands would be met. According to the San Francisco *Examiner*, 500 of the 1,000 Italians present ran from the building shouting at the top of their voices that they were being betrayed into the hands of the capitalists. They voted to continue the strike, although many workers did go to work the next day, while mediators, labor leaders, and lawyers met to discuss the situation.[58]

Both Italian papers accused the English-speaking press of conspiring with the cannery owners in reporting that the strike had ended before the strikers had decided to return to work. Rumors to this effect were simply used to intimidate the workers, they claimed, and should be ignored. In a letter to the editor of *La Voce del Popolo*, one cannery worker wrote, "It doesn't matter what the cannery officials say. Their goal is to create discord among the workers to better subjugate them. But the workers know very well this trick and they know well what these people are trying to get at."[59]

If the cannery officials and the government were indeed setting out to create discord among the workers, the issue of patriotism became a convenient tool. One of the strike mediators, Ralph Merritt, referred to as the "dictator of food supply" by *L'Italia*, made the following speech to the workers during the strike:

> What the government wants you to do and what the government is interested in is that you listen to us as we are the representatives of the poor people of the United States and it is they who are going to be affected by this strike. Also, if the fruit is not packed, we are going to lose the war and if you do not want it said that the Italians of California lost the war you must listen to us and not ask what is right.[60]

Articles in the San Francisco and San Jose papers exploited the patriotism question in a more subtle manner. Rather than malign the "unpatriotic" activities of the Italian strikers, they repeatedly glorified the efforts of those who helped out in various ways during the strike. When the workers were still out on strike, middle-class women in the area took some

[57] *L'Italia*, July 31, 1917.   [58] *San Francisco Examiner*, July 28, 1917.
[59] *La Voce del Popolo*, July 30, 1917.   [60] *San Jose Mercury Herald*, July 28, 1917.

steps to save the fruit crop. One article described the bravery of women from the Oakland Defense Unit, who "risked their lives and led 100 housewives to work in the canneries." The article claimed that the Italian women workers—who had been frightened by IWW threats but were back at work already—were relieved to see such acts of patriotism and heroism. The middle-class women gave "confidence and a feeling of security to the workers."[61] Students from the University of California also took time off from their schoolwork to go into the canneries for a few days to prevent any fruit that was under government contract from spoiling.

Patriotism became an advantageous tool to pit the "loyal" middle class against the "suspect" Italian workers. Sensitive to accusations of "un-Americanism," the Italians became the victims of a psychological weapon meant to discourage working-class solidarity. Women of Alameda County advocated a plan to set up distribution centers in Oakland where women could buy the fruit to can at home. The San Francisco *Labor Clarion*, the official organ of the AFL San Francisco Labor Council, showing little sympathy for the efforts of the Toilers, made one of its few references to the strike by supporting the home-canning drive as a patriotic wartime undertaking. It even suggested that each neighborhood arrange "canning bees."[62]

La Voce del Popolo responded to this strike-breaking activity with reports that the women and students were not taking the work seriously and were unconscious of the fact that they were taking jobs away from workers who needed them. Similarly, the *Tri-City Labor Review* of the Alameda Labor Council satirically called the middle-class women "saviors of our apricots" who "scabbed for the miserable half-starved crew of striking women in the canneries."[63] Oakland's socialist newspaper exclaimed that the "society women" had no shame and decried "these women who have all the luxuries of life, working for those who really need to make the money." The newspaper suggested that if these women wanted to help they should look into the conditions of the canneries and "expose the dirty deal the workers get in these scab holes of California."[64]

By July 31 the mediation team had reached an agreement with eleven canning companies in and around San Jose. On behalf of the Toilers, the

---

[61] *San Francisco Examiner*, August 1, 1917.   [62] *Labor Clarion*, August 17, 1917.
[63] *Tri-City Labor Review* August 1, 1917.   [64] *The World*, August 3, 1917.

AFL agreed to represent only the male workers.[65] Although the evidence is inconclusive, it appears that the Toilers made this concession in order to stay within the AFL. The Toilers agreed that the men would be paid no less than 30 cents an hour up to January 1, 1918. The women workers would be represented by the Industrial Welfare Commission, an informal member of the mediation process which the AFL accepted as their "legitimate" voice. The commission raised the hourly rate from 16 cents to 17½ cents, and the piece-rate scale was raised a few cents per box. The companies agreed to abide by the decisions until the first of the year, and the workers agreed to work without striking for that period. In addition, all strikers were to be reemployed without discrimination. However, the employers did not recognize the Toilers of the World. They feared that union recognition would lead to annual negotiations and further labor trouble.[66]

It is not possible to understand the 1917 strike and its aftermath without examining both the influence of the radical IWW and the fear it engendered. It would have been tactically inconceivable for the Toilers to acknowledge any IWW involvement in their union. Likewise, it is understandable that the Italian press, striving to promote a respectable image for the Italians, continually stressed the absence of the IWW from the Toilers' rank and file. Despite these consistent denials, federal investigators and secret-service agents employed by the large corporations initiated a probe of IWW activities in California, Oregon, and Washington immediately after the strike's conclusion. By mid-1917 the government was harassing and prosecuting IWW members in every western state for treason in aiding and abetting the enemy.

At this point, we can only speculate how much the IWW was actually involved with the Toilers, but the fear was real, and the Toilers lost support as a viable labor union because of it. The San Francisco *Labor Clarion* never reported the chartering of the Toilers of the World and reported—briefly—on the strike only after it was over. On the other hand, the Alameda Labor Council paper covered the Toilers and the strike extensively. The Toilers had successfully penetrated the canning industry in the Bay Area and Santa Clara County, so the paper's attention to their activities is not surprising. What is unusual is the *Clarion's* curious silence.

---

[65] Brown, 375.   [66] *San Francisco Examiner*, August 1, 1917.

It is possible that the *Clarion* did not cover the cannery workers' strike because the Toilers was a federal union of unskilled workers. More likely, however, the *Clarion* was reluctant to report on a union that might have connections with what the *Clarion* editor called "the combination of mental defectives known as the Industrial Workers of the World." Referring to the formation of the United Railroad Workers union, the *Clarion* wrote, "The truth is, these persons with IWW proclivities never produce anything but trouble."[67]

Perhaps the AFL leaders in San Francisco thought that the rhetoric of the Toilers of the World resembled too closely the radical language of the IWW, particularly on the issue of labor's commitment to the war effort. Frequent editorials in the *Labor Clarion* pledged organized labor's support for the war. "Labor has ever been true to democracy," began one editorial, "and has never faltered when the call came for sacrifices to preserve or promote free institutions." The author boldly insisted, "If the captains of industry and commerce will stand as loyally and unselfishly by their country as do the workers there will be no cause for complaint and a speedy and victorious war will be the result."[68]

The language of the Toilers was much stronger and less obsequious:

[The cannery employer] who would deny his help a portion of his war profits is guilty of treason and should be so handled. The unprincipled operators of trade and stock exchanges, who dealing in foodstuffs have gambled, robbed and speculated, are the real traitors to the government and should be given short life, as aiders and abettors of the enemy.[69]

Decrying the inequity of profits and advocating profit distribution must have sounded too close to IWW philosophy.

AFL leaders were not alone in their desire to dissociate trade unionism from IWW radicalism. The state bureaucracy, embodied in the California Commission of Immigration and Housing, was equally interested, albeit for different reasons. The commission believed that IWW radicalism was eroding the potentially harmonious agricultural labor relations upon which their anti-union strategy rested. The IWW represented, according to commission member Carleton Parker, "an unfortunately valuable symptom of a diseased industrialism."[70] In order to uncover the

---

[67] *Labor Clarion*, July 21, 1917.
[69] *Tri-City Labor Review*, July 27, 1917.

[68] Ibid., April 13, 1917.
[70] Daniel, 98.

extent of IWW influence among the agricultural workers, the commission began covert investigation of IWW operations in 1914, which continued until the end of World War I.

J. Vance Thompson, a secret investigator employed by the commission, wrote regular, detailed reports on Bay Area labor activities, including the canning industry. Because he was paid to find evidence of IWW activity, his reports should be treated with circumspection. In May 1919 Thompson reported that a "well-organized insidious propaganda" was being spread among all agricultural and migratory workers. Supplying detailed evidence of the involvement of specific IWW members, Thompson argued that "their peculiar psychology of destruction furnishes effective avenues for successful operation by those designing to hamper the efforts of our government for efficiency."[71]

Thompson followed the meetings of the Toilers of the World and the strike very closely. It is likely that his reports to the commission encouraged its attempts to keep the conflict unpublicized. In one report on IWW activities in the Bay Area, he wrote that the IWW thrived on press publicity, "the more adverse, the more useful to their ends." According to Thompson, publicity only rallied sympathy for martyrdom and should be avoided at all costs. "New idols and new issues," he wrote, "are essential to the continuous success of the movement." He specifically suggested that to stop the spread of "noisy radical propaganda it will be necessary to eliminate the food upon which the movement thrives; namely, press publicity and the creation of martyrs."[72]

Thompson feared IWW sabotage and likened the situation in the Bay Area to a "dormant volcano." He believed that the Italians were particularly susceptible to IWW influence because "the majority of cannery workers are illiterate and frequently subject to ruthless exploitation." He elucidated the system of sabotage, known in IWW language as "wearing of the wooden shoe," and described in detail methods for burning store houses, barns, and fields. He also learned of the more subtle methods of destruction, such as filling a boiler with water in the winter and waiting for the frost to cause an explosion. According to this spy, not only were the Wobblies in San Francisco opposed to the U.S. involvement in

[71] J. Vance Thompson to George Bell, May 30, 1917, Simon Lubin Papers, CCIH, Bancroft Library.
[72] Ibid., June 18, 1917.

the war and outspoken in their sympathies for the kaiser, they were sabotaging the war effort by destroying crops and transportation facilities and, as the cannery strike revealed, curtailing food supplies.[73] Thompson admitted, however, that the presence of a strong AFL in San Francisco severely hindered IWW activity. He wrote, "The IWW complain bitterly against the friction between themselves and the AFL unionists, admitting that the strength of the latter around San Francisco hampers the activities of the Wobblies; they being kept too busy fighting the AFL to pay much attention to the Sab Cat (sabotage)."[74] According to Thompson, the IWW tried to persuade the cannery workers to leave the Toilers of the World and join the IWW by charging, "The AFL loses for you by selling you out. The IWW will win for you because we oppose the boss and demand full product of our toil." Circulars had been ordered, he reported, which would show the cannery workers "how their strike was sold just when they had the industry crippled, and victory in sight." The circulars were to be distributed in conjunction with IWW efforts to create dissatisfaction or partial stoppage at the plants and perhaps to agitate for another strike before the prune crop came in. Thompson credited the IWW for the success of the cannery strike and believed that "the Wobs had made the situation in San Jose impossible of being handled by any AFL official."[75]

In the end, Thompson did not provide a conclusive answer to the question of whether the IWW was involved in the Toilers. He maintained that when the cannery workers did not leave the Toilers as the IWW urged, the IWW then urged its own members to join the AFL in their respective crafts, including canning, and to get themselves elected as delegates and to official positions. Thompson buttressed his argument by claiming that efforts to destroy the California fruit crop were widespread and threatening and that the sabotage was "AFL in name, Wobblie in action."[76] Moving into the AFL would have been a major departure from IWW policy, which had always been to have nothing to do with the AFL and to repudiate the "boring from within" strategy.[77] If Thompson's

---

[73] Ibid., March 26, 1917.   [74] Ibid.
[75] J.V. Thompson, Notes on IWW Activities, n.d., Simon Lubin Papers, CCIH, Bancroft Library.
[76] J.V. Thompson, Notes on Industrial Situation, August 7, 1917; Thompson, Brief Report of IWW Situation in California at Present Date, July 18, 1917, Simon Lubin Papers, CCIH, Bancroft Library.   [77] Foner, 415–34.

report was true, it no doubt reflected serious differences within the IWW which came in response to the mass wartime hysteria aimed directly at crushing the organization. But however internal divisions may have weakened the IWW, they only contributed to its demise. Although the Wobblies in California tried repeatedly to revive their organizing campaign among agricultural workers, federal repression rid the state of all IWW activists, making questions of organizing strategy moot.

The Toilers of the World did not last much longer. In 1918 the union called another strike over wages and hours in an Oakland cannery, but it ended quickly, arbitrated by the same mediation team that had ended the 1917 strike. The Toilers left the AFL in 1918 but continued to push for $3.50 for an eight-hour day. A year later the union, now known as the Fruit Workers Union, returned to the AFL, which then tried to organize all the local unions in California under the name of the Fruit and Vegetable Workers Union. That union gave up its charter in 1922 when agricultural prices declined sharply and its organization crumbled. In 1920 Gov. Hiram Johnson ordered the Industrial Welfare Commission to set wage rates for the entire fruit and vegetable industry. It adjusted grievances throughout the state in cooperation with the cannery owners and without the interference of trade unionists. The canners were pleased with this arrangement and complied with the commission's rulings throughout the 1920s.[78]

Following the Industrial Welfare Commission's lead, the canning companies tried to appease the workers in order to avoid further labor unrest. After the merger of California's four leading canneries, the new Del Monte Corporation was as interested in presenting the image of one unified national brand to its employees as it was to the consumer. Eager to develop harmonious labor relations, Del Monte tried to create a sense of family, camaraderie, and devotion to a larger entity.

In 1918 a committee of management employees began publishing a monthly periodical financed by the corporation and entitled *Del Monte Activities*. Written by and for middle management, the magazine reported the social activities of each department, usually rumors of romances between floors, and the scores of company baseball games. The workers

---

[78] Kenneth Smith, "Industrial Relations in the California Fruit and Vegetable Canning Industry" (M.A. thesis, University of California, Berkeley, 1949), 103–8.

in the canning plants were rarely mentioned. In one issue, however, the editors printed a poem written by "a young lady whose thoughts . . . though she is busy selecting quality fruits for Del Monte consumers, turn to the patriotic aspect of the work":

> Merrily we work along
> work along
> work along
> In the cannery.
> The fruit we can is Del Monte
> Del Monte
> Del Monte
> The best brand in the land.[79]

In 1919 the editors of the *Del Monte Activities* announced the addition of *The Lug Box*, a newspaper intended to tie the "home office" with the "outside employees." The majority of the articles were in English, and since some reports suggest that most of the Italian workers read only Italian, it is likely that they never even read the paper. There was, however, one section translated into Italian, Spanish, and Portuguese, designed to convey a message about workers' roles in the plant. One article explained, "Irrespective of what your work may be, yours is the most important work in the plant. If you do not do your own work carefully and thoroughly, you are a weak link in the chain."[80] Another article that might well have been titled "From Stockboy to Superintendent," outlined "steady but sure progress" in the career of one Italian cannery worker. His promotions over the years exemplified, according to *The Lug Box*, the truth that:

> The heights by great men reached and kept
> Are not attained by sudden flight;
> But they, while their companions slept,
> Were toiling upwards through the night.[81]

The lessons were clear: work hard, and maybe one day you will be promoted to foreman of the plant. The paper explained that to work at Del

---

[79] *Del Monte Activities*, July 1918, Del Monte Archives.
[80] *The Lug Box*, September 1919, Del Monte Archives.
[81] Ibid., July 1919.

Monte meant more than just having a job. Workers were to think of themselves as part of a much larger organization, dedicated to the common cause of packing the world's finest fruits and vegetables.

The development of labor relations within the canning industry and the program of protective labor legislation initiated by the state filled the gap left by the demise of the trade unionists and the IWW. In the 1920s welfare capitalism replaced collective economic and political action. It was not until the crisis of the 1930s that worker militancy and the radical leadership of the communists, built upon the ruins of the IWW insurgency, altered the state's agricultural sector, and led to the organization of the Cannery and Agricultural Workers' Industrial Union.

But in 1917, the cannery workers had no such powerful and committed leadership. The AFL was unwilling to organize and support agricultural and unskilled workers wholeheartedly. It was reluctant to organize women. And it was leery of the Toilers' possible association with IWW radicalism. In the eyes of the AFL, the Toilers of the World was a renegade union. The IWW, in contrast, was eager to organize unskilled agricultural workers and made a special effort to organize women. Yet the Toilers were not willing to give their full allegiance to the IWW.

The Italian cannery workers were caught in the middle of a labor movement riven with conflict. Aggravating their situation was the need to assert their class interests and yet gain respect as patriotic Americans. The Italian press expressed this tension, supporting the strike and the workers' class consciousness, but always with ambivalence. The Italians were torn both between two different tendencies in the American labor movement and between their own conflicting desires.

I would like to thank Professor Lawrence Levine's research seminar at the University of California, Berkeley. Special thanks to Stephen Aron, Dario Biocca, Gordon Huckins, Nina Silber, Stanley Tamarkin, and John Torpey.

Go East, Paesani
EARLY ITALIAN AMERICAN
MAJOR LEAGUERS
FROM THE WEST COAST

By Lawrence Baldassaro

I N RECENT YEARS, the ethnic and racial dimension of baseball has become a frequent subject of serious scholarly inquiry. To date, however, little attention has been paid to the history of Italian Americans in major league baseball. This essay will examine the crucial role that players from the San Francisco area played in the evolution of Italian American participation in major league baseball.

The origins of baseball are typically associated with New York, since baseball as we know it was first codified in the 1840s by the Knickerbocker Club. Even Italian American ballplayers are likely to be thought of as New Yorkers, since so many of the prominent players, such as Joe DiMaggio, Yogi Berra, Phil Rizzuto, and, more recently, Mike Piazza, have played for New York teams over the years.

However, for many years virtually all of the important Italian American major leaguers were to come from the San Francisco Bay Area, but they played, of course, in the East. Until 1958, there were no major league teams west of St. Louis. Of the six players who made their major league debut between 1910 and 1920, three were from San Francisco, and two of the other three were also from California (Napa and Santa Barbara). By 1930, only one Italian American born in New York City had made it to the major leagues. And even by 1940, by which time more than forty Italian Americans had appeared on major league rosters, only four were from metropolitan New York.

By that time, at least sixteen players from the San Francisco Bay Area had played in the big leagues, as well as at least four others from other parts of California. Several of them had long and successful big league careers, and three of them (Tony Lazzeri, Ernie Lombardi, and Joe DiMaggio) ended up in the Hall of Fame. Their journey east, to make a living playing the game that for many was the very symbol of America, was an ironic reversal of the long westward journey their parents had made from Italy a generation earlier in search of the American Dream.

As with Italian Americans in general, Italian American baseball players are typically associated in the public's mind with eastern cities. Think of all the prominent figures, such as Joe DiMaggio and Carl Furillo, who have played for New York teams over the years. Yet, after Ed Abbaticchio—a native of Pennsylvania who made his major league debut in 1897—it was to be a long time before another Italian American from the East Coast would have a significant major league career. By 1940, by which time more than forty Italian Americans had appeared on major league rosters, only four were from metropolitan New York.

Why did such an apparently unlikely place as San Francisco prove to be so fertile a breeding ground for major leaguers of Italian descent? There are at least two elements that help account for the city's prominent place in Italian American baseball history: a large Italian population and a strong baseball tradition that fostered, more than in large eastern cities, the development of players from that population.

The origins of baseball have always been associated with the East Coast, but baseball made its way to the West Coast prior to the Civil War. By 1866, several Bay Area teams had formed the Pacific Base Ball Convention, and by 1867, there were about one hundred organized clubs in California. California became a hotbed of amateur and semi-pro baseball, particularly in San Francisco. As in other cities and towns across America, youth teams were sponsored by civic and fraternal groups, businesses, and churches. By the mid-1880s, there were two professional leagues in the state, the California League and the California State League, each with three franchises in San Francisco, the Pacific Coast

Oakland baseball player Ernie Lombardi, the only catcher to win two batting titles, was one of the stars of the Pacific Coast League. Minor League clubs enlisted the talents of locals who had honed their skills In the sand lot baseball of San Francisco and adjacent Bay Area communities. *California Historical Society, FN-40010.*

League was recognized by organized baseball in 1904 as a Class A league, at that time the highest minor league classification.[1]

ITALIANS IN CALIFORNIA

AT THE SAME TIME that baseball was planting its roots on the West Coast, Italians were settling in California in increasing numbers. In many ways, their experience differed from that of their counterparts in the East. As many historians have pointed out, Italians in San Francisco generally encountered less hostility and enjoyed more opportunity than did their counterparts in large eastern cities.

By 1920, San Francisco had the sixth-largest Italian community in the United States, with 24,000 immigrants and another 22,000 American-born. Italians accounted for 16 percent of San Francisco's foreign-born population; only New York City had a higher percentage. Italians in San Francisco were also less segregated than in other cities, though the heaviest concentration lived in the North Beach area, not far from Fisherman's Wharf. While North Beach was generally a low-rent neighborhood, it was a far cry from the squalid tenement districts that so many immigrants occupied in the large urban centers of the East. Even for struggling newcomers, the American experience was generally less oppressive than it was for so many Italians elsewhere.[2]

BASEBALL IN SAN FRANCISCO

ACCORDING TO HISTORIAN STEVEN RIESS, the primary reason why so few children of eastern and southern European immigrants played professional baseball in the first three decades of the twentieth century was the lack of facilities in the inner cities where they lived. It was difficult to acquire the experience and skills needed to play at the profes-

---

[1] For the history of baseball in California, see Dick Dobbins and Jon Twichell, *Nuggets on the Diamond: Professional Baseball in the Bay Area from the Gold Rush to the Present* (San Francisco, 1994); Dennis Snelling, *The Pacific Coast League: A Statistical History, 1903–1957* (Jefferson, N.C., 1995); and Paul J. Zingg and Mark D. Medeiros, *Runs, Hits, and an Era: The Pacific Coast League, 1903–58* (Urbana, Ill., 1994).
[2] Dino Cinel, *From Italy to San Francisco* (Palo Alto, Calif., 1984), 19–21.

sional level by just playing in the streets and alleys.[3] Unlike those crowded inner cities, San Francisco had numerous playgrounds where boys could play baseball.

The availability of such facilities in San Francisco, together with a relatively mild climate, undoubtedly contributed to the development of baseball talent among young Italian Americans. Andrew Rolle, in his study of Italian immigrants in the West, noted that boys in San Francisco "played the game in an environment bereft of slums in the usual sense." The Italian quarter of San Francisco "seemed less cluttered, depressing, and confusing than the Columbus Squares of eastern metropoli."[4]

One of the city's playgrounds sat right in the middle of the Italian quarter of San Francisco. It was at the North Beach Playground (now called the Joe DiMaggio Playground) where many of the Italian American children who later became professional ballplayers first learned to play the game. There they played on blacktop, but nearby, on the western edge of North Beach, was Funston Playground, another training ground for young Italian American ballplayers, but one that had two authentic baseball diamonds.

For the Italian American kids growing up in the neighborhood, playing ball was *the* thing to do. One of those kids was Dario Lodigiani, who grew up a few blocks from the DiMaggio family in the North Beach neighborhood and went on to play in the major leagues for six years beginning in 1938. He played on the local playgrounds with both Joe and Dom DiMaggio. "Things were kind of tough," he recalled when I interviewed him last year.[5] "We played a lot of ball. There was nothing to do. A lot of us couldn't afford the price of going to different places, so we stuck around Funston Playground, North Beach Playground, and the different playgrounds around San Francisco.

"Of course, the Italian ballplayers came out of mostly Italian neighborhoods, like all of North Beach and the Marina. At that time we were just a bunch of friends playing, not knowing that we were going to have one of the most famous players of all time playing with us."

---

[3] Steven A. Riess, *City Games: The Evolution of American Urban Society and the Rise of Sports* (Urbana, Ill., 1989), 104.
[4] Andrew F. Rolle, *The Immigrant Upraised: Italian Adventurers and Colonists in an Expanding America* (Norman, Ok., 1968), 290.
[5] Dario Lodigiani, personal interview, October 2, 2000.

Lodigiani recalled the amateur baseball scene in San Francisco in the twenties and thirties. "No matter what park you went to there was a ballgame going on. There was always some place to play. On Sunday, they started at 8 in the morning, then 10, 12, 2, and 4. If you showed any kind of ability you always had a place to play."

Well aware that he is part of the Italian American baseball tradition of San Francisco, Lodigiani can name all the local players who made it to the big leagues, as well as those who never got beyond the Pacific Coast League. But as a kid playing at the North Beach Playground he never dreamed that he, or any of his friends, would become big-league players. "The Coast League was really the big thing out here when we were kids," he said. "We never thought of New York, Philadelphia, Chicago, or anything."

Most of the Italian American ballplayers from California who did make it to one of the big-league cities played in the Pacific Coast League on their way up.[6] The vitality of the minor leagues in California was possible because of the rich pool of talent that was nourished first on the local sandlots and then in the amateur and semi-pro leagues that flourished in California, nowhere more so than in the San Francisco area.

In his 1994 history of professional baseball in San Francisco, *Nuggets on the Diamond*, Dick Dobbins, who grew up in Oakland, confirmed Lodigiani's assessment of the local amateur baseball scene. "The early phenomenon of sandlot baseball—a term that originated in San Francisco—became an institution here," he wrote. Dobbins, in fact, was convinced that, as children playing on those sandlots, he and his buddies were "growing up in the richest baseball center in the world. The game may have been 'invented' in upstate New York and played professionally for the first time in Ohio, but the true heart of American baseball is right here in the Bay Area."[7]

---

[6] Some Italian American ballplayers spent all or most of their careers in the Pacific Coast League. Billy Raimondi, an Oakland native, played for twenty-one years in the PCL (1932–53) and was one of the league's most popular players. A catcher who wore glasses, he was a PCL All-Star sixteen times. Three of his brothers—Ernie, Al, and Walt—also played in the PCL. Art Garibaldi, of San Francisco, compiled a .293 lifetime average playing as an infielder for three PCL teams between 1931 and 1942. In 1936, he appeared in seventy-one games for the St. Louis Cardinals and hit .276.

[7] Dick Dobbins and Jon Twichell, *Nuggets on the Diamond: Professional Baseball in the Bay Area from the Gold Rush to the Present* (San Francisco, 1994).

The availability of playing facilities, the large number of amateur teams and leagues, and a moderate climate enabling year-round play were all factors that contributed to a high level of competition that, in turn, enabled young players to hone their skills. Only the most talented and dedicated players could succeed as they grew into their teens and faced stiffer competition from the best players in the Bay Area. At the same time, the increase in the number of organized teams at the amateur level made it more likely that talented players would be seen and recommended by local scouts. And the increase in the number of minor leagues after the turn of the century (including the Pacific Coast League) meant that there were more opportunities for young men to make a living playing the game. It was because of that baseball-rich environment that San Francisco, and not New York, Philadelphia, or Chicago, produced the preponderance of early Italian American major leaguers.

Ping Bodie

As noted earlier, by 1940 sixteen Italian Americans from the San Francisco Bay Area had played in the major leagues. Many of them went on to have notable careers in the major leagues. The most famous, of course, was Joe DiMaggio. But there were also his brothers, Vince and Dominic, and Dolph Camilli, Ernie Lombardi, the only catcher to ever win two batting titles, and several others. But here I shall only speak briefly of two players.

The first San Francisco native of Italian descent to make his way from the sandlots to the major leagues was also the first Italian American, after Ed Abbaticchio, to have a notable big-league career. He would also prove to be one of the most colorful characters in baseball history, but fans would not have known from his name alone that he had a drop of Italian blood in his veins. He played his entire professional career as Ping Bodie, but he was born as Francesco Pezzolo.

After originally immigrating to New York, by 1876 his parents had moved to Bodie, California, a booming and lawless gold-mining settlement that obviously became the source for Ping Bodie's baseball pseudonym. In the early 1880s, the family moved to what was then known as the Cow Hollow district of San Francisco and opened a grocery store. It was there that Francesco was born in 1887.

San Francisco Seals players Babe Pinelli and Ping Bodie, who went on to play for several major league clubs, were part of a vigorous Bay Area baseball tradition. As early as the 1880s San Francisco had six teams franchised by the California League and the California State League. Of the six Italian American players who debuted in the major leagues between 1910 and 1920, five were from San Francisco or nearby communities. *California Historical Society, FN-40015.*

A right-handed hitting outfielder, Bodie began his professional career in 1908 with the San Francisco Seals of the Pacific Coast League. By 1911, he was in the big leagues with the Chicago White Sox, then later played for the Philadelphia Athletics. Then, in 1918, his contract was purchased by the New York Yankees. The New York press heralded the arrival of Bodie, who by then had established a reputation as both a hard-hitting outfielder and a colorful character. A *New York Times* story on March 8, 1918, ran under the headline: "Pacific Coast Italian Welcomed by Huggins as Asset to Team."

Bodie, who stood five feet eight inches tall and weighed 195 pounds, was variously described in the press as stout, rotund, and even roly poly; one writer called him "one of New York's most famous spaghetti destroyers." Not surprisingly, given his ample physique, Bodie was not the swiftest of base runners. His lack of speed led to one of the more memorable lines in baseball lore. Following a failed stolen-base attempt, sportswriter Bugs Baer wrote: "Ping had larceny in his heart, but his feet were honest."[8]

In 1920, Bodie got a new teammate when the Yankees purchased Babe Ruth's contract from the Red Sox. Bodie's name will forever be linked with that of Ruth because of one of the most frequently quoted lines in baseball literature. Bodie was Ruth's roommate for a time, before the Babe decided to room by himself. When a reporter asked Bodie what it was like to room with the freewheeling Ruth, who rarely spent time in his hotel room when on the road, he replied: "I don't room with him, I room with his suitcase." [There are several variations of this quotation. According to Frank Graham, in his *New York Yankees* (1943), the question was posed as "Who are you rooming with, Ping?" the reply was "With a suitcase." In a 1953 interview Bodie claimed it was in answer to a question posed by a writer when he was playing minor league ball in Wichita Falls, Texas after his major league career ended.[9]

After his nine-year major league career ended in 1921, Bodie spent the next seven seasons playing minor league ball in the Pacific Coast,

---

[8] *The Sporting News*, December 27, 1961.
[9] Robert W. Creamer, *Babe: The Legend Comes to Life* (New York, 1983), 222. Incidentally, one of Babe Ruth's nicknames, "the Bambino" (Italian for "baby"), was apparently the creation of his Italian American fans.

Western, and Texas leagues, In 1928, at the age of 41, he finished his professional career by hitting .348 while playing for San Francisco in the Pacific Coast League.

WHAT'S IN A NAME?

I WANT TO SAY A FEW WORDS about Bodie's name, not only because he was the first of many Italian American ballplayers to change his name, but also because it offers an example of the pressure to assimilate that so many Italian Americans faced. Obviously Bodie played under an assumed name because he felt it was desirable to conceal his ethnic identity so as to appear more "American" and therefore acceptable and mainstream. The bias against foreign-sounding Italian names was so blatant that in a story that appeared on May 12, 1918, New York *Tribune* reporter Wood Ballard could write of Bodie: "Ping needs a stage name. Pezzolo wouldn't look well in a box score."

Bodie's father, by the way, was never pleased that his son abandoned the family name, so much so that he kept him out of his will. In a telephone interview, Bodie's nephew, Joseph Pezzolo, told me that his grandfather said of Ping: "If my name isn't good enough for him, neither is my money."[10]

It is ironic that the first of what was to be a large number of Italian American players to have an impact in New York, with its huge Italian population, played under an assumed name. To add to the irony, even though Ping Bodie abandoned his family name, he was proud to think of himself (mistakenly) as the first Italian to play in the big leagues. In his obituary in *The Sporting News*, Bodie is quoted as acknowledging that his father had been angry about the name change, "because I became a national figure and the first player of Italian descent to reach the majors."[11]

Though his claim of being first was inaccurate, Bodie was a pioneer. He was the first Italian American ballplayer from the West Coast to gain national attention, and he was the first to break into the big show out East. In that way, he opened the door for the many others from San

[10] Joseph Pezzolo, telephone interview, August 16, 1999.
[11] *The Sporting News*, December 27, 1961.

Francisco and other parts of California who would make a living playing baseball, either in the major leagues or in the Pacific Coast League.

TONY LAZZERI

BY THE MID-TWENTIES no more than thirteen players identifiable as
Italian Americans had ever played in the major leagues. Then, along
came Tony Lazzeri, the first Italian American to become a major league
star. A native of San Francisco, Lazzeri began his professional career in
the Pacific Coast League in 1922. In 1925, the right-handed-hitting second baseman hit sixty home runs for the Salt Lake City Bees. (No one
in professional baseball at any level had ever hit that many home runs.)
He joined the Yankees in 1926, stepping right into the starting lineup,
and was a key member of the famed 1927 "Murderer's Row" Yankees,
thought by many to be the greatest team of all time.

In his rookie year, he hit eighteen homers (third in the American
League) and drove in 114 runs (trailing only Babe Ruth in the American League). In each of the next four years he hit over .300, reaching a
career-high of .354 in 1929. Over the course of his fourteen-year career,
Lazzeri compiled a lifetime average of .292. On May 24, 1936, he became
the first player in major league history to hit two grand slams in one
game, and he set the still-standing American League record with eleven
runs batted in.

At five feet eleven inches and 160 pounds, Lazzeri surprised observers
with his power; his work as a boiler maker's assistant had given him
tremendous strength in his forearms. Lazzeri was a tough kid from the
streets of San Francisco. "It was always fight or get licked," recalled
Lazzeri, "and I never got licked."[12] But as a major leaguer Lazzeri never
got into fights. On the field he was a no-nonsense, hard-nosed player,
but he was mild-mannered and quiet, well-liked and respected by both
teammates and opponents.

Photos of Tony Lazzeri often remind me of those of Italian immigrants at the turn of the century; he gazes straight into the camera with
doleful eyes and shows little or no trace of a smile, looking somewhat
apprehensive, even insecure. Even in his early photos, he does not look

---

[12] *The Sporting News*, December 11, 1930.

like a boy playing a game for the fun of it, but a man going about the serious business of working to make a living. He was, I think, the perfect hero for the children of immigrants who inherited their parents' stern work ethic.

True to the image conveyed in those photos, he was also a man of few words. As one writer put it, "trying to interview Tony Lazzeri is like trying to mine coal with a comb and a nail file." Another wrote, "Italians are noted for their volatile nature and excitability. In the main they are a joyous race. Lazzeri, however, moves in an atmosphere of settled calm, verging upon melancholy."[13]

But there was also a surprisingly mischievous spirit lurking behind the serious facade. Lazzeri was a notorious locker room prankster. One of his favorite targets was none other than Babe Ruth. In addition to nailing the Babe's shoe to the floor of his locker, Lazzeri liked to "doctor" Ruth's eye drops. When Ruth would come into the clubhouse after a long night on the town, he would clear his eyes with the drops, saying, "These are what makes the Babe hit." But before Ruth came in, Lazzeri had already emptied the solution from the bottle and filled it with water. Ruth apparently never knew the difference.[14]

From the beginning of his career the press took note of Lazzeri's ethnicity. When he hit his first home run as a rookie in a pre-season game against the Dodgers, a subhead in *The Sporting News* story on April 8, 1926, read: "Walloping Wop Comes Through," establishing an alliterative nickname that other writers would borrow in the future. The ethnic references would continue throughout Lazzeri's career; he was variously identified as "Signor Lazzeri," "the bronze Italian," "the hardhitting Italian," and the "favorite son of Italy." Even Paul Gallico, the first important sportswriter of Italian descent, followed suit in the October 9, 1927, issue of the New York *Daily News*, calling him 'The Wonderful Wop."

As both the statistics and the testimony of his contemporaries confirm, Tony Lazzeri was a key player on a Yankee team that won six pen-

---

[13] Frank Graham, *The New York Yankees: An Informal History* (New York, rev. ed., 1958), 115; F. C. Lane, "A Great Natural Ball Player is Tony Lazzeri," *Baseball Magazine* (December 1927), 305.

[14] Dario Lodigiani, telephone interview, March 6, 1999. Lodigiani was recounting a story he had heard from his friend, Frank Crosetti, Lazzeri's Yankee teammate.

nants and five World Series in his twelve years in New York. He was one of the most productive hitters on one of the most powerful teams of all time. In fact, his home-run and RBI statistics between 1926 and 1937 put him in the company of the game's most elite sluggers of that time. Over that period, only five players in the American League, all Hall of Famers, drove in more runs. And in that same span he hit more home runs than all but six American Leaguers.

He was also recognized by his peers and the press as a natural leader who possessed one of the keenest baseball minds of his time. When Lazzeri died, *New York Times* columnist Arthur Daley wrote: "He evoked infinitely greater admiration from the other athletes than he ever did from the fans." He was "a money player almost without equal and one of the smartest athletes ever to patrol the diamond. . . . Tony was one of the fastest thinkers baseball ever has had."[15] (Incidentally, Lazzeri played his entire career as an epileptic, though he never suffered a seizure on the playing field.)

Of all the ballplayers I have studied and written about, none fascinates me more than Tony Lazzeri. He is, I think, one of the best "forgotten" players in major league history. It was not until 1991, forty-six years after his death, that he was elected to the Hall of Fame by the Veterans' Committee. The problem was that he played in the gigantic shadows of his teammates, Babe Ruth and Lou Gehrig, the most potent one-two punch in baseball history. Lazzeri was no match for either their statistics or their "star power."

Ruth was in a class by himself, the lovable bad boy who captivated the entire nation. Gehrig was the strong, silent hero. For all that he did on the field, Lazzeri could never have been an equal member of that trinity of Yankee stars. Even though Gehrig, like Lazzeri, was the son of immigrants, he had gone to Columbia University, an automatic passport to American respectability. As an Ivy Leaguer, he was the embodiment of the fully assimilated second-generation ethnic. And, as a German American, his ethnicity was never a matter of note. Like the Irish, Germans had been so prevalent in major league baseball for so long that their ethnic background was no longer remarkable.

Lazzeri, on the other hand, was identified as an *Italian* ballplayer

---

[15] *New York Times*, August 9, 1946, p. 23.

throughout his career and was never able to transcend his role as an ethnic hero. That identity was perhaps inevitable, at least initially, since he was the star the Yankees had sought to draw Italian American fans to the ballpark. But continuing references to his ethnicity were also a sign of the times, when anti-immigrant feelings were still widespread. (Lazzeri was in his second season as a Yankee the year that Sacco and Vanzetti were executed.) Ruth was the "Babe," Gehrig the "Iron Horse"; neither was identified as "the German," much less as "the kraut." But for many, both in the media and in the stands, Tony Lazzeri was always the "wop" or the "dago," and therefore not qualified to be an authentic American hero no matter how well he played.

The time may not have been right for the son of Italian immigrants to be accepted as a full-fledged national hero, but it is difficult to exaggerate Lazzeri's significance in the evolution of Italian American participation in major league baseball. He was the first to achieve star status, and he was the first to draw large numbers of Italian fans to the ballpark. Both by his accomplishments and his demeanor, Lazzeri paved the way for the man who would enjoy the All-American status that eluded him. In 1936, he was joined in the Yankee lineup by another San Francisco native, Joe DiMaggio, who was destined to become an American cultural icon. But that's a story for another time.

PART FIVE

Italians Who Made a Difference

I N 1893 A JUNIOR PROFESSOR, Frederick Jackson Turner, presented a
seminal paper before the American Historical Association in which
he declared that the frontier—that area of free land at the distant
perimeter of American settlement—not only lured Americans westward,
but in the process, that frontier had uniquely influenced the American
personality.

The availability of free land in an area of low population density beck-
oned to the recently arrived and the urban dispossessed to seize the
opportunities it offered to assure their economic security. That free land
also attracted those eager to structure a society that embraced the prin-
ciple of democratic equality. Democracy, Turner contended, came not
from European theories reinterpreted at Jamestown or Plymouth Plantation, but rather it emerged from the West. He further contended that
in the West democracy was more strongly regenerated each time newcomers settled another frontier, where inherited class structures proved
inappropriate and traditional economic practices were outmoded. Ultimately, these western Americans were made equal by the success of their
endeavors and their worth was measured by their practical mastery of
the challenges confronting them.

Interacting with an environment abundant in resources but daunting in its vastness and unfamiliarity, settlers soon discovered that traditional behaviors did not bring about expected results. The challenges
posed by the frontier environment turned aside inherited traditions and
rewarded instead practical, innovative solutions to immediate problems.

The West's more fluid social order also offered greater opportunities
for social mobility. At the same time, the expanse of land allowed unprece-

dented physical mobility, resulting in often only temporary attachments to place and impermanence in relationships. A result of such detachment was a greater reliance on self and a stronger emphasis placed upon inner motivation and individualism.

On the western frontier, change, not conformity, was the order of the day. Newly discovered resources inspired imaginative entrepreneurs. Land and opportunity attracted diverse communities transported across the land by an expanding railroad network. The towns that emerged reflected the varied backgrounds and experiences of the settlers who gave expression to the place.

The result was a combination of diverse nationalities with the unique bond resulting from a common westering experience. Into the vacuum resulting from confrontation with the new, they thrust both their diversity and their shared experiences in the new land. Whether German, Bohemian, or Italian, to some degree each frontier settler reflected a self-reliant spirit and a concentration on the practical process. Consequently, a premium was placed upon equality and the importance of self-improvement.

The immigrant vanguard was a self-selected group. These migrants were daring enough to abandon the familiar for the unknown. They were unintimidated by change and unafraid to start over. To be willing to cross an ocean, travel endless miles on foot, on a wagon, or by train; to claim a homestead in an inhospitable setting—all required bravura, supreme self-confidence, admirable flexibility, and an unerring sense of independence.

The pioneer migrants admired the same characteristics in their heroes, including wilderness politician Davy Crockett, folk hero Paul Bunyan, the literary creations in James Fenimore Cooper's *Leather Stocking Tales*, and the dime novel swashbucklers created by Erastus Beadle. These admired frontier characteristics are also reflected among the Italian and Italian American settlers whose stories are told in the following selections.

Count Leonetto Cipriani captured a zest for life. He also displayed a wide range of talents and was successful in what he undertook. Cipriani's overland diaries, written between 1853 and 1871, record the frontier travels of a well-known leader of the Italian unification movement and an ally of the Bonapartes of France. In his efforts to achieve an independent Italy, Cipriani supported the Kingdom of Sardinia. But when Austrian forces gained the advantage by occupying Florence, resulting in the peace of Villa Franca, he temporarily decamped for Gold Rush San Francisco, where he served as consular representative of the king of Sardinia.

Cipriani returned to Paris in 1855, receiving the warmest welcome from his friends, the Bonapartes. To one member of the family, Jerome, former king of Westphalia, he described his stately home in Belmont, which he had shipped in 1,200 prefabricated sections, later assembled using 700 hooks and 26,000 screws. He also suggested the economic opportunities California offered. After overseeing marriage negotiations between Prince Napoleon of France and the House of Savoy, and participating in an exploratory voyage to a region of the North Sea, Cipriani returned in 1858 to California, where he joined Domenico Ghirardelli in establishing the Italian Hospital of San Francisco.

While traveling again to Europe to join the struggle of France and Sardinia against the Austrian occupiers, the mustachioed forty-seven-year-old Cipriani interrupted his travels long enough in Baltimore to marry the twenty-three-year-old Mary Tolley Washington, a descendant of Martha Washington, whom he had met in Paris. After a two-week respite, he departed for the war he had waited years to wage. Shortly thereafter Napoleon II appointed him governor of the former papal territory of Romagna.

Within the year factional bickering and the death of his young wife in childbirth caused Cipriani to sail again for America. Settling once more in California, he spent four years farming and mining, ignoring the occasional gaffs hurled by anti-monarchist Italian settlers from nearby San Francisco.

In 1864 the *Alta California* reported his departure for Italy, where he was declared count hereditary, appointed to the Italian senate, and given the honorary rank of general. Cipriani returned twice more to California, where he discovered the proverbial mining bonanza valued at more than $100,000. He subsequently withdrew to his castle, Bella Vista, near Centuri on the Corsican coast, where he spent his retirement with his second wife and nine children.

The dashing Cipriani, who stood six feet four inches, made several trips to the United States beginning in 1833–34 when he traded goods in New Orleans. But he is most noted for being the first Italian to describe the crossing of the Great Plains as part of a wagon train. His diary suggests that he was subject to the same vagaries of travel as other frontiersmen driving a herd of cattle westward, although his ire toward unscrupulous merchants who sold him rotten goods may have been expressed with greater eloquence. With rare literary fluency and acute attention to detail, he describes encounters with the Mormon community, the condition of the immigrant Chinese, and the development of the Italian community in the region around San Francisco. He is particularly affecting in describing the plight of Italian argonauts who did not meet with success in California.

In her autobiography, *At the End of the Santa Fe Trail*, Sister Blandina Segale clearly demonstrated that during her long life, which spanned two centuries, she possessed the independent spirit typical of frontier folk. She was unquestionably devoted to the three traditional vows made by all Daughters of Charity of St. Vincent de Paul, along with obedience to an additional religious rule that discouraged attachment to any particular place. Sister Blandina's deep religious commitment led her from her birthplace in Genoa where she was baptized Rosa Maria in 1854, and a childhood home in Ohio to the unfamiliar mining towns of southwestern Colorado and railroad outposts of New Mexico, where she labored for two decades.

Despite the limitations imposed by the rules of religious life, Sister Blandina was not constrained by the dictates of the "cult of true womanhood," which dominated nineteenth-century middle-class American culture. Sister Blandina enjoyed a greater latitude of action and expression, for her work as a missionary required that she exercise economic initiative. It also directed that she be enterprising in establishing outposts for her order's ministry. All of these were patterns of behavior shared with the self-made citizens of the West.

When directed by her order to relocate to Santa Fe, Sister Blandina grappled with the challenges of settling an unfamiliar land described by many single woman homesteaders. She displayed self-reliance and resourcefulness as she served on the battlefield, instructed the disadvantaged, and cared for the needy. As Sister Theresa Martin describes in her life sketch of Sister Blandina, her practical, independent turn of mind even led her to organize a bucket brigade to quench a fire enveloping the convalescent wing of her railroad workers hospital. In another case she may have saved the lives of four Colorado doctors whom Billy the Kid had vowed to scalp for refusing to treat one of his wounded gang members. Sister Blandina averted the scene by intervening and treating the man herself. Clearly, though obedient to her vows, Sister Blandina Segale, once assigned to her frontier outposts, led a uniquely self-directed life of accomplishment that was a priority among the emerging western values.

Frontier values were also reflected in the life of another Italian citizen of the West. According to the dean of western writing, J. Frank Dobie, Johnny Siringo was the first authentic cowboy to publish an autobiography. *Texas Cowboy or Fifteen Years on the Hurricane Deck of a Spanish Cow Pony* is a landmark contribution to the genre of cowboy literature. It accurately captures the life of a western cowboy, as do *Nine Scars Make a Man*, *Lone Star Cowboy*, *The History of Billy the Kid* and many more.

Siringo, the son of an Italian father and an Irish mother, was christened Charles Angelo. At eleven he had already become an able wrangler. In the course of his labors along the cattle trails he befriended the famed Billy the Kid and, finally, entrusted his memories to narrative and became an extremely popular writer.

Like so many other multifaceted individualists, while still young he embarked upon another career. At thirty Siringo became a Pinkerton detective, a member of the most effective crime-fighting agency in the United States at the time. He rose quickly through the ranks, in the process introducing such innovations as the well-known Rogues Gallery. Siringo even became a national hero when he singlehandedly foiled an assassination attempt on the president of the United States.

Distressed by what he perceived to be the government's harsh response to a legitimate labor protest, he returned to writing, recapturing his experiences in a series of volumes avidly read by the American public. His fans included oilman Edward Doheny and William S. Hart, a Shakespearean actor who became the consummate Hollywood cowboy. As a friendship developed between the actor and the writer, Siringo became a film consultant, assuring that such Hollywood films as *Tumbleweeds* captured an authentic western tone. In the following essay about Charles A. Siringo, "the daring adventurer in the old West," Neil M. Clark captures the myriad facets of a cowboy hero who, like the West itself, appears larger than life.

On ten acres of agricultural land north of Fresno, Baldassare Forestiere built an elaborate labyrinth of rooms connected by more than one hundred tunnels. This site served as his home for much of Forestiere's adult life.

From the 1920s until 1954 Simon Rodia labored to accent the south Los Angeles skyline with three 80-foot towers, along with fourteen other structures and a surrounding wall. These he covered with a colorful mosaic medley made from artfully combined pottery shards, shells, broken glass, and discarded artifacts. In his essay Ken Scambray explains that Simon Rodia's imaginatively crafted structures bear testimony to an expansive use of space and the creation of a prismatic variety of multi-hued surfaces that both reflect and refract the light of the sun.

In unique ways both Italian migrants created monuments to the new social order developed in the American West. They benefitted from its characteristic acceptance of independence, individualism, and free expression and the West's tolerance for the reformulation of traditional ways of doing things.

Scambray traces the lives of the two men, noting those elements that were of basic importance to the immigrant as he created a new world for himself in America: land, an opportunity to achieve, and a latitude for individual expression. Thus the Italian immigrant could succeed and prosper in a manner unique to his own personal vision.

Forestiere drew his inspiration for his labyrinth from mythology that constituted part of his native Sicilian oral tradition. As the author points out, Rodia uniquely expressed his own cultural assimilation by reinterpreting the tower celebrated in his native town of Nola by creating the Watts Towers, which were accented by artistic motifs created with the found objects of modern industrial America. The open expanse of the American West permitted each man to impart a unique individuality to the particular space around him.

The folk art, or perhaps "grass-roots art," created by these two Italian Americans embodies the essence of the new life of the Trans-Mississippi West, with the self-affirmation and self-assurance that the West's endless horizons of opportunity have nurtured. It explains the proposition understood by these men: where one came from was not as important as what one could do to solve the challenges one now confronted.

Arrival in San Francisco

EXCURSIONS INTO
THE INTERIOR OF CALIFORNIA

An excerpt from
California and Overland Diaries of
Count Leonetto Cipriani from 1853 through 1871

Translated and edited by Ernest Falbo

THE NEXT MORNING I went around the city, looking for an inn where I might stay under cover and take meals at a reasonable cost. In American inns, room and board cost thirty dollars a day, plus fifteen for our servant.

I avoided them like the plague, and asked to be taken to an Italian inn recommended by the coach driver. It was kept by a man named Martin,[1] of Genoese origin.

The next day, I took a letter of introduction given to me by Baron Brenier to Mr. Dillon,[2] the French consul, and I was received with the

---

[1] Martin—1852 San Francisco Directories list Frank Martin as the operator of a restaurant on Montgomery Street near California, probably the same Francesco Martini, proprietor of the Barnum Hotel restaurant on Commercial Street, which was destroyed by fire in 1857. The 1858 directory lists him as operator of a lodging house on the southwest corner of California and Montgomery Street. The 1860 directory lists Francesco Martini as proprietor of Martin's Restaurant, 153 Commercial and furnished rooms, 60 Sansome.

[2] Guillaume Patrice Dillon—French consul in San Francisco from 1850 to 1856, acting consul for Sardinia from 1853 to 1856 in San Francisco.

Count Leonetto Cipriani, a patriot
who was a leader in the Italian unification movement and a close advisor
to the Bonaparte family of France,
had many memorable adventures
during his several sojourns in the
United States. He married Mary
Tolley Washington, a descendant of
Martha Washington, who bore him
a son before her death. Not far from
his prefabricated villa at Belmont,
Cipriani extracted a fortune estimated to
be approximately $100,000 from his min-
ing operations in the Mother Lode.

utmost cordiality. Returning to the inn, I found Mr. Grover,[3] consul-
general of Austria, waiting there for me with Nicola Larco[4] and Ottavio
Cipriani.[5]

Grover introduced himself not so much as a colleague, but as an Englishman born in Leghorn. He was an intimate friend of the Bartolom-

---

[3] S. J. Gower—Listed as consul for Austria in San Francisco city directories for 1852 and 1854. Gower
apparently lived in California for a fairly long period and is recorded as having been an artist
and an early member of San Francisco's Bohemian Club.

[4] Nicholas Larco—Until his bankruptcy in 1873, probably the wealthiest Italian in California and
mentioned frequently in Sardinian consular dispatches. He is variously listed as a commission
merchant, importer, shipowner, and landowner. He invested heavily in mining and in silkworm growing. (See obituary notice, *Alta California*, March 14, 1878.)

[5] Ottavio Cipriani—Listed in San Francisco directories from 1850 to 1859 (no entries for 1856–57),
from 1852 to 1854 with the firm of Hinrichsen, Reincke & Co., commission merchants. Also
an advertisement of an O. F. Cipriani in the steamer edition of the San Francisco *Pacific News*,
March 1, 1850, p. 4, col. 4.

mei, so he knew all about me. Friends of my friends are friends of mine, and as such I proffered my hand. But as a consul, I never set foot in his house, for which reason we never saw each other again.

Nicola Larco was the richest Italian merchant in the city. He was a simple, frank, and goodhearted man. Ottavio Cipriani was my second cousin, the only son of the eldest son of my father's brother, Francesco Cipriani. Nicola and Ottavio were at the same time my fortune and my despair in California, There was no limit to the cordiality that they lavished upon me, but, on the other hand, thinking of my own interests they dissuaded me from buying land for speculation and so prevented me from accumulating an immense fortune in just a few years' time.

A few days after my arrival, the "Distruzione" docked in San Francisco. My household then had increased by four persons, so it was no longer possible for me to stay at the inn. We rented a small unfurnished frame house and slept on mattresses from aboard ship and did our own cooking.

Meanwhile, the cargo was unloaded and transported to the lot that I had purchased. We pitched our tents, which served as our residence while assembling my house.

The daily salary of bricklayers was $20, of carpenters $15, and $10 for manual laborers, so we had to resign ourselves to doing everything alone. So Garbi, Del Grande, Crespino Bizzarri and wife, Gosto, and I rose at dawn and worked until nightfall. It was hard work, and none of us was accustomed to it, but finally, by the end of June 1852, my house was put up, furnished, and occupied.

Where the city of San Francisco stands today there were, in 1848, only a few unpretentious houses and some Indian huts. The San Francisco mission was three miles inland. Soon after the discovery of gold in the West, San Francisco was organized municipally as an American city. But at the outset the city's growth was not rapid, since gold was discovered a hundred to three hundred miles in the interior and near navigable rivers, and the more practical Americans (Lord knows how marvellously practical they are!) were deceived by the example set by the Atlantic states, where the great commercial cities are located on the rivers and not on the

---

[6] March 9, 1852. (L. Cipriani, letter to Sardinian Ministry of Foreign Affairs, July 28,1852.)
[7] Morgan's San Francisco Directory 1853–2 lists Cipriani, Leonette, [*sic*] Sardinian consul, Sutter and Dupont.

coast. Furthermore, for more than a year, those who arrived in San Francisco hurried off to the interior, fearful of not getting there in time to participate in the gold harvest. Even the ships' crews deserted, and by 1850 there were more than a thousand abandoned ships in the bay.

Gradually, however, the city became populated, and as houses and public buildings were built, the value of property in the center increased proportionately. Within a short time, it had increased a hundred-fold. But in the outlying areas of the city, property values were low, since no one believed in the prodigious growth that the city was to have later. Besides, land values had undergone tremendous fluctuations, ruining many speculators.

Even Nicola Larco and Ottavio Cipriani, who had been in business for two years in San Francisco, had lost money in that type of speculation. When I explained to them that I had made the long journey for the express purpose of purchasing land, they were so strongly opposed to my plan that they ultimately dissuaded me from buying any land at all. In the end, I bought only a single lot, paying $1,000 for it, and on this lot I put up my house.

I then ventured into buying some vast extensions of land outside the city suitable for farming. But I failed there, too, since the owner and I could not agree on the price. It was a real shame, too. I offered $8,000 for the land to the $12,000 he wanted for it. Fifteen years later it sold for $200,000. Another ranch selling for $16,000 was sold for $300,000 ten years later.

After these failures, I decided to make another attempt further inland, and one night I went on horseback to visit the *rancho* of Gabilan,[8] which was located on a range in the California Sierra. Accompanying me was an Indian guide, sent by the ranch owner. We travelled all night, over mountains and plains, and the next morning, when the Indian still had not spoken of stopping anywhere, I asked him where he meant to have breakfast.

"Aqui cerquito," he answered, "Not far from here."

---

[8] A land grant, *Cienaga del Gabilan*, was granted October 26, 1843. The range was called Sierra de Gavilan in the 1840s (Castro Docs., II, 44), is mentioned as San Juan or Gavilan or Salinas range by Blaske in 1857, and is shown as Sierra Gabilan on Goddard's maps. Erwin G. Gudde, *California Place Names, A Geographical Dictionary* (Berkeley and Los Angeles, 1949), 276.

That *cerquito* turned out to be a ride until noon. We reached a beautiful valley filled with cattle, where we saw the place, a little house with smoke coming from the chimney. It was another *rancho* belonging to the same owner. There was much excitement, as a *rodeo* was going on.

To reassure our empty stomachs, quarters of oxen and deer were hanging from the trees. But there was neither bread nor wine. Everyone selected the meat he preferred, then cut away the piece he liked best and impaled it on a stick. Then, after roasting it over the coals of one of several fires, we ate the meat while it was still dripping. I did like the others, and ate that blood-dripping meat, which made up for the lack of wine.

After that meal fit for a cannibal, the Indians and more than a hundred other participants began horseback races and jousted with one another until nightfall. Then everyone, wrapped in his blanket, stretched out on the ground to sleep, I slept soundly from seven o'clock that evening until eight the next morning.

After a heavy breakfast of more of the same meat, the Indian went to the slaughter house and sliced thirty pounds of meat as if it were sausage, rolled it up, and tied it behind the saddle. That was to be our food supply for two days, in the unlikely event that we would not find game along the way.

Very late in the evening, we came to a wide valley. The Indian announced, "We're here," and dismounted at once. He put hobbles on the horses, lighted a fire and started to roast part of the "sausages." The meat could be considered already "cooked" by the sun and the horses sweat. The Indian offered it to me, with words of praise for its flavor, but I hesitated. It was not the half-raw meat which disturbed me, but the stink of horse hairs that had become entangled with the meat and roasted with it. My stomach was revolted, but at the same time it was rumbling from hunger, so without so much as a word, I took a piece and closed my eyes. Despite my first impression, I finally ate more than the Indian did.

Towards midnight, when I had just fallen asleep, I was awakened by horses' hooves pounding around the fire. There was no word or sign from the Indian; I lifted my head and saw, in the brilliance of the flame, shadows moving slowly. I reached for my carbine, but the Indian, as quick as lightning, took it from my hand. "*Por Dios! Que hace usted?*" he said, "Look at them. They're not men, they're bears. Let them stay, and go to sleep."

His was sound advice, based on experience. Bears left in peace never come near a fire, but once provoked, even slightly grazed by a bullet, they become ferocious and dangerous.

Being new to that kind of company, I did not sleep all night and thus could observe at my ease the habits of bears in those special circumstances. There were six of them, four big ones and two little ones, walking in groups of three. All night long they kept going around the fire, stopping only when the Indian threw more wood on the flame. At daybreak they disappeared, one after another, into the thick foliage.

Aware of my repugnance for his filthy meat, the Indian, on arising, took his carbine and went out, returning shortly with half a bear on his shoulders and a quarter of a deer in his hand. He then began to demonstrate his talent as a savage cook.

He cut off the head of the bear, wrapped it in damp grass, covered it with ashes and let it cook among the hot coals. He spitted the deer on a pole that was stuck at an angle in the ground, and kindled a fire under it.

Half an hour later, the roast was ready, burned from without but delicious inside. As for the bear's head, not only was it delicious, but it was white like pig heads when skinned in hot water. The bear head gave off an aroma that would have aroused the appetite of a dying man.

We rode all day across the tableland. It was one of those enchanting alpine sites—abundant water, a crystal lake filled with trout, wild game galore, hare and partridge by the thousands; and groves of pine trees along the summit. And in the valley there were meadowlands, where the horses half-disappeared in the verdure. Huge oak trees rose here and there, like in the parks of Europe, and in the distance towered the Sierra Nevadas with their eternal snows, and at their feet, in the immense plain, was the San Joaquin River, the largest in California. Altogether it was a magnificent sight. How was I to know then that in that very plain I would have found, in time, ample reward for all my efforts?[9]

[9] "On November 18, 1867, he (Cipriani) found gold there." (L. Cipriani, *Avventure*, vol. 2, p. 82n.) Possibly in or near Altaville in Calaveras County, California. The only reference other than the above footnote to Cipriani's sojourn in California from 1867 to 1868 concerns a ring, once the property of the Empress Josephine, which was lost in a fire at Altaville. (*Avventure*, vol. I, p. 74.) A footnote further explains: "Altaville, gold mine in Calaveras County, California. A fire on April 24, 1867, destroyed the house in which Cipriani and his son were living.

At two in the afternoon, after travelling the entire Gabilan range from north to south, we rode eastward to return to the *rancho* where the Indian hoped to arrive that same evening. At seven, however, my horse was too exhausted to go further. The Indian went on alone, promising to return as soon as possible with another horse for me. I waited for the Indian until ten o'clock, and then continued on the way until I was so tired, and the horse even more so, that I had to stop. I built two big bonfires, ate a piece of bear meat and, wrapped up in my blanket, I fell asleep. I slept soundly, making up for my loss of sleep the previous night caused by the bears.

At about two in the morning, I heard sounds. I thought it was the Indian, but instead realized that they had come from my horse, rearing and striking, defending himself from a dozen wolves.

The lesson I had learned the night before was of use to me now. I quickly stoked the fire around the base of the tree where I had been lying. Then, taking my carbine and pistols, I climbed into the tree and sat on a branch, with my back against the trunk. From that vantage point, I could study the lupine society at my ease, just as I had studied the bears the night before. The wolves struggled with the horse, and finally devoured it. Towards me, the wolves were of a rudeness without equal; they paid no heed to me at all, just as if I were not there. The wolves got along well among themselves, as long as there was meat enough for all of them, but when they got down to the bones, hostilities began. They howled and bit, grabbing the prey from one another's mouths.

They narrowly escaped with their lives." A search of Calaveras County records failed to disclose any mining claims or properties filed by Cipriani or by his friend, Nicholas Larco. (Letter of Sept. 5, 1958, Basil E. Esmond, County Recorder, San Andreas.) However, Larco, who managed Cipriani's investments, is listed as occupant (with Prince, B. R.) of the Altaville Quartz-Mills Company, in the *Pacific Coast Business Directory, 1867*, p. 73.

D. C. Demarest, 1865 Yosemite Road, Berkeley, an old-time resident of Altaville, letter to Calaveras County Historical Society, San Andreas, October 4, 1957, wrote:

"My father told me many times, about the early-days' operation of the Cherokee Mine by an Italian nobleman, whose name I have forgotten, but which I presume was Colonel Leonetto Cipriani, as Mr. Falbo has it. As my father related the story to me, the operation of the Mine at that time was profitable, and rumor had it that when the Italian gentleman quit the Mine to return to Italy, he was taking with him a large amount of recovered gold—perhaps as much as $100,000 in value. . . . I was always under the impression that when the Colonel left California for Italy, he transferred the Cherokee Mine to B. R. Prince. As far back as I can remember, Prince owned the Mine which was located on the Tucker Ranch, about a half-mile due west of the Altaville school house (brick structure built in 1858)." Mr. Demarest's father was superintendent of the Altaville–Angels Camp ditches for the Union Water Company in the 1860s.

Finally, at daybreak, the wolves ran off at the appearance of some *rancheros* who had come to take me to the *rancho*. Once at the ranch, I told them what had happened. It was then the poor Indian who spent an unhappy quarter of an hour. The overseer, without saying so much as "Hey, there," took his hatchet and threw it at the Indian, breaking his shoulder and calling, "Wild shameless dog!" The Indian deserved punishment for leaving alone in that wolf-infested valley a gentleman entrusted to his care by the master. And he deserved it even more for not having returned that same night as he had promised. But when I saw that the overseer was reaching for his rifle, I intervened for the Indian's sake, feeling that he had already been punished enough. The next day, I returned to San Juan, where the owner asked $5,000 for the Gabilan land.[10] I accepted, on the condition that the land titles be examined first by my lawyer. When I found out that though the land grant had been requested, it had not been confirmed by decree of the Viceroy of Mexico, I decided not to continue the transaction.

A month later, after recovering from the physical and emotional exhaustion of the first venture, I made another trip to northern California to look at several *ranchos* that were offered to me at moderate prices. Among these was the Clear Lake *rancho*,[11] about two hundred miles from San Francisco.

With my friends Megas[12] and Tintenmaker,[13] who wanted to come with me, I took a steamboat as far as Napa, and from there we travelled

---

[10] Probably San Juan Bautista in San Benito County.

[11] Obviously *Clear Lake* Rancho.

[12] Very likely Mezes, Simon Monserat. In Cipriani's handwriting "g" and "z" look alike, cause confusion. A receipt for taxes on this land reads "Received from G. H. Howard Esquire Two hundred and fifty seven 81/100 Dollars on a/c of Clear Lake taxes. San Francisco Nov. 24, 1855. S. M. Mezes, by O. Cipriani." (California Historical Society, San Francisco.) Mezes, born in Spain, became an influential banker in Puerto Rico. He arrived in California February 23, 1850, and organized the firm of Ranke, (?) Cipriani and Mezes, real estate operators. Died in 1884. The Cipriani referred to above is Octavius (Ottavio in Italian) Cipriani, Leonetto's cousin. For biography of Mezes, see Bailey Millard, *History of the San Francisco Bay Region*, vol. 3 (Chicago, 1924), 382–83.

[13] Teschemacher? (No "Tintenmaker" listed in San Francisco directories.) H. F. Teschemacher (1823–1904), prominent citizen and mayor of San Francisco during the Civil War, arranged the peace treaty between the white settlers and Clear Lake Indians in 1851 (?), and later, in 1852, was a claimant for Rancho Lupyomi (south shore of Clear Lake), then Napa County. Mildred B. Hoover, *Historic Spots in California* (Palo Alto, 1948), 247. Also, Bancroft's *History of California*, vol. V, p. 745.

on horseback with two Americans, who knew the country well, serving as guides.

The first night we spent at the abandoned "Rancho de las Putas," so disreputably designated because of a nearby Indian tribe living in a brutal state of nature.[14] We spent the second night at a hot springs, sulphur water at forty degrees centigrade, which was to become very famous later as baths for the treatment of rheumatism and the scrofula.[15] On the third day, we reached the shores of the lake, where we found the house of an American who served as doctor to the Indian tribes of the surrounding area.

The next day, following the north bank of the lake, we came to a beautiful valley, so beautiful that I named it "Paradise Valley," the name it was to retain, and as such it is marked on maps of California.[16]

The valley was semi-circular, facing east. We entered from a narrow canyon through which a precipitous stream emptied into the lake. The valley itself was a meadowland of about a square league. Brooks ran through the meadow and huge plain; green oak trees, with hanging branches like those of the weeping willow, stood along the banks. Here and there a stately cedar towered over all. Surrounding the valley were sloping hills, with groves of magnificent cherry trees, wild pear and apple trees no higher than half a meter but laden with fruit. What was most amazing were the multitudes of fawn, which resembled African gazelles, innocently grazing on the hillside. They drew near to us, like sheep do at the morning arrival of the shepherdess who comes to look after them. We were all carrying arms, but no one thought of shooting the fawns. How true it is that even with cruel man, and man is cruel toward wild

---

[14] In Berryessa Valley, Napa County, California. (See Erwin G. Gudde, *California Place Names, A Geographical Dictionary* (Berkeley and Los Angeles, 1949), 276. Also, Myrtle Garrison, *Romance and History of California Ranchos* (San Francisco, 1935), 165.)

[15] Calistoga, Napa County. In the 1850s, Sam Brannan bought the land then called *Agua Caliente*, or Hot Springs, and developed it into a resort. (See Erwin G. Gudde, ibid., p. 51.) Calistoga Springs was advertised for its "infallible cure for rheumatism" and scrofula. (See adv. in J. C. Fergusson, *Alta California Pacific Coast and Transcontinental Railroad Guide*. San Francisco, 1871.)

[16] Paradise Valley is on the east shore of Clear Lake, opposite Mt. Konocti. The Ukiah state highway (route 20) goes through it. Immediately west of Paradise Valley is Floyd Mountain, sometimes called Red or Bald Mountain.

animals, those appealing and harmless beasts can bring out gentleness. That valley was a reserve for the Indian tribes who came to hunt game when stormy weather prevented them from fishing in the lake.

Crossing the stream, the horses suddenly refused to go any further. "There's a bear!" the doctor shouted. And, as a matter of fact, reaching the far bank we saw a dozen bears, some in the branches of an old oak tree, others below eating acorns. Everyone immediately started shooting. Three bears were killed, and the others fled. It was the first time that I had the pleasure of seeing a bear at my feet felled by my own carbine. It was an enormous animal, weighing more than a thousand pounds.

After exploring the valley, we went out through the canyon from which we had entered. Going along the very edge of the lake, we saw at a certain point the six Indian canoes that the doctor had gotten ready for us for crossing the lake.

On earlier voyages to the New World, I had often embarked in other canoes, dug out of huge trunks, which are as safe as a ship with three decks. But these canoes are made of pieces of straw, rolled tightly round and round, like the straw plating used for hats, and joined with three or four more layers. The layers are put together and mounted on a framework of willows, like a breadbasket. It is difficult to understand how, but the fact remains that these canoes can carry two or three people easily.

It was a nice ride, and that evening we arrived at the doctor's house. Two Indian tribes were camped nearby around big bonfires.

During the night, there was a continual beat of drums and wailing of flutes. In the morning, the Indian men went out fishing and hunting for game to offer us as their customary gifts and to receive in exchange a hundred miscellaneous objects. Meanwhile, the doctor had disposed under thick green oak boughs all the gifts intended for the Indians, consisting of tobacco, blankets, handkerchiefs, knick-knacks, and other objects of little value.

Six runners on horseback, clothed in mantles of black and white feathers, announced the arrival of the tribes. The chiefs approached first, mounted on fine beautiful horses and followed by the warriors. Then came the most beautiful young Indian maidens carrying on their heads great baskets filled with fish, game, and wild fruit. Finally came the old people and the rabble with a throng of dogs, inseparable friends of the Indians.

Having placed the gifts in good order, the chiefs, one after the other, made speeches that I thought had two merits: one, they were brief; two, I did not understand a thing. The doctor answered on behalf of all of us, and then a strange thing happened. The two chiefs came up to me to give me a handshake, which is an American greeting, and to rub noses, an Indian greeting.

I do not know whether this had been planned earlier or whether my being taller and more military-looking than my companions struck the imagination of those savages (I was wearing a wide blue silk scarf around my waist), but the fact remains, they took me for a chief and presented me with the finest gift.[17]

My gift was a fair young beautiful Indian maid as naked as a fish, but covered from head to foot by her long black tresses. She knelt before me, and an old woman, priestess of the tribe, poured on her head a bowl of water in a solemn rite that testified that she was a maiden.

I did not expect such an honor, nor such a gift. But I did not lose my composure. I took off my coat, covered her, and had her sit at my feet. A cry of joy arose from the gathering, sounding like two thousand possessed with the devil. Then the chiefs had the cane flutes sounded, and the games began while the old women prepared the wild game which had been brought as a gift to us. The warriors on horseback took part in a game that consisted of running head on, at full speed, and trying to throw each other off their horses as they passed. For the others, the entertainment was dancing and somersaults, accompanied by the discordant sounds of the instruments.

When the roast was ready, the old women began to shout a word that sounded like *piro piro*, a sound that our Italian housewives are wont to use when calling the chickens. At the call, everyone left what he was doing and came rushing. My companions and I sat on one side and the Indians on the other, and we all began to feast. Those exquisite meats, the trout, weighing from ten to fifteen pounds, had been wrapped in aromatic herbs and roasted on the coals. The flavor would have had to concede nothing to the best dishes prepared by the most famous chefs of France. And the excellent wild fruits, too, made that spectacular banquet one of the episodes which has most impressed me.

---

[17] Cipriani was slightly less than six feet four inches tall. (L. Cipriani, *Avventure*, vol. 1, p. 7n.)

Afterwards came the distribution of gifts, which was accomplished in hierarchical order. And then came night, which would have been the hour of rest, had it not been for those two thousand bedeviled Indians, drunk with joy, who did nothing but jump and shout and carry on until morning.

Not knowing what to do with the Indian girl, I asked the doctor how I could let her go without offending the sensitivity of the Indian tribe, and the doctor advised me to give her to an Indian boy who was in love with her and who would have given his life to have her. He warned me, however, that in his presence I should pour on her head a glass of water to demonstrate that I was giving her to him as pure as when I had received her. Thus it was done, to the great joy of everyone.

The next morning we left, and on the third day we were back in San Francisco.

Although I was deeply taken with that *rancho*, I did not buy it, because of its great distance from the city, which did not give any great hope for a quick increase in land value. Besides, the Indians would have been bad neighbors, either as friends or enemies. But fourteen years later, in 1866, the Clear Lake valley contained a small city of three thousand inhabitants, more than three hundred farms, and a borax mine that brought in several million dollars annually![18]

---

[18] Probably Lakeport in Lake County. Lakeport had 512 farms, valued at $1,892,000, and a population of 2,970 in 1870. (See Bancroft, *History of California*, vol. 6, pp. 509–10. San Francisco, 1884.)

Life Sketch of
Sister Blandina Segale
1850–1941

By Sister Theresa Martin, S.C.

"GESU" WAS THE FIRST WORD the little Italian child, Rosa Maria Segale, learned to write at her home in the hilly village of Cicagna, Italy, Lingering over the sweetness of its sound, she smiled at her accomplishment and then laboriously added, "Madre."

Nearly a century later when she lay dying in the infirmary at the motherhouse of the Sisters of Charity near Cincinnati, Ohio, Rosa Maria Segale, now known as Sister Blandina, serenely whispered, "Gesu, Madre," smiled, turned her head, and died.

Rosa Maria Segale was born on January 23, 1850, in the northern Italian village of Cicagna, which lies about fifteen miles above Genoa in the thickly populated section of the Ligurian hills. Her mother, Giovanna Malatesta, was noble and good. To her the elder Genoese women came for wise counsel in Italy and later in America. Sister Blandina wrote of her mother, "My father kept secret my mother's illustrious family name, for those were days of revolution in Italy. In the Middle Ages my mother's family had absolute control or they would know why."

Francesco, her father, was a proficient overseer and owner of two well-cultivated orchards. For generations the Segale family had lived and died in their stone houses in the rocky and rugged Ligurian hills. Known to the villagers as *Il Signorino* (The Little Lord), Francesco was quiet, refined, sensitive, and adored by his five children.

After the baby Rosa Maria was baptized, Giovanna took her, as was her custom, to the mountain sanctuary of Mont' Allegro, to present her to our Lady Santa Maria. Over the high altar of the church is the Byzantine painting *The Dormition of the Virgin*, which legend decrees was miraculously transported from Dalmatia. Offering her newly born, Giovanna prayed, "To help mankind, *Madre mia*, to comfort the sorrowful . . . to harbor the harborless . . . to visit the sick . . . to teach your ways to mankind."

When Rosa was four years old her father and mother gave away their stone house and their orchards, and left revolution-tossed Italy for America. Accompanied by Andrea, 11; Maria Maddelena, 8; Catalina, 6; and Rosa, they set sail from Genoa and landed at New Orleans three months later. Cincinnati was their objective. A few Genoese had preceded them there, and the city appealed to them because Giovanna hoped to be able to help her countrymen there, and because the Segales had heard that Cincinnati was built upon seven hills. "It will remind us of Cicagna," Giovanna had encouraged Francesco,

The early Cincinnati days were filled with loneliness, language difficulties, dire poverty. Concerned about her children's future, Giovanna hired an English teacher and somehow managed to pay for the lessons. The Segales all lived in one room at Main and Canal streets. There little Catalina died. An immigrant, Mr. Novello, finally prevailed upon a friend to allow Francesco to open a fruit stand on his corner, Front and Sycamore streets. From the beginning Francesco's business thrived, and when Bartolomeo, the older boy, completed his studies in Italy and came to America, he persuaded his father to open a confectionery store. From then on Francesco was quite successful.

Little Rosa made her First Holy Communion after a year of preparation on April 21, 1861, at the Cathedral of St. Peter in Chains. She was confirmed that same afternoon by the Most Reverend Archbishop John Baptist Purcell. She attended schools conducted by the Notre Dame Sisters, the Sisters of Mercy, and Hughes Intermediate School. Meanwhile the Segales had purchased a home at 461 West Fifth Street. There the other children were born. When Rosa completed grammar school, she was allowed to attend Mt. St. Vincent Academy, Cedar Grove, a school

Rosa Maria Segale, born near
Genoa in 1854, settled with her
family in Cincinnati, Ohio. She
joined the Daughters of Charity
of St. Vincent de Paul and after
her novitiate Sister Blandina
Segale was assigned to teach in
Trinidad, Colorado. For twenty-
one years she ministered to Italian
immigrants who had made their
way to the Southwest following
the Santa Fe Trail.

conducted by the Sisters of Charity, in Cincinnati. Ever since she had
come to Cincinnati, Rosa had observed the Sisters of Charity as they went
about performing works of mercy, working among the sick, the orphans;
and she loved them. She knew that during the Civil War they nursed the
soldiers on the battlefields. One day she surprised her father by saying,
"Father, as soon as I am old enough, I shall be a Sister of Charity." After
completing her musical course at Cedar Grove, she entered the Sisters of
Charity motherhouse at the age of sixteen, September 13, 1866. Her beloved
sister and lifelong companion, Maria Maddelena, refused several marriage offers that same month and followed her younger sister to the Sisters of Charity motherhouse. She was known as Sister Justina.

   After pronouncing their holy vows on December 8, 1868, Rosa secretly prayed to be sent to the faraway West—Santa Fe—where the Sisters
of Charity had gone in 1865. Sister Blandina's desire was fulfilled in 1872,

after she had been on mission in Dayton and Steubenville, Ohio. During her twenty-one years in the West. Sister Blandina kept a journal of her experiences, which were published in 1932 under the title, *At the End of the Santa Fe Trail.*

Recalled to the motherhouse in 1894, Sister Blandina's next missions were in Ohio, at Fayetteville and Glendale. In August 1897, Mother Mary Blanche, mother general, entrusted the care of the Italians in Cincinnati to Sister Blandina and Sister Justina. From this time on the two sisters were never separated. This work of reconverting the immigrant Italians was dear to the heart of the Archbishop of Cincinnati, William Henry Elder, who had watched anxiously as proselytism spread among the Italian people. The work of bringing their own people back into the Faith was a labor that kept Sister Blandina in the basin of the city for thirty-five busy years. Never did she slacken in her work. She herself gave instructions to 80 percent of the Italians in the city. Her battle cry, "The Charity of Christ Urges Us," was well lived.

During that first hard year in the basin of the city. Sister Blandina wrote,

> What we really need is not a school, but a center; a cheery, homey place where the immigrants can come; where the poor can receive charity and the rich bestow it. The Italian immigrants are so lonely. If we care for the children's religious life they will make good Catholics but the parents will draw within themselves and become very bitter unless we help them. . . . If this is His work it will succeed despite all opposition; if it is not His work we do not want it to succeed.

The present home of the Santa Maria Institute at 21 West Thirteenth Street is a far cry from those first cross-filled years. Their first institute for their people opened in 1899 at the old motherhouse of the Sisters of the Poor of St. Francis at Third and Lytle streets, Through the kindness of Archbishop Elder and the Sisters, this property was placed at their disposal. From 1897 to 1899, Sister Blandina and Sister Justina lived with the Sisters of Charity, using the convent as headquarters for their school and social work. They opened three schools for Italians: at Springer Institute, Holy Trinity, and at Lytle Street.

It would be impossible to enumerate all the works undertaken by the Sisters at the Santa Maria Institute from 1897 to the present, because according to Sister Blandina's philosophy, individual needs are sufficient reason for the inauguration of a work. By 1905, the Sisters were able to report to the papal delegate, Archbishop Diomede Falconio, when he visited the Santa Maria, that there was no organized proselytism in Cincinnati. However, proselytism did not cease. Far from it. In 1912, it ran rampant through the city, and to combat the new menace, the Sisters moved from their second home at 534 West Seventh Street to 640 West Eighth Street, where their property finally included four houses.

Among the undertakings of the Sisters, the following are typical: handling of juvenile court cases; Americanization centers at Walnut Hills and Fairmount; free employment bureau; reclamation of girls and women; classes for all nationality groups; day nursery; kindergarten; milk station; housing of homeless girls and women; visitation of the sick, the imprisoned, the unfortunate; distribution of food, free clothes, books; Sunday School classes; Boy and Girl Scout troops; Legion of Mary; classes in homemaking, singing, dramatics; clubs; Braille work.

When the juvenile court was organized in Cincinnati, Sister Blandina was asked to be present at the first meeting. Later the court appointed her a Cincinnati probation officer. The Santa Maria had its own juvenile court. In five years' time the Sisters had restored 157 women to normal living. In an attempt to rid the city of white slavery, Sister Blandina brought a case to court. Her action was highly commended by local attorneys, especially Mr. Ledyard Lincoln, prominent lawyer.

In September 1916, their golden jubilee as Sisters of Charity dawned, 1866–1916. Sister Blandina briefly records the day: "Fifty years ago we made our Holy Vows on the Feast of the Immaculate Conception with a number of other Sisters. Several of them have been called Home. Today our people have given us $125.00. I am deeply moved. We shall use this money to provide books for poor children." Six years later their own Santa Maria celebrated its silver jubilee. That occasion was heralded throughout Cincinnati, and the Sisters were delighted. High Masses of Thanksgiving were sung at the convent, 640 West Eighth Street; St. Anthony Welfare Center; and Sacre Cuore Church. On December 10, there was an elaborate celebration in Memorial Hall. The night of the celebration the Sisters quietly reminisced in their convent home. Rarely were they present at the harvest. The harvest belonged to God and to whomsoever He chose. Theirs was the laborer's part; theirs to bear the heats of the blistering sun; the ingratitude of those who did not understand. But they knew that they were indeed rich, and they wondered at the magnitude of their happiness.

The extent of Sister Blandina's dependence on Sister Justina came as a terrific blow when, on July 31, 1929, Sister Justina died at the Good Samaritan Hospital in Cincinnati. Her illness was brief; an appendectomy performed July 20, and eleven days later, at the age of 83, she was dead. . . .

When she was 81, Sister Blandina went to Rome. As the news of her intended journey became known, a highly esteemed writer of the *Cincinnati Post*, Alfred Segal, wrote the following in his column, "Life as He Sees It":

> Sister Blandina starts back to Italy Sunday, after seventy-seven years. . . . Four years old she was when she left her native land; at eighty-one she returns.
>
> She is going to see the Pope about placing Mother Elizabeth Seton among the Saints, but people say that Sister Blandina is saint enough herself, canonized by sixty years of faithful doing,
>
> Trinidad, Colorado, knew her for a saint sixty years ago when she went there to teach. And if Trinidad was a rough place when she entered it, gentler it was when she departed. Rude men reverenced her walking among them as she did, unafraid; she offered a holy presence by which the power of pistols was shamed. She built a schoolhouse at Trinidad and went her way.
>
> She went to New Mexico and established a trade school for Indians. She made a hospital for the workmen who were building the Santa Fe Railroad and were dying in numbers from the hardships of the trail. The Apache Indians were in truculent mood; Sister Blandina went into the wilderness to meet their scouts and by gentle words made peace.
>
> Cincinnati became aware of Sister Blandina some thirty-five years ago. She came here with her sister, Maria Maddelena, also a nun, by name Sister Justina, and founded a social center for Italian immigrants which they called the Santa Maria Institute. . . . They offered shelter to women stranded and without work; gave food to hungry men and found them jobs; guarded the children of working women in their day nursery; visited homes, looked after erring children, visited prisons. . . . Thirty-five years of this.

One day in March 1933, on the feast of St. Patrick, to be exact, her summons came to return to the motherhouse. She delayed not a moment, and two days later she left the Santa Maria Institute and returned to the motherhouse of the Sisters of Charity at Mount St. Joseph, a suburb of Cincinnati. Change of residence did not change Sister Blandina. Her fingers were ever busy, her correspondence enormous. People sought her sage advice, and younger people found in her a kindred spirit; for her interest in youth and their problems was ever of paramount importance,

The aged Sister spent hours in the motherhouse chapel praying for God's holy will to be done in all things. Frequently she would plead, "Remember, my *Gesu*, to send our Community sufficient and worthy aspirants to the religious life so that we can adequately care for our work for You." And then she would smile quickly as she added, "And don't forget the Santa Maria Institute, nor the West, my *Gesu*."

The radio she loved, and the operas, which she knew thoroughly, were her special delight. Political speeches she listened to with avidity. The Rt. Rev. Fulton J. Sheen, speaking over the Catholic Hour, held first place. The last program she listened to was Monsignor Sheen's, Before his talk the next Sunday she was dead.

One day before a fall, in 1937, which resulted in a broken hip and almost a year of complete inactivity, Sister Blandina walked across the beautiful motherhouse grounds, past the academy, the college, and on out the tree-lined road below which the Ohio river flows. Climbing a little hill, she paused before the delicately wrought iron crucifix guarding the entrance to the Sisters' cemetery. El Campo Santo, they used to call it in Santa Fe. . . .

The end came February 23, 1941, just a month after the celebration of her ninety-first birthday. Her Sisters in Christ and her friends watched and prayed. And throughout the city news spread that Sister Blandina was dying. Men bared their heads, went into churches, and knelt in quiet corners with bowed heads and aching hearts. The Italians of Cincinnati were grief stricken. Had she not instructed 80 percent of them herself?

But Sister Blandina was worrying about neither past nor future. She was a little girl again in Cincinnati, sitting in a fruit wagon and looking into the faces of the first two Sisters of Charity she had ever seen. And then she was turning to *Il Signorino* her father, and saying to him, "Father, as soon as I am old enough I shall be a Sister of Charity."

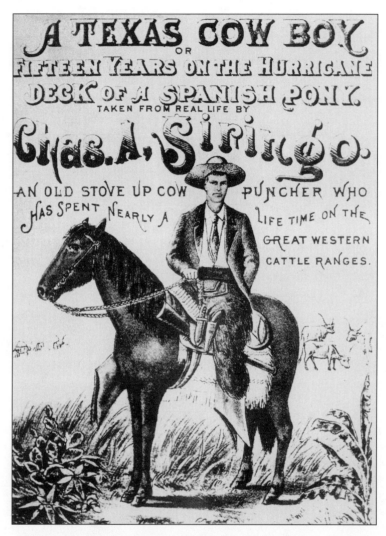

Frontier cowhand and notable Pinkerton detective Charlie A. Siringo is best remembered for bringing the cowboy into western legend in a number of books beginning with *Texas Cowboy*. Few lived the life of a cowboy as fully or as completely as Siringo, nor shared those first-hand experiences compellingly as did this western writer.

Close Calls

AN INTERVIEW
WITH CHARLES A. SIRINGO,
DARING ADVENTURER IN
THE OLD WILD WEST

By Neil M. Clark

OWN IN THE STATE UNIVERSITY at Austin, Texas, they have
dedicated six bronze tablets to men representing the forces that
went into the building of that state; on one of the six is inscribed
simply: "Charlie Cowboy."

Those who know the literature of the cowboy's West need no introduction to "Charlie Cowboy," or, to give him his full name, Charlie A.
Siringo. The very name is synonymous with every vivid phase of the old
West that is now history: buffalo-hunting, cow-punching, Indian-fight-
ing, the Chisholm Trail, broncho-busting, Billy the Kid, No-Man's-
Land, John Wesley Hardin, sheep and cattle wars, rustling, sharpshooting,
prairie fires, stampedes. Few lived as fully and daringly as Charles Siringo
the varied lives of those colorful days; few went so far afield and knew
so many of the men, both good and bad, whose names are indelibly symbols of their generation and place; and none, probably, has told so well,
out of a wealth of first-hand experience, the thrilling and romantic story
as it really happened.

Siringo was born in 1855 in Matagorda County, in the extreme southern part of Texas. At the age of twelve he hired out as a cowboy at ten

dollars a month, to rope and brand the maverick mustangs and long-horned cattle which then abounded in that country. Moving to Illinois with his mother a year later, he was thrown on his own at the age of fourteen, and for a couple of years wandered far, free, and lonely, earning his board and bed in various ways: by work on a farm, as a bell boy in a St. Louis hotel, as a roustabout on river boats to and from New Orleans; and once, after sleeping out on bales of cotton and going hungry a couple of days, he even took a turn at going to school, exchanging hand work for head work for a spell.

In 1871 he returned to Matagorda and the life of a puncher. Here he soon became a full-fledged son of the range. He broke wild ponies at two dollars and a half a head, skinned dead cattle and sold the hides, registered his own brand and raised a few cattle under it. In 1876 he made his first trip with a herd up the famous Chisholm Trail. He held many jobs in the following years, as drifting, carefree punchers often did, and won a reputation as a dead-center shot with rifle or six-gun. At the age of twenty-two he began working for David T. Beals, owner of the huge LX Ranch near Amarillo, and advanced in responsibility until he was one of the company's most trusted men. He quit cowpunching finally to become a merchant in Caldwell, Kansas, prospering for a couple of years.

In 1886, however, he sold his store and moved to Chicago to go into a similar line of business there. But after a brief experience with city merchandising, which convinced him that the saddle was where he really shone, he joined the Pinkertons, became a cowboy detective, and for twenty years and more participated in scores of famous and thrilling western manhunts involving rustlers, bank and train robbers, mine thieves, dynamiters, and murderers, putting his neck in jeopardy a thousand times, and playing parts, in order to acquire the needed facts, ranging from hobo to broncho-buster, to pretended outlaw, and to wealthy mine or ranch owner.

In this many-sided experience, the total amount of formal education that Charlie Siringo found it possible to squeeze in would be equal to perhaps three or four months in a modern grade school. He learned to read and write and figure—that was about all. But he found life itself a grand schoolmaster, and nature had made him a willing pupil, with a seeing eye and a yarn-spinning tongue. So, though scarcely knowing the first principles of composition, he sat down and wrote in the 1880s, in the intervals of keeping store in Caldwell, a book about his own experiences. *Fifteen Years on the Hurricane Deck of a Spanish Pony*, he called it; and it became, and remains, one of the classics of cowboy literature. Over a million copies were sold before the copyright period expired, and it would be difficult to say how many more have been sold since. He has not written many books, but, as Will Rogers wrote about him about his latest, "Riata and Spurs":

> Why, if you lived to be a thousand years old you couldn't write a bad book about the cowboys—the stuff they did might be bad, but you could tell it so well it would almost sound respectable.

A small man, weighing barely a 130 pounds, but wire-tough, brown of face, and keen of eye, with humor still invincible in spite of his seventy-two years, and a mind razor-sharp for accuracy and pertinent detail, Charlie Siringo is found today by his friends—and there is a host of them!—in his "Den" at Venice, California, convenient to Hollywood and his special cronies, Bill Hart, Will Rogers, and many more.

"Close calls," said Charlie to me when I broached the story of his experiences to him, "I've had hundreds of 'em. Once I had to hunt my hole when a mob had the amiable intention of burning me at the stake. Several times, too, men were hired to kill me. And they came pretty near succeeding—too near for my comfort. But few of the bad men," he went on, "were really as bad as they're painted. Their deeds were exaggerated by rumor. I found them good fellows at heart, who simply hadn't learnt to control their impulses, and after getting into one desperate scrape, they went from bad to worse on false trails hoping to save their skins.

"It was while I was still in my teens and was shipping cattle for Mr. Wiley Kuykendall in southern Texas that a stranger one day rode into camp. Mr. Kuykendall, who knew him, introduced him by some fictitious name and he spent the night. We found him a well-spoken chap. Next day he mounted his pony and rode on.

"'Boys',' said Mr. Kuykendall, after he had gone, 'do you know who that is? That's John Wesley Hardin.'"

No bad man's name in that day was better known or more generally feared. First and last, Hardin killed thirty-four men. And how did he get his start on the outlaw trail? By an impulsive crime that probably nine out of ten men of spirit would have committed under similar circumstances.

"Hardin was a young man of good blood in postwar New Orleans, when Northern politicians of the 'carpet-bagger' stripe were running things with a high hand. These political scamps put in, as supposed guardians of peace and the law, men—even negroes—who were least qualified and most irritating to the people. Becoming involved in a fracas with one of these policemen, Hardin made his first killing. He realized that justice would not be tempered with mercy under the existing regime, so he fled. Most of his later killings were the result of his effort to make good his escape and to prevent people from capturing him for the sake of the big price on his head.

"Hardin was a fairly true type of the Western bad man, and he was the only one, I suppose, who ever made Wild Bill Hickok put up his guns. Wild Bill was the fast-shooting and fearless officer who kept the peace in Abilene, the famous cow town, and John Wesley Hardin, in the course of his travels, came to Abilene. He entered a saloon with a friend; this friend got into a ruckus with one of Hickok's deputies. Hardin intervened, took the officer's guns, kicked him out and said:

"'Tell your long-haired boss'—meaning Hickok—'that if he comes around I'll treat *him* the same way.'

"The message, of course, was not long delayed in delivery. Knowing that to enter the saloon could only mean a shooting, Wild Bill waited for his man outside. Presently Hardin came out, alone, bound for another saloon. Hickok covered him, and told him to withdraw his guns from the holsters, being very careful to make no false move, and to hand them over, butt ends first.

"Now, though Wild Bill was not aware of it at the time, John Wesley Hardin was the man who invented the trick, devised for just such emergencies, of flipping the guns over, business ends to the front, just as the officer was about to take them. So, when Wild Bill momentarily lowered his own guns to seize Hardin's he suddenly found himself gazing into twin muzzles of death. Admiration, rather than fear, was the famous marshal's reaction to this display.

"'You are the bravest boy I ever saw,' he said.

"Wild Bill was carrying a printed circular in his pocket at that very moment, offering twenty-five thousand dollars for the apprehension of Hardin. But he promptly forgot it.

"'Put up your guns,' he said; 'you and I are friends. You can stay in Abilene as long as you please. Keep the peace, and I will not molest you.'

"So the famous outlaw and the famous marshal became friends. Wild Bill kept his word.

"Hardin's end, however, was typical of the fate of most of the men I knew who persistently defied the law and the sanctity of human life. He was captured later and sentenced to the penitentiary. While serving his time, he studied law. Being pardoned eventually, he went to El Paso to practice. But one day a gunman with an old grudge fired a bullet into the back of his head and killed him. No doubt the murderer thought he would never be bothered for killing so notorious a person as Hardin; but he was held for trial. However, before the trial came off, he in turn was shot and killed. So it went, with most of the wanton gunmen."

Mr. Siringo, without self-excuses, harked back to an incident occurring in Bat Masterson's saloon and dance hall in Dodge City, in order to show how impulsive actions, if the result had been only slightly different, might have lent a conspicuously different shade to his own career.

"The typical cowboy," he said, "was wolf-wild and free as the wind, and generally he had the grim determination to see his friends through any scrapes they got into. Early in May, 1877, I found myself footloose near the Chisholm Trail, and picked up a job with a northbound herd. We headed up the Chisholm Trail at first, but after a while branched off in the direction of Dodge City, Kansas, taking that route because settlers were coming in, even then, and cutting up the old drive trail with plowshares and fences.

"We had a hard time on the trail with thirty-five hundred head of wild Texas steers, especially in the Indian Territory, where we encountered many swollen rivers and had to plunge into the water ourselves, in order to get the herd across. We arrived at Dodge City on July 3d. After sixty days with wild steers, wild Indians, and wild rivers, some of us were ready to unbend. So Wess Adams, my cowboy chum, and I drew our pay and quit the job, determined to celebrate the glorious Fourth in proper style in Dodge City.

"Wess and I chose the Lone Star dance hall for our operations, and soon were swinging our partners in free and easy style. Bat Masterson, the proprietor, was there in person, wearing an apron and helping to serve the drinks. Presently I noticed Wess, at the opposite of the hall, making signs to attract my attention. As soon as I could, I went over.

"'Come on, Charlie,' he said, 'let's get our horses from the livery stable and tie them out in front.'

"'What's up?' I asked.

"'Oh,' said he, 'I just want to show some of these buffalo hunters that they're not in the cowboy class.'

"It appeared that a long-haired hunter had grabbed off the girl Wess favored, and the cowboy didn't like the transaction one bit. It wasn't my quarrel, of course, but he was my chum.

"When we got back from the livery stable, Wess's girl was sitting on the buffalo hunter's knee. I watched Wess go to the bar and order a big stein of beer. He poured out the liquor and I wondered what he had in mind, but kept my eyes peeled, knowing that trouble was bound to come soon.

"Wess walked up to the buffalo hunter and ran the fingers of one hand through his long hair. With the other hand, he brought the stein crashing down on the man's skull. The hunter was a big, powerful man, and would have made two of Wess, but his actions were somewhat hampered by having the girl on his knee. One of his men drew his hunting knife and planted it deep in Wess's back.

"After that, things popped for fair. Bat Masterson, knowing I was with Wess, picked up a handful of beer glasses and began hurling them at me. One cut a gash in my forehead, and the blood streamed down into one eye. With Wess at my elbow, guns in hand, we retreated to the door and ran to our horses.

"A town marshal tried to stop us as we rode off, but we flourished our guns and ran him up an alley, then galloped whooping and shooting out of town, and rode twenty miles to a cow camp. Wess lost a lot of blood on the way, but was all right again in two weeks, and the buffalo hunter slept off his headache in the course of time."

The wild, foolish, impulsive escapade of two boys full of hot blood and high spirits!

"I've often wondered," Mr. Siringo said, "what difference it might have made in my life if I had accidentally let a bullet slip into some man's heart that night and had had a price put on my head. Who knows!

"My reasoned conclusion from a long experience with many kinds of men is, not to judge too harshly the chap who makes one slip, but to try to understand him. Take the cowboy: to be sure, he did lots of raw things. But he lived in the rawest surroundings, out on the edge of society; and personally, I shouldn't be at all surprised to learn that, behind the closed doors of polite society today, just about as many things are done on impulse, which are fully as bad, considered morally, as anything the cowboys pulled in their wild, free, open style.

"Take Billy the Kid. Billy is one of the legends of the West today. Indeed, he was a good deal of a legend even before he died, being considered by many the worst of the bad men. But some of us who knew Billy as a man, ate with him, practiced shooting with him, considered him what I still believe him to have been, a real prince of a human being, who got off on the wrong foot.

"It was late in 1878 that I finished a 225-mile horseback ride from Dodge City to the LX Ranch headquarters, and saw a dozen or more men playing cards under the cottonwoods. I was told they were Billy the Kid and his gang of warriors from Lincoln County, New Mexico. When the cook banged his dinner gong, they raced for the table with the rest of us, and I found myself seated next to Billy the Kid. His real name, by the way, was William H. Bonney, and he was born in New York City.

"I had just been to Chicago with a trainload of fat steers and had brought back a box of cigars as a treat for the bunch. I opened them after supper and passed them around. In Chicago, with a high-heeled cowboy's disregard for expense, I had also bought a meerschaum cigar holder for ten dollars. Billy wanted to try it and liked it so well that he asked me to make him a present of it which I did. In return, he gave me a finely bound novel that he had just finished reading, autographing it for me, with the date of presentation.

"In the next few weeks he and I became quite chummy. As I was something of a shot, we used to practice with our six-guns, shooting at a mark. The universal practice of wearing guns, of course, was what really made the bad men of the West seem so bad. They always had the tool at hand to give a mortal wound in exchange for an affront, provided better judgment didn't check the hasty impulse.

"A good many fictions have grown up about the cowboy bad man and his guns. It is perfectly true that men got so they could draw fast and shoot with remarkable accuracy, but nothing like the way they tell about it in some of the stories, where the action is too fast for the eye—or the brain, either!—to follow. Billy the Kid was about the fastest man with a gun I ever shot against. Often at the LX Ranch he would point out a knothole, or a mark on a fence post, and say:

"'Charlie, when I count three, let's shoot and see who hits it.'

"We'd both draw and fire at the same instant. I don't mind saying that I could shoot as straight as Billy; but he could plant two bullets in the mark to my one.

"Offhand shooting of this sort, when done skillfully, was a knack that a man acquired only by practice and the wish to do it well; just as the cowboy learned by practice to throw a rope and catch a steer where and when he wanted it. With thumb on the hammer the very momentum of the gun on its downward arc helped in cocking it, and the bullet sped on its way in a marvelously short space of time, with high accuracy, at short range.

"At close range, some killers fired from the hip on the upward arc, with a view of hitting the opponent at the waistline.

"I have known a few men who could shoot two pistols at the same time, with accuracy. Billy the Kid, however, was not a two-gun man; John Wesley Hardin was.

"A blacksmith's son in Jackson County, Texas, used to be able to fire two powder-and-ball Colt's pistols, one after the other, and do great execution. He once won a bet of $250 that he could kill six quails out of a flock sitting on the ground, before they could get away.

"Billy the Kid, though not a two-gun man, had fatal skill with one gun. As far as I know, he never killed wantonly, but shot only men who he thought needed shooting. Most of his killings, which numbered twenty-one in all, took place in the so-called Lincoln County War, inaugurated by him to avenge the slaying of his friend and employer, an Englishman named Tunstall. But at last friendly, lovable, magnetic, misguided Billy the Kid stepped one night into a betraying patch of moonlight, and Sheriff Pat Garett's bullet ended his career. Billy was four years younger than I; yet it is more than forty-seven years, now, since they laid him away at Fort Sumner by the side of his chum, Tom O'Phalliard, who also died from a bullet wound. The killer's life, if a wild one, was usually short."

Speaking of another wholly different type of bad man, Jim Miller, Mr. Siringo revealed an unrecorded bit of western history, and incidentally shed light on the typical fate of one man who chose the vicious way to wealth. Sheriff Pat Garett himself was assassinated, several years after writing the final chapter in the career of Billy the Kid. Garett was Siringo's friend, and, he says, one of the most fearless law officers of that time and region.

Wayne Brazil, a goat man, had leased a ranch from Garett, and was accused of his assassination. Brazil pleaded guilty, but claimed self-defense as his motive and was acquitted. It was Charlie Siringo, in his capacity of detective, rather than of cowboy, many years later, after all those immediately concerned in the deal were dead, dug up the true facts, which led to Miller.

"Jim Miller," Mr. Siringo said, "was one of the few genuinely cold-blooded killers I knew. He could be, and was, hired to do murder; that was his profession.

"It was Jim Miller, hidden in a clump of willows by the roadside, who fired the shot that killed Pat Garett. The man who hired him to do it, a banker with a grudge of many years' standing, had been riding in the buggy with Garett just a few minutes previously. Wayne Brazil was an entirely unexpected factor in the party. He rode alongside on horseback at the critical moment, and began arguing with Garett about the terms of his lease. Garett and the banker got out of the buggy and stood in the road to stretch their legs. It was then that Miller, from his place of concealment, shot Garett through the back with a rifle. The wound was mortal; but before he died the courageous sheriff tried to reach his gun with the evident intention of shooting Brazil, who, no doubt, he thought was to blame. Brazil pulled his own gun first, however, and shot Garett through the head.

"No doubt Wayne Brazil was paid handsomely to accept the responsibility for this crime, though there is no direct evidence to prove it. At any rate, the fact that there was a rifle bullet as well as a revolver bullet in Garett's body was not brought out and questioned at the trial, and I was not even aware of it, myself, until years later. Hence, at the time, nobody had any reason to suspect Jim Miller.

"As it happened, however, fate took a queer and quick revenge on Miller, the real killer. Ten thousand dollars was deposited to his credit in the bank, as the price of this killing. Before he had a chance to touch a penny of it, however, he was called away to Ada, Oklahoma, to kill the marshal, Bob Gossett.

"He shot from ambush. Gossett fell on his back, his hat sliding down in such a way that it shaded and hid his eyes. Though his wound was mortal, Gossett did not die immediately, and retained consciousness. So it happened that when Miller rode out of the woods to take a look at him, the fallen marshal recognized him.

"For a moment. Miller appeared undecided. Without guessing, of course, that the marshal was observing him all the while, Miller drew his gun, apparently with the intention of firing a second shot; but decided against it, believing the marshal was thoroughly dead.

"After Miller rode away, Gossett managed to drag himself some distance to the cabin of friends. Before he died, he was able to tell what had occurred. A posse was formed, Jim Miller was tracked and taken, and was hanged with little formality from a beam in a barn, together with the three men who, he confessed, had hired him to commit the murder."

Even in the gun-toting West, though, Mr. Siringo pointed out, the real bad men were merely highlights. They weren't dangerous, except on rare occasions.

"A man who attended to business and kept a good hold on himself," he said, "had nothing much to fear from them. It was only once in a long, long time that a real dead-in-earnest human 'critter' undertook the job of salivating you. If I tried to pick and choose the closest among the many narrow escapes from death that I personally had, only a few would be cases where my life was threatened by other men; the majority would be accidents and freaks of nature.

"Once, for example, I was out hunting a buffalo steak for supper. I sighted a herd, and stalked it down a dry wash. From cover along the bank, I shot a bull which was standing not far from me and a little apart from the rest of the herd. The wounded bull, infuriated, charged directly toward me, leaped into the wash, and tumbled down dead a few feet away.

"Evidently he was the leader of the herd. At any rate, the rest all stampeded in the same direction, leaping right over me in my hiding place. I hugged the bank for dear life, and for several minutes all I could see was flying hoofs and the bellies of buffalo. Had the bank suddenly caved in, or had one of the beasts missed his footing and fallen on top of me, that would have been the end of Charlie Siringo!

"Or take another time, when I was caught in front of a prairie fire, with a high wind blowing. That was about as narrow a squeak as any, I expect. Wolves and wild cattle were running with me, doing their best to escape being burned to death. My horse was so tired at the last that I could scarcely spur him to a gallop. The flames weren't more than a hundred yards behind me when, by pure luck, I ran into a weedy wallow covering maybe half an acre of ground and full of water. The wet reeds wouldn't burn, of course. So I sat still in the saddle, and in a minute or two, the fire had roared by and was *ahead* of me.

"Of the men I knew," Mr. Siringo went on, "there was one whom I always considered about the ablest manager and best cowman of the whole West; and yet he made a terrible mess of his life, simply because of his inability to control his impulses. When he saw red, he killed. The man's name was William C. Moore, made an outlaw by his own hasty acts, but a born leader.

"Outlaw Bill Moore's first bad fall from grace occurred in California, where he shot and killed his brother-in-law. He fled to Wyoming, where he became the manager of one of the biggest cattle companies in the West; but one day in a mad fit he killed his negro coachman and had to light out again. He reached the LX Ranch one day on a worn-out pony, practically broke, and went to work for a cowboy's wages. Inside of a year he was manager of the ranch, and in a few years more he sold the interests which he had managed to accumulate on his own account, for the sum of seventy thousand dollars. With this money he bought himself a ranch in western New Mexico. There again, however, his lack of control got the better of him, and he killed two men. A big price was put on his head and he had to pull out, a jump or two ahead of the law. The last time I saw Bill Moore he was a broken, unhappy old fellow living under an assumed name a long, long ways from the country where his best work was done.

"I remember an exciting experience in the Coeur d'Alene country in 1892, during the strike between the miner's union and the owners. In the end, they discovered that I was a detective. It was then that I was threatened with burning at the stake, and narrowly escaped.

"During the troubles that followed, which were long drawn out and became so serious that finally United States troops had to be brought in to restore order, I was compelled, in order to save my life, to take to the hills, and at one time had for companion in escape a young man named Frank Stark. We were skirting a mountain one night, and upon reaching a certain footpath which we had to cross or else go a long ways around, we found it guarded by three men with rifles. I told Stark it would be better to have a quick fight with them than to make the long climb up the steep mountain.

"I tried a trick. We two were well hidden. So, in a loud voice, I said:

"'You shoot the one on the right; I'll kill the fellow on the left.'

"I thought the remark might have some effect; and it certainly did! All three jumped as if really shot and started running down the canyon for dear life. They dropped their rifles and even tripped and turned somersaults, in their eagerness to get away. And Stark and I went on unmolested.

"The only kind of hasty impulse that it pays to heed is *the impulse you know is right*. When you're sure, go ahead and forget every doubt. If, for instance, when I had tough jobs of work to do on the range, or in trailing criminals, I had ever stopped to figure on the possible *dangers* to be met, instead of thinking of doing the job the best way, I never would have amounted to a row of rowels on a Mexican spur."

So that, in brief, is the story of Charlie Siringo, around whose person clings so much that is a vivid reminder of the Old West. Wild, free, and untamed were the men of that world he knew so well—but, by and large, they were sound to the core.

With the memory of long days and nights under lonely skies still shining vividly in his eyes, Mr. Siringo says calmly that when the time comes for him to cross the Great Divide, there are four verses that he hopes will be inscribed on his tombstone. Of the four, this is the last:

> Let cattle rub my headstone round,
> And coyotes wail their kin,
> Let bosses come and paw the mound,
> But don't you fence it in.

Creative Responses to the Italian Immigrant Experience in California

Baldassare Forestiere's "Underground Gardens" and Simon Rodia's "Watts Towers"

By Kenneth Scambray

BALDASSARE FORESTIERE's Underground Gardens and Simon Rodia's Watts Towers are two works of "grassroots art" that express the conflicted and often bifurcating experience of Italian immigration to America. Under a ten-acre parcel of land in rural north Fresno, California, Baldassare Forestiere (1879–1946) dug over one hundred underground tunnels and rooms where he lived throughout his life. While living in suburban Watts near Los Angeles from 1921 to 1954, Simon Rodia (1879–1965) built three towers reaching over eighty feet surrounded by numerous other forms all enclosed by a six-foot wall. He decorated his towers, forms, and walls with broken glass, pottery, shells, and other artifacts that he scavenged from the neighborhood and landscape around him in Southern California.

Adjustment for Italian immigrants became a complex process that included at the same time the adaptation of Old World culture in the new land and assimilation into New World society.[1] But recollections of the

---

[1] John Higham, *Strangers in the Land: Patterns of American Nativism, 1860–1925* (New Brunswick, 1988), 234–64.

past and settlement in the New World were not often easily reconcilable for the immigrant or even later generations.[2] Together, the iconography of Rodia's towers and Forestiere's grottoes express the tension between hope and memory that is central to the bicultural, immigrant experience. As Jerre Mangione wrote about his relatives in *Mount Allegro*, they liked to tell stories about Italy, "a past they had long ago romanticized," in spite of the poverty they left behind.[3] Forestiere's life and Underground Gardens articulate in their form the conflict between the past and present, while Rodia's life and his Watts Towers more successfully merge that past with his hope for a better life in Southern California. Neither the Underground Gardens nor the Watts Towers can be fully appreciated without an understanding of the heritage, geography, and communities that influenced the lives of Baldassare Forestiere and Simon Rodia.

BALDASSARE FORESTIERE'S "UNDERGROUND GARDENS"

BALDASSARE FORESTIERE WAS BORN July 8, 1879, in Filari, a small village in the Peloritani Mountains in the province of Messina. Baldassare's tyrannical father, Rosario, owned an olive-processing factory and adjacent groves, which provided a reliable income for the Forestiere family. However, he was unwilling to share his economic resources with his four sons, Antonio, Baldassare, Giuseppe, and Vincenzo.[4] Unable to foresee any opportunity for himself within his father's business or elsewhere in Sicily, in 1902, at the age of twenty-one Baldassare emigrated, along with his older brother, Antonio, to America.[5]

[2] Rudolph J. Vecoli, "The Search for an Italian American Identity: Continuity and Change," in *Italian Americans: New Perspectives in Italian Immigration and Ethnicity*, ed. Lydio Tomasi (New York, 1985), 94–95.

[3] *Mount Allegro: A Memoir of Italian Life* (New York, 1981), 204.

[4] Elena Faulks, telephone interviews, July 1998 and 2001. Elena is Baldassare Forestiere's niece and "Ric" Forestiere's sister; Silvio Manno, "Forward: California: Earthly Paradise" (Unpublished t.s.), 2. Baldassare had five siblings: in their order of birth, Antonio, Baldassare, Giuseppe, Rose, Vincenzo, and Nicolina. Vincenzo settled in Boston, and Giuseppe settled in Fresno. After leaving Fresno, Rose lived in northern California, where Elena currently resides. Only Nicolina remained in Italy. Faulks, interview, 2001.

[5] Rosario "Ric" Forestiere, Contribution and Italian translation by Silvio Manno, "In Search of Baldassare: Twelve Days in Sicily," Travel diary 10 Sept. 1999–21 Sept. 1999 (Unpublished t.s.) 6; Manno, "Forward: California: Earthly Paradise," 2. "Ric" Forestiere, son of Giuseppe and

After working on the East Coast and the central California coast, Forestiere finally settled in Fresno in 1906. Settling in the far north end of Fresno, he was far removed from the Italian community located approximately ten miles southwest of him in the immigrant neighborhood known as the West Side. Forestiere lived a relatively isolated life in his new home.[6] From this remote plot of land he would begin his own version of the immigrant success story. He first worked for others. In typical immigrant fashion, he lived frugally, saved his money, and gradually began purchasing vineyards. By the time of his death, he would own more than 1,000 acres of valley farmland.

Though the dry, semi-arid climate of the valley contrasted with the mild climate of his native Filari, Fresno had one major resource that Sicily historically did not provide for its peasants: an abundance of cheap land. Soon after purchasing the parcel, Forestiere built a small, wooden house on the barren land in advance of planting an orchard. He would soon find that the valley heat during the summer in his new home (which he often referred to as his "little sweat house") made living intolerable. To support himself upon his arrival in Fresno, he worked as a leveler and a grafter for other valley farmers.[7] However, when Forestiere began planting his own orchard, he soon discovered that approximately twenty-four inches below the topsoil was a thick layer of impermeable hardpan, a concrete-like packed clay that underlies many sections of the valley floor. His land was not suitable for trees. Perhaps the low cost of the acreage should have raised the suspicions of this poor, Sicilian immigrant. Forestiere never planted his orchard. Instead, after work each day, he returned to his small wooden house and began digging his caverns under his isolated ten-acre plot of land near the corner of Shaw and Cornelia avenues. Forestiere would spend the next forty years, until his death in 1946, living in and digging what would become known as the Underground Gardens.

---

nephew of Baldassare; and the Underground Gardens' docent, Silvio Manno, traveled to Filari in 1999, which has been abandoned and is now in ruins. See also: Andrew Rolle, *The Italian Americans: Troubled Roots* (Norman, Ok., 1980), 34; and Denis Mack Smith, *A History of Sicily: Medieval Sicily 800–1713*, vol. 1; *A History of Sicily: Modern Sicily After 1713*, vol. 2 (New York, 1968) 499–501.
[6] Michael La Sorte, *La Merica: Images of Italian Greenhorn Experience* (Philadelphia, 1985), 37–60.
[7] Manno, "Forward," 3.

The stories that circulated within Fresno's Italian community depicted Forestiere as an eccentric. During his lifetime, he became an embarrassment to some, but not all, members of his family. A few of his relatives even urged him to stop digging his grottoes.[8] As word spread of his work on his caverns, local residents in the Italian community were quick to label him the "human mole," a term that has unfortunately come to characterize his life to a wider public.[9] But the reality is that Forestiere's life was in many respects similar to that of most Italian immigrants, both in what he accomplished in his over forty years as a successful farmer in the San Joaquin Valley and what his remarkable Underground Gardens expresses to us today.

By day, Forestiere worked in his remote vineyards. Each night after work, he descended and dug with his pick and shovel. Their muted scraping against the valley's loamy subsoil below the thick layer of hardpan was the only sound that accompanied him in his isolated life underground. He explained to his relatives that his project was his relaxation after a hard day in his vineyards.[10] In his imagination he took the religious and secular forms—arches and grottoes—of his remembered Sicily and recreated them in his tunnels. Forestiere's grottoes became for him the private world of his past, which he would inhabit nearly exclusively until his death in 1946.

While Forestiere's life underground may appear eccentric to his observers, his grottoes have cultural and historical antecedents in Sicily. In the first place, in ancient Greek myth, many of its gods and demigods lived underground and in grottoes, some even under the sea. The fabled giant shepherds, the Cyclopes, from Homer's *Odyssey*, lived in the bowels of Mount Etna, where they forged Zeus's thunderbolts.[11] In Sicily these legends formed part of the general cultural milieu of peasants, as well as land-owning *latifundi*, who learned these tales in school. The region that surrounds Forestiere's native village also contains many underground dwellings and structures. The hillsides near the village of Rometta Marea, for example, contain a vast number of Saracen caves in which

[8] Manno, "Forward," 24.
[9] Rolle, *The Italian Americans*, 35; Charles Hillinger, "The Human Mole," *Dream Streets: The Big Book of Italian American Culture*, ed. Lawrence DiStasi (New York, 1989), 21.
[10] Faulks.
[11] Thomas Bulfinch, *Bulfinch's Mythology* (New York, 1970), 237–40, 920.

he and his brothers played as children.[12] Dating from the ninth century, when the Arabs invaded and colonized Sicily, these caves, dug out of the limestone cliffs, served originally as storage depots for food and armaments, as well as housing for Saracen soldiers. As late as the nineteenth century, these caves provided storage for grain and shelter for shepherds tending their flocks on the remote hillsides.[13] South of Messina, Syracuse contains a plethora of catacombs, grottoes, sepulchers, and mines. Over the centuries these underground structures have been used as prisons, garrisons, work places, and domestic dwellings.

Certain aspects of the Underground Gardens bear a resemblance to the catacombs of San Giovanni in Syracuse. The catacombs' "conic-tapered *venturi*" constructed for light and to enhance airflow are remarkably similar to the skylight openings that Forestiere designed in his chambers.[14] Just as important, the asymmetrical pattern of Forestiere's tunnels and grottoes reflects as well the sometimes "confusing geometry" of the San Giovanni catacombs.[15] Further, in the late nineteenth century, when Sicily's sulfur mining industry employed nearly 250,000 people, many miners, including entire families, lived in "underground grotto[e]s."[16] In his youth, Forestiere was adventuresome. Sleeping whenever he could, he would disappear for days in his explorations of the surrounding hillsides and neighboring towns and villages.[17]

Forestiere's grottoes have both practical and aesthetic dimensions. He devoted the first ten years to excavating his living quarters. To escape the searing summer heat, he fashioned a kitchen with a properly vented wood-burning stove, a chamber with two beds, and finally a living room.[18] Adjacent to his living quarters, he constructed what he called the "Sunrise Plaza," designed to capture the morning sun. The "Sunrise Plaza" also contains a small fishpond in which Forestiere placed fish, which he caught in nearby rivers and lakes, until he was ready to eat them.[19] One bed was adjacent to a window that overlooks the Sunrise

---

[12] Forestiere, 12.   [13]Manno, "Forward," 28–29.
[14] Forestiere, 3.
[15] David D. Hume, *About Sicily: Travelers in an Ancient Land* (New Hampshire, 1999), 141.
[16] Smith, 475–77.
[17] Manno, "Forward," 30.
[18] Silvio Manno, "The Forestiere Underground Gardens: A Pictorial Journey, April 1, 2001" (Unpublished t.s.), 1–7.   [19] Manno, docent, Underground Gardens.

Plaza and was designed to let in the light and warmth of the spring and summer months. During the long valley winter months when bright sunlight was less frequent and valley temperatures plummeted, he slept in his winter bed, which was located deep inside the bedchamber and closer to the stove. He also dug a room for the storage and production of wine and cheese and the curing of meat, important aspects of the Sicilian culture he had left behind in Filari. In the evenings throughout the year, when he was not digging in the dark recesses of his caverns, he was able to rest comfortably in his living quarters and work on his English by reading an occasional newspaper by kerosene lantern.[20]

Beyond his living quarters, he continued for the next thirty years to dig approximately ninety more grottoes. The ten barren acres under which he dug his Underground Gardens became a place of refuge, even from his expansive vineyards. His underground home became "a place representing a simpler and more harmonious life."[21] Though he labored for long hours during the day as a farmer, Forestiere replicated a garden to recall yet another aspect of the Sicily he remembered. Since the ninth century and the Arabic invasion of Sicily, the island has been idealized as the Mediterranean's "garden paradise." On the land surrounding Palermo, which became known as the *"conca d'oro,"* the Arabs introduced the first lemon and citrus groves, as well as a variety of other fruits and nuts.[22] However, by the end of the nineteenth century, in both agricultural productivity and diversity of crops, the province of Messina had surpassed Palermo.[23] His father's property surrounding the olive factory was planted with a large olive grove.[24] This is the Sicily that he wished to recreate in his Underground Gardens.

At selected spots throughout his grottoes, Forestiere cut round holes in the ceiling for light for the lemon, orange, tangerine, lime, and grapefruit trees he had planted in many parts of the underground gardens. The horticultural knowledge he acquired as a farmer served him well in the creation of his gardens. Forestiere grafted one tree with as many as eight different varieties of fruit. The conical shape of the skylights allowed

[20] Faulks.
[21] Luisa Del Gludice, "The 'Archvilla'": An Italian Canadian Architectural Archetype," *Studies in Italian American Folklore*, ed. Luisa Del Giudice (Logan, 1993), 61
[22] Smith, 8.   [23] Smith, 473, 497.   [24] Forestiere.

for an increase flow of air and controlled the entrance of rainwater.[25] Forestiere's clever engineering and design of the skylights and the planters constituted an efficient drainage and irrigation system. The skylights funneled rainwater into the planters, thus irrigating the trees and preventing flooding in the chambers and tunnels.[26] His plants also benefited from the grottoes' ambient temperature, which varied little more than ten degrees throughout the year.[27]

Forestiere dug an "Aquarium Chamber" filled with fish with an "Aquarium Viewing Chamber" where observers could view the fish above through glass covering an opening in the bottom of the pond. In the "Boat Planter" grotto, he constructed a planter in the shape of a boat to recall his own, and millions of other immigrants', passage to America. The elaborate labyrinth of tunnels led also to an "Auto Tunnel," actually an open-air space where Forestiere parked his car. To complement his Sunrise Patio, he created the "Sunset Patio" on the west end of the grottoes. The approximately thirty-square-foot space, open to the sun, has a central planter that contained originally an orange tree that Forestiere had grafted with grapefruits, kumquats, and lemons. In the center of the planter, he planted three grape vines. At the far west end of the gardens, below ground level and directly adjacent to the grottoes, Forestiere planted another, larger garden with an assortment of fruit trees, vines, and decorative plants.

Forestiere completed his tunnels and grottoes with a "room" one hundred feet long and thirty-five feet wide. Some have called this an auditorium or a dance hall.[28] No one is certain what Forestiere intended. The room contrasts with the intimate nature of the rest of the chambers. But observers of the room fail to take into account that originally there was no roof on the space. After Forestiere's death, Giuseppe, who scavenged the trusses from an abandoned airplane hangar at a local airfield, added the roof, windows, and flooring.[29] Without the roof, it can be read as one more iconic representation of an important aspect of the life that Forestiere left behind him in Sicily: the communal life of Filari.

---

[25] Manno, "Forward," 23.   [26] Manno, docent.
[27] Catherine Monson Rehart, *The Valley's Legends and Legacies* (Fresno, 1996), 189.
[28] Manno, "The Forestiere," 52.
[29] Manno, docent.

In Forestiere's Underground Gardens, it serves as the "piazza," the place of communal gathering. The piazza is yet another aspect of Forestiere's recollections of his youth in Filari not accessible to him in his remote and isolated location on the far north end of Fresno.

The interplay between light and darkness is a central feature of the Underground Gardens. Between the hours of nine in the morning and three in the afternoon, sunlight shines through the skylights of the various grottoes and permeates the Sunrise Patio, the Sunset Patio, and the larger garden area on the west end of the site. From late spring to late autumn in Fresno, before the shortened winter days and fog return to the valley, throughout the grottoes there is a contrasting display of sunlight and shadows. The Underground Gardens have a monastic-like atmosphere conducive to retrospection. Yet they also capture, at least for part of the day and part of the year, the light of the countryside surrounding them. The contrast between light and darkness characterizes Baldassare Forestiere's inner and outer life. At night he dug his grottoes, recalling his past, and by day, as a successful valley farmer in Fresno, he labored in the full sun of his vineyards.

Forestiere's retrospective arches and gardens express that contrast between the Old World and the New World. Isolated in a dry valley in the extreme edge of the North American continent, he recreated a part of that Sicily of his youth. But for the Italian immigrant, the past can also represent discord and hardship. The problematic nature of the past is a seminal theme that runs throughout Italian American literature. While Forestiere dug, hauled, carved, and built to reconstruct his Gardens, he was also expressing, paradoxically, that other impulse to escape from the bitter aspects of his past.

As Gennaro's rebellious son, Emilio, says in Garibaldi Lapolla's *The Grand Gennaro*, what past should the Italian immigrant recall: "The Roman past and the past of the sixteenth century? Or the past of their miserable enslavement? Or the past of their recent history—the betrayal of Garibaldi and the republican hopes of Mazzini?"[30] Similarly, Jo Pagano writes in *Golden Wedding* that his Simone family before coming to America had lived for centuries "in a condition that amounted to feudal serfdom."[31]

[30] Garibaldi Lapolla, *The Grand Gennaro* (New York, 1935), 323.
[31] *Golden Wedding* (1943. New York, 1975), 4.

Baldassare and his brother left Italy to escape the patriarchal order that his oppressive father represented. While his vineyards recalled the labor of his past and even created for Forestiere another kind of serfdom, his grottoes were his castle: *In casa sua ciascuno è re.*[32] His grottoes allowed him to live comfortably between two worlds: his livelihood as a successful San Joaquin Valley farmer and his memories of Sicily.

SIMON RODIA'S WATTS TOWERS

THE WATTS TOWERS IS AS MUCH a story about Italians in Southern California as it is about Simon Rodia, the Italian immigrant who built them. Forestiere's solitary life and Underground Gardens in many respects contrasted with the communal lives of Fresno Italians at the time. Rodia's life and towers, on the other hand, more positively reflect the immigrant experience in Southern California and ultimately the experiences of most Italian immigrants throughout America at mid-century. Though the immigrant assimilation process was often presented as problematic in the works of such Italian American writers as Pascal D'Angelo, Antonia Pola, and Pietro Di Donate, western Italian American writers such as Angelo Pellegrini, Jo Pagano, and John Fante generally expressed hope and optimism in their works. The dramatization of immigrants' and their offsprings' pursuit of the American Dream in Italian American literature contrasted with the theme of alienation expressed by those members of the Lost Generation of the 1920s and 1930s who had exiled themselves to Europe out of protest over what they perceived to be the parochialism of American culture. In fact, Pagano in *Golden Wedding* parodied the "fatuous, over-indulged prima donnas" of the 1920s, including, presumably, their anti-democratic, caustic oracle, H. L. Mencken.[33] Looking back to the pre–World War period, Angelo Pellegrini wrote that for many immigrants "economic gain is no more than marginal relevance" in their struggle for success. For him in Seattle, Washington, throughout the twenties and thirties the American dream was "the inalienable right to seek happiness in self-realization."[34] Similarly, for both Pagano and Fante, California was not the terminus, geographical or oth-

---

[32] Del Giudice, 55; "In a home of one's own, each one is king," Del Giudice, 92.
[33] Pagano, 263.
[34] *American Dream* (San Francisco, 1986), 5–6.

erwise, of the American Dream.[35] In *Golden Wedding* Pagano's characters are on a quest that takes them beyond the traditional concepts of the
family and gender roles. As a Southern California writer, Pagano tells us
that his characters' experiences were "a part of that glittering, reckless
world of the future, a world whose history was a history of light."[36] Rodia's
towers reflect this same optimistic spirit that is expressed by the writers
of the period, including a very creative use of sunlight.

One of four children, Rodia was born in 1879 into a poor peasant family in Ribottoli, Campania, a village with few resources. Rodia followed
an older brother in 1894 to Philadelphia, where he began his American
odyssey. Over the next fifteen years he moved from northern California to the southwestern United States and back to California, where in
1917 he settled in Long Beach. In 1921 he relocated again when he bought
a small house on 107th Street in the Watts section of Los Angeles, at
the time a largely Mexican immigrant neighborhood.[37] Impetuous and
difficult to get along with, he divorced his third and last wife shortly
after moving to Watts. Alone but not isolated in his community, after
work each day at a Santa Monica tile factory Rodia worked for the next
thirty-four years on his towers. Then one day in 1955, having finished
the towers, he simply abandoned them. He gave the property to a neighbor and disappeared. For many years, his whereabouts was unknown.
He was even presumed dead. But in the early 1960s he was discovered
alive and well in Martinez, California. He had lived just long enough
to be recognized and honored for his remarkable towers.[38]

Rodia's Los Angeles is characterized by capacious space and the
omnipresence of sunlight. Light played a significant role in Rodia's selec-
tion of materials for his towers and other sculptures. He traveled daily
through neighborhoods that often contained large open spaces between
residential developments and commercial and industrial sites.[39] The

---

[35] Gloria Ricci Lothrop, ed., *Fulfilling the Promise of California: An Anthology of Essays on the Italian American Experience in California* (California Italian American Task Force; Spokane, Wash.,
2000), 235.   [36] Pagano, 284.
[37] Bud Goldstone and Arloa Paquin Goldstone, *The Los Angeles Watts Towers* (Los Angeles, 1997)
27–35.
[38] Goldstone, 84.
[39] Rosalind Giardina Crosby, "The Italians of Los Angeles, 1900," in *Struggle and Success: An Anthology of the Italian Immigrant Experience in California*, ed. Paola A. Sensi-Isolani and Phylis Cancilla Martinelli (New York, 1993), 42–43.

In 1921 Simon Rodia acquired an oddly shaped property in Watts south of downtown Los Angeles. There until 1954 he created seventeen sculptures Including three towers reaching up to ninety-nine feet. He embellished the surfaces with fragments of tile, glass, sea shells, pottery, and more in what has been described as an excellent example of "grassroots art." *Photo by Luisa Del Giudice, Italian Oral History Institute (www.italianlosangeles.com).*

houses were single-story bungalows that lined quiet, sunny streets. Before World War I, the motion-picture industry moved from the northeast to Hollywood mainly because of the reliability of sunlight in which to do location shooting.[40] In *Golden Wedding* Pagano used the phrase "history of light" in reference to the reason the motion-picture industry moved from the East to Los Angeles. For the nickels it cost to see a movie in the 1920s and 30s, Hollywood's films worked a similar kind of magic for immigrant Italians. They could see all those who had already "made America."

The mythology of success has deep roots in American culture. As one European observer said in the 1920s, "The idea of success is in the blood of the nation, for the nation itself is success—the most gigantic success history has ever recorded."[41] Likewise, the mythology of success is recorded in Italian American literature, from the eastern works of D'Angelo and Lapolla to the California novels of Dorothy Bryant, Steve Varni, John Fante, Jo Pagano, and Lawrence Madalena. In both their detail and their extraordinary height, Rodia's towers express his dream of success in America, as well as his recollection of his past.

Light and the abundance of space were central to the form and content of the towers. The capacity to reflect light would be an important aspect of the materials he selected to festoon his seventeen different sculptures, including three towers standing between fifty-five- and nearly one-hundred-feet tall. Rodia collected fragments of glass, pop bottles, pottery, cups, plates, automobile glass, window glass, mirrors, bottoms of bottles, teapots and tiles, as well as seashells he gathered during his walks on Southern California beaches. The tiles, whole and fragments, came from a variety of manufacturers in Southern California. He placed these in bins on the site and carefully selected the fragments for their placement. He kept a fire burning on the back of his property, where he melted glass into free forms before he embedded them into the walls of his sculptures. He used household and industrial objects to press designs into his drying mortar, from the backs of ice cream parlor chairs, wire rug beaters, and faucet handles, to gears, iron gates, grills, baskets, and cooking utensils. He poured mortar into cast-iron corn bread bakers, removed the

---

[40] Gerald Mast, *A Short History of the Movies* (Indianapolis, 1996), 118.
[41] Richard Hubbard, *The American Idea of Success* (New York, 1971), 184.

dried mortar, and inserted the panels into his sculptures. On other surfaces he inscribed freehand designs into his wet mortar. Into sections of his exterior wall, he pressed images of his tools—hammers, pliers, and files—signs of his immigrant working-class values.

But Rodia's site is not just a random collection of junk. It is a controlled work created from the many carefully selected materials collected from his surroundings. As the Southern California light passes over the multicolored surfaces of his sculptures during the day, it creates a polyphonic luminosity. The combination of free-form glass and tile fragments reflects the Southern California light in harmonic tones and shades. The elongated, arched buttresses that crisscross the site and that also form the round circles on the towers cast a network of changing shadows across the site. Like Southern California around it and like Rodia's own life, the sculptures are not static. They change with the movement and intensity of the sun. Though made of reinforced concrete, the giant towers appear light and airy, more celestial than earth bound.

Just as important, many of the soft drink bottles are placed with their labels showing. The colorful fragments of the cups, saucers, tiles, plates, vases, and utensils are a cross section of the consumer life of the twenties and thirties. The objects that Rodia pressed into his sculptures have their identifiable sources in the community and industries that surrounded him in Southern California. Nevertheless, his sculptures transcend the period in which they were constructed and leave an indelible record of an immigrant mind that went beyond the parochial and the mundane. R. Buckminster Fuller credited Rodia with making innovations in his structural engineering. But Fuller was quick to add that Rodia's innovations were "intuitive" and not just technical. The towers are a masterpiece of "grassroots art" that have permanently captured a record of both the era and the immigrant experience.

While the towers are the creation of one man, they also express the recollections and hopes of generations of Italian immigrants in the New World. They are the paean of an Italian immigrant to both his past and his life in Southern California. Like Forestiere's Underground Gardens, they express the psychological dislocating experience of immigration. But unlike Forestiere's grottoes, Rodia's towers provide a resolution to the problematic nature of the bicultural experience. Rodia collected the discards of modem America and organized them into a new form. At the same time, his construction, while it represents the present in its accumulation of contemporary artifacts, also recalls the past.

Folklorists I. Sheldon Posen and Daniel Ward have suggested that Rodia's towers were based on the ceremonial *gigli* (lilies) annually paraded around the town of Nola, not far from his native village, in honor of the local patron saint, St. Paulinus. Each year around June 22, on the occasion of the feast honoring St. Paulinus, ceremonial *gigli*, towers that stood more than six stories high, and a ship are paraded around the streets of the town. The ceremony is referred to as the "Dance of the *Gigli*." The bearers of the *gigli* towers "dance" through the streets to the accompaniment of a lively brass band. Since at least the sixteenth century, the "Dance of the *Gigli*" feast was organized by Nola's eight craft guilds. The *gigli* represent the guilds and the ship symbolizes the return of St. Paulinus after his and other villagers' kidnapping, liberation, and return from captivity during the fifth century. The shape of Rodia's towers, especially the central tower, and the ship are nearly identical copies of the ones carried through the streets of Nola. Rodia named his ship the *Marco Polo* after the great explorer who opened western culture to a world beyond its borders.

If we look at the immigrant literature of the period, what motivated him becomes as transparent as the iconography of his work. It is remarkable that one man built the towers without help from others or assistance from machinery. The Italian immigrants who flooded America at the turn of the century were little more than, in D'Angelo's words, "pick and shovel" laborers. Even so, in spite of their hardships in the New World, like Pagano's immigrants in *Golden Wedding*, they set out on another kind of voyage. As Lapolla explains in *The Grand Gennaro*, once settled, immigrants worked with a vengeance to overcome their historical subaltern status in Italy and in America. Lapolla's main character, the Grand Gennaro, pounds his chest and boasts, "I, I made America, and made it quick." Lapolla writes, "if one said of himself that he had made America, he said it with an air of rough boasting, implying 'I told you so' or 'Look at me.'" It is often reported that Rodia wanted people to know how hard he had labored. He never failed to point out that he built his towers alone. Rodia was quoted as saying, "I'm gonna do something. . . . This is a great country." Once someone showed Rodia a picture of Antonio Gaudi's Church of the Sagrada Familia in Barcelona. Rodia asked, "Did he have helpers?" When he was told a crew of workers had built it, unimpressed, Rodia said, "I did it myself."

Rodia's creation contrasts in important ways with Forestiere's in Fresno. Though he owned considerable land in the San Joaquin Valley, Forestiere confined himself to a restricted space for his chambers. Though his one hundred grottoes underlie acres of land, spaciousness is not each individual room's major characteristic. The visitor must duck at times to pass through a tunnel, and the majority of the rooms are little more than fifty to one hundred square feet. Forestiere remained isolated underground as he focused on those recollections of his village life in Filari. His signature was the black smudges that his lantern left on the arches of his tunnels. While Forestiere's grottoes are characterized by a combination of seasonal light and darkness, by contrast, Rodia's Towers are bathed daily in total sunlight, which is nearly constant in Southern California. Rodia inscribed his work with a public sign, *Nuestro Pueblo*, an appropriate name considering the towers' public location in the middle of his suburban, ethnic neighborhood.

Forestiere's and Rodia's creations contrast in their light/dark and public/private dimensions. However, what brings their two works together is that they also represent "home" for the two immigrant wayfarers. Forestiere's Underground Gardens narrates for us the interior, private aspect of separation that characterizes all immigrant experiences in America. There is something fundamentally sad about a man who spent the better part of his life underground, recalling a past he could only revisit in its derivative forms. But there is also something joyful in the gardens he planted and in his successful efforts to bring the sunlight, if only seasonally, into his underground grottoes and planters.

Both men narrated in their respective "dialects," their inner turmoil inspired by the bicultural experience of Italian immigration. Rodia was surrounded by suburban and industrial America; Forestiere was surrounded by a rural landscape. Rodia merged the common images from his regional ceremonial spires with the found objects of modem industrial America. With his hand tools, the pick, shovel, and wheelbarrow,

Forestiere used his hardpan "bricks," the most abundant resource he had, to create the arches and gardens of his Sicilian memories. Both men engaged in what can only be termed, without fear of hyperbole, a Herculean labor. Work was a primary value that immigrant Italians brought with them as peasants to the New World. Rodia's Watts Towers, in their unique decoration with the materials he found around him in Los Angeles, and their soaring heights, speak more eloquently to that dream of success that most immigrants brought to the New World than do Forestiere's retrospective underground arches. Ultimately, both Simon Rodia and Baldassare Forestiere transcended their parochial, subaltern origins in Italy and inscribed a timeless message about the immigrant experience in their unique works.

Bibliography

Baldassaro, Lawrence. "Go East Paisani: Early Italian American Major
Leaguers from the West Coast." In *Italian Immigrants Go West*, edit-
ed by Janet Worrall, Carol Albright, and Elvira G. Di Fabio. Staten
Island, New York: American Italian Historical Association, 2003.

Bolton, Herbert Eugene. *The Padre on Horseback: A Sketch of Eusebio
Francisco Kino*. San Francisco: Sonora Press, 1932.

Breidenbach, Flora. "Samuel Charles Mazzuchelli: Gifted Pioneer of
the Midwest." In *Italian Americans and Their Public and Private Life*,
edited by Frank J. Cavaioli, Angela Danzi, and Salvatore J. LaGu-
mina. Staten Island, New York: American Italian Historical Association, 1993.

Case, Lynn M. "The Middle West in 1837: Translations From the Notes
of an Italian Count, Francesco Arese." *Mississippi Valley Historical
Review* 20 (December 1983): 381–99.

Clark, Neil M. "Close Calls: An Interview with Charles A. Siringo,
Daring Adventurer in the Old Wild West." *America Magazine*: 173–85.

Cofone, Albin J. "Reno's Little Italy: Italian Entrepreneurship and Culture in Northern Nevada." *Nevada Historical Society Quarterly* 26
(Winter 1983): 97–110.

Espinosa, J. M. "The Neopolitan Jesuits on the Colorado Frontier
1868–1919." *Colorado Magazine* 15 (March 1938): 64–73.

Falbo, Ernest, trans. and ed. *California and Overland Diaries of Count
Leonetto Cipriani From 1853 Through 1871*. Portland, Oregon: The
Champoeg Press, 1962.

Martin, Sr. Theresa, S.C. "Life Sketch of Sister Blandina Segale
1850–1941." In *At the End of the Santa Fe Trail* by Sister Blandina
Segale, S.C. Milwaukee, Wisconsin 1948, 1–10.

Martinelli, Phylis C. "Italian Immigrant Women in the Southwest." In *The Italian Immigrant Woman in North America*, edited by Betty B. Caroli, Robert F. Harney and Lydio F. Tomasi. Toronto, Canada: The Multicultural History Society of Ontario, 1978.

Owens, Sister M. Lilliana. "Frances Xavier Cabrini: Foundress of the Queen of Heaven Institute." *Colorado Magazine* 22 (July 1945): 171–78.

Pumroy, Eric. "Francesco Vigo: Italian on the American Frontier," in *Support and Struggle: Italians and Italian Americans in a Comparative Perspective*, edited by Joseph Tropea, James E. Miller and Cheryl Beattie-Repetti. New York: American Italian Historical Association, 9–21, 1986.

Reis, Elizabeth. "The AFL, the IWW and Bay Area Cannery Workers." *California History* 64 (Summer 1985): 174–91 and 241–42.

Rusich, Luciano G. "Giacomo Costantino Beltrami and the Indians of North America." In *The Italian Americans Through the Generations*, edited by Rocco Caporale. New York: American Italian Historical Association, 4–19, 1986.

Scambray, Ken. "Creative Responses to the Italian American Experience in California: Baldassare Forestiere's 'Underground Gardens' and Simon Rodia's 'Watts Towers.'" *Italian American Review* 8 (Autumn/Winter 2001): 113–40.

Smith, G. Hubert. "Count Andreani: A Forgotten Traveler." *Minnesota History* 19 (March 1938): 34–42.

Speroni, Charles. "California's Fishermen's Festivals." *Western Folklore* 14 (April 1955): 77–89.

Worrall, Janet E. "Adjustment and Integration: The Italian Experience in Colorado." In *New Explorations in Italian American Studies*, edited by Richard N. Juliani and Sandra P. Juliani. New York: American Italian Historical Association, 195–208, 1992.

Index

Abbaticchio, Ed: 260, 265
Abiati, A.: 184
Accolti, Fr. Michael: 17, 98
Ada, Ok.: 308
Adams, Wess: 303–4
Agricultural Workers' Organization: 242
agriculture: 15, 149, 152, 179–80
Albertini, Mother Luigina: 143
Albi, Mrs. Rodolfo: 168
Albi, Peter: 180
Albuquerque, N.M.: 155, 159, 161, 162, 168, 170
Alfieri, Vittorio: 44
Alsatians: 73
Alta California: 22
Alta California (newspaper): 275
Altar River: 93, 107
American Federation of Labor: 207, 251, 253, 255, 256
American Fur Company: 79–80, 82
American Historical Association: 273
American Philosophical Society: 25, 47
American Protective Association (APA): 174, 184–86

American Revolution: 30
Americans: 74, 76
Anaconda Copper Mining Company: 206
Andreani, Count Paolo: 24–25, 44; other travels of, 47–48; studies of, 46–47; travels to the Great Lakes of, 45–47
Angelo, Charles. *See* Siringo, Johnny
Anthropologie der Naturvölker (book): 66
Anthony, Donald: 238
Anzalone, Brother Cherubin: 132
Apache tribe: 112
Arata, Daniel: 185–86
architecture: Italian influence on, 14
Arese, Count Francesco: 26, 71; studies of, 71–72
Arizona: 101–2, 158
Asians: 154
Askin, John: 34, 35–36, 41
Assiniboin tribe: 56
Associazione Italiana di Mutua Protezione Cristoforo Colombo: 164

Asti Winery: 210
Astor, John Jacob: 79–80
"Astronomical explanation of the
    comet . . .": 105
At the End of the Santa Fe Trail
    (autobiography): 159, 276, 294
Austin, Nev.: 189
Avansino family: 192
Aztec tribe: 60

Bachechi, Maria: 168
Bairo, Angelina: 168
Baja California: 93–94, 208
Baldassarre, Father: 134
Balzar, Fred: 200
Bancroft, Anne: 18
Bancroft, Hubert Howe: 66
Bandini, Fr. Pietro: 152, 153
Bandini, Juan: 210
Bank of America. *See* Bank of Italy
Bank of Italy: 15
Bardone, Genevieve: 165
Bardone, Mary: 165
Barsanti, Alexander: 165
Barzini, Luigi: 18
baseball: 212, 259–72
Basques: 192
Bauer, Sister Orsolina: 143
Bavarians: 93
Beals, David T.: 300
Beckx, Fr. P. J.: 130–31
Belgians: 93, 131
Beltrami, Giacomo Costantino:
    25–26; background of, 51–52;
    influence of studies of, 65–69;
    studies of Mexican Indians of,

60–61, 64–65; studies of North
    American Indians of, 55–59,
    61–64, 65–66; travels of, 52–54
Benavente, Fr. Toribio de
    (Motolinia): 60
Benenato, Frank: 166
Benenato, Giusseppa: 166, 172
Bensherod (steamboat): 79
Benzoni, Girolamo: 22
Bergamo, Italy: 25, 51
Berra, Yogi: 259
Bertino, Felix: 166–67
Biesta, Federico: 209
Bigando, Kate: 168
Billings, Mont.: 206
Billy the Kid: 159, 276, 305–6, 307
Biscacianti, Eliza: 212
Bisceglia Brothers Cannery: 244
Bitch Lake. *See* Itasca Lake, Minn.
Bizzarri, Crespino: 281
Bizzarri, Gosto: 281
"Black Robes." *See* Jesuits
Blackfoot tribe: 97
Blacks: 26, 154, 176
Blandina, Andrea: 292
Blandina, Catalina: 292
Blandina, Francesco: 291–92, 293
Blandina, Giovanna Malatesta: 291,
    292
Blandina, Maria Maddelena: 292
Blue Fox: 16
Bodie, Calif.: 265
Bodie, Ping: 265–68; photo of, 266
Bogan, Sister J. Berckmans: 143
Bohemians: 93, 274
bois-brûlés: 53–54

Boldrina, Sister Clemenza: 142
Bollettino del Nevada (newspaper):
  195, 198, 200–1
Bonney, William H. *See* Billy the
  Kid
Book of Mormon: 151
Botta, Carlo: 22
Botta, Paolo Emilio: 22, 208
Boturini, Lorenzo Benaducci: 23, 64
Bourbourg, Brasseur de: 69
Boy Spies of America: 247
Brazil, Wayne: 307–8
Brennan, C. F.: 185
Brinker, Fr. John: 134
British: 24, 29, 30, 31, 32, 33, 34, 35,
  37, 39, 40, 45, 48, 74, 173–74
Brown, Patrick: 38
Brunetti, Joe: 197
Bucola, Anthony: photo of, 164
Bucola, Nellie Rietta: photo of, 164
Buffalo, N.Y.: 90
Bunker Hill, Calif.: 18
Bunyan, Paul: 274
Bureau of Labor: 239

Cabrini, Mother Frances Xavier:
  99, 100, 139–46, 171, 182; canon-
  ization of, 100, 146, 156; photo of,
  141
Cabrini, Rose: 139
Cafferata, Manuel: 192
Cahokia, Ill.: 29, 30
Calabria, Italy: 152
Caldwell, Kans.: 300
Calhoun (ship): 52
California: 15, 98, 101–2, 106, 110,
  208, 209–10, 210–11, 240, 252, 259,
  275, 281, 319–20; climate of, 14;
  similarity to Italy, 14
California Commission of Immi-
  gration and Housing (CCIH): 241,
  248
California Food Control Depart-
  ment: 249
California Fruit Canners Associa-
  tion (CFCA): 236, 244
California League: 260
California Packing Corporation. *See*
  Del Monte Company
California State League: 260
Camilli, Dolph: 265
Campania, Italy: 155, 166
Campietta, Mother Umilia: 142
Campobasso, Italy: 178
Campos, Fr. Agustín de: 112, 113, 114
Canestrelli, Fr. Philip: 97
Canners League of California: 248
canning industry: 235–42
Capra, Frank: 16
Carbonelli, Fr. Antonio: 95
Cardon, Rosa: 152
Cardone, Paul: 169
Cardone, Susanna: 169
Careri, Giovanni: 22
Carli, Gian Rinaldo: 64
Carson, Kit: 150
The Case of the Well Dressed Corpse
  (novel): 195
Casonato, Sister Taresia: 143
Cass, William: 61, 83
Cassinella, William: 191
Cataldo Mission: 99

Cataldo, Fr. Joseph (Giuseppe): 18, 96, 99

Catholic Church: 100, 119–20, 123, 129–30, 135, 159, 173–74, 181, 182, 184–85

Cavour, Count Camillo: 209

Ceschetti, Francisco: 165

Cherokee tribe: 153

Chicago: 85–86, 88, 300

Chickasaw tribe: 39, 153

Chinese: 17, 176, 192, 276

Chippewa tribe: 54, 55, 58, 59, 65–66, 68, 118–19, 121

Chisholm Trail: 300, 303

Choctaw tribe: 39

Chouteau, René Auguste: 80

Christian Brothers: 137

Cicagna, Italy: 291

Cicognani, Fr. Amletto Giovanni: 146

Cincinnati, Ohio: 72, 73, 118, 135, 159, 291, 292, 293

Cipriani, Count Leonetto: 209, 274–76, 279–80; drawing of, 280

Cipriani, Francesco: 281

Cipriani, Mary Tolley Washington: 275

Cipriani, Ottavio: 280, 281, 282

City of Naples (fishing boat): 223

Clark, George Rogers: 24, 30–31, 32–33, 36, 39, 42

Clark, William: 52, 61

Clavigero, Fr. Francesco: 95

Clay, Henry: 74

Clear Lake Rancho: 286

Cleveland, Ohio: 89

Cloudy-Weather (Chippewa chief): 58

Coeur d'Alene tribe: 96

Colombo Hotel: 194–95

Colombo, Sister Rosario: 143

Colorado: 15, 145, 156, 158, 159, 173, 207–8, 276

Colorado Fuel and Iron Company (CF&I): 174, 175

Colorado River: 22, 93, 94, 107, 110, 113

Colorado Springs, Colo.: 179

Columbia Basin: 98

Columbus Day: 182–84, 217

Commentary on the Sunday Epistles and Gospels (*Postila sobre las Epistolas y Evangelios Domenicales*) (publication): 61

Como, Perry: 18

Compagnoni, Countess Geronima: 55, 59

Comstock Lode, Nev.: 189, 207

Conejos mission: 131–32

Congiato, Fr. Nicholas: 98

Congress: 33, 40–41

Cooper, James Fenimore: 66–67, 274

Corbin, Austin: 205

Corriere de Trinidad (newspaper): 177

Cors, Edward: 18

Corsicana, Tex.: 153

Crescenzo, Samuel: 189

Crockett, Davy: 150, 274

Crooks, Ramsay: 79–80

Cuneo, Gian: 161

Cuneo, Louisa: 161

D'Aponte, Father: 133
Dakota tribe. *See* Sioux tribe
Damascio, Frank: 181, 184
Dante Alighieri Society: 169, 200
Dayton, Nev.: 188
Dazzini, Sister Raphael: 143
de Attelis, Orazio, Marquis de Santangelo: 23
De Blieck, Fr.: 131
De Lorenzo, Sister Mercedes: 143
De Mateis Winery: 199
De Smet, Fr. Pierre Jean: 96, 132
Denver, Colo.: 95, 100, 130, 131, 133, 134, 135, 137, 138, 139, 142, 143, 144, 145, 155, 156, 161, 162, 165, 168, 169, 170, 173, 177, 178, 179, 182, 184–86
Denver & Rio Grand Western Railroad: 17
Denver, South Park and Pacific Railroad: 176
Detroit, Mich.: 24, 30, 32, 33, 34, 35, 37, 38, 39, 48, 89, 120
Di Giorgio Corporation: 15
A Dictionary of the Kalispel or Flathead Indian Language (book): 97
Dakotas: 206
"Dance of the Gigli" feast: 324
Daughters of Charity of St. Vincent de Paul: 276
Dayton, Ohio: 294
Del Monte Company: 235, 237
Del Vecchio, Liberato : 208
Depot Hotel: 196–97
Diamond, Wash.: 206

A Dictionary of the Nez Perce Language (book): 97
DiFiore Company: 244
Di Giorgio, Rosario: 210
Dillon, Guillaume Patrice: 279
DiMaggio, Dominic: 263, 265
DiMaggio, Joe: 16, 259, 260, 263, 265, 272
DiMaggio, Vince: 265
Diomedi, Fr. Alexander: 97
Dodge City, Kans.: 303
Doheny, Edward: 277
Dominican Sisters: 99, 120, 122
Dominicans: 93, 99, 117–18
Dominis, John: 151
Donatelli, Nicola: 212
Donofrio, Charles: 167
Dormio family: 196
Dotta, Emilio: 189
Dubuque, Iowa: 119
Duhaut-Cilly, Auguste: 22
Dupaix, Guillermo: 69
Dutchmen: 103–4

Earl of Selkirk: 45–46
Elder, Archbishop William Henry: 294
Elko, Nev.: 189
Endeavor (fishing boat): 225
Eskibugekogé (Chippewa chief): 55
Eureka, Nev.: 189
Europa Hotel (Reno, Nev.): 196–97
Europa Hotel (Sparks, Nev.): 197

Falconio, Archbishop Diomede: 295
Farfariello: 212

Farnese, Miss: 168
Favores Celestiales (book): 103
Fayetteville, Ohio: 294
Federal Food Administration: 233
Federal Labor Union. *See* Toilers of
   the World
*Fifteen Years on the Hurricane Deck of
   a Spanish Pony* (book): 301
Figliolino, John: 179
Figliolino, Tom: 179
Filottrano, Italy: 51
Fior D'Italia: 16
First National Bank: 191
fishermen's festivals: 216–17, 217–19,
   219–21, 228–31
fishing industry: 16, 151. *See also*
   Monterey, Calif., fishermen's fes-
   tival of; Point Loma, Calif., fish-
   ermen's festival of; San Francisco,
   Calif., fishermen's festival of
Flathead tribe: 96, 97, 98
Folle Avoine tribe. *See* Menomeni
   tribe
Fond du Lac, Wisc.: 48
Fontana, Marco: 210, 236
Foreign Miners Tax: 209
Forestiere, Antonio: 312
Forestiere, Baldassare: 278, 311,
   312–19, 323, 325
Forestiere, Giuseppe: 312, 317
Forestiere, Rosario: 312
Forestiere, Vincenzo: 312
Forgnone, Angelo: 189–90
Forsyth and Richardson: 46
Fort Armstrong, Ill.: 55
Fort Edward: 55

Fort Snelling, Minn.: 25, 52, 53, 54,
   55, 58
Fort St. Anthony. *See* Fort Snelling
Fort Wayne, Ind.: 34
Fox tribe: 55, 66
Franciscans: 93, 95
Frederic, François Alexandre, Duke
   de la Rochefoucauld Liancourt:
   25, 45, 48
French: 18, 22, 23, 24, 28, 29, 30, 31,
   32, 36, 38, 40, 41, 43, 46, 53, 55, 59,
   69, 71, 72, 77, 81, 82, 85, 93, 103–4,
   192
Fresno, Calif.: 311, 313
Fuller, R. Buckminster: 323
Funston Playground: 263
fur trade: 23–24, 25, 27, 30, 34, 34–36,
   37–38, 40, 45, 48–49, 49–50, 53,
   79–80, 82, 118, 148
Furillo, Carl: 260

Galena, Ill.: 119, 123
Gallo family: 15
Garaventa family: 192
Garbi, Alessandro: 204
Gardella family: 192
Garett, Pat: 306, 307–8
Garramone, Elvira: 180
Garramone, Mike: 179–80
Garramone, Tony: 179–80
Gasparri, Father: 132, 134
gastronomy: 16
Gay, Greer: 195
Gehrig, Lou: 271
Gelmini, Fr. Dominic: 140
Genoa, Italy: 13, 151, 180, 196, 276

Germans: 18, 73, 75, 84, 149, 173, 274
Gerstl, Father: 103–4, 105
Ghiglieri family: 192
Ghirardelli, Domenico: 16, 209, 275
Giannini, Amadeo P.: 15
Giglio, Fr. S.: 136
Gila River: 93, 94, 107
Giomi, Angelina: 160
Giomi, Girolamo: 160
Giorda, Fr. Giovanni: 98
Giorda, Fr. Giuseppe: 96
Giragi, Carmel: 17
Giragi, Columbus: 17
Girot, Ellen: 166–67
Glendale, Ohio: 294
gold rush: 16, 98, 148, 281
Gonzaga University: 18, 98, 99
Gossett, Bob: 308
Gower, S. J.: 280–81
Granata, John: 197–98, 201
Grand Army of the Republic (GAR): 185, 186
Grand Portage, Mich.: 45, 47, 48, 49
Great Lakes: 23, 24, 34, 47, 72, 91
Great Northern Railroad: 152
Greeks: 176
Green Bay, Wisc.: 84, 85
Gregory, Thomas: 248
The Griffin (ship): 23
Griffin-Skelley plant: 244
Griffith, David W.: 212
Grosso, Michael: 167
Grosso, Teresa: 157, 167–68
Guaragna, Salvatore. *See* Warren, Harry
Guasti, Secondo: 15, 199, 210–11

Gubitosi, Fr.: 144
Guida, Father: 134–35
Gunnison, Colo.: 176
Guscetti, Frank: 197
Guscetti, Louis: 197

Hamilton, Henry: 30, 31
Hamtramck, John Francis: 37, 38, 39
Hardin, John Wesley: 301–2, 306
Harmar, Josiah: 37, 39
Harrison, William Henry: 24, 41
Hart, William S. "Bill": 277, 301
Hay Ranch: 189
Haymarket Riot: 277
Héros (ship): 22
Hickok, Wild Bill: 302–3
Holy Ghost: 229, 230
Hotel Italia: 185
Hoover, Herbert: 249
Houston, Sam: 150
Hudson's Bay Company: 24, 53
Humphreys, David: 45

Il Circolo Filodrammatico: 169
Il Correo Atlantico (newspaper): 23
Il Grido del Popolo (newspaper): 180
Il Risveglio (newspaper): 180
Illinois: 152
Ince, William: 212
Indian treaties: 61
Indian wars: 40
Indians: 15, 25, 29, 32, 36–37, 38, 39, 48, 52, 53, 55, 61–62, 62–64, 65, 94–95, 98, 99, 107, 109, 112, 119–20, 125, 148, 153, 154, 158, 282–86, 288–90; birthplace of,

68–69; languages of, 98, 99, 119, 120–21. *See also* individual tribes
Industrial Welfare Commission (IWC): 241, 242, 243, 248, 252, 256
Industrial Workers of the World (IWW): 206, 207, 233, 234, 235, 240, 242–43, 244, 247, 248–49, 252, 253–56, 258
International Hotel: 189
Iowa: 205–6
Iowa City, Iowa: 123–24
Irish: 84, 173–74
Iroquois tribe: 96
Italian American Bank: 161
Italian Benevolent Society: 209, 244
The Italian Chain Store Company: 197
Italian Fishermen's Protective Association: 211
Italian Hall: 164
Italian Hospital: 275
Italian Hospital Association: 209
Italian Protective and Benevolent Association: 207
Italian Women's Club: 169
Italian-language newspapers: 16, 161, 177, 180, 187–88, 194–95, 198, 209, 234, 235, 245–47, 248, 250, 252, 257
Italians: 15, 142, 148, 157–58, 274; as artists, 212, 278; as baseball players, 212, 259–72; as cannery workers, 233, 235, 240–41, 243, 244, 245, 246, 249, 250, 252, 254, 257, 258; as farmers, 204–5, 205–6, 209, 210; as fishermen, 209, 211, 215–17; as hoteliers, 194–97, 207, 279; as landowners, 24, 178, 188, 190, 313;

as loggers, 206; as miners, 205, 206, 207–8; as railroad workers, 176–77, 206; as steel workers, 177; as vintners, 199, 210–11, 314; assimilation of culture of, 191, 198, 200–1, 203, 210, 249, 272, 311–12, 319–20; communities in U.S. of, 17, 149–50, 150–51, 155, 160–62, 164–65, 165–67, 169, 170, 181, 184, 191–93, 197–98, 200–1, 210, 262, 276; discrimination against, 15, 154, 175, 176, 184–86, 205, 207, 209–10, 268; immigration of, 14; in Arizona, 17; in Arkansas, 152, 204–5; in California, 14, 15–16, 18, 22, 93–95, 98, 101, 102, 106–13, 151, 152, 204, 208–12, 213–21, 234–35, 240–41, 245–47, 248–49, 251, 258, 259–262, 263–72, 275, 277–78, 279–90, 311–12, 313–26; in Colorado, 15, 95, 129, 130, 131–38, 142–46, 156, 173–86, 207–8, 270; in Illinois, 99, 119; in Indiana, 30–31, 33, 40, 42; in Iowa, 99, 123–24; in Kansas, 152, 205; in Kentucky, 36, 38, 73–75, 205; in Louisiana, 23, 204; in Michigan, 34–35, 49; in mining, 174–76, 178, 189; in Minnesota, 25, 205; in Missouri, 205; in Montana, 17, 97, 98, 206; in Nevada, 17, 154, 187–201; in New Mexico, 17, 131, 153–54, 207, 276; in Ohio, 72–73, 292–97; in other industries, 207, 208–9, 210; in the Southwest, 157–172, 206–7; in Texas, 23, 153, 204, 299–310; in Utah, 17, 151–52, 208; in Washington, 205; in Wisconsin, 118–19, 122; influence on U.S. of, 15–16, 18; languages of, 166, 178, 180, 193–94, 197, 200, 203, 250; motivations for emigrating of, 14, 148–52, 154–55, 159, 173, 203–4, 206, 210, 273–74, 318–19, 319–20; nativist hostility toward, 156; religion of, 159, 164, 173; women, 155, 156, 157, 158–62, 165, 166–72, 240, 243, 245

Italy: 18, 23, 44, 68, 95, 97, 101, 118, 125, 127, 140, 158, 177, 192, 223, 225, 270, 275, 296, 319, 326; central Italy, 179; climate of, 14, 51–52; culture of, 165, 167, 190, 198, 200, 312; government of, 130, 131, 191, 274, 291, 292; northen Italy, 16, 25, 27, 168, 169, 205, 206, 208; southern Italy, 178, 203, 214, 215

Itasca Lake, Minn.: 54

Jacova tribe: 55
Jamaica: 48
James Cafferata: 192
Jano tribe: 112
Japanese: 175, 176, 211
Jenks, Albert E.: 68
Jesuits: 17–18, 93, 94, 95–99, 101–2, 118, 153, 164, 207, 208; in Colorado, 95, 129–38
Jocome tribe: 112
Joe DiMaggio Playground: 263, 264
Jogues, Fr. Isaac: 96
Johnson, Hiram: 241, 256
Johnston, John: 46
Jones, George Wallace: 121
Justina, Sister: 293, 294, 296

Kansas: 152, 205
Kansas City, Mo.: 152
Kartschoke-Peterson Brickyard: 244
Kaskaskia, Ill.: 29, 30, 31, 32, 38
Kelly, Father. See Mazzuchelli, Fr. Samuel Charles
Kelly, Fr. Massy. See Mazzuchelli, Fr. Samuel Charles
Kelly, Fr. Mathew. See Mazzuchelli, Fr. Samuel Charles
Kentucky: 24, 26, 30, 32, 33–34, 36, 37, 38, 73, 74, 75, 76, 81, 84, 118
King Ferdinand VII: 94
King Victor Emmanuel II of Sardinia: 209
Kingdom of Sardinia: 274
Kino, Fr. Eusebio: 22, 93–94, 153; as explorer, 103, 104–5, 107, 110–11, 114–15; as missionary, 103, 107–10, 111–13; as student, 102–3; character of, 113–15; portrait of, 102; studies of, 94, 105; voyage to America of, 103–5
Kitci-Okiman (the Great Warrior). See Beltrami, Giacomo Costantino
Knights of Liberty: 247
Ku Klux Klan (KKK): 174, 185, 186
Kuykendall, Wiley: 301

L'Eco della Colonia (newspaper): 209
L'Italia (newspaper): 245–47, 248–49, 249–50
L'Unione (newspaper): 177
La Capitale (newspaper): 180
La Democrazia (ship): 204, 251
La Frusta (newspaper): 180
La Guardia, Fiorello: 153–54

La Nazione (newspaper): 181
La Nuova Italia (women's club): 169
La Pointe, Wisc.: 46, 47, 48
La Roma (newspaper): 180
La Salle, Robert de: 23
La Società Sant' Anna: 169
La Società Santa Margherita: 169
La Stella (newspaper): 180
La Voce del Popolo (The Voice of the
    People) (newspaper): 245–46, 247,
    249, 250
Labor Bureau: 237
Lake Erie: 48, 89
Lake Huron: 48, 55, 89
Lake Julia: 26
Lake Michigan: 55
Lake Ontario: 48, 58
Lake Superior: 25, 43, 46, 47, 50, 88
Lake Winnipeg: 58
Lambert, Captain J. J.: 133
Larco, Nicholas (Nicola): 2029, 280,
    281, 282
Las Vegas, N.M.: 136–37
Lazarist Order: 96
Lazzeri, Tony: 260, 269–72
Le Méxique (two-volume book): 59,
    64, 65, 66
Leandri, Giovanni Batista: 210
Lee, Richard Henry: 44
Lelia Byrd (ship): 222
Leone, Fr. Alejandro: 132
LePore, Fr. Mariano: 142, 181, 184
Lewis, Meriwether: 61
Lexington: 73, 74
Leyba, Don Fernando de: 30, 33
Liberty League: 247

"Life in the Rocky Mountains"
    (article): 97
Lightfoot, B. C.: 185
Liguria, Italy: 155, 165
Lincoln County War: 306
Lincoln, Ledyard: 295
"Little Italies": 154, 161, 165, 170, 181,
    184; in Reno, Nev., 187–201
Locantro, Sister Filomena: 143
Lodi, Italy: 146
Lodigiani, Dario: 263–64
Logan, Utah: 169
Lombardi, Ernie: 260, 265; photo
    of, 261
Lombardi, Fr. Jesus: 94–95
Lombardy, Italy: 16, 139
Long, Stephen H.: 25, 53, 54
Los Angeles, Calif.: 208, 320
Louisiana: 29, 30, 152
Louisiana Purchase: 61
Louisville, Ky.: 38, 52, 74–75, 76, 77
Loyola Church: 135
Luca, Don Guiseppe De: 142
Lucca, Italy: 162
Lucchese: 162
Ludlow massacre: 15, 156, 174, 175, 177
LX Ranch: 300, 305, 306, 309

Macerata, Italy: 51
Machebeuf, Bishop Joseph P.: 130,
    131, 132, 133, 134, 136
Mackinac Island: 88–89, 118
Macomb, Alexander: 34
Madison, James: 25, 44, 47
Magdalena River: 93, 107
Maggio, Joseph: 15

Magniani, Oduardo: 165
Malaspina, Alessandro: 22, 208
Manale, Sister Imelda: 143
Manchester (cruiser): 226
Mancini, Frank: 18, 180
Maraschi, Fr. Anthony: 17, 98
Maria (fishing boat): 225
Maria Santissima del Lume: 217
Martin, Dean: 18
Martin, Frank: 279
Martinelli, Mother Maddalena: 143
Martinez, Calif.: 320
Martini family: 15
Mary Blanche, Mother : 294
Massari, Vincent: 177
Masterson, Bat: 303, 304
Matz, Fr. Nicholas C.: 142–43, 144
Mayan civilization: 69
Mazza, Frank: 184
Mazzei, Phillip: 44
Mazzella, Fr. Camillus: 134
Mazzuchelli, Fr. Samuel Charles:
    99, 205–6; and Native Americans,
    118–20, 120–21, 122–23, 124, 125; as
    builder, 123–24; background of,
    117–18
McDonald, Jesse: 184
McIntyre, Cardinal James Francis:
    226–27
Medici-Spada, Countess Giulia: 26,
    54
Memorie (book): 97
Menante, Harry: 191
Mengarini, Fr. Gregorio: 96, 98
Menominee tribe: 55, 118–19
Merritt, Ralph: 249, 250

Mexicans: 154, 174, 175
Mexico: 22, 52, 55, 59–60, 64, 66, 69
Miami Company: 35, 36, 41
Miamis. *See* Fort Wayne, Ind.
Michilimackinac, Mich.: 32, 34, 48
Midwest: 27
Milan, Italy: 117–18
Miller, Jim: 307–8
Milwaukee, Wisc.: 85
Minasi, Fr.: 134
mining: 17, 136, 148, 153, 154, 160,
    174, 178, 208, 275
Minutili, Fr. Geronimo: 95
Mission Caborca: 110, 111, 112
Mission Cocóspora: 107–8, 109–10
Mission Dolores: 107–8, 108–9,
    110–11, 113
Mission Guebavi: 107
Mission Imuris: 112
Mission Magdalena: 112, 114
Mission Remedios: 107–8, 109–10
Mission San Ignacio: 112
Mission San Xavier del Bac: 107,
    110, 111
Mission Tubutama: 111, 112
Mission Tumacácori: 107, 110, 111, 112
Missionaries of Saint Charles: 99
Missionary Sisters of the Sacred
    Heart: 99–100, 140, 143, 156
Mississippi River: 23, 24, 25, 27, 37,
    52, 76–77; search for source of, 54,
    58, 62
Mississippi Valley: 72
Missouri: 205
Missouri Province: 131, 138
Missouri River: 15

Mondavi family: 15
Mondovi, Piedmont, Italy: 27
Monserat, Simon: 286, 287
Montana: 17, 97, 98, 206
Monterey, Calif.: 106, 208, 211; fishermen's festival of, 219–21
Montgomery, John: 36
Montreal: 48, 49
Moore, William C.: 309
Mormons: 151–52, 158, 276
Morse, Jedidiah: 62
Morvillo, Fr. Anthony: 97
Mosconi, Luigi: 184
Mother Cabrini High School: 146
Mother Lode: 208, 280
Mount Carmel School: 171, 182
Mt. St. Vincent Academy: 292
Mundelein, Archbishop George Cardinal: 146
Munnecum, Fr.: 133
Musso and Frank Restaurant: 16
Mussolini: 198–200
mutual-aid societies: 161

Napa Valley, Calif.: 16
Naples, Italy: 23, 130, 152
Napoli, Fr. Ignacio: 95
The Native Races of the Pacific States of North America (book): 66
Nebraska: 205
Neri, Fr. Joseph: 98
Nevada: 154, 187, 188, 189
New Mexico: 153, 158, 207, 276
New Mexico–Colorado Mission of the Neapolitan Province of the Society of Jesus: 131, 132, 137–38
New Orleans, La.: 23, 27, 39, 48, 152

New Orleans Province: 131, 138
Nez Perce tribe: 96
Niagara Falls: 48, 90–92
Nizza, Fray Marco da: 21–22, 153
Nobili, Fr. Giovanni (John): 17, 96, 98, 151
Noce, Angelo: 156, 180, 182–84
Nocera, Sister Lucida: 143
Nola, Italy: 278
Nolan, Edward J.: 135
North Beach Playground. See Joe DiMaggio Playground
Northern Europeans: 175–76
Northwest: geography of, 43
Northwest Company: 46, 49, 53
Northwest Passage: 22
Notre Dame Sisters: 292
Novello, Mr.: 292

O'Phalliard, Tom: 306
Oakland, Calif.: 224, 232, 236, 238, 244–45, 247, 251, 256, 261, 264
Ocangra Aramee Wawakakara (book): 120–21
Ohio: 74, 75, 276
Ohio River: 37, 38, 52, 72–73, 75–76, 76–77
Ohio Valley: 24, 72
Oregon Territory: 97
Oregon Trail: 148
organized labor: 15, 174–76, 177, 205, 206, 207–8, 210, 233–34, 235, 243–56
Ottawa tribe: 55, 88–89, 118–19
Our Lady of Mt. Carmel Church: 181, 182
Our Lady of Mt. Carmel School: 143, 144

Pacific Base Ball Convention: 260
Pacific Coast League: 260–61, 264,
  265, 267, 268, 269
Packet Pennsylvania (steamboat):
  84–85
Palma, Italy: 195
Pantanella, Fr. Dominic: 95, 137, 144
Paradise Valley, Nev.: 189–90
Paradise, John: 44
Paris Inn: 16
Parma, Italy: 51
Pastorino, Frank: 189
patron saints: 213–15, 219–20, 227–28,
  229, 324
Patti, Madame Adelina: 18, 204, 212
Peabody, James H.: 175
Pecetti family: 192
Perazzo, Carlo: 160, 165
Perazzo, Fredrica: 160
Perazzo, Henry: 160
Perazzo, Louisa: 160
Perazzo, Paolo: 160
Perazzo, Virginia: 160
Perino, Alex: 16
Personé, Fr. Salvatore: 95, 132, 133
Petri family: 16
Pezzolo, Francesco. See Bodie, Ping
Philadelphia, Pa.: 47, 52
Phoenix, Ariz.: 155, 157, 160, 161, 165,
  166, 165–67, 168, 170, 171
Piazza, Mike: 259
Piazza, Santino: 196
Piccolo, Fr. Francesco Maria: 94–95
Piedmont (Piemonte), Italy: 16, 27,
  96, 155, 158, 165, 169
Piemonte Hotel: 197
Pike, Zebulon M.: 61

A Pilgrimage in America Leading to
  the Discovery of the Sources of the
  Mississippi and Bloody River; with
  a Description of the Whole Course of
  the Former; and of the Ohio (narra-
  tive): 55, 58, 59, 62
Pima tribe: 94, 101, 108, 110, 112–13
Pimeria Alta: 93–94, 107
Pincolini (Mizpah) Hotel: 194–95
Pincolini, Aldevado: 195
Pincolini, Bruno: 195
Pincolini, Guido: 195
Pinelli, Babe: photo of, 266
Pinkerton Agency: 17, 277, 300
Pinto, Father: 133, 136
Piretto family: 192
Pittman, Key: 198–200
Piuma's Italian Pharmacy: photo of,
  202
Piuma, Giovanni: 202
Pizzati, Salvatore: 23
Platt, Sam: 198–200
Point Loma: 228; fishermen's festi-
  val of, 228–31
Pojero, Francesco Varvaro: 147
Polish: 175
Politi, Leo: 18
Polk, James K.: 23
Pollock, Oliver: 31
polygamy: 158–59
Ponziglione, Fr. Paul: 95–96
Pope Leo XIII: 140
Pope Pius XI: 146
Pope Urban VIII: 229
Popul-Vuh (Mayan epic): 69
Portuguese: 217, 229, 230
Potenza, Italy: 166

Potomawa tribe: 55
Prairie du Chien, Wisc.: 55
Pratt-Low Cannery: 247
Principessa Jolanda (women's club):
    169
Pueblo, Colo.: 169, 174, 177
Pueblo Smeltermen's Union: 177
Purcell, Archbishop John Baptist: 292

Queen Margerita: 153
Queen of Heaven Mother Cabrini
    Memorial School: 144, 145
Queen of Heaven Orphanage: 171,
    182
Questa, Camella: 191
Questa, Edward: 191–92
Questa, Fred: 191
Quilici, Hugo: 191

Racine, Wisc.: 85
Raffeto family: 192
Raggio family: 192
railroads: 147, 154, 162, 176, 178, 206
Ramelli, C.: 197
ranching: 111–12
Ravalli, Fr. Anthony (Antonio): 96,
    98
Recanzone family: 190
Recanzone, Batista: 189–90
Red Lake, Minn.: 54
Red River basin: 53
Regis College. See Sacred Heart
    College
Regis University: 182
Reno, Nev.: 187, 190, 191, 192–201
Renville, Mr.: 57
Repetto, Alessandro: 210

Rizzuto, Phil: 259
Rocca, Salvatore: 210
Rocky Mountain News (newspaper):
    186
Rodia, Simon (Sam, Sabato): 18, 278,
    311, 322–25; background of, 319–20
Rogers, Will: 301
Roman Capitol Mine: 189
Romanelli, Carlo: 212
Roncaglia, Agostino: 184
Rosati, Bishop Joseph: 96
Rossi family: 16
Rossi, Adolfo: 176
Rotary Club: 247
Rovere, Bert: 16
Russians: 173
Ruth, Babe: 267, 269, 270, 271

Sacred Heart Church: 181
Sacred Heart College: 95, 136, 137, 181
Saetta, Fr. Francesco Saverio: 94–95
Sahagún, Fray Bernardino de: 61, 65
St. Paulinus: 324
Saint Francis Hotel: 196
Saint Ignatius College. See Univers-
    ity of San Francisco
A Salish or Flathead Grammar
    (book): 97
St. Clair, Arthur: 39
St. Clara's School: 99, 122
St. Ignatius College: 98
St. Ignatius Mission, Colo.: 96–97,
    133
Saint Isabel: 229, 230
St. Louis, Mo.: 23–24, 26, 29, 30, 31,
    32, 33, 34, 52, 69, 71, 77, 79, 81, 83
St. Louis (steamboat): 79

St. Mary's College: 96
St. Mary's Mission: 96
Salari, Charles: 165
Salari, Rebecca: 165
Salish tribe. *See* Flathead tribe
Salvatierra, Fr. Juan Maria (Giovanni): 94, 101
Salvatore Fallico family: photo of, 163
Samuel, Father. *See* Mazzuchelli, Fr. Samuel Charles
San Diego, Calif.: 208, 211
(San Diego) *Union* (newspaper): 230–31
San Francisco, Calif.: 18, 209, 211, 239, 242, 259, 262, 279–80, 281–82; baseball in, 260–62, 22–65; fishermen's festival of, 217–19
(San Francisco) *Examiner* (newspaper): 250
San Giovan Giuseppe della Croce (John Joseph of the Cross): 227
San Jose, Calif.: 244
San Juan, Calif.: 286
San Marco: 196
San Pedro: 221–25; fishermen's festival of, 211, 221–28
(San Pedro) *News Pilot* (newspaper): 222
San Rocco: feast of, 161, 182
Santa Barbara: 211
Santa Clara, Calif.: 247
Santa Cruz, Calif.: 106
Santa Fe, N.M.: 130, 131, 137, 159, 276, 293–94
Santa Maria Institute: 294–95
Santa Rosalia: 219

Saturday Evening Post (magazine): 237
Saturno, Leopoldo (Pete): 196
Saturno, Teresa: 196
Sauki tribe: 55
Sbarboro family: 16
Scalabrini, Bishop Giovanni Battista: 99
Scandinavians: 147, 149, 173, 206
Scarpi, Maria: 171–72
School of the Sacred Heart: 135
Sedition Slammers: 247
Segal, Alfred: 296
Segale, Rosa Maria. *See* Segale, Sister Blandina
Segale, Sister Blandina: 153, 159, 276–77, 291–97; photo of, 293
Segale, Sister Maria Maddalena: 159
Segno, Italy: 101
Seminole tribe: 153
Senator Hotel: 196
Seven Years' War: 23, 27
Sicily: 152, 153, 155, 166
silk industry: 169
Silver Plume, Colo.: 178
Silver State Flour Mill: 190
Sinatra, Frank: 18
Sinsinawa Mound: 121
Sinsinawa, Wisc.: 120
Sioux tribe: 53, 54, 55, 56, 57, 58, 59, 61, 66, 68; sketch of: 57
Siringo, Charles A. "Johnny": 17, 149, 157, 277, 301–10; background of: 299–300
Sisters of Charity: 133–34, 135, 159, 291, 293–94, 295

Sisters of Loretto: 133
Sisters of Mercy: 292
Sisters of the Sacred Heart: 182
Sketches of Modern Indian Life
  (book): 97
slavery: 29
Slavs: 174
Slovenians: 175
smallpox: 48, 139
Snelling, Josiah: 53
Snow, Lorenzo: 158
Società Regina Elena, Sorelle di
  Colombo: 169
Society of Jesus. *See* Jesuits
Society of Maria Santissima del
  Lume: 217–18
Sonoma Valley: 16
Sonora: 101–2
Sorice, Giuseppe: 181
South Platte River: 178
Southern Europeans: 176
Southern Pacific Railroad: 152
Southwest, 157–172, 206–7
Spanish: 21, 22, 23, 24, 27, 29, 30, 31,
  33, 36, 37, 39, 40, 60, 93, 95, 102,
  129–30, 137
Sparks, Nev.: 188, 197
Stambaugh, Colonel: 120
Stark, Frank: 310
steamboats: 77–79, 80–81, 82, 89
Stenterello: 212
Steubenville, Ohio: 294
Stiles, Ezra: 44
Sunnyside, Ark.: 205
Swiss American House: 197

Tagliaferro, Lawrence: 25, 52, 58

Taranto, Giuseppe: 151–52
Tardiveau, Bartholomei: 36, 40
Temperance Society: 83, 84
Tempest (steamboat): 78–79
Territorial Enterprise (newspaper): 189
Teschemacher, H. F.: 286, 287
Tetrazzini, Luisa: 212
Texas: 23, 153, 204, 299–310
*Texas Cowboy or Fifteen Years on the
  Hurricane Deck of a Spanish Cow
  Pony* (autobiography): 149, 277;
  cover image of, 298
Texas League: 268
Ticino, Italy: 165
Tisserant, CardinalEugene: 225
Todd, McGill & Company: 35
Toilers of the World: 233, 234, 243,
  244, 252, 253, 254, 255, 256, 258
Tombstone Epitaph (newspaper): 17
Tommasini, Fr. Francis X.: 134, 136
Tonka-Wasci-cio-honska (the
  Great Chief from a Far Coun-
  try). *See* Beltrami, Giacomo
  Costantino
Tonti, Enrico (Henri): 23, 152
Torino, Italy: 159
Torre, Italy: 197
Torquemada, Fray Juan de: 60
Toscano Hotel: 194–95
Travatore Hotel: 196–97
Treaty of Greenville: 40
Trent, Italy: 101
Trinidad, Colo.: 120, 133, 134, 136,
  137, 159, 175, 177
Tucson, Ariz.: 110
Tuscany (Toscana), Italy: 16, 23, 155,
  165–66

Udine, Italy: 51
Underground Gardens: 311, 313, 314,
    315–19, 323, 325
Union Pacific Railroad: 17, 176
United Mine Workers of America
    (UMW): 174–75, 175–76
United States: 61
United States (steamboat): 52
United States Topological Expedi-
    tion: 25
University of San Francisco: 17
University of Santa Clara: 98
Utah: 17, 151–52, 158, 208

Veteran (fishing boat): 224
Vignolo, Roberto: 212
Vigo, Francesco: 23–24, 148; as a
    landowner, 40–41; as fur trader,
    27, 29–30, 33–39, 41; as U.S.
    agent, 39–40; background of,
    27–29; finances of, 33, 40–41,
    41–42; in the American Revolu-
    tion, 30–33
Vincennes, Ind.: 24, 28, 29, 30–31,
    31–32, 32–33, 33–34, 35, 36–37, 38,
    40, 40–41, 42
Virginia (steamboat): 25, 52–53
Virginia City, Mont.: 98
Virginia City, Nev.: 189, 192
Viscount of Kingsborough: 69

Wabash River: 29
Wabiscihouwa (Sioux chief): 55
Waitz, Theodore: 66
Waldensians: 151–52, 158, 205
Walsenburg, Colo.: 134
Wanotan (Sioux chief): 53, 57

Warren, Harry: 18
Washington, 205
Washington, George: 25, 39, 44, 45
Watts Towers: 18, 278, 311, 319,
    322–24; photo of, 321
Watts, Calif.: 311
Wayne, Anthony: 39–40
Weinstock, Harrison: 249
Western Explorer (fishing boat): 226
Western Federation of Miners:
    246–47
Western League: 268
Wheatland Riot: 241, 242
Whirling Thunder (Winnebago
    member): 118
Winnebago tribe: 55, 118–19
Wisconsin: 118, 122, 152
Woascita (daughter of Cloudy-
    Weather): 58
Wobblies. *See* Industrial Workers of
    the World (IWW)
women: 156. *See also* Italians, women
World War I: 233, 235

XY Company: 46

Yosti, Emilien: 29
Young, Brigham: 169
Yugoslavs: 211
Yuma tribe: 110

Zarlengo Brothers Contracting
    Company: 178
Zarlengo, Charles (Gaetano): 177–78
Zarlengo, Elizabeth Fabrizio: 178
Zarlengo, Francesco: 178
Zarlengo, George: 178

*The Land Beyond: Italian Migrants in the
Westward Movement—An Anthology of Essays
on the Italian Settlers' Experience in the American West*
edited by Gloria Ricci Lothrop, introduction by Andrew Rolle,
has been produced in an edition of one thousand copies.

𝄢   𝄢   𝄢

The book is set in Caslon Old Style type with Hoefler Ornaments.
Design by Ariane C. Smith, Spokane, Washington.
Printing by Cushing-Malloy, Inc., Ann Arbor, Michigan.